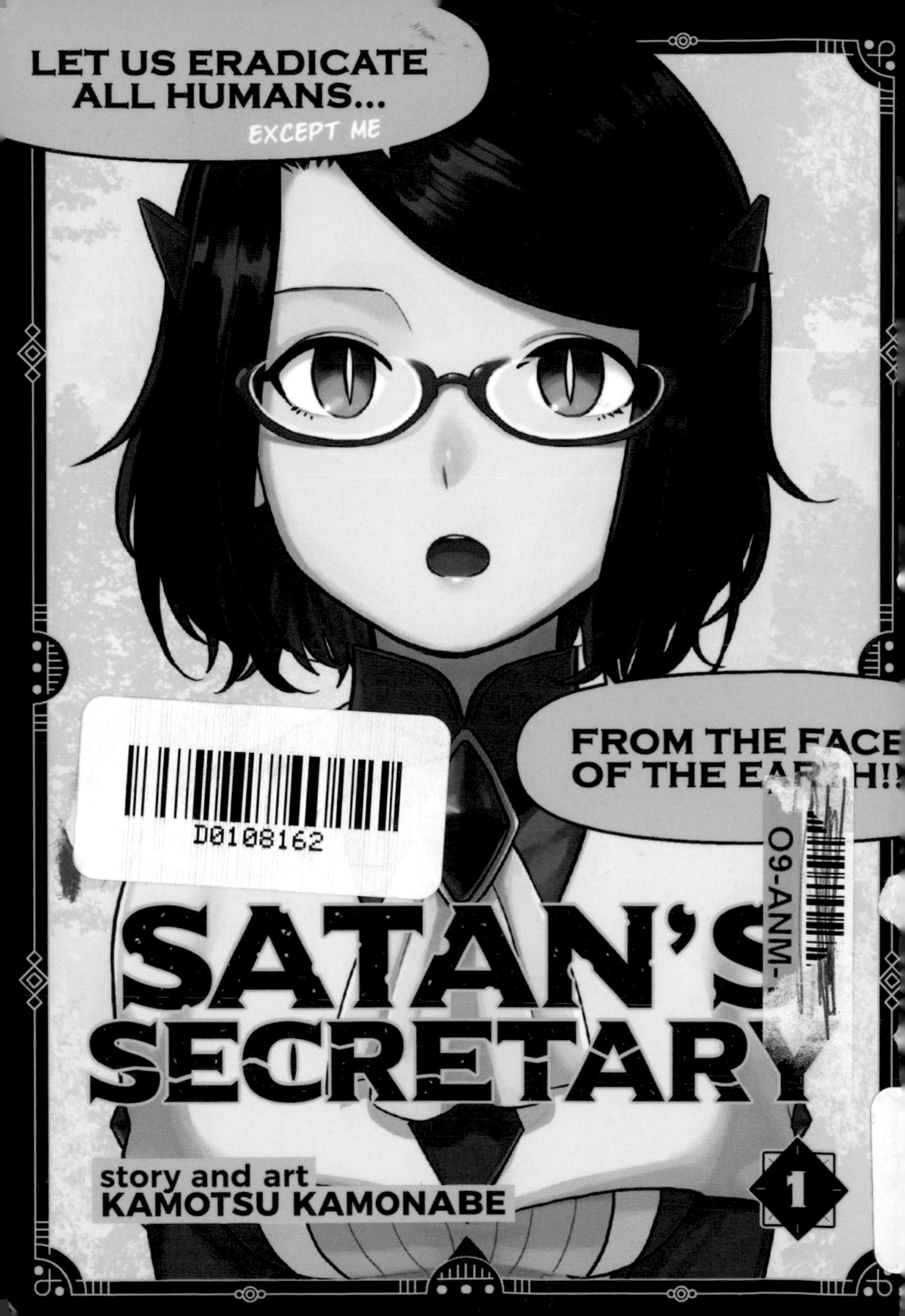
LET US ERADICATE ALL HUMANS...
EXCEPT ME
FROM THE FACE
OF THE EA H!!
SATAN'S SECRETARY
1
story and art
KAMOTSU KAMONABE

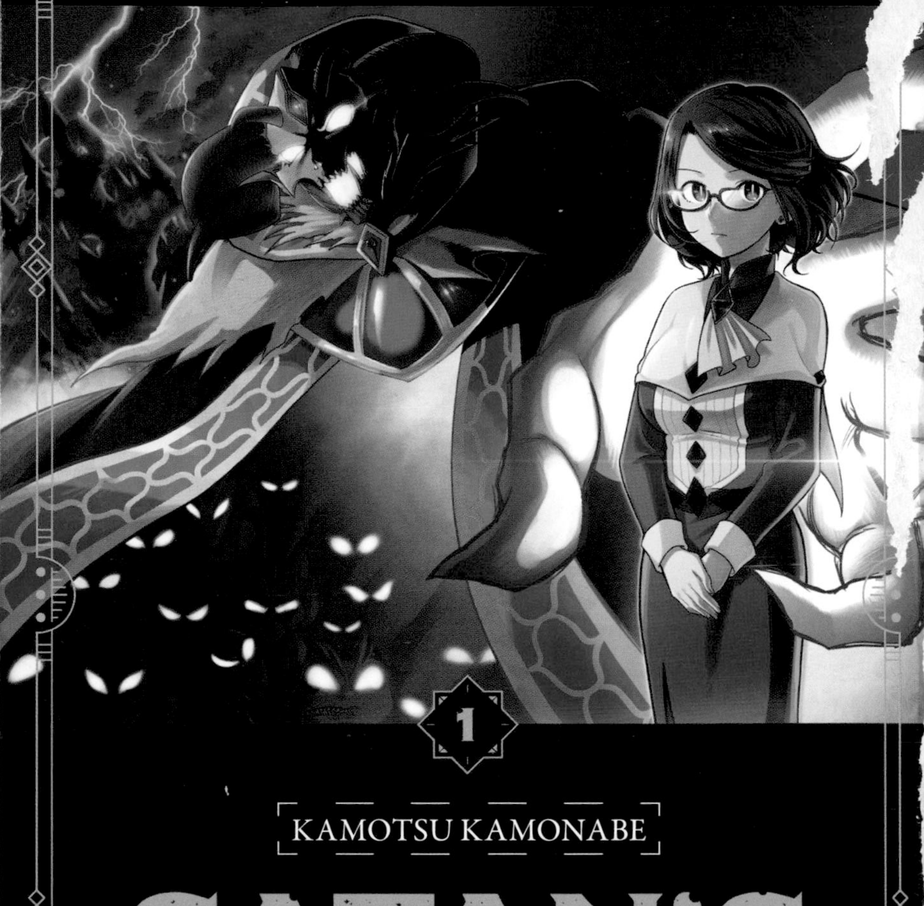

1

KAMOTSU KAMONABE

# SATAN'S SECRETARY

PRESENTED BY KAMOTSU KAMONABE
VOLUME ONE

# SATAN'S SECRETARY

## CONTENTS

SATAN'S SECRETARY
Presented by Kamotsu Kamonabe
Volume One

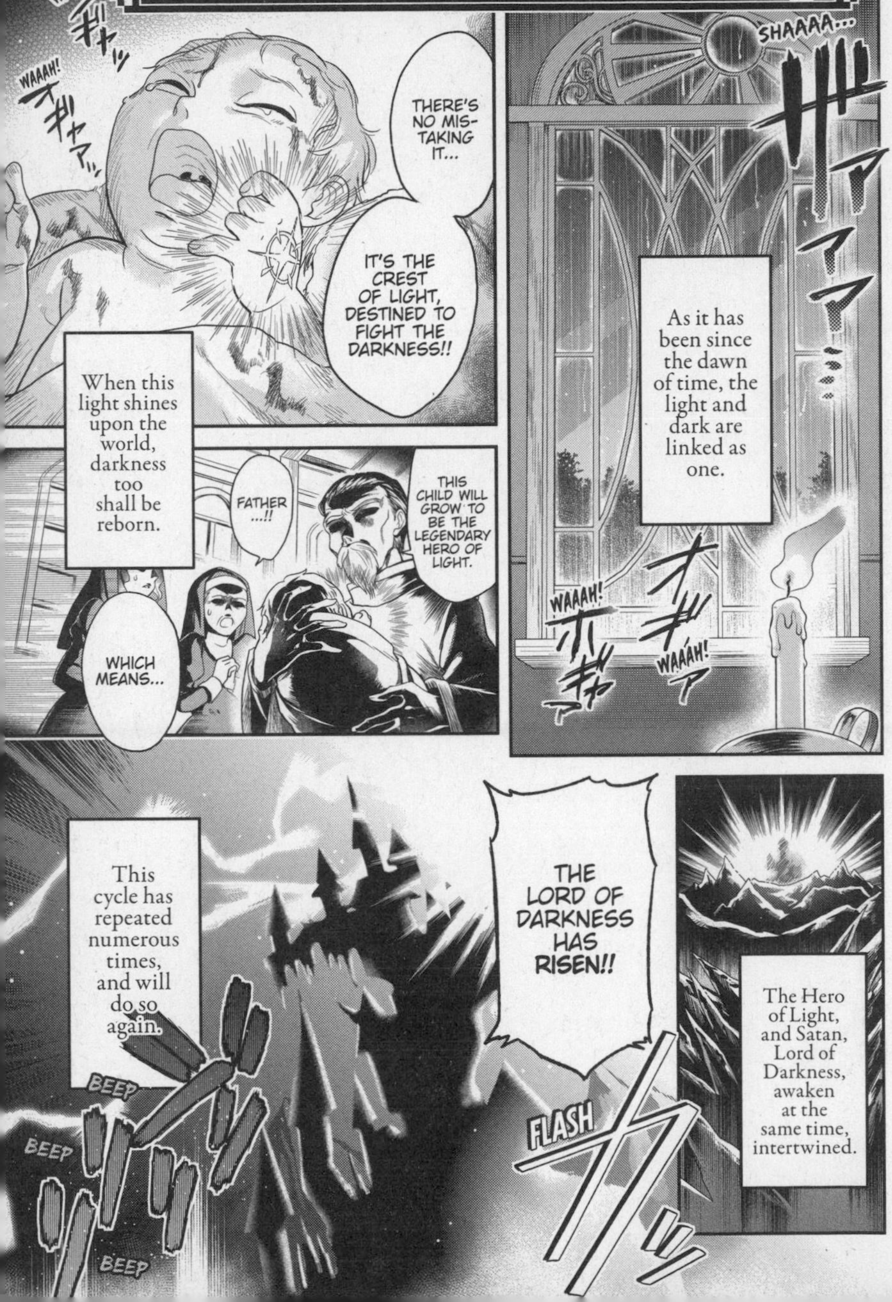
SHAAAA...
As it has been since the dawn of time, the light and dark are linked as one.
WAAAH!
WAAAH!
WAAH!
WAAAH!
THERE'S NO MIS-TAKING IT...
IT'S THE CREST OF LIGHT, DESTINED TO FIGHT THE DARKNESS!!
When this light shines upon the world, darkness too shall be reborn.
THIS CHILD WILL GROW TO BE THE LEGENDARY HERO OF LIGHT.
FATHER ...!!
WHICH MEANS...
The Hero of Light, and Satan, Lord of Darkness, awaken at the same time, intertwined.
THE LORD OF DARKNESS HAS RISEN!!
This cycle has repeated numerous times, and will do so again.
FLASH
BEEP
BEEP
BEEP

# CHAPTER 1: THE WORLD CAN BE SAVED. BUT ONLY WITHOUT THE SECRETARY.

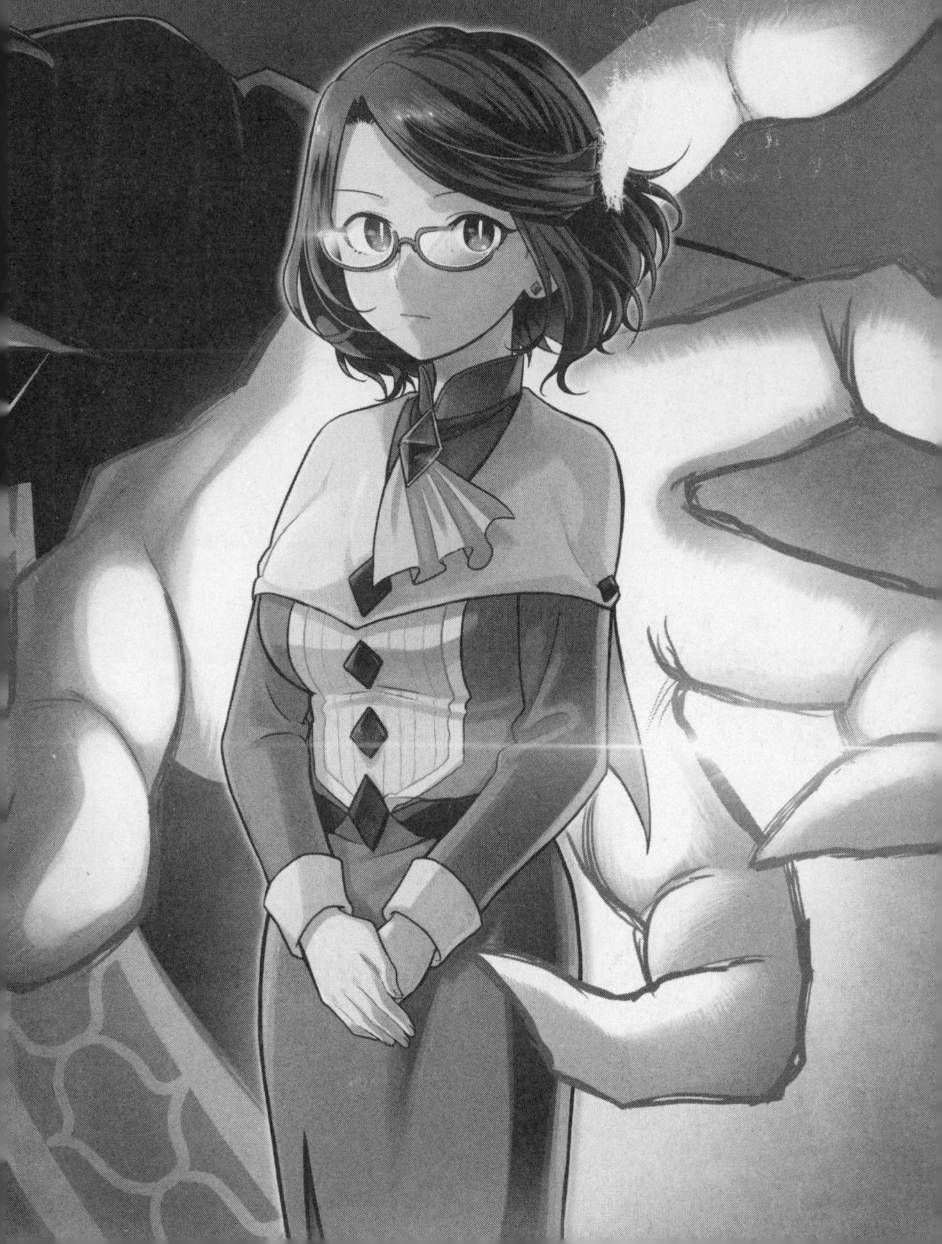

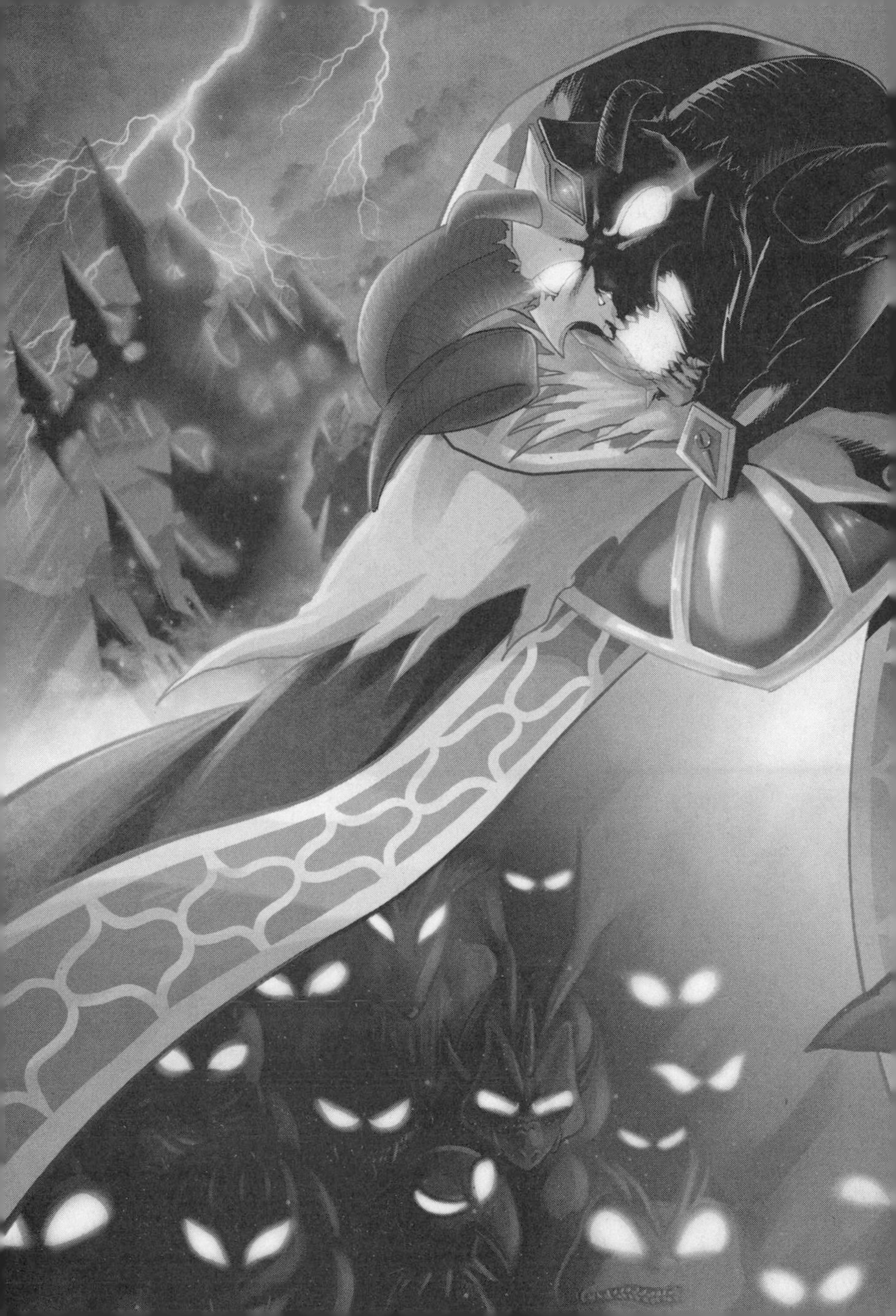

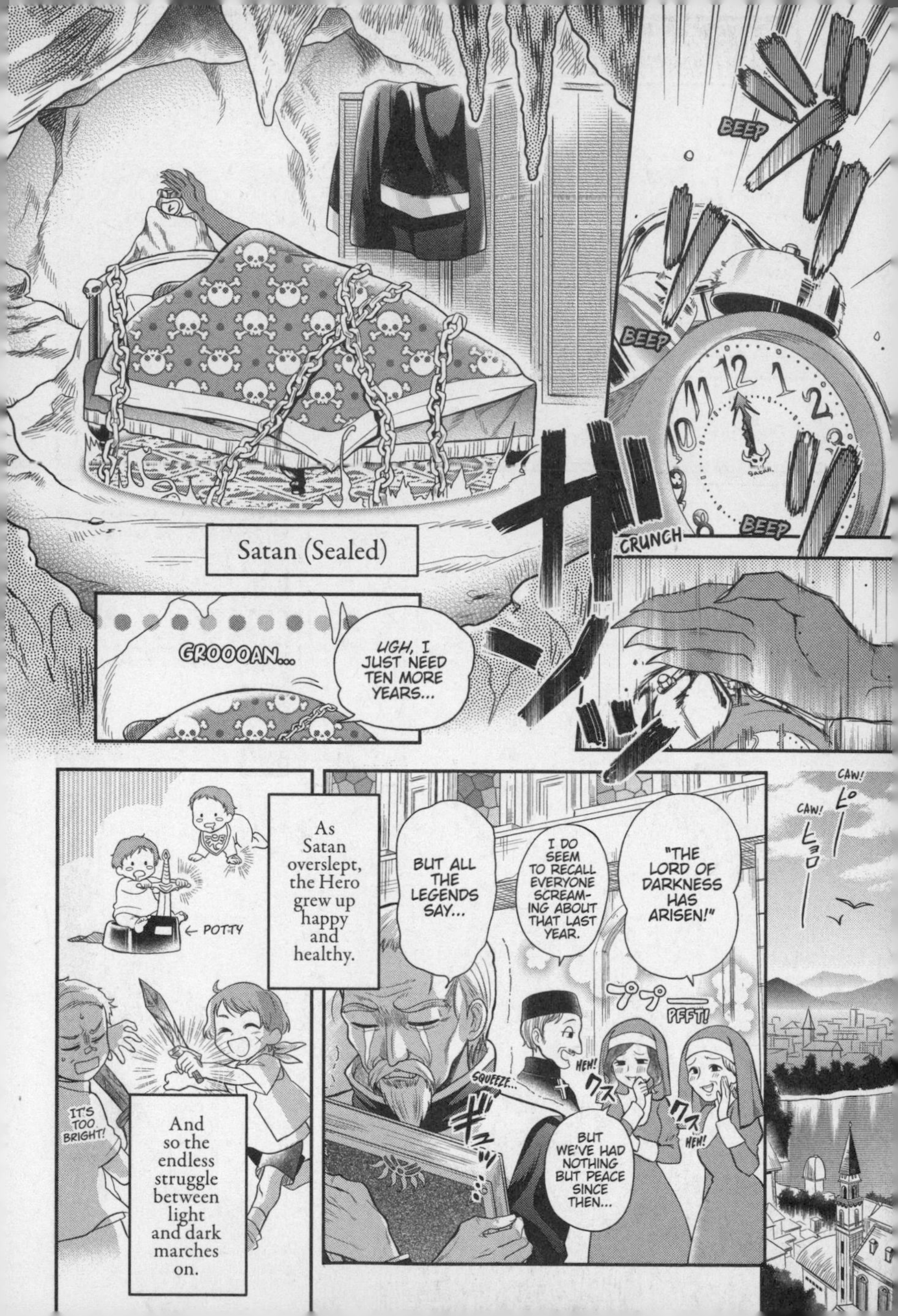
BEEP
BEEP
BEEP
CRUNCH
Satan (Sealed)
GROOOAN...
UGH, I JUST NEED TEN MORE YEARS...
CAW!
CAW!
"THE LORD OF DARKNESS HAS ARISEN!"
I DO SEEM TO RECALL EVERYONE SCREAMING ABOUT THAT LAST YEAR.
BUT ALL THE LEGENDS SAY...
PFFT!
HEH!
HEH!
SQUEEZE...
BUT WE'VE HAD NOTHING BUT PEACE SINCE THEN...
As Satan overslept, the Hero grew up happy and healthy.
POTTY
And so the endless struggle between light and dark marches on.
IT'S TOO BRIGHT!

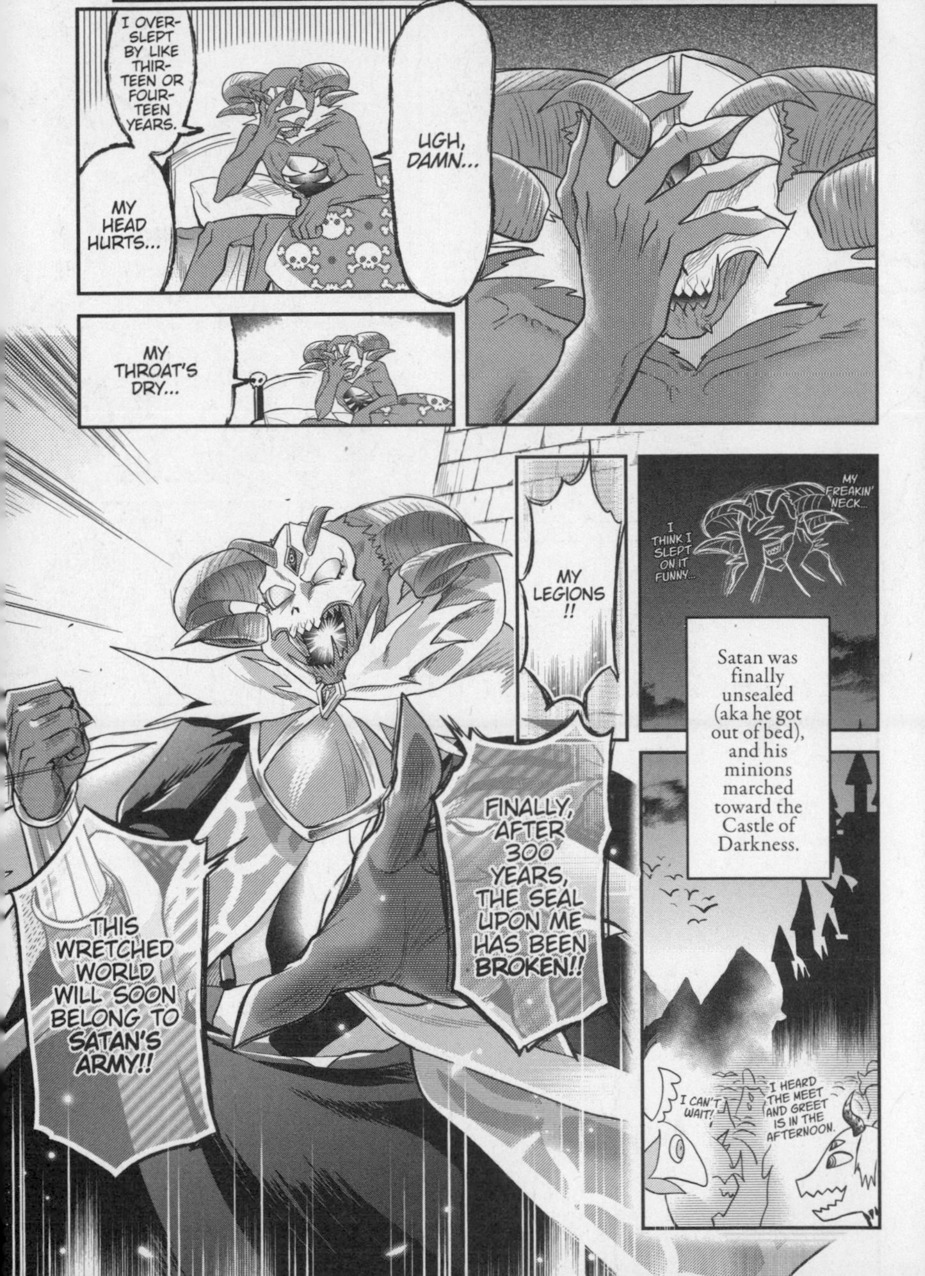
UGH, DAMN...
I OVERSLEPT BY LIKE THIRTEEN OR FOURTEEN YEARS.
MY HEAD HURTS...
MY THROAT'S DRY...
MY FREAKIN' NECK...
I THINK I SLEPT ON IT FUNNY...
Satan was finally unsealed (aka he got out of bed), and his minions marched toward the Castle of Darkness.
I HEARD THE MEET AND GREET IS IN THE AFTERNOON.
I CAN'T WAIT!
MY LEGIONS!!
FINALLY, AFTER 300 YEARS, THE SEAL UPON ME HAS BEEN BROKEN!!
THIS WRETCHED WORLD WILL SOON BELONG TO SATAN'S ARMY!!

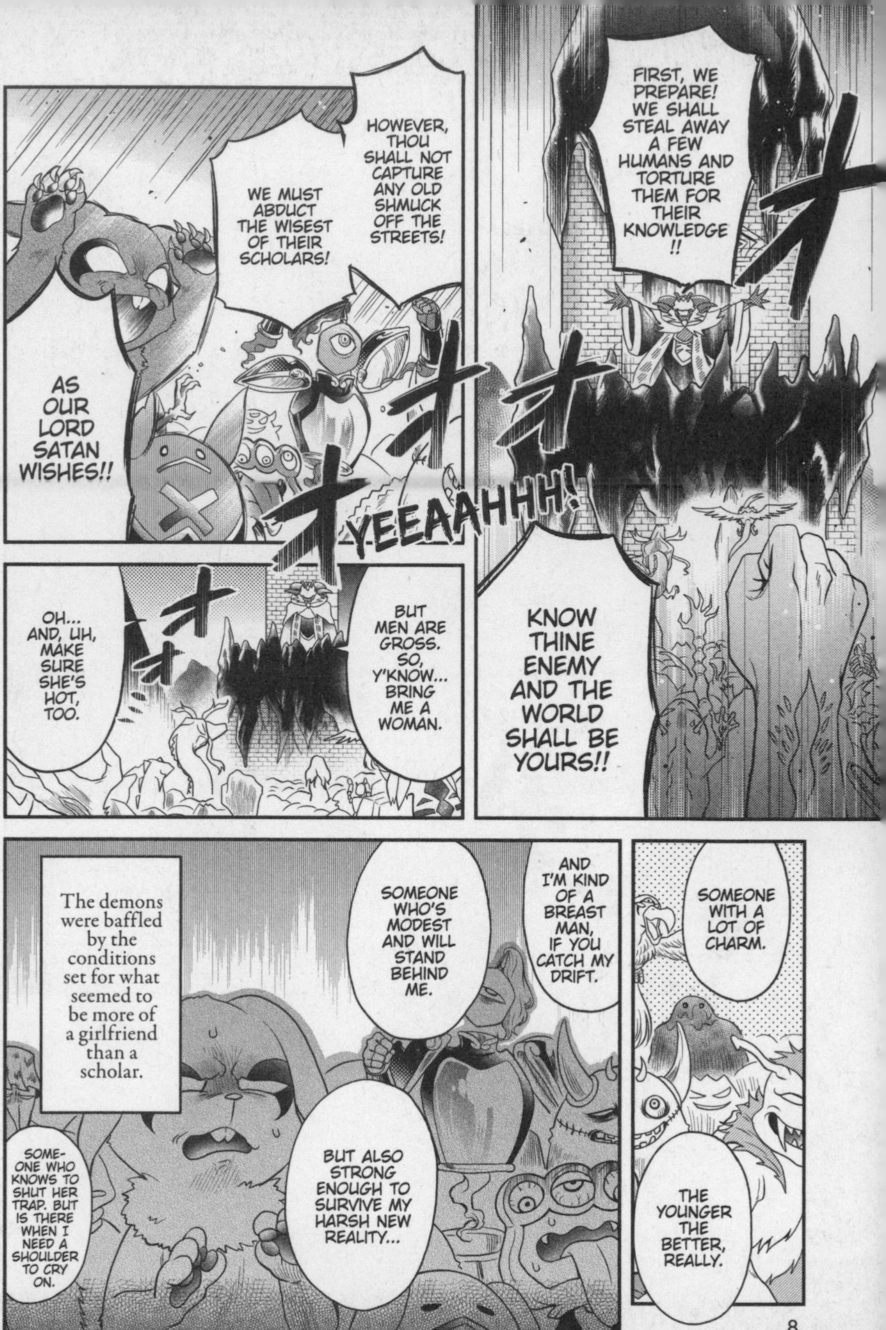
FIRST, WE PREPARE! WE SHALL STEAL AWAY A FEW HUMANS AND TORTURE THEM FOR THEIR KNOWLEDGE !!
HOWEVER, THOU SHALL NOT CAPTURE ANY OLD SHMUCK OFF THE STREETS!
WE MUST ABDUCT THE WISEST OF THEIR SCHOLARS!
AS OUR LORD SATAN WISHES!!
YEEAAHHH!
KNOW THINE ENEMY AND THE WORLD SHALL BE YOURS!!
BUT MEN ARE GROSS. SO, Y'KNOW... BRING ME A WOMAN.
OH... AND, UH, MAKE SURE SHE'S HOT, TOO.
SOMEONE WITH A LOT OF CHARM.
THE YOUNGER THE BETTER, REALLY.
AND I'M KIND OF A BREAST MAN, IF YOU CATCH MY DRIFT.
SOMEONE WHO'S MODEST AND WILL STAND BEHIND ME.
The demons were baffled by the conditions set for what seemed to be more of a girlfriend than a scholar.
BUT ALSO STRONG ENOUGH TO SURVIVE MY HARSH NEW REALITY...
SOME-ONE WHO KNOWS TO SHUT HER TRAP. BUT IS THERE WHEN I NEED A SHOULDER TO CRY ON.

## CUTTING TO THE CHASE!

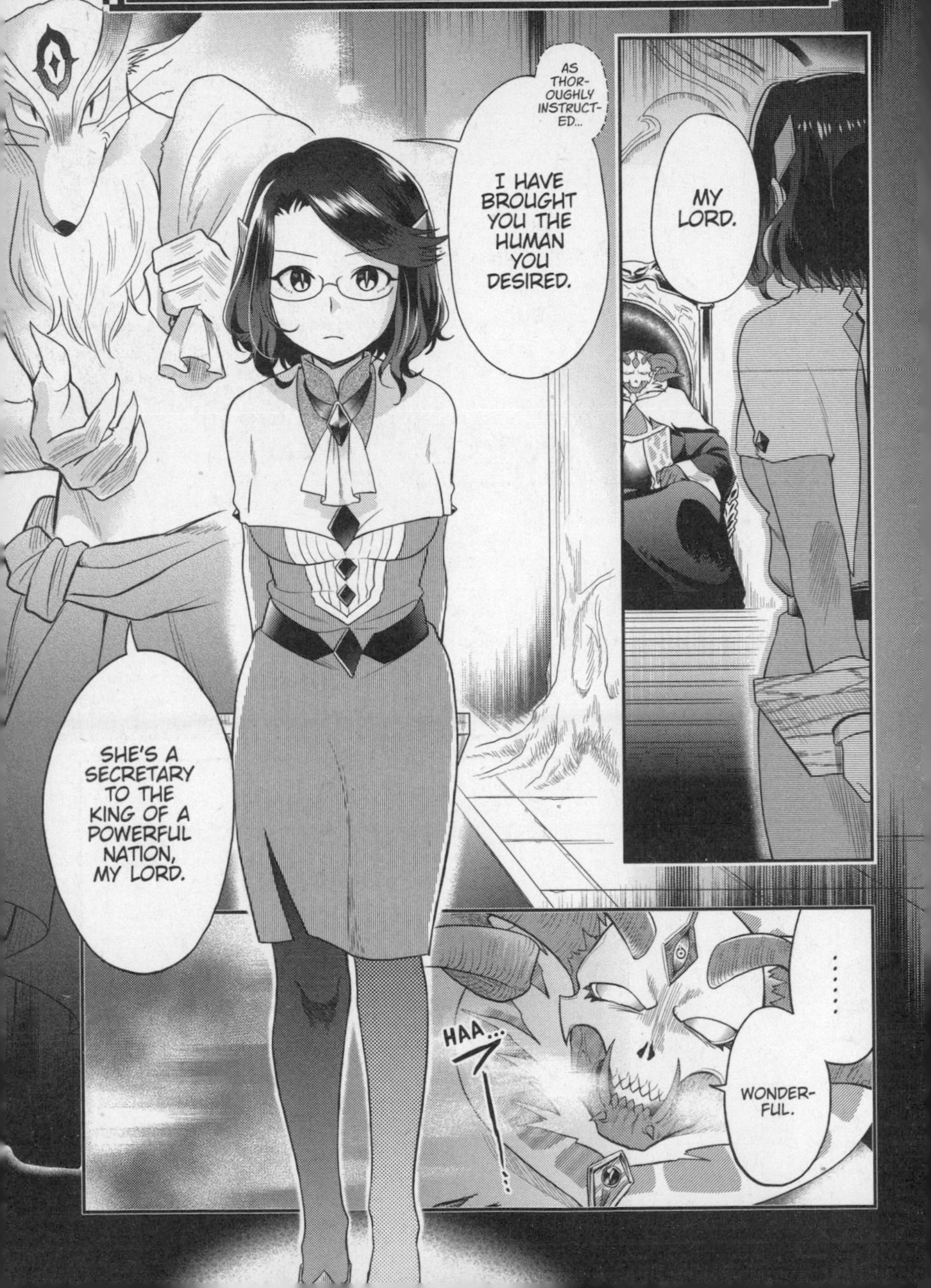
MY LORD.
AS THOROUGHLY INSTRUCTED...
I HAVE BROUGHT YOU THE HUMAN YOU DESIRED.
SHE'S A SECRETARY TO THE KING OF A POWERFUL NATION, MY LORD.
......
HAA...
WONDERFUL.

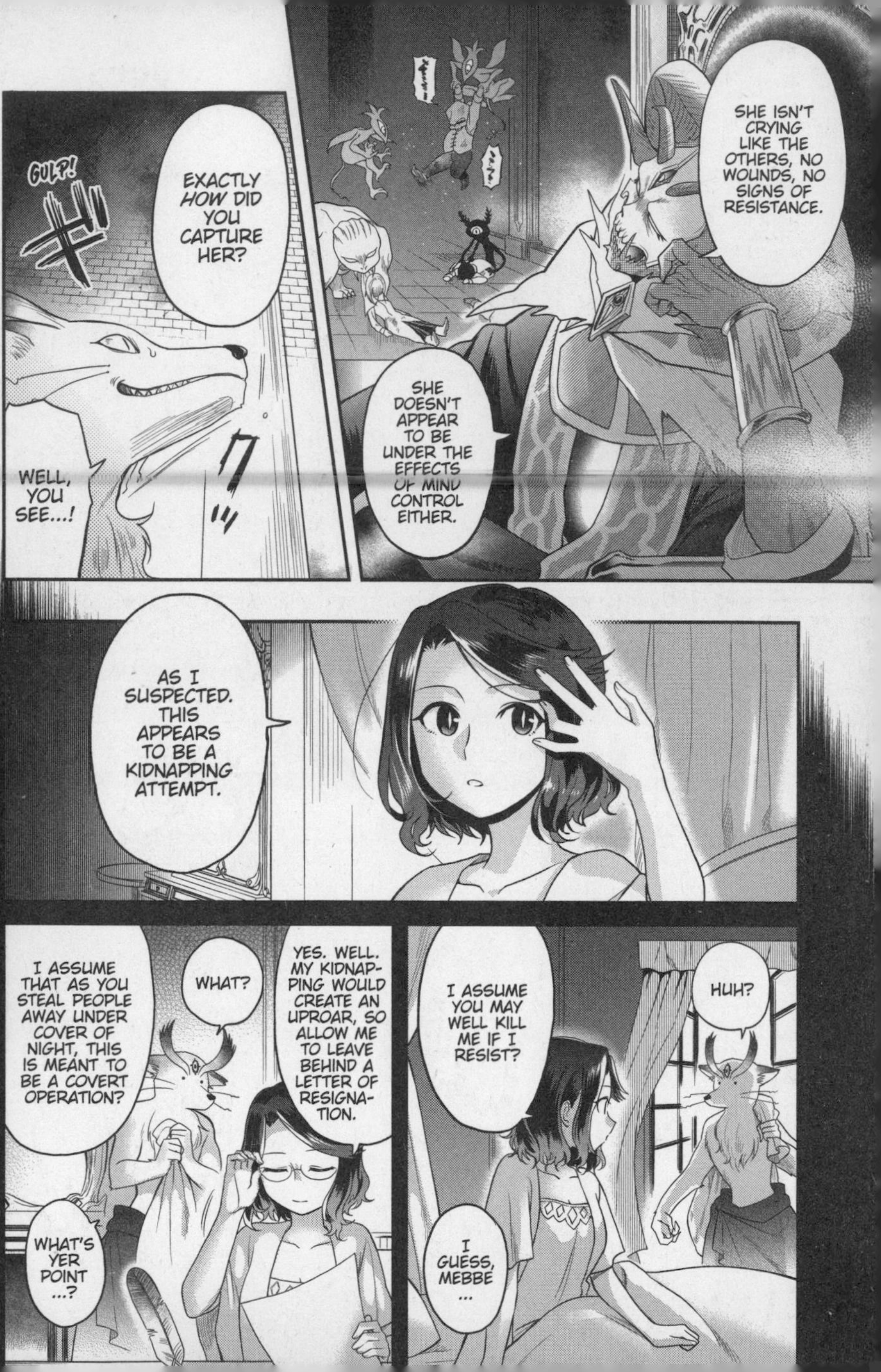
SHE ISN'T CRYING LIKE THE OTHERS, NO WOUNDS, NO SIGNS OF RESISTANCE.
SHE DOESN'T APPEAR TO BE UNDER THE EFFECTS OF MIND CONTROL EITHER.
EXACTLY HOW DID YOU CAPTURE HER?
GULP!
WELL, YOU SEE...!
AS I SUSPECTED. THIS APPEARS TO BE A KIDNAPPING ATTEMPT.
I ASSUME YOU MAY WELL KILL ME IF I RESIST?
HUH?
I GUESS, MEBBE ...
I ASSUME THAT AS YOU STEAL PEOPLE AWAY UNDER COVER OF NIGHT, THIS IS MEANT TO BE A COVERT OPERATION?
WHAT?
YES. WELL. MY KIDNAPPING WOULD CREATE AN UPROAR, SO ALLOW ME TO LEAVE BEHIND A LETTER OF RESIGNATION.
WHAT'S YER POINT ...?

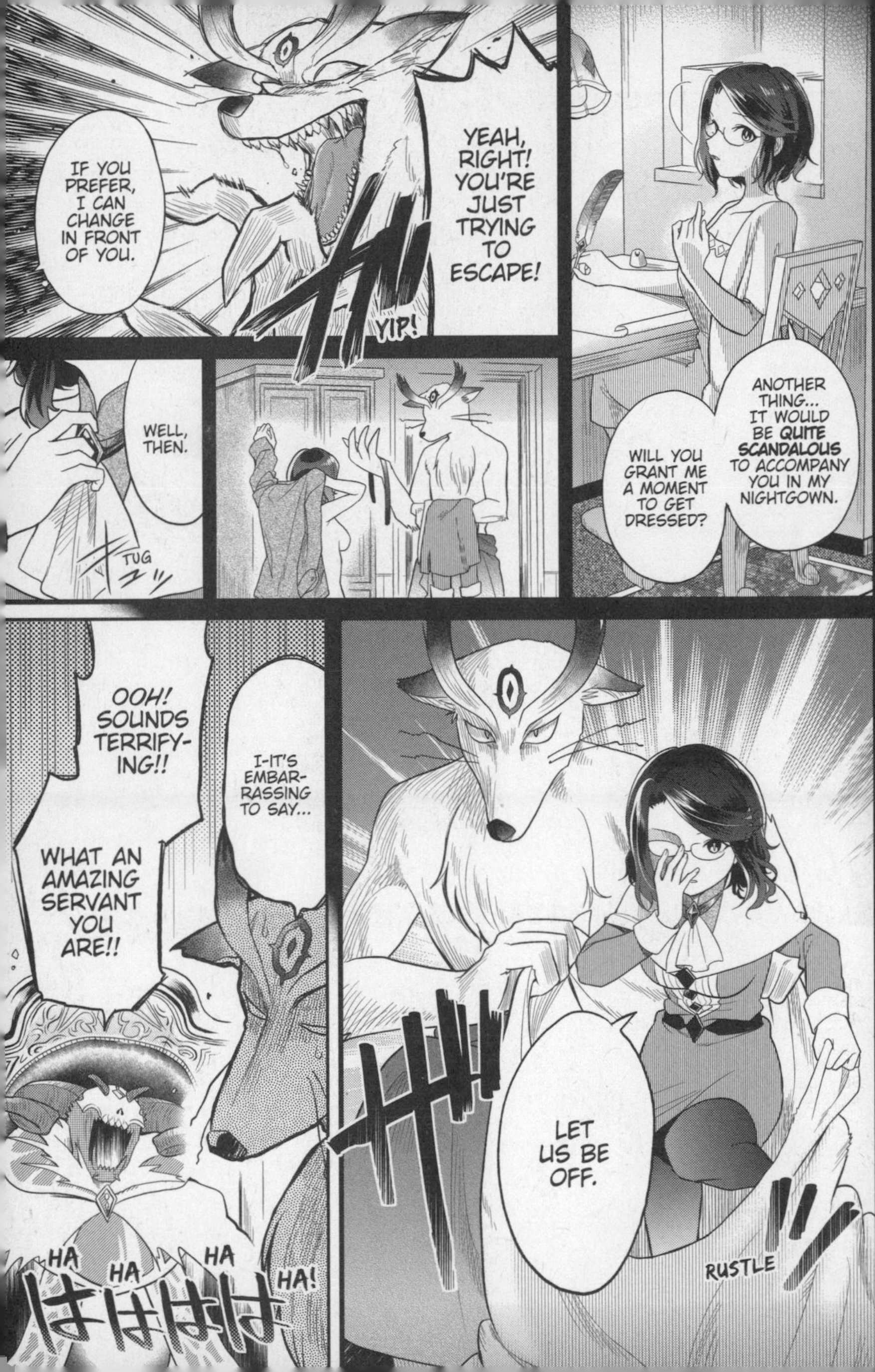
ANOTHER THING... IT WOULD BE **QUITE SCANDALOUS** TO ACCOMPANY YOU IN MY NIGHTGOWN.
WILL YOU GRANT ME A MOMENT TO GET DRESSED?
YEAH, RIGHT! YOU'RE JUST TRYING TO ESCAPE!
YIP!
IF YOU PREFER, I CAN CHANGE IN FRONT OF YOU.
WELL, THEN.
TUG
LET US BE OFF.
RUSTLE
I-IT'S EMBARRASSING TO SAY...
OOH! SOUNDS TERRIFYING!!
WHAT AN AMAZING SERVANT YOU ARE!!
HA HA HA HA!
はははは

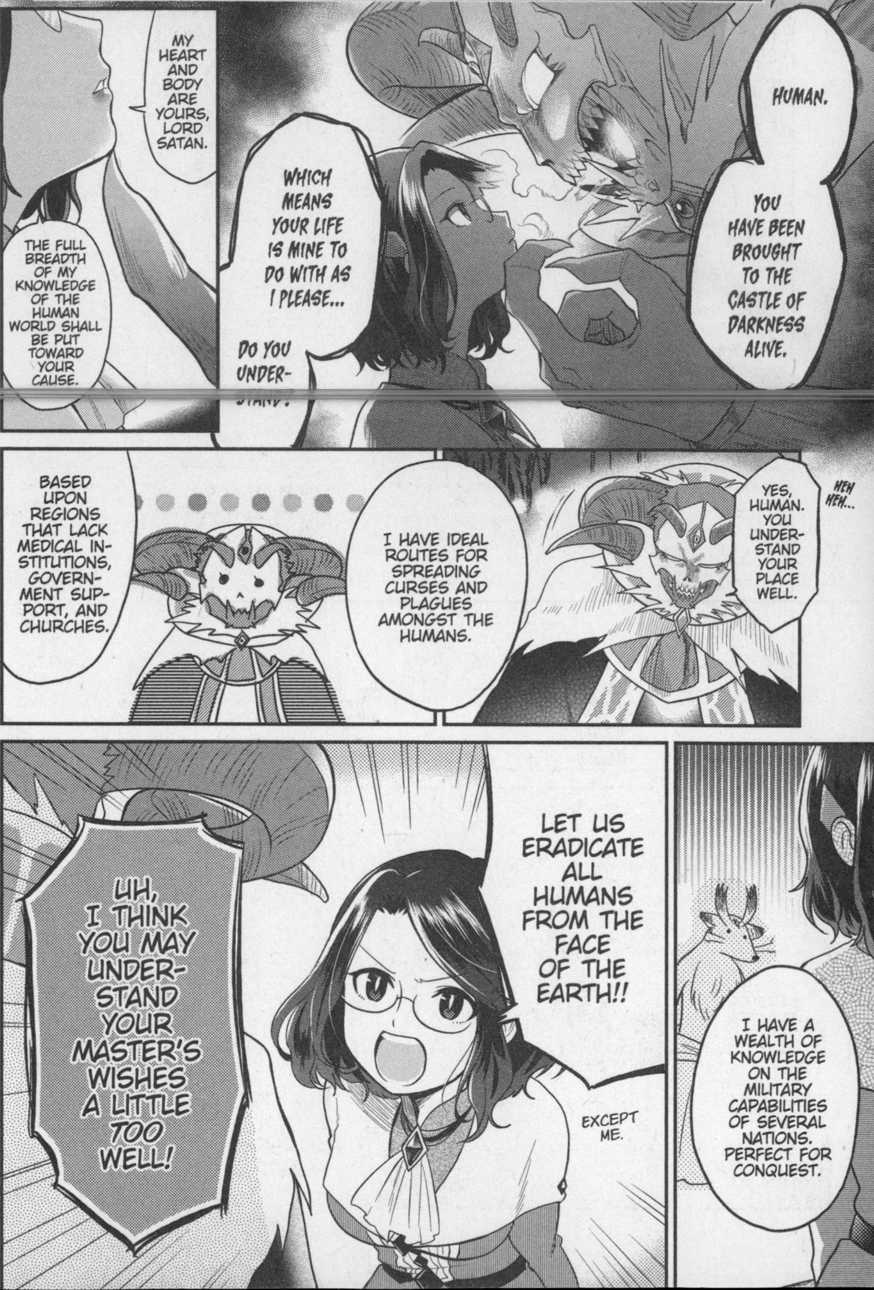
HUMAN.
YOU HAVE BEEN BROUGHT TO THE CASTLE OF DARKNESS ALIVE.
WHICH MEANS YOUR LIFE IS MINE TO DO WITH AS I PLEASE...
DO YOU UNDER-STAND?
MY HEART AND BODY ARE YOURS, LORD SATAN.
THE FULL BREADTH OF MY KNOWLEDGE OF THE HUMAN WORLD SHALL BE PUT TOWARD YOUR CAUSE.
HEH HEH...
YES, HUMAN. YOU UNDER-STAND YOUR PLACE WELL.
I HAVE IDEAL ROUTES FOR SPREADING CURSES AND PLAGUES AMONGST THE HUMANS.
BASED UPON REGIONS THAT LACK MEDICAL IN-STITUTIONS, GOVERN-MENT SUP-PORT, AND CHURCHES.
I HAVE A WEALTH OF KNOWLEDGE ON THE MILITARY CAPABILITIES OF SEVERAL NATIONS. PERFECT FOR CONQUEST.
LET US ERADICATE ALL HUMANS FROM THE FACE OF THE EARTH!!
EXCEPT ME.
UH, I THINK YOU MAY UNDER-STAND YOUR MASTER'S WISHES A LITTLE TOO WELL!

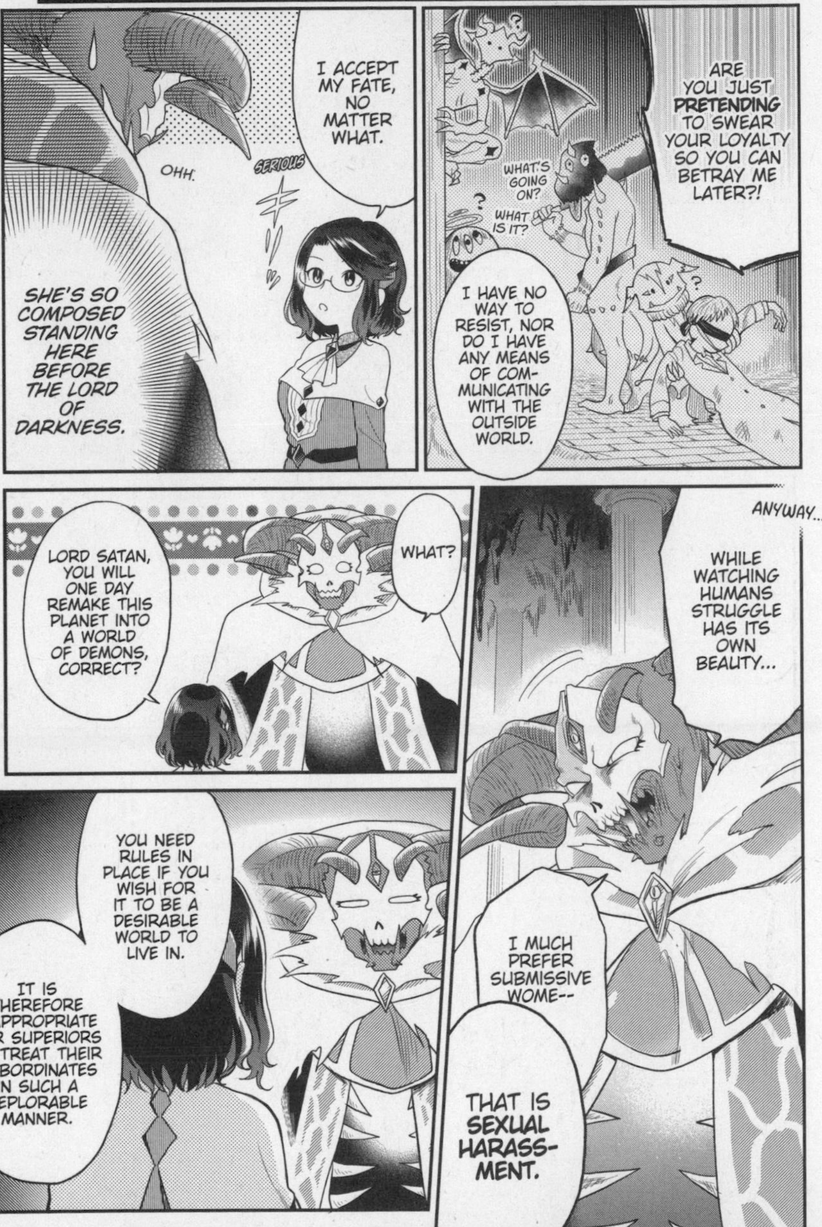
ARE YOU JUST PRETENDING TO SWEAR YOUR LOYALTY SO YOU CAN BETRAY ME LATER?!
WHAT'S GOING ON?
WHAT IS IT?
I HAVE NO WAY TO RESIST, NOR DO I HAVE ANY MEANS OF COM-MUNICATING WITH THE OUTSIDE WORLD.
I ACCEPT MY FATE, NO MATTER WHAT.
OHH.
SERIOUS
SHE'S SO COMPOSED STANDING HERE BEFORE THE LORD OF DARKNESS.
ANYWAY...
WHILE WATCHING HUMANS STRUGGLE HAS ITS OWN BEAUTY...
I MUCH PREFER SUBMISSIVE WOME--
THAT IS SEXUAL HARASS-MENT.
WHAT?
LORD SATAN, YOU WILL ONE DAY REMAKE THIS PLANET INTO A WORLD OF DEMONS, CORRECT?
YOU NEED RULES IN PLACE IF YOU WISH FOR IT TO BE A DESIRABLE WORLD TO LIVE IN.
IT IS THEREFORE INAPPROPRIATE FOR SUPERIORS TO TREAT THEIR SUBORDINATES IN SUCH A DEPLORABLE MANNER.

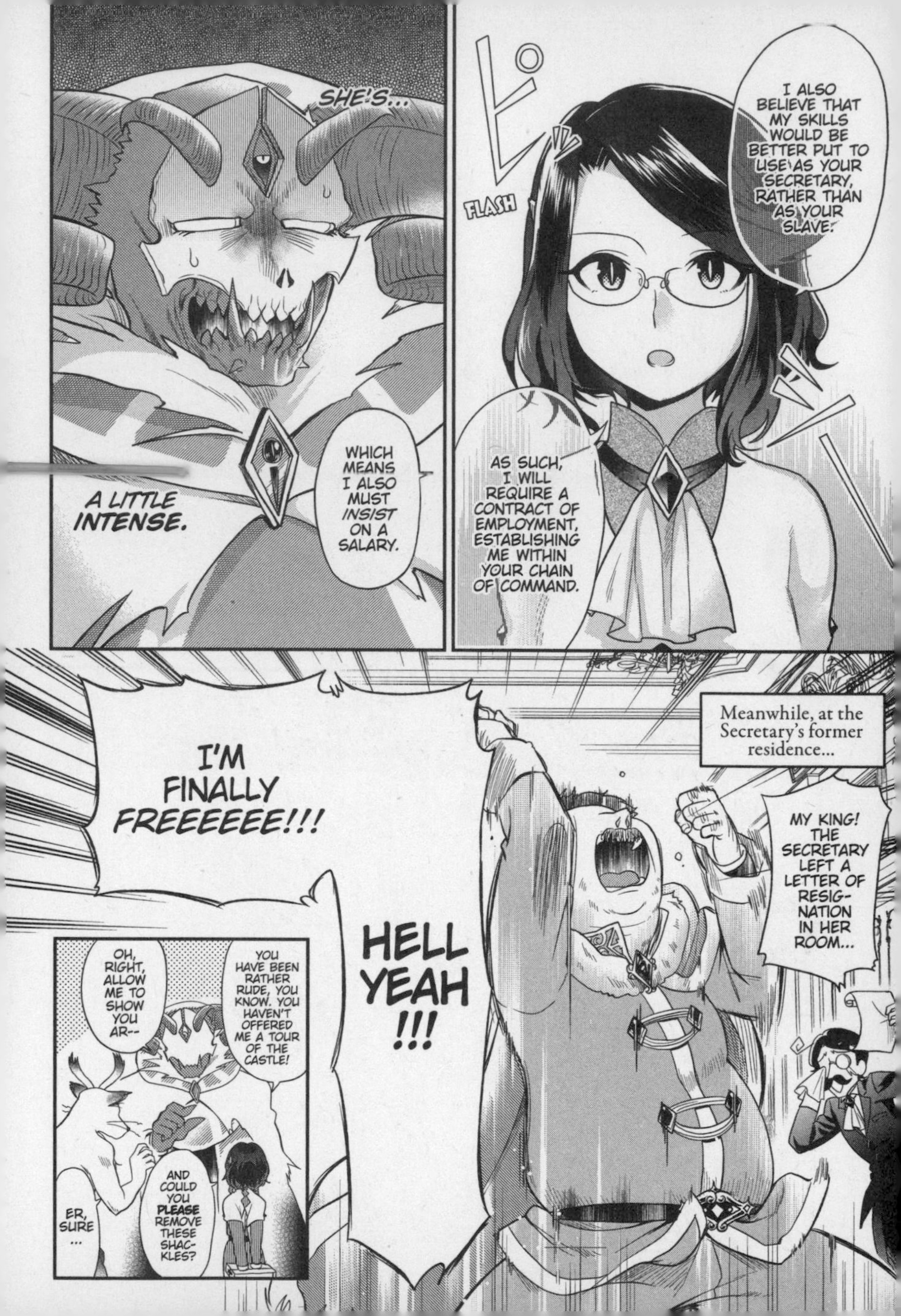
FLASH
I ALSO BELIEVE THAT MY SKILLS WOULD BE BETTER PUT TO USE AS YOUR SECRETARY, RATHER THAN AS YOUR SLAVE.
AS SUCH, I WILL REQUIRE A CONTRACT OF EMPLOYMENT, ESTABLISHING ME WITHIN YOUR CHAIN OF COMMAND.
SHE'S...
WHICH MEANS I ALSO MUST *INSIST* ON A SALARY.
A LITTLE INTENSE.
Meanwhile, at the Secretary's former residence...
MY KING! THE SECRETARY LEFT A LETTER OF RESIGNATION IN HER ROOM...
I'M FINALLY FREEEEEEE!!!
HELL YEAH!!!
YOU HAVE BEEN RATHER RUDE, YOU KNOW. YOU HAVEN'T OFFERED ME A TOUR OF THE CASTLE!
OH, RIGHT, ALLOW ME TO SHOW YOU AR--
AND COULD YOU **PLEASE** REMOVE THESE SHACKLES?
ER, SURE...

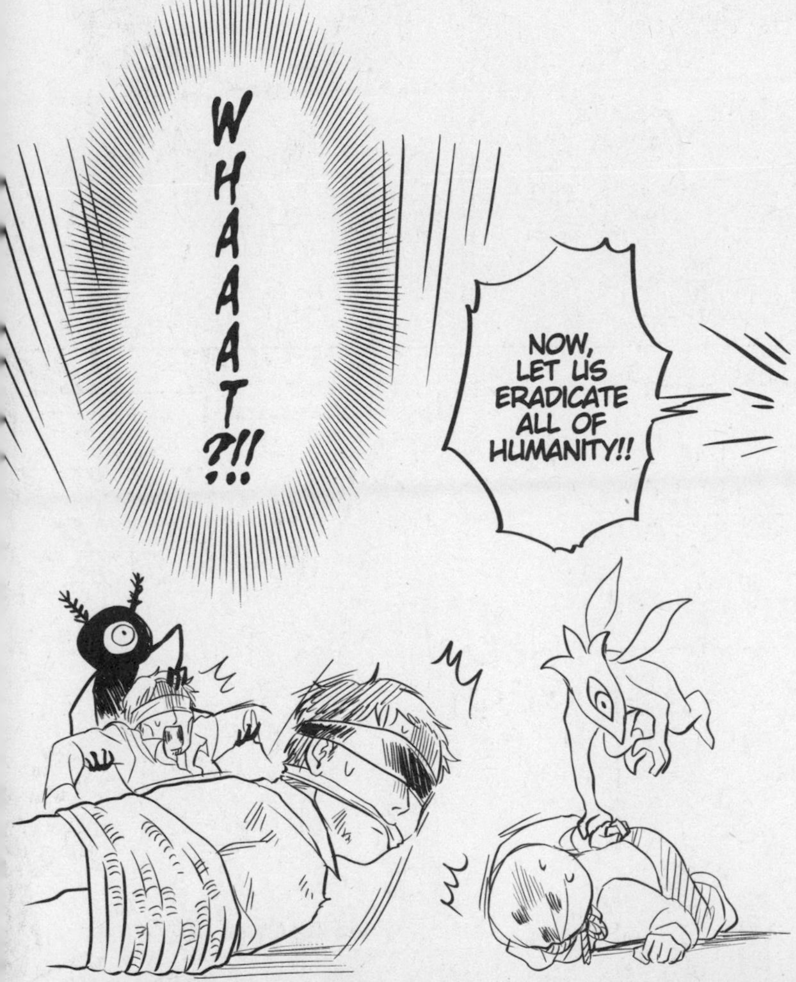
NOW, LET US ERADICATE ALL OF HUMANITY!!
WHAAAAT?!!
THE OTHER HUMANS WHO WERE CAPTURED

# SATAN'S SECRETARY

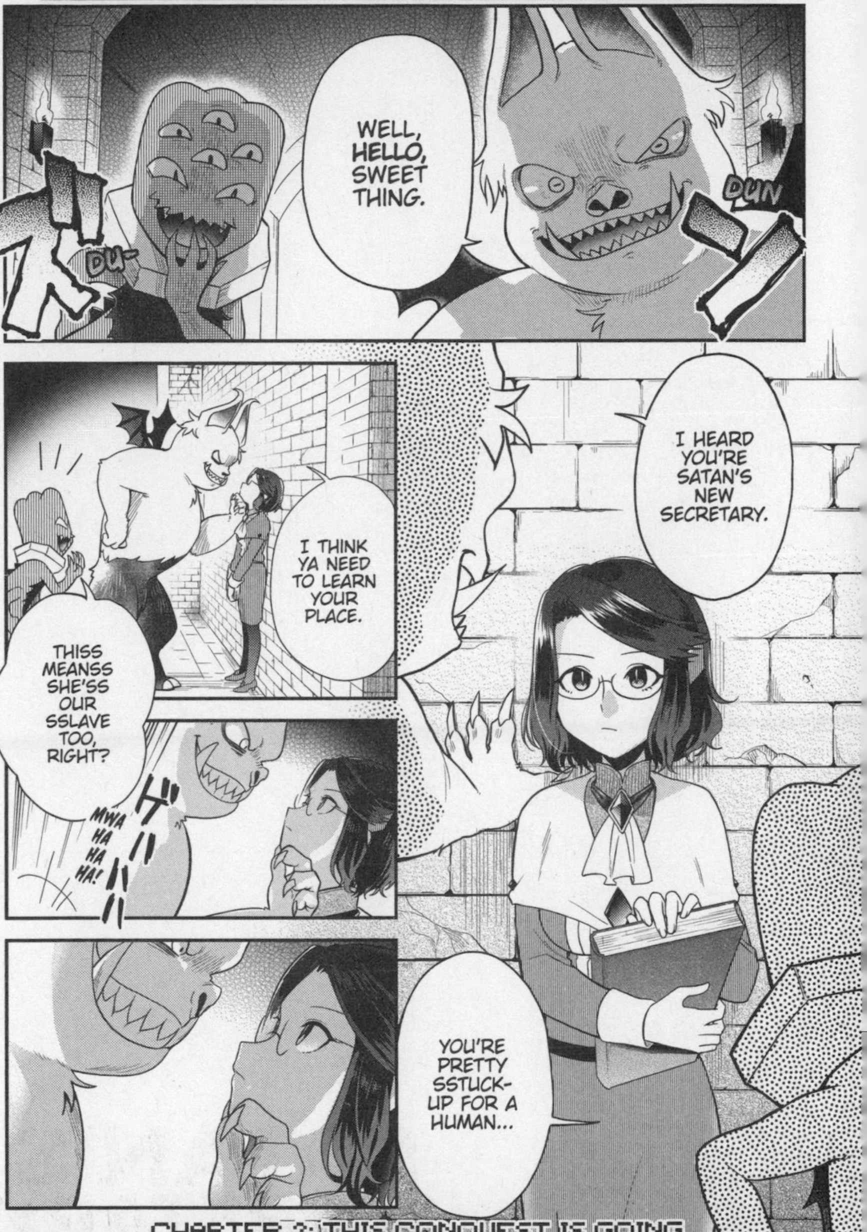
WELL, HELLO, SWEET THING.
DUN
DU-
I HEARD YOU'RE SATAN'S NEW SECRETARY.
YOU'RE PRETTY SSTUCK-UP FOR A HUMAN...
I THINK YA NEED TO LEARN YOUR PLACE.
THISS MEANSS SHE'SS OUR SSLAVE TOO, RIGHT?
MWA HA HA HA HA!

## CHAPTER 2: THIS CONQUEST IS GOING TO TAKE SOME WORK

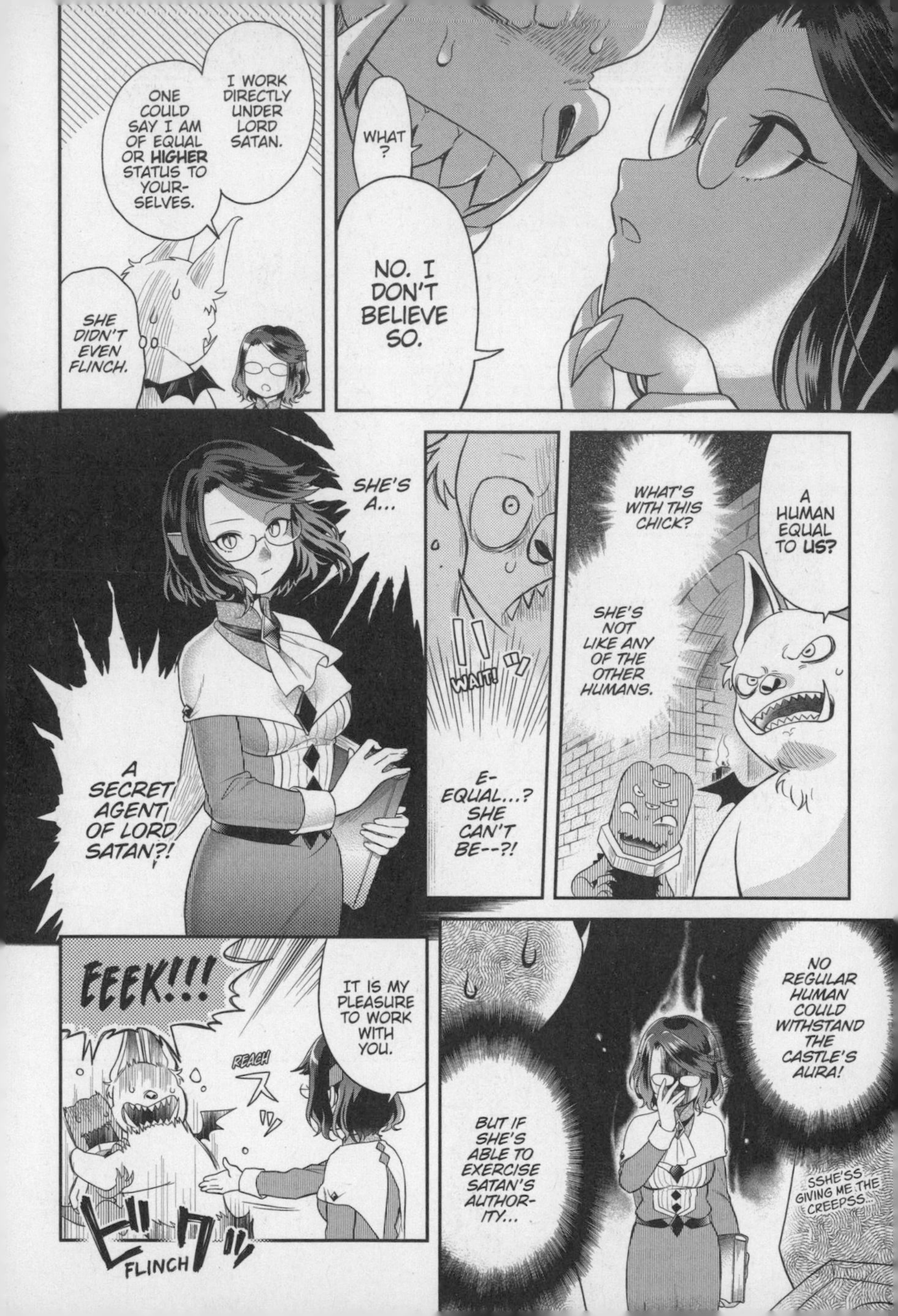
WHAT?
NO. I DON'T BELIEVE SO.
I WORK DIRECTLY UNDER LORD SATAN.
ONE COULD SAY I AM OF EQUAL OR HIGHER STATUS TO YOUR-SELVES.
SHE DIDN'T EVEN FLINCH.
A HUMAN EQUAL TO US?
WHAT'S WITH THIS CHICK?
SHE'S NOT LIKE ANY OF THE OTHER HUMANS.
E-EQUAL...? SHE CAN'T BE--?!
WAIT!
SHE'S A...
A SECRET AGENT OF LORD SATAN?!
NO REGULAR HUMAN COULD WITHSTAND THE CASTLE'S AURA!
BUT IF SHE'S ABLE TO EXERCISE SATAN'S AUTHOR-ITY...
SSHE'SS GIVING ME THE CREEPSS...
IT IS MY PLEASURE TO WORK WITH YOU.
REACH
EEEK!!!
FLINCH

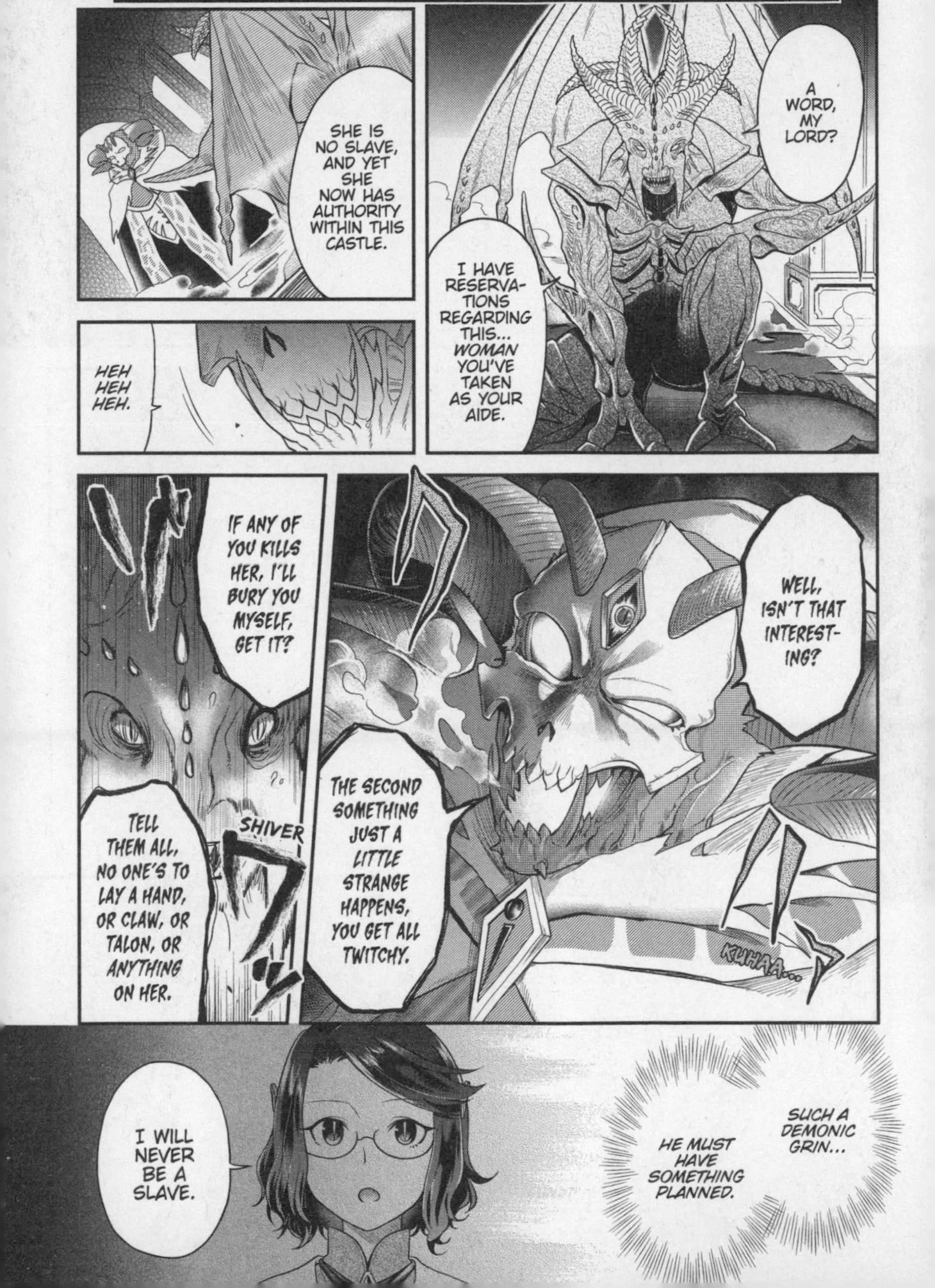
A WORD, MY LORD?
I HAVE RESERVATIONS REGARDING THIS... *WOMAN* YOU'VE TAKEN AS YOUR AIDE.
SHE IS NO SLAVE, AND YET SHE NOW HAS AUTHORITY WITHIN THIS CASTLE.
HEH HEH HEH.
WELL, ISN'T THAT INTERESTING?
THE SECOND SOMETHING JUST A LITTLE STRANGE HAPPENS, YOU GET ALL TWITCHY.
KUHAA...
IF ANY OF YOU KILLS HER, I'LL BURY YOU MYSELF, GET IT?
SHIVER
TELL THEM ALL, NO ONE'S TO LAY A HAND, OR CLAW, OR TALON, OR ANYTHING ON HER.
SUCH A DEMONIC GRIN...
HE MUST HAVE SOMETHING PLANNED.
I WILL NEVER BE A SLAVE.

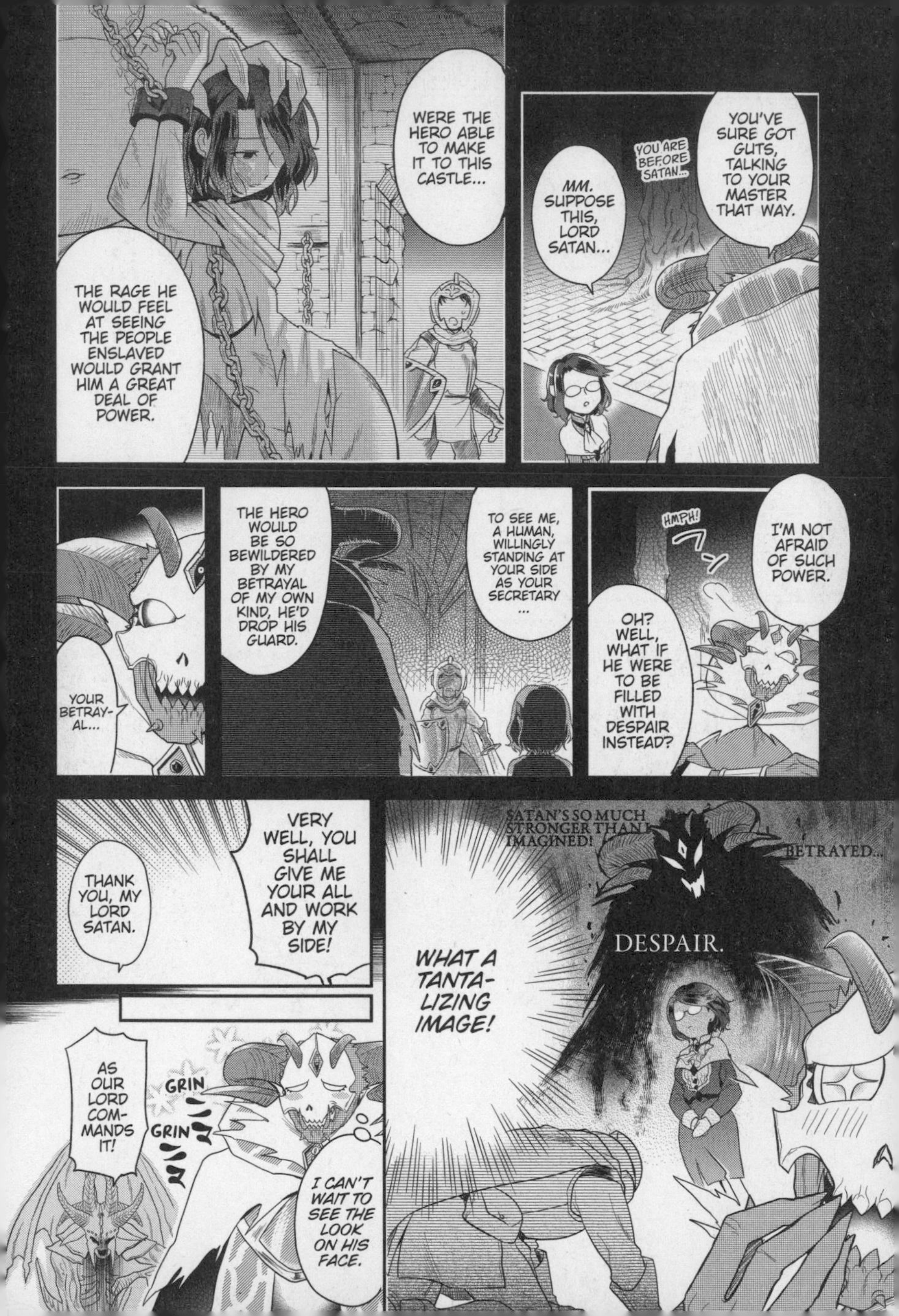
YOU'VE SURE GOT GUTS, TALKING TO YOUR MASTER THAT WAY.
YOU ARE BEFORE SATAN...
MM. SUPPOSE THIS, LORD SATAN...
WERE THE HERO ABLE TO MAKE IT TO THIS CASTLE...
THE RAGE HE WOULD FEEL AT SEEING THE PEOPLE ENSLAVED WOULD GRANT HIM A GREAT DEAL OF POWER.
HMPH!
I'M NOT AFRAID OF SUCH POWER.
OH? WELL, WHAT IF HE WERE TO BE FILLED WITH DESPAIR INSTEAD?
TO SEE ME, A HUMAN, WILLINGLY STANDING AT YOUR SIDE AS YOUR SECRETARY...
THE HERO WOULD BE SO BEWILDERED BY MY BETRAYAL OF MY OWN KIND, HE'D DROP HIS GUARD.
YOUR BETRAY-AL...
SATAN'S SO MUCH STRONGER THAN I IMAGINED!
BETRAYED...
DESPAIR.
WHAT A TANTA-LIZING IMAGE!
VERY WELL, YOU SHALL GIVE ME YOUR ALL AND WORK BY MY SIDE!
THANK YOU, MY LORD SATAN.
GRIN
GRIN
I CAN'T WAIT TO SEE THE LOOK ON HIS FACE.
AS OUR LORD COM-MANDS IT!

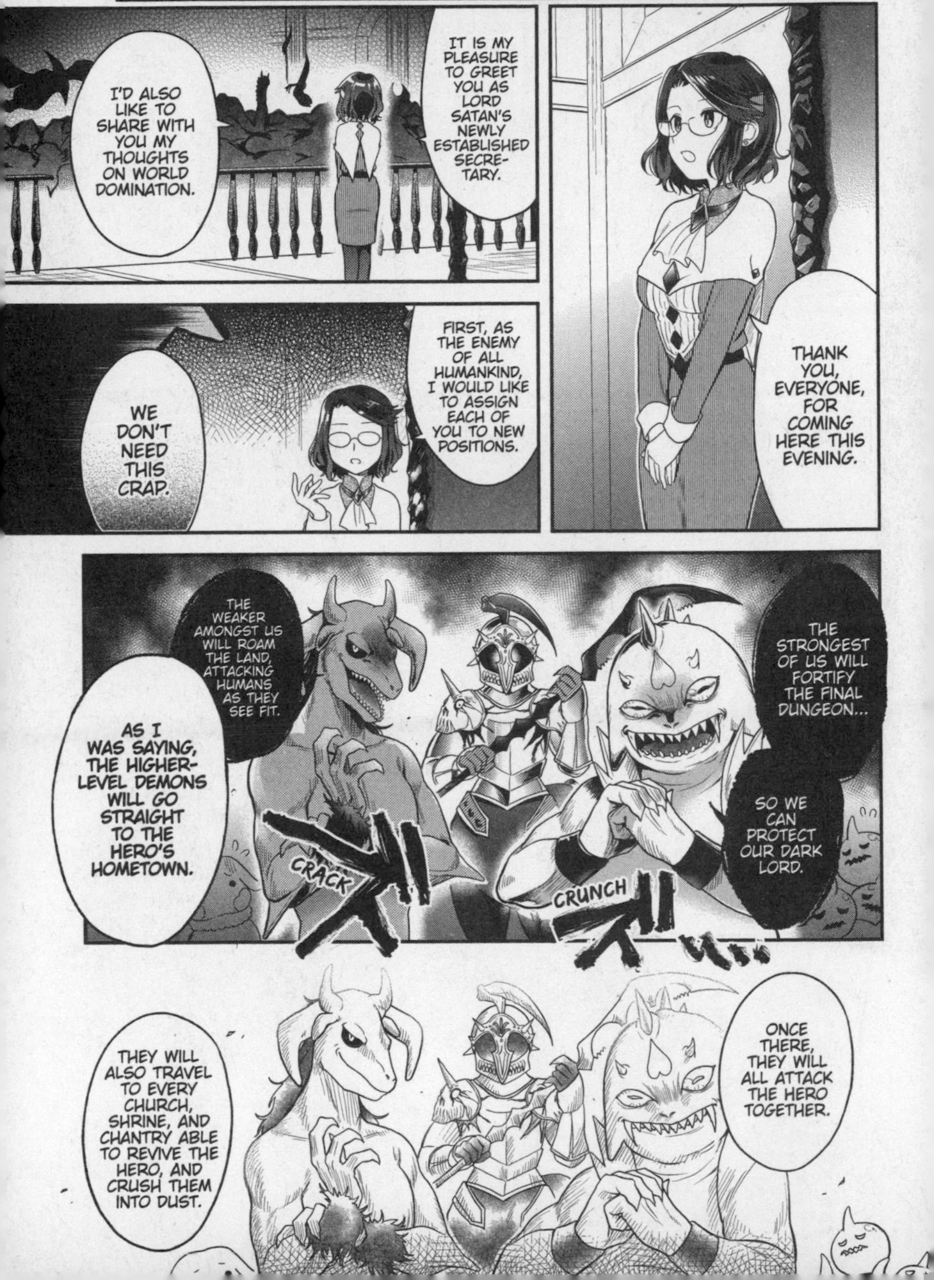
THANK YOU, EVERYONE, FOR COMING HERE THIS EVENING.
IT IS MY PLEASURE TO GREET YOU AS LORD SATAN'S NEWLY ESTABLISHED SECRE-TARY.
I'D ALSO LIKE TO SHARE WITH YOU MY THOUGHTS ON WORLD DOMINATION.
FIRST, AS THE ENEMY OF ALL HUMANKIND, I WOULD LIKE TO ASSIGN EACH OF YOU TO NEW POSITIONS.
WE DON'T NEED THIS CRAP.
THE STRONGEST OF US WILL FORTIFY THE FINAL DUNGEON...
SO WE CAN PROTECT OUR DARK LORD.
THE WEAKER AMONGST US WILL ROAM THE LAND, ATTACKING HUMANS AS THEY SEE FIT.
AS I WAS SAYING, THE HIGHER-LEVEL DEMONS WILL GO STRAIGHT TO THE HERO'S HOMETOWN.
CRUNCH
CRACK
ONCE THERE, THEY WILL ALL ATTACK THE HERO TOGETHER.
THEY WILL ALSO TRAVEL TO EVERY CHURCH, SHRINE, AND CHANTRY ABLE TO REVIVE THE HERO, AND CRUSH THEM INTO DUST.

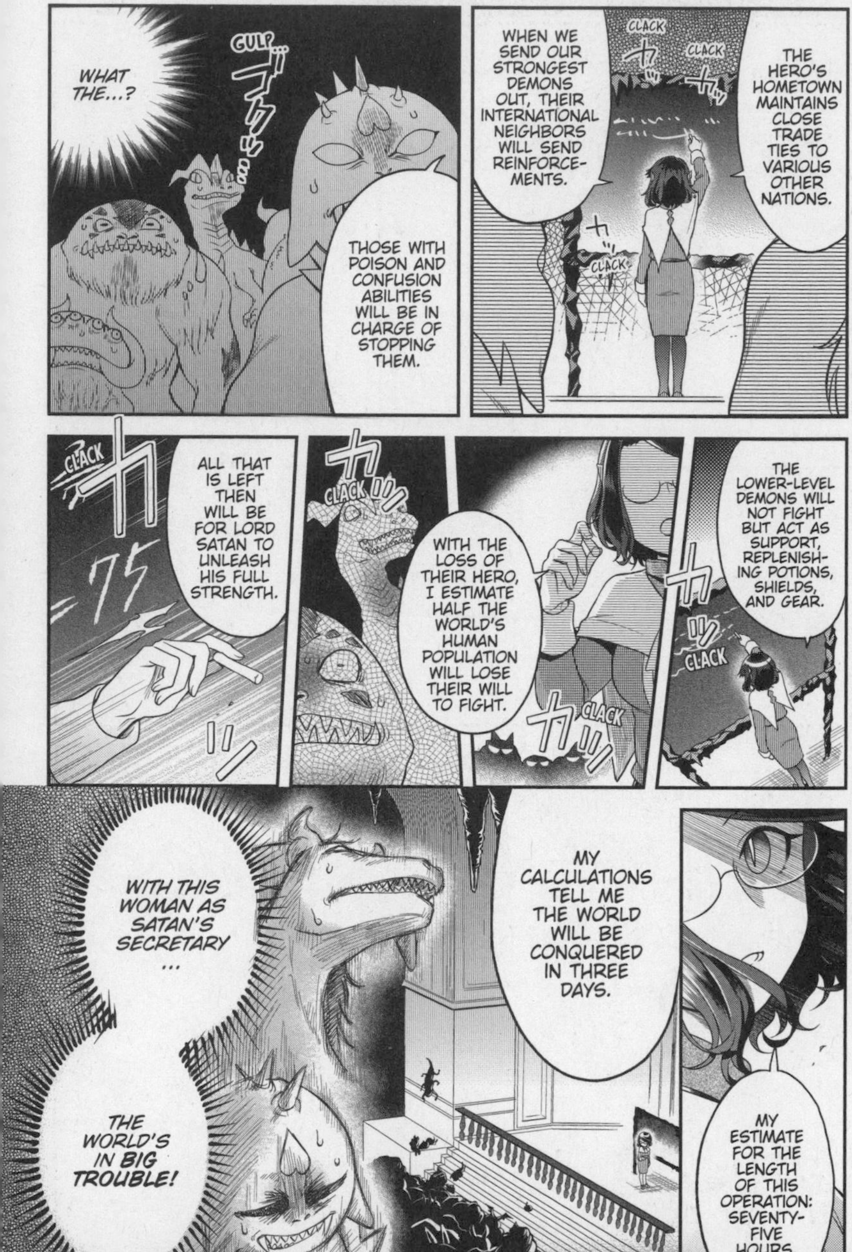
CLACK
CLACK
THE HERO'S HOMETOWN MAINTAINS CLOSE TRADE TIES TO VARIOUS OTHER NATIONS.
WHEN WE SEND OUR STRONGEST DEMONS OUT, THEIR INTERNATIONAL NEIGHBORS WILL SEND REINFORCE-MENTS.
CLACK
THOSE WITH POISON AND CONFUSION ABILITIES WILL BE IN CHARGE OF STOPPING THEM.
GULP...
WHAT THE...?
THE LOWER-LEVEL DEMONS WILL NOT FIGHT BUT ACT AS SUPPORT, REPLENISH-ING POTIONS, SHIELDS, AND GEAR.
CLACK
CLACK
WITH THE LOSS OF THEIR HERO, I ESTIMATE HALF THE WORLD'S HUMAN POPULATION WILL LOSE THEIR WILL TO FIGHT.
CLACK
ALL THAT IS LEFT THEN WILL BE FOR LORD SATAN TO UNLEASH HIS FULL STRENGTH.
CLACK
75
MY ESTIMATE FOR THE LENGTH OF THIS OPERATION: SEVENTY-FIVE HOURS.
MY CALCULATIONS TELL ME THE WORLD WILL BE CONQUERED IN THREE DAYS.
WITH THIS WOMAN AS SATAN'S SECRETARY...
THE WORLD'S IN BIG TROUBLE!

# THE MEET AND GREET LATER...

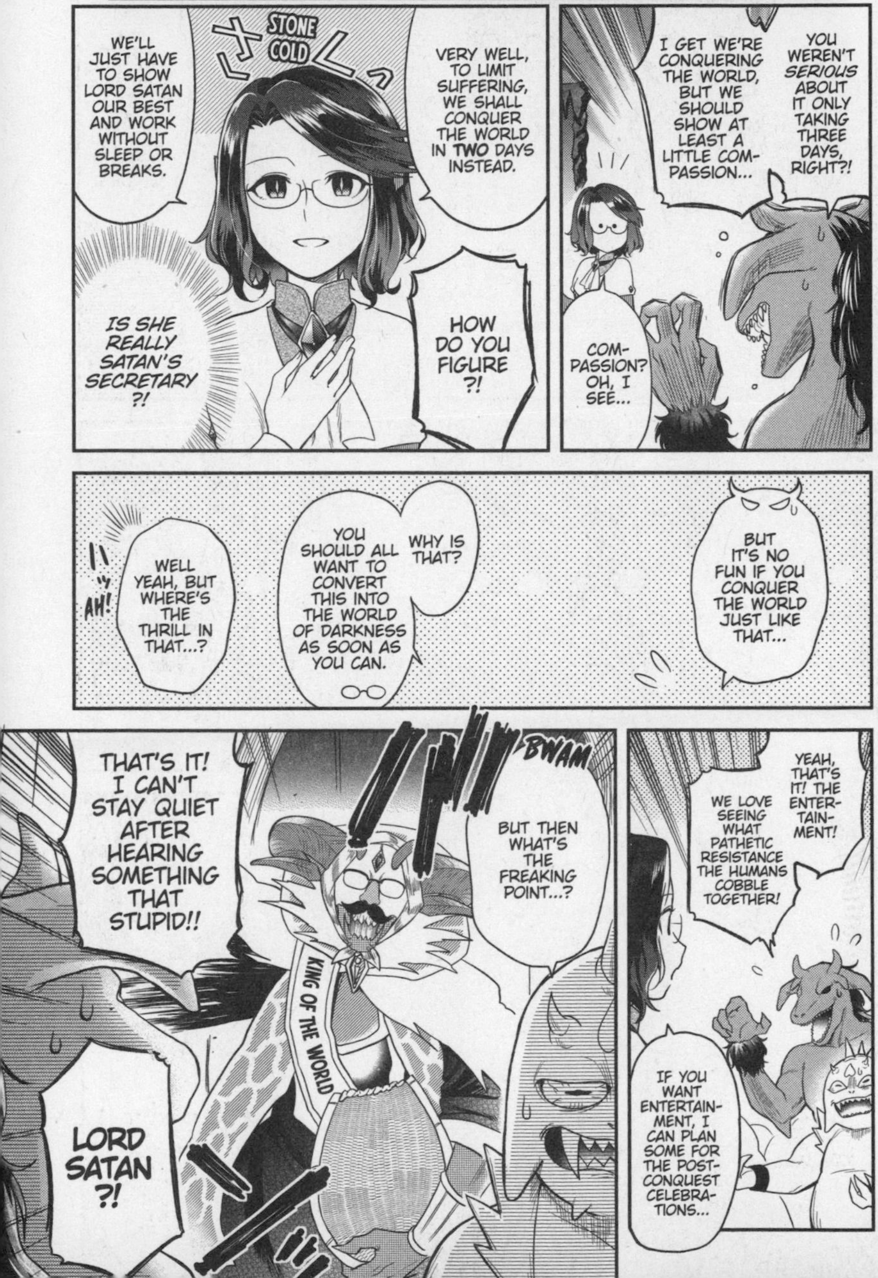
YOU WEREN'T SERIOUS ABOUT IT ONLY TAKING THREE DAYS, RIGHT?!
I GET WE'RE CONQUERING THE WORLD, BUT WE SHOULD SHOW AT LEAST A LITTLE COMPASSION...
COMPASSION? OH, I SEE...
VERY WELL, TO LIMIT SUFFERING, WE SHALL CONQUER THE WORLD IN TWO DAYS INSTEAD.
STONE COLD
WE'LL JUST HAVE TO SHOW LORD SATAN OUR BEST AND WORK WITHOUT SLEEP OR BREAKS.
HOW DO YOU FIGURE?!
IS SHE REALLY SATAN'S SECRETARY?!
BUT IT'S NO FUN IF YOU CONQUER THE WORLD JUST LIKE THAT...
WHY IS THAT?
YOU SHOULD ALL WANT TO CONVERT THIS INTO THE WORLD OF DARKNESS AS SOON AS YOU CAN.
WELL YEAH, BUT WHERE'S THE THRILL IN THAT...?
AH!
YEAH, THAT'S IT! THE ENTERTAINMENT!
WE LOVE SEEING WHAT PATHETIC RESISTANCE THE HUMANS COBBLE TOGETHER!
IF YOU WANT ENTERTAINMENT, I CAN PLAN SOME FOR THE POST-CONQUEST CELEBRATIONS...
BWAM
BUT THEN WHAT'S THE FREAKING POINT...?
THAT'S IT! I CAN'T STAY QUIET AFTER HEARING SOMETHING THAT STUPID!!
KING OF THE WORLD
LORD SATAN?!

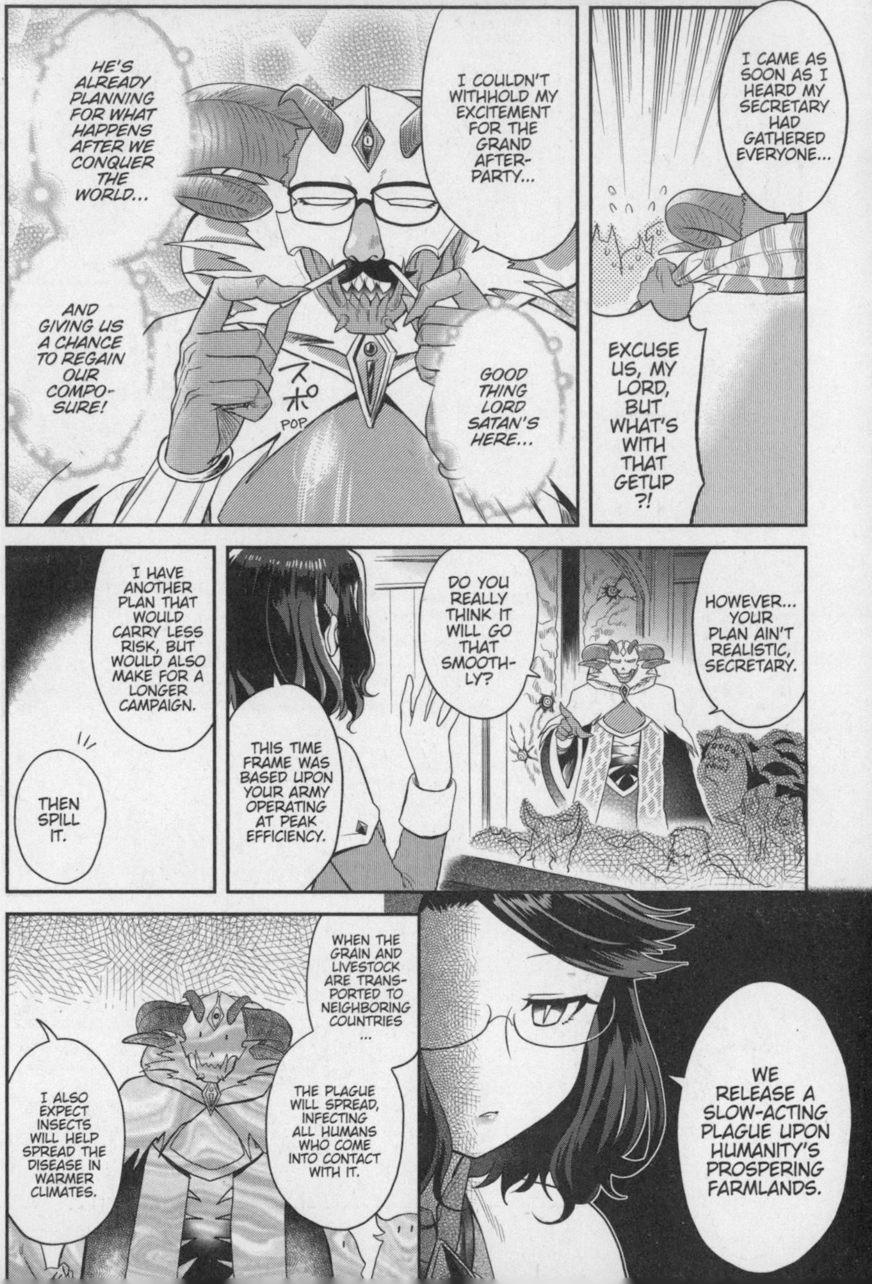
I CAME AS SOON AS I HEARD MY SECRETARY HAD GATHERED EVERYONE...
EXCUSE US, MY LORD, BUT WHAT'S WITH THAT GETUP?!
I COULDN'T WITHHOLD MY EXCITEMENT FOR THE GRAND AFTER-PARTY...
HE'S ALREADY PLANNING FOR WHAT HAPPENS AFTER WE CONQUER THE WORLD...
GOOD THING LORD SATAN'S HERE...
スポ
POP
AND GIVING US A CHANCE TO REGAIN OUR COMPOSURE!
HOWEVER... YOUR PLAN AIN'T REALISTIC, SECRETARY.
DO YOU REALLY THINK IT WILL GO THAT SMOOTHLY?
THIS TIME FRAME WAS BASED UPON YOUR ARMY OPERATING AT PEAK EFFICIENCY.
I HAVE ANOTHER PLAN THAT WOULD CARRY LESS RISK, BUT WOULD ALSO MAKE FOR A LONGER CAMPAIGN.
THEN SPILL IT.
WE RELEASE A SLOW-ACTING PLAGUE UPON HUMANITY'S PROSPERING FARMLANDS.
WHEN THE GRAIN AND LIVESTOCK ARE TRANSPORTED TO NEIGHBORING COUNTRIES...
THE PLAGUE WILL SPREAD, INFECTING ALL HUMANS WHO COME INTO CONTACT WITH IT.
I ALSO EXPECT INSECTS WILL HELP SPREAD THE DISEASE IN WARMER CLIMATES.

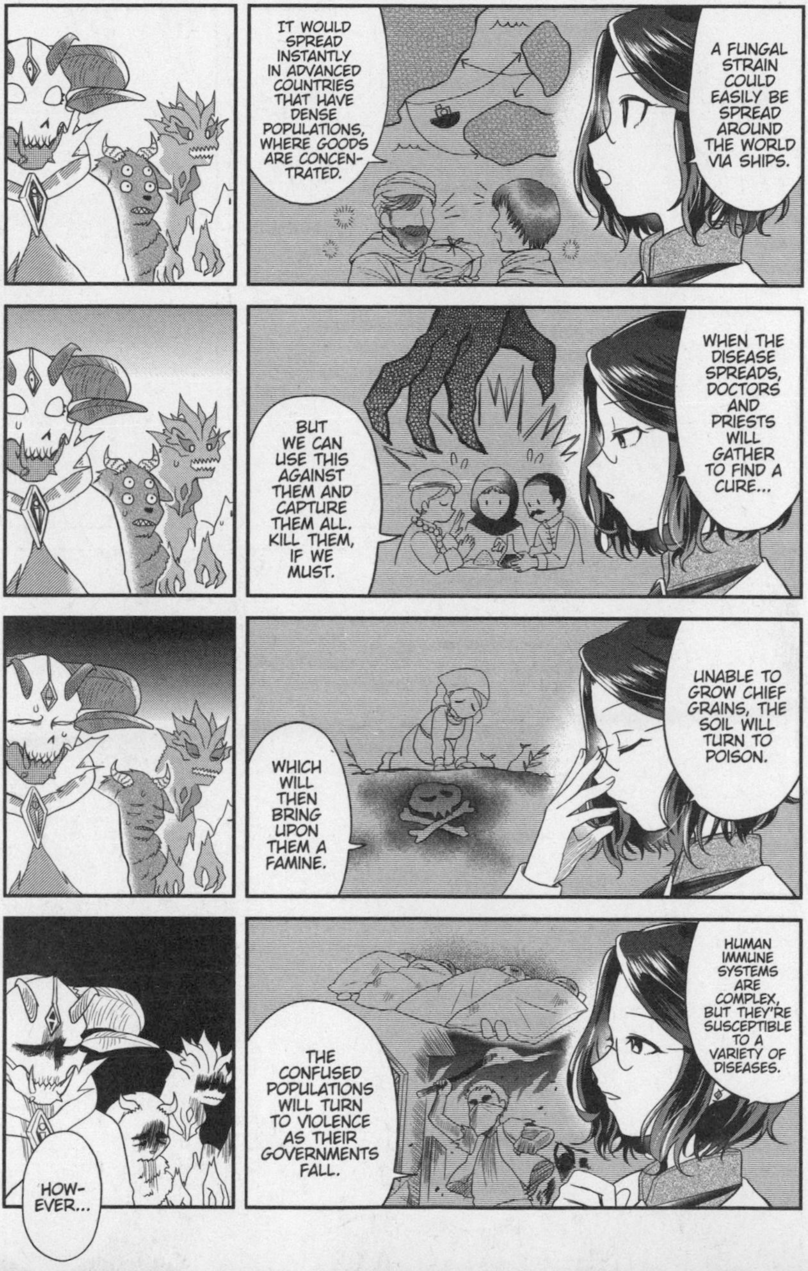
A FUNGAL STRAIN COULD EASILY BE SPREAD AROUND THE WORLD VIA SHIPS.
IT WOULD SPREAD INSTANTLY IN ADVANCED COUNTRIES THAT HAVE DENSE POPULATIONS, WHERE GOODS ARE CONCEN-TRATED.
WHEN THE DISEASE SPREADS, DOCTORS AND PRIESTS WILL GATHER TO FIND A CURE...
BUT WE CAN USE THIS AGAINST THEM AND CAPTURE THEM ALL. KILL THEM, IF WE MUST.
UNABLE TO GROW CHIEF GRAINS, THE SOIL WILL TURN TO POISON.
WHICH WILL THEN BRING UPON THEM A FAMINE.
HUMAN IMMUNE SYSTEMS ARE COMPLEX, BUT THEY'RE SUSCEPTIBLE TO A VARIETY OF DISEASES.
THE CONFUSED POPULATIONS WILL TURN TO VIOLENCE AS THEIR GOVERNMENTS FALL.
HOW-EVER...

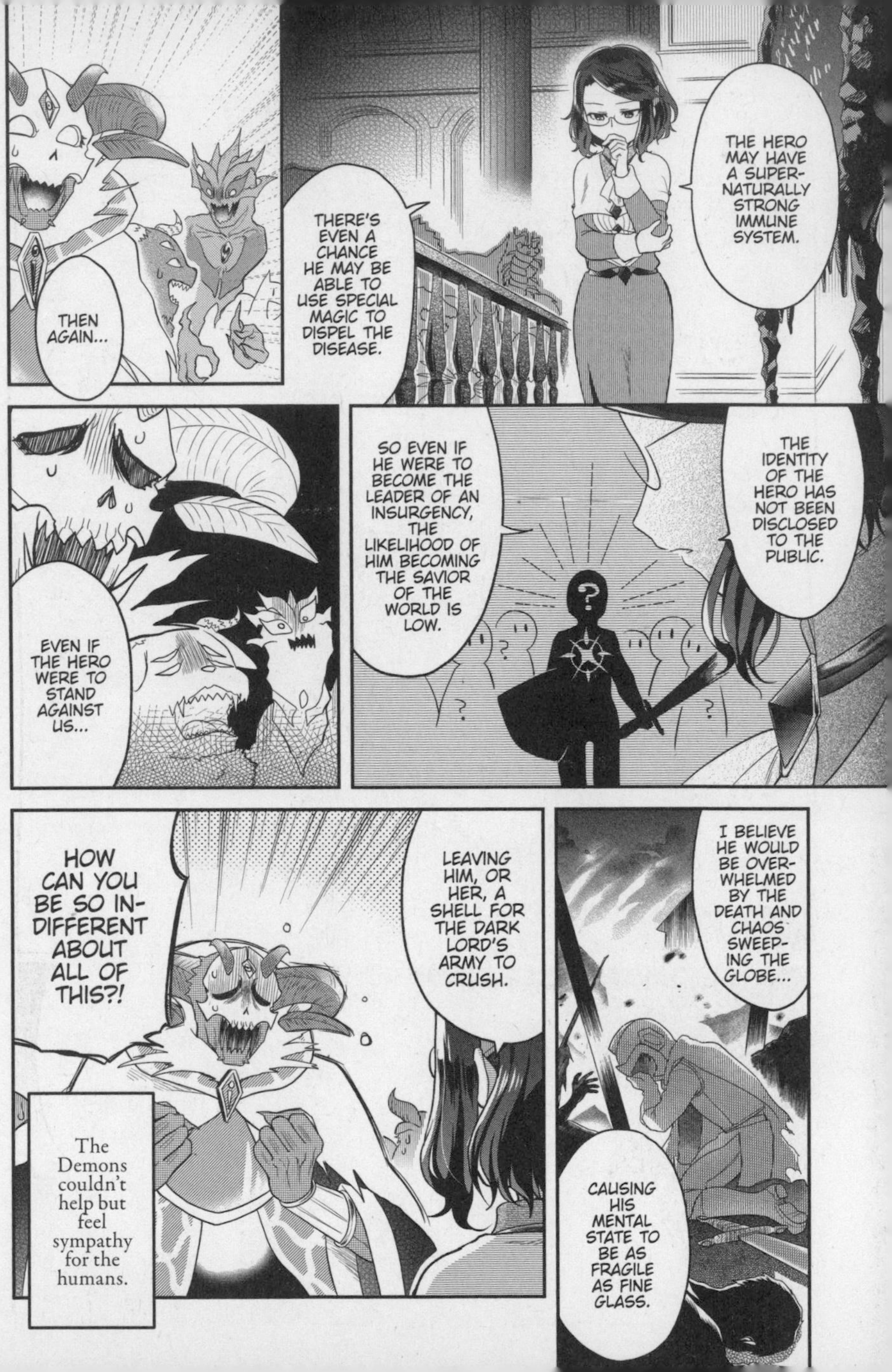
THE HERO MAY HAVE A SUPER-NATURALLY STRONG IMMUNE SYSTEM.
THERE'S EVEN A CHANCE HE MAY BE ABLE TO USE SPECIAL MAGIC TO DISPEL THE DISEASE.
THEN AGAIN...
THE IDENTITY OF THE HERO HAS NOT BEEN DISCLOSED TO THE PUBLIC.
SO EVEN IF HE WERE TO BECOME THE LEADER OF AN INSURGENCY, THE LIKELIHOOD OF HIM BECOMING THE SAVIOR OF THE WORLD IS LOW.
EVEN IF THE HERO WERE TO STAND AGAINST US...
I BELIEVE HE WOULD BE OVER-WHELMED BY THE DEATH AND CHAOS SWEEP-ING THE GLOBE...
CAUSING HIS MENTAL STATE TO BE AS FRAGILE AS FINE GLASS.
LEAVING HIM, OR HER, A SHELL FOR THE DARK LORD'S ARMY TO CRUSH.
HOW CAN YOU BE SO IN-DIFFERENT ABOUT ALL OF THIS?!
The Demons couldn't help but feel sympathy for the humans.

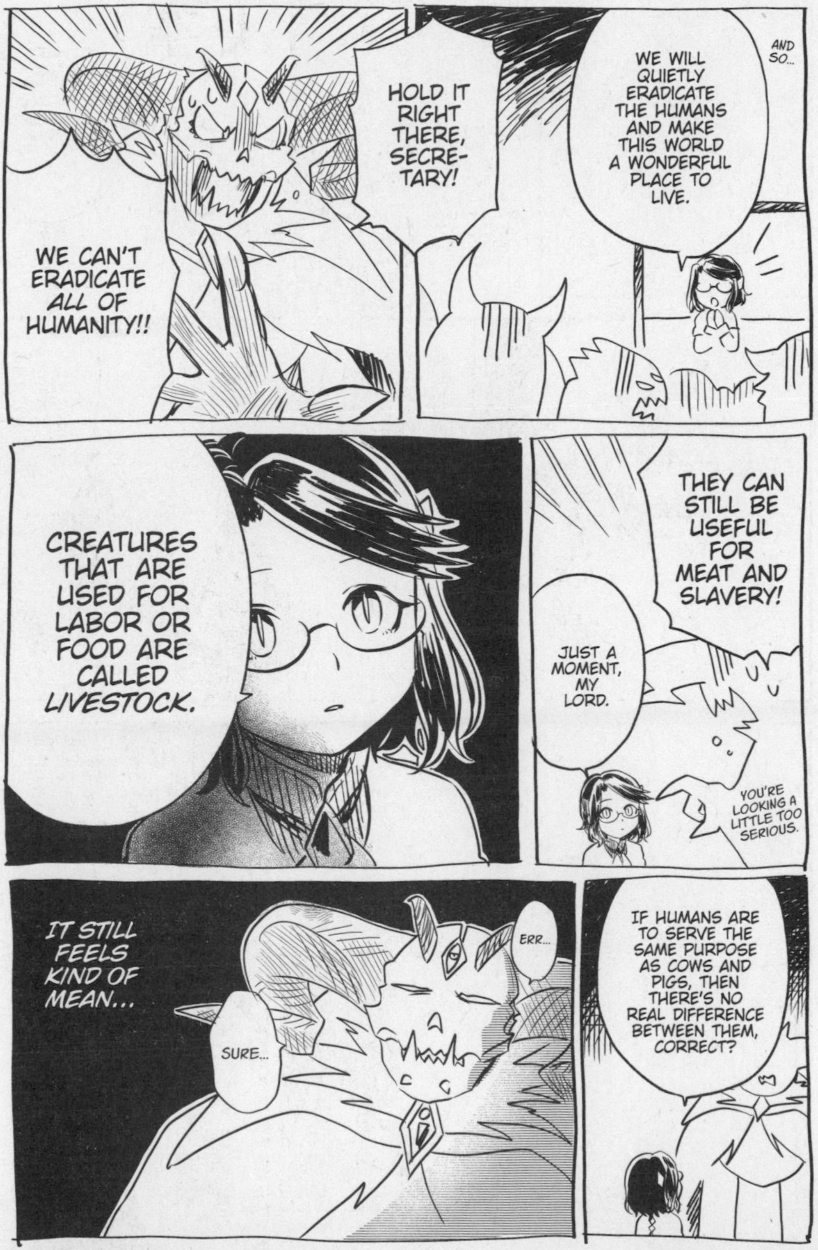
AND SO...
WE WILL QUIETLY ERADICATE THE HUMANS AND MAKE THIS WORLD A WONDERFUL PLACE TO LIVE.
HOLD IT RIGHT THERE, SECRETARY!
WE CAN'T ERADICATE ALL OF HUMANITY!!
THEY CAN STILL BE USEFUL FOR MEAT AND SLAVERY!
JUST A MOMENT, MY LORD.
YOU'RE LOOKING A LITTLE TOO SERIOUS.
CREATURES THAT ARE USED FOR LABOR OR FOOD ARE CALLED LIVESTOCK.
IF HUMANS ARE TO SERVE THE SAME PURPOSE AS COWS AND PIGS, THEN THERE'S NO REAL DIFFERENCE BETWEEN THEM, CORRECT?
ERR...
SURE...
IT STILL FEELS KIND OF MEAN...

**SATAN'S SECRETARY**

# ZERO POINTS FOR SERVICE

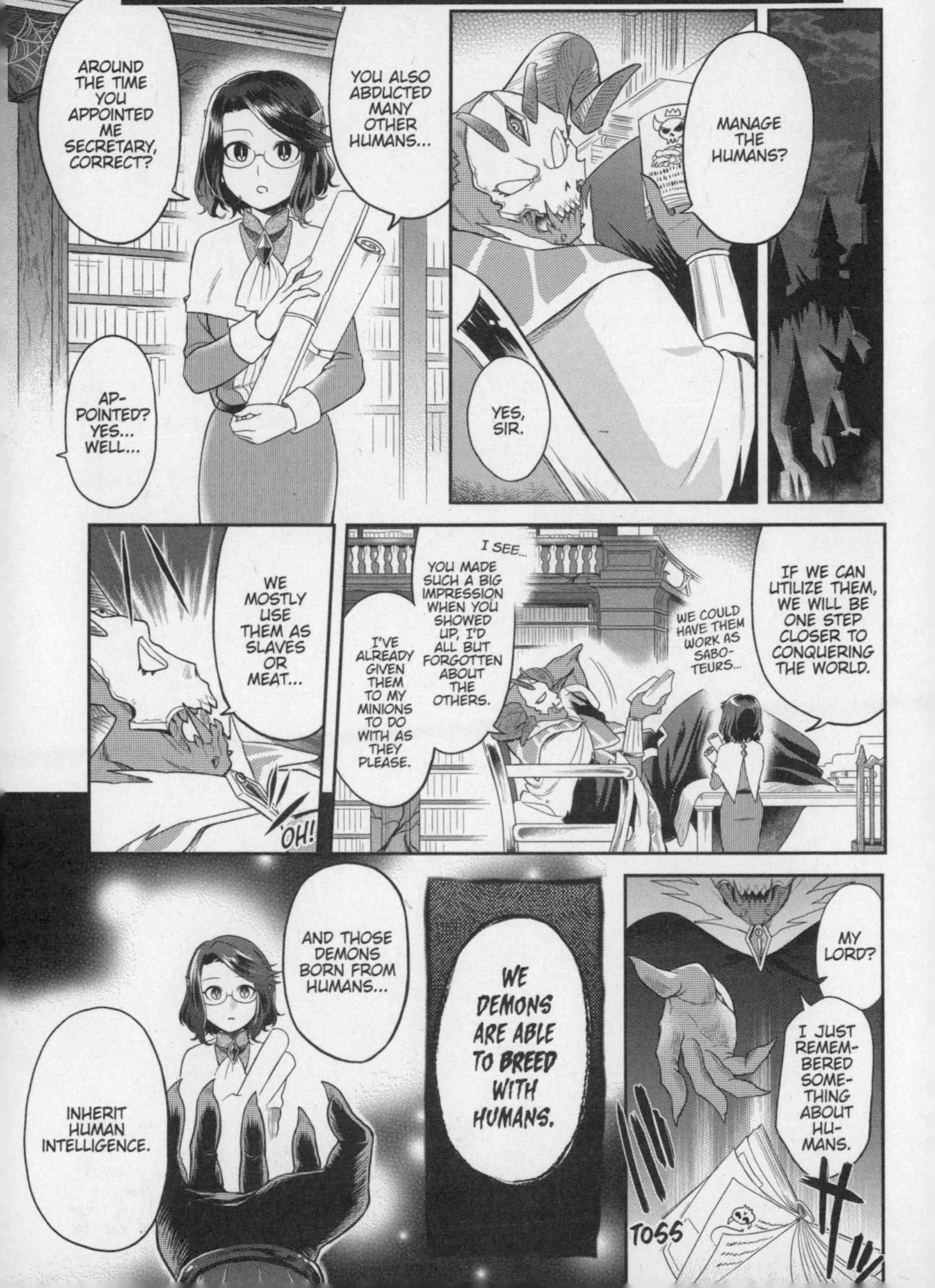
MANAGE THE HUMANS?
YES, SIR.
YOU ALSO ABDUCTED MANY OTHER HUMANS...
AROUND THE TIME YOU APPOINTED ME SECRETARY, CORRECT?
AP-POINTED? YES... WELL...
IF WE CAN UTILIZE THEM, WE WILL BE ONE STEP CLOSER TO CONQUERING THE WORLD.
WE COULD HAVE THEM WORK AS SABO-TEURS...
I SEE... YOU MADE SUCH A BIG IMPRESSION WHEN YOU SHOWED UP, I'D ALL BUT FORGOTTEN ABOUT THE OTHERS.
I'VE ALREADY GIVEN THEM TO MY MINIONS TO DO WITH AS THEY PLEASE.
WE MOSTLY USE THEM AS SLAVES OR MEAT...
OH!
MY LORD?
I JUST REMEM-BERED SOME-THING ABOUT HU-MANS.
TOSS
WE DEMONS ARE ABLE TO BREED WITH HUMANS.
AND THOSE DEMONS BORN FROM HUMANS...
INHERIT HUMAN INTELLIGENCE.

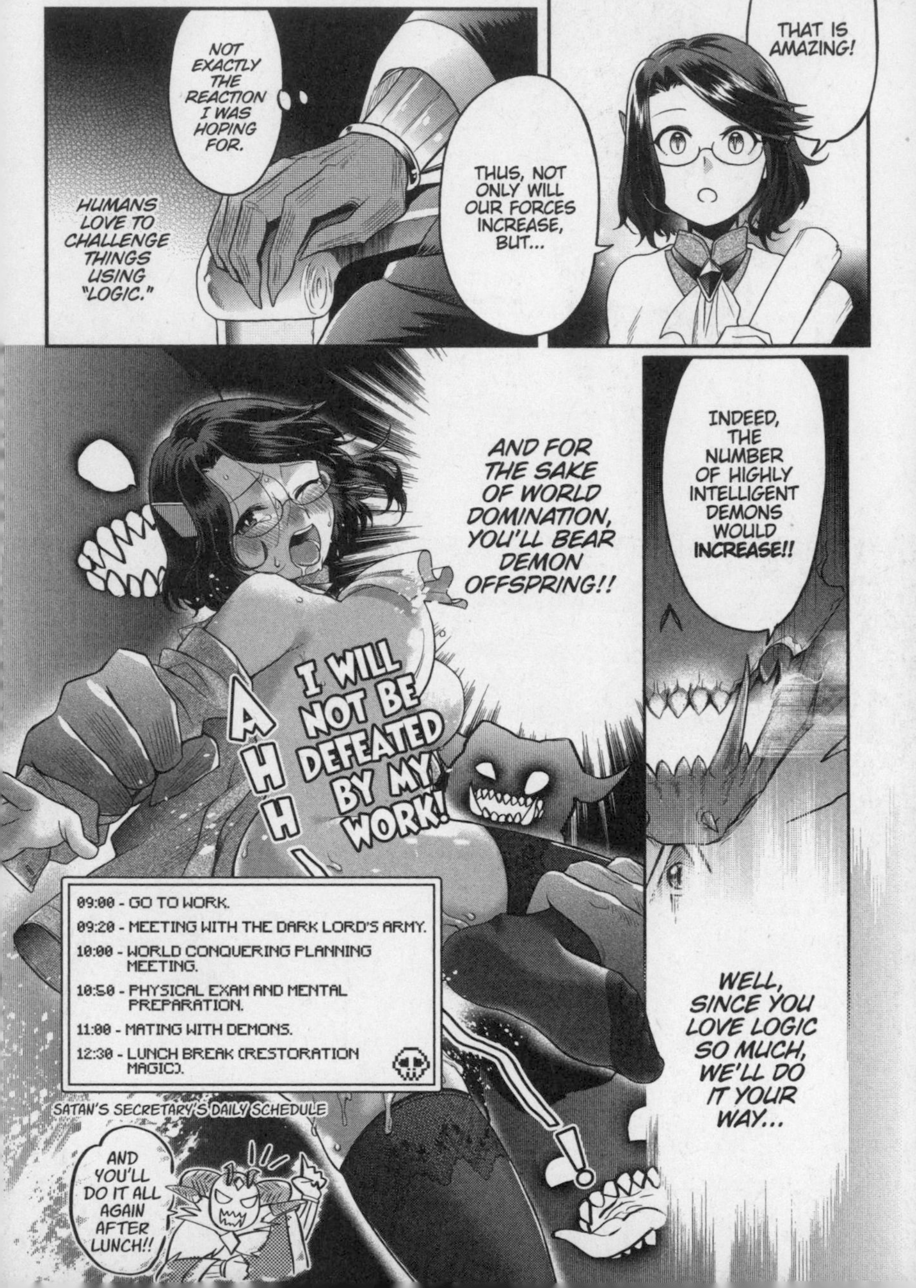
THAT IS AMAZING!
THUS, NOT ONLY WILL OUR FORCES INCREASE, BUT...
NOT EXACTLY THE REACTION I WAS HOPING FOR.
HUMANS LOVE TO CHALLENGE THINGS USING "LOGIC."
INDEED, THE NUMBER OF HIGHLY INTELLIGENT DEMONS WOULD INCREASE!!
WELL, SINCE YOU LOVE LOGIC SO MUCH, WE'LL DO IT YOUR WAY...
AND FOR THE SAKE OF WORLD DOMINATION, YOU'LL BEAR DEMON OFFSPRING!!
I WILL NOT BE DEFEATED BY MY WORK!
AHH
09:00 - GO TO WORK.
09:20 - MEETING WITH THE DARK LORD'S ARMY.
10:00 - WORLD CONQUERING PLANNING MEETING.
10:50 - PHYSICAL EXAM AND MENTAL PREPARATION.
11:00 - MATING WITH DEMONS.
12:30 - LUNCH BREAK (RESTORATION MAGIC).
SATAN'S SECRETARY'S DAILY SCHEDULE
AND YOU'LL DO IT ALL AGAIN AFTER LUNCH!!

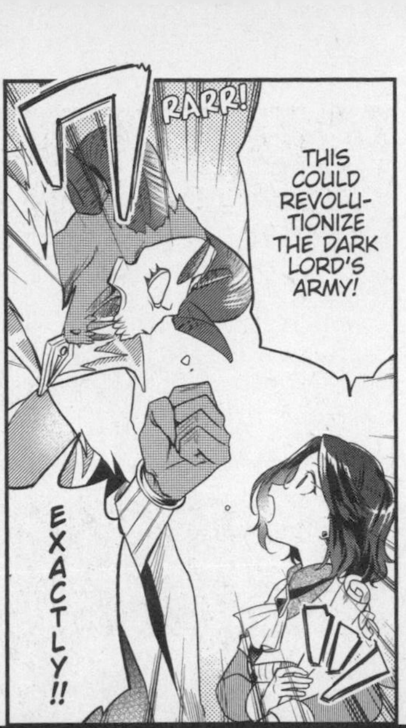
RARR!
THIS COULD REVOLUTIONIZE THE DARK LORD'S ARMY!
EXACTLY!!

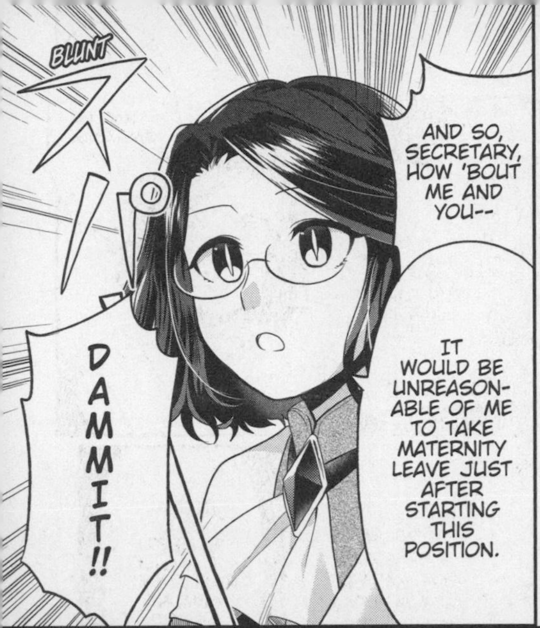
AND SO, SECRETARY, HOW 'BOUT ME AND YOU--
IT WOULD BE UNREASONABLE OF ME TO TAKE MATERNITY LEAVE JUST AFTER STARTING THIS POSITION.
BLUNT
DAMMIT!!

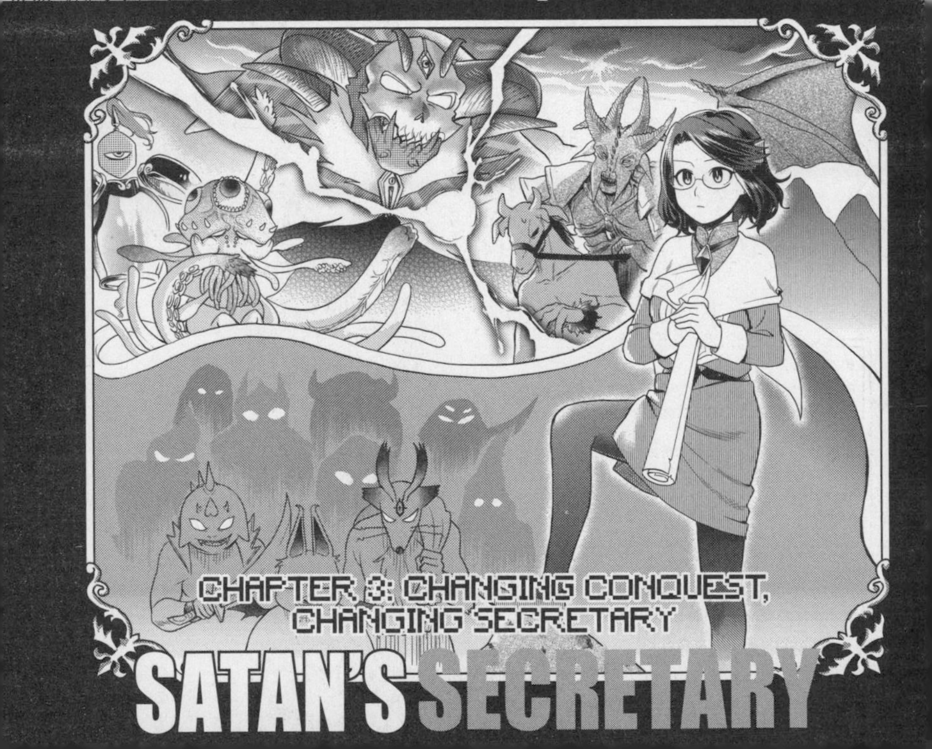
CHAPTER 3: CHANGING CONQUEST, CHANGING SECRETARY
SATAN'S SECRETARY

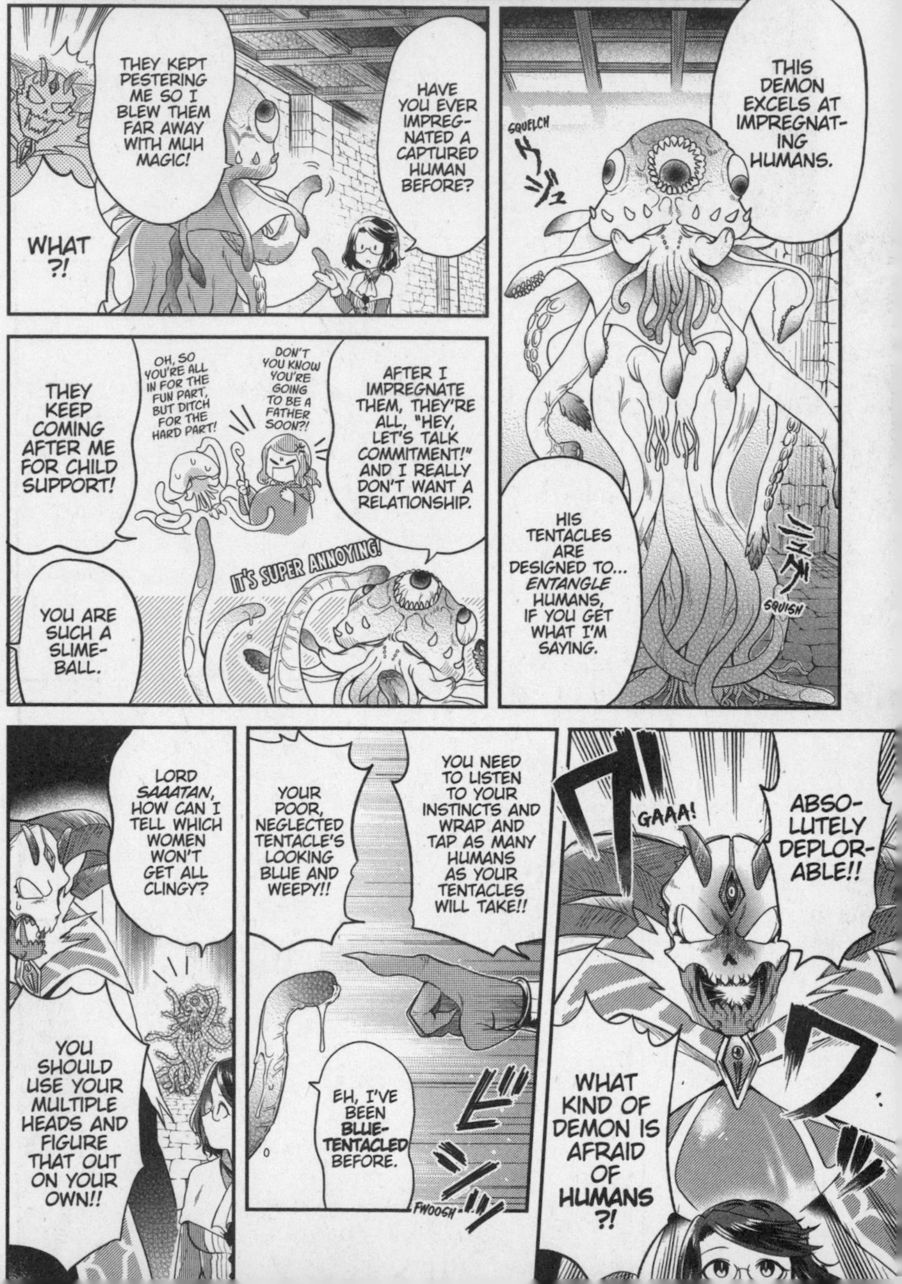
THIS DEMON EXCELS AT IMPREGNATING HUMANS.
SQUELCH
HIS TENTACLES ARE DESIGNED TO... *ENTANGLE* HUMANS, IF YOU GET WHAT I'M SAYING.
SQUISH
HAVE YOU EVER IMPREGNATED A CAPTURED HUMAN BEFORE?
THEY KEPT PESTERING ME SO I BLEW THEM FAR AWAY WITH MUH MAGIC!
WHAT?!
AFTER I IMPREGNATE THEM, THEY'RE ALL, "HEY, LET'S TALK COMMITMENT!" AND I REALLY DON'T WANT A RELATIONSHIP.
DON'T YOU KNOW YOU'RE GOING TO BE A FATHER SOON?!
OH, SO YOU'RE ALL IN FOR THE FUN PART, BUT DITCH FOR THE HARD PART!
THEY KEEP COMING AFTER ME FOR CHILD SUPPORT!
IT'S SUPER ANNOYING!
YOU ARE SUCH A SLIMEBALL.
GAAA!
ABSOLUTELY DEPLORABLE!!
WHAT KIND OF DEMON IS AFRAID OF HUMANS?!
YOU NEED TO LISTEN TO YOUR INSTINCTS AND WRAP AND TAP AS MANY HUMANS AS YOUR TENTACLES WILL TAKE!!
YOUR POOR, NEGLECTED TENTACLE'S LOOKING BLUE AND WEEPY!!
EH, I'VE BEEN **BLUE-TENTACLED** BEFORE.
FWOOSH
LORD *SAAATAN*, HOW CAN I TELL WHICH WOMEN WON'T GET ALL CLINGY?
YOU SHOULD USE YOUR MULTIPLE HEADS AND FIGURE THAT OUT ON YOUR OWN!!

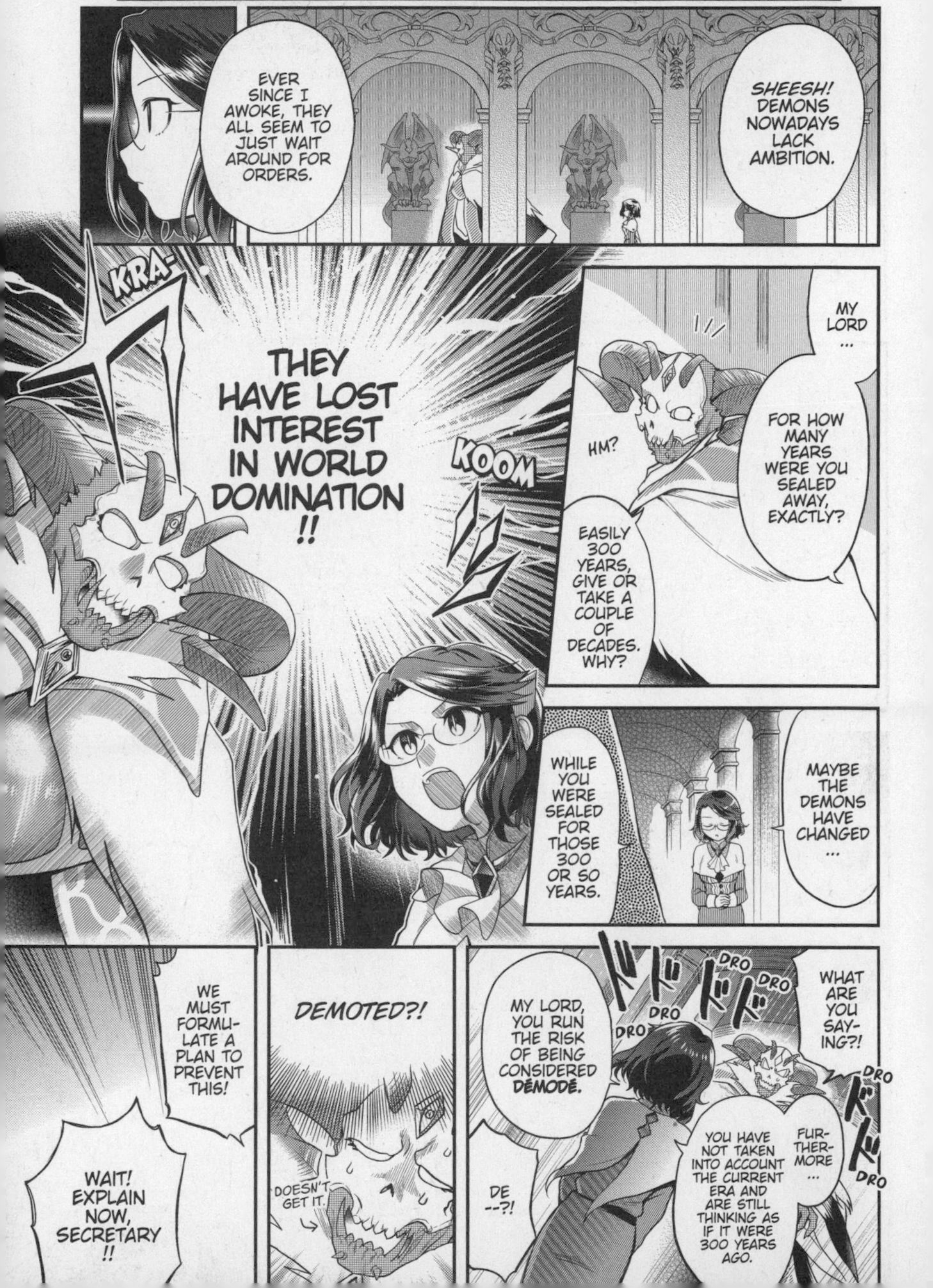
SHEESH! DEMONS NOWADAYS LACK AMBITION.
EVER SINCE I AWOKE, THEY ALL SEEM TO JUST WAIT AROUND FOR ORDERS.
MY LORD ...
FOR HOW MANY YEARS WERE YOU SEALED AWAY, EXACTLY?
HM?
EASILY 300 YEARS, GIVE OR TAKE A COUPLE OF DECADES. WHY?
MAYBE THE DEMONS HAVE CHANGED ...
WHILE YOU WERE SEALED FOR THOSE 300 OR SO YEARS.
KRA-
KOOM
THEY HAVE LOST INTEREST IN WORLD DOMINATION !!
WHAT ARE YOU SAYING?!
DRO DRO DRO DRO
MY LORD, YOU RUN THE RISK OF BEING CONSIDERED DÉMODÉ.
FURTHERMORE ...
YOU HAVE NOT TAKEN INTO ACCOUNT THE CURRENT ERA AND ARE STILL THINKING AS IF IT WERE 300 YEARS AGO.
DRO DRO
DE --?!
DEMOTED?!
DOESN'T GET IT.
WE MUST FORMULATE A PLAN TO PREVENT THIS!
WAIT! EXPLAIN NOW, SECRETARY !!

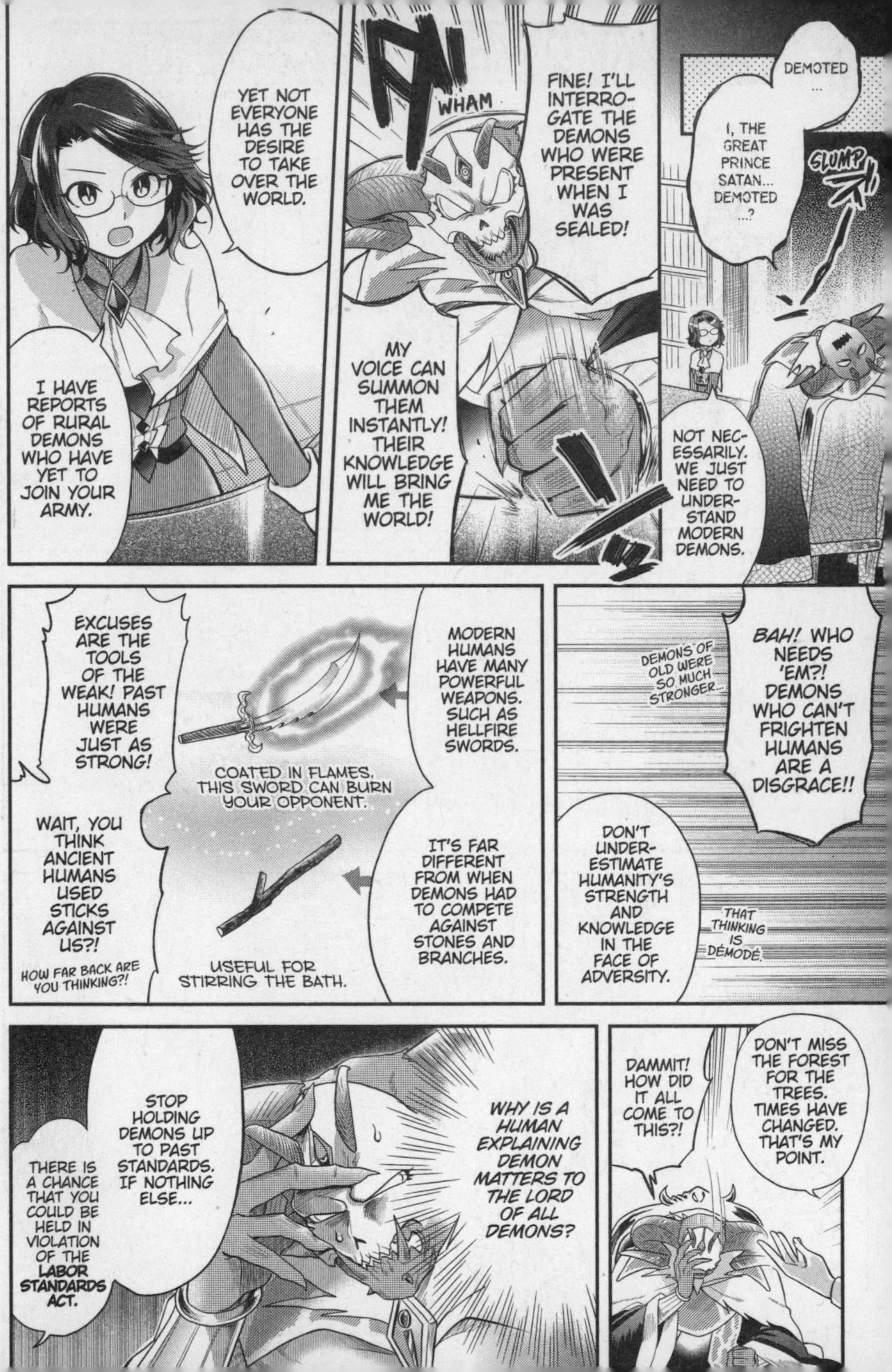
DEMOTED ...
I, THE GREAT PRINCE SATAN... DEMOTED ...?
SLUMP
NOT NECESSARILY. WE JUST NEED TO UNDERSTAND MODERN DEMONS.
WHAM
FINE! I'LL INTERROGATE THE DEMONS WHO WERE PRESENT WHEN I WAS SEALED!
MY VOICE CAN SUMMON THEM INSTANTLY! THEIR KNOWLEDGE WILL BRING ME THE WORLD!
YET NOT EVERYONE HAS THE DESIRE TO TAKE OVER THE WORLD.
I HAVE REPORTS OF RURAL DEMONS WHO HAVE YET TO JOIN YOUR ARMY.
BAH! WHO NEEDS 'EM?! DEMONS WHO CAN'T FRIGHTEN HUMANS ARE A DISGRACE!!
DEMONS OF OLD WERE SO MUCH STRONGER...
DON'T UNDERESTIMATE HUMANITY'S STRENGTH AND KNOWLEDGE IN THE FACE OF ADVERSITY.
THAT THINKING IS DÉMODÉ.
MODERN HUMANS HAVE MANY POWERFUL WEAPONS. SUCH AS HELLFIRE SWORDS.
COATED IN FLAMES. THIS SWORD CAN BURN YOUR OPPONENT.
IT'S FAR DIFFERENT FROM WHEN DEMONS HAD TO COMPETE AGAINST STONES AND BRANCHES.
USEFUL FOR STIRRING THE BATH.
EXCUSES ARE THE TOOLS OF THE WEAK! PAST HUMANS WERE JUST AS STRONG!
WAIT, YOU THINK ANCIENT HUMANS USED STICKS AGAINST US?!
HOW FAR BACK ARE YOU THINKING?!
DON'T MISS THE FOREST FOR THE TREES. TIMES HAVE CHANGED. THAT'S MY POINT.
DAMMIT! HOW DID IT ALL COME TO THIS?!
WHY IS A HUMAN EXPLAINING DEMON MATTERS TO THE LORD OF ALL DEMONS?
STOP HOLDING DEMONS UP TO PAST STANDARDS. IF NOTHING ELSE...
THERE IS A CHANCE THAT YOU COULD BE HELD IN VIOLATION OF THE LABOR STANDARDS ACT.

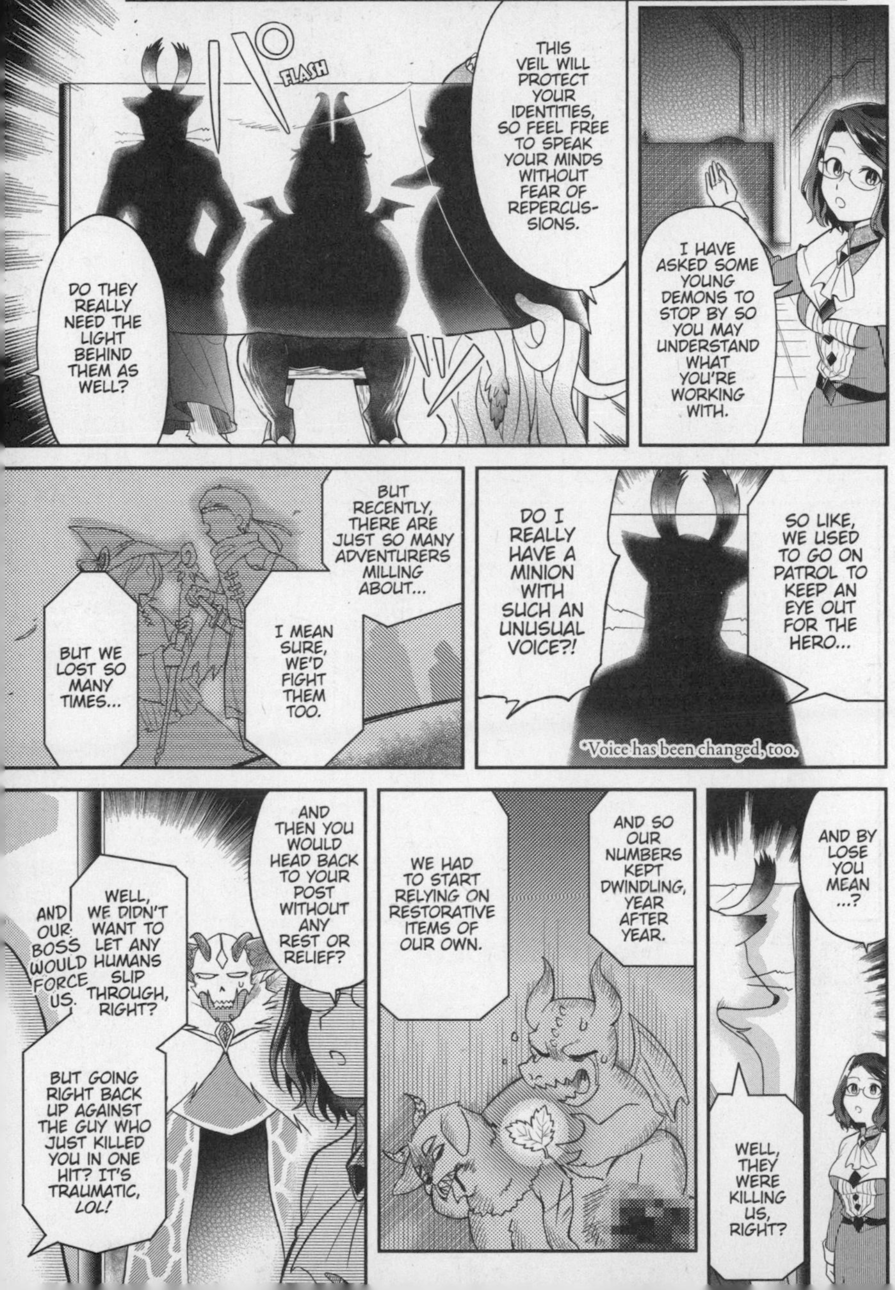
I HAVE ASKED SOME YOUNG DEMONS TO STOP BY SO YOU MAY UNDERSTAND WHAT YOU'RE WORKING WITH.
THIS VEIL WILL PROTECT YOUR IDENTITIES, SO FEEL FREE TO SPEAK YOUR MINDS WITHOUT FEAR OF REPERCUSSIONS.
FLASH
DO THEY REALLY NEED THE LIGHT BEHIND THEM AS WELL?
SO LIKE, WE USED TO GO ON PATROL TO KEEP AN EYE OUT FOR THE HERO...
DO I REALLY HAVE A MINION WITH SUCH AN UNUSUAL VOICE?!
*Voice has been changed, too.
BUT RECENTLY, THERE ARE JUST SO MANY ADVENTURERS MILLING ABOUT...
I MEAN SURE, WE'D FIGHT THEM TOO.
BUT WE LOST SO MANY TIMES...
AND BY LOSE YOU MEAN ...?
WELL, THEY WERE KILLING US, RIGHT?
AND SO OUR NUMBERS KEPT DWINDLING, YEAR AFTER YEAR.
WE HAD TO START RELYING ON RESTORATIVE ITEMS OF OUR OWN.
AND THEN YOU WOULD HEAD BACK TO YOUR POST WITHOUT ANY REST OR RELIEF?
WELL, WE DIDN'T WANT TO LET ANY HUMANS SLIP THROUGH, RIGHT?
AND OUR BOSS WOULD FORCE US.
BUT GOING RIGHT BACK UP AGAINST THE GUY WHO JUST KILLED YOU IN ONE HIT? IT'S TRAUMATIC, LOL!

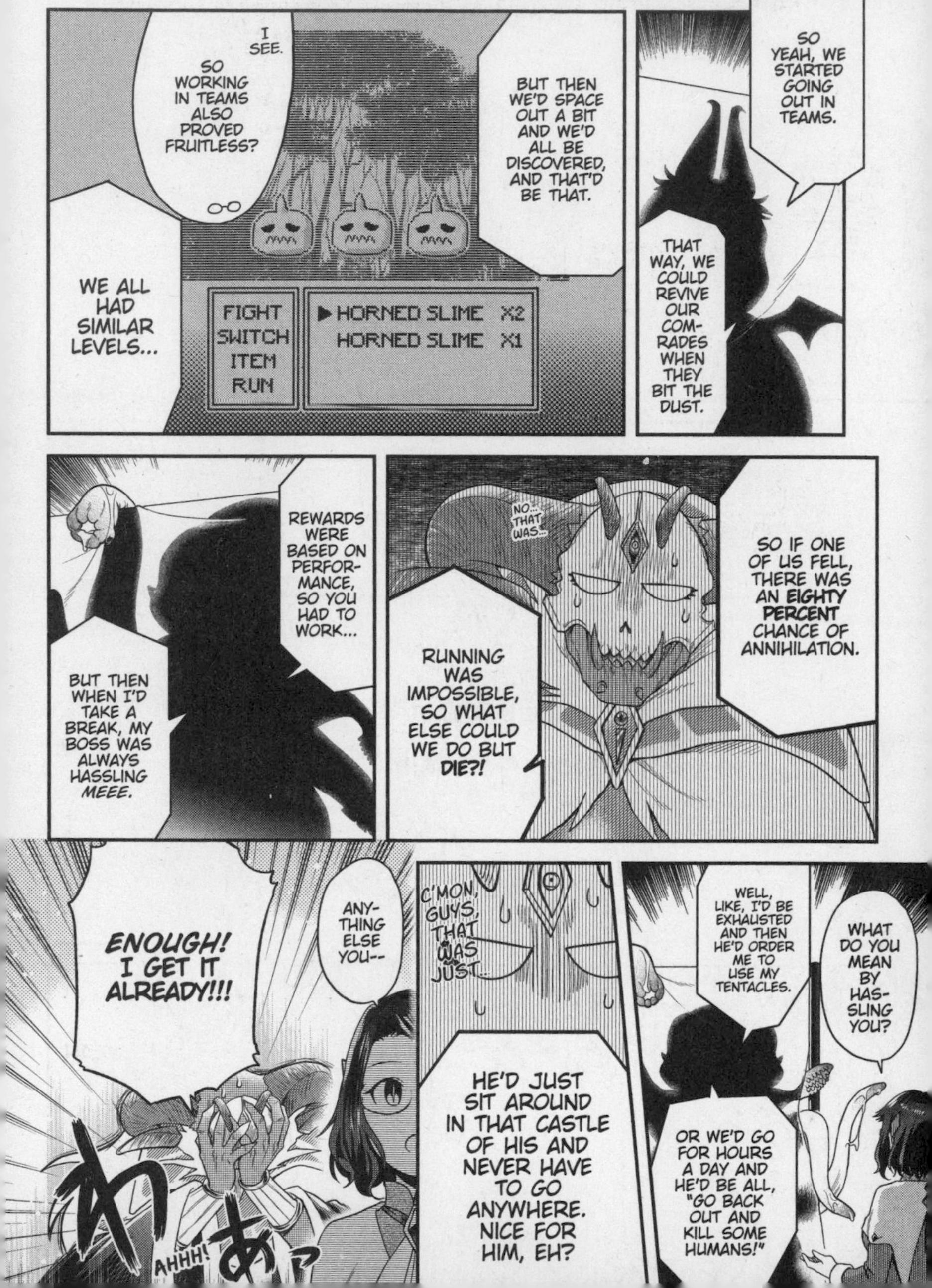
SO YEAH, WE STARTED GOING OUT IN TEAMS.
THAT WAY, WE COULD REVIVE OUR COMRADES WHEN THEY BIT THE DUST.
WE ALL HAD SIMILAR LEVELS...
FIGHT
SWITCH
ITEM
RUN
▶HORNED SLIME X2
HORNED SLIME X1
BUT THEN WE'D SPACE OUT A BIT AND WE'D ALL BE DISCOVERED, AND THAT'D BE THAT.
I SEE.
SO WORKING IN TEAMS ALSO PROVED FRUITLESS?
SO IF ONE OF US FELL, THERE WAS AN **EIGHTY PERCENT** CHANCE OF ANNIHILATION.
NO... THAT WAS...
RUNNING WAS IMPOSSIBLE, SO WHAT ELSE COULD WE DO BUT **DIE?!**
REWARDS WERE BASED ON PERFORMANCE, SO YOU HAD TO WORK...
BUT THEN WHEN I'D TAKE A BREAK, MY BOSS WAS ALWAYS HASSLING MEEE.
WHAT DO YOU MEAN BY HASSLING YOU?
WELL, LIKE, I'D BE EXHAUSTED AND THEN HE'D ORDER ME TO USE MY TENTACLES.
OR WE'D GO FOR HOURS A DAY AND HE'D BE ALL, "GO BACK OUT AND KILL SOME HUMANS!"
C'MON, GUYS, THAT WAS JUST...
HE'D JUST SIT AROUND IN THAT CASTLE OF HIS AND NEVER HAVE TO GO ANYWHERE. NICE FOR HIM, EH?
ANYTHING ELSE YOU--
*ENOUGH! I GET IT ALREADY!!!*
AHHH!

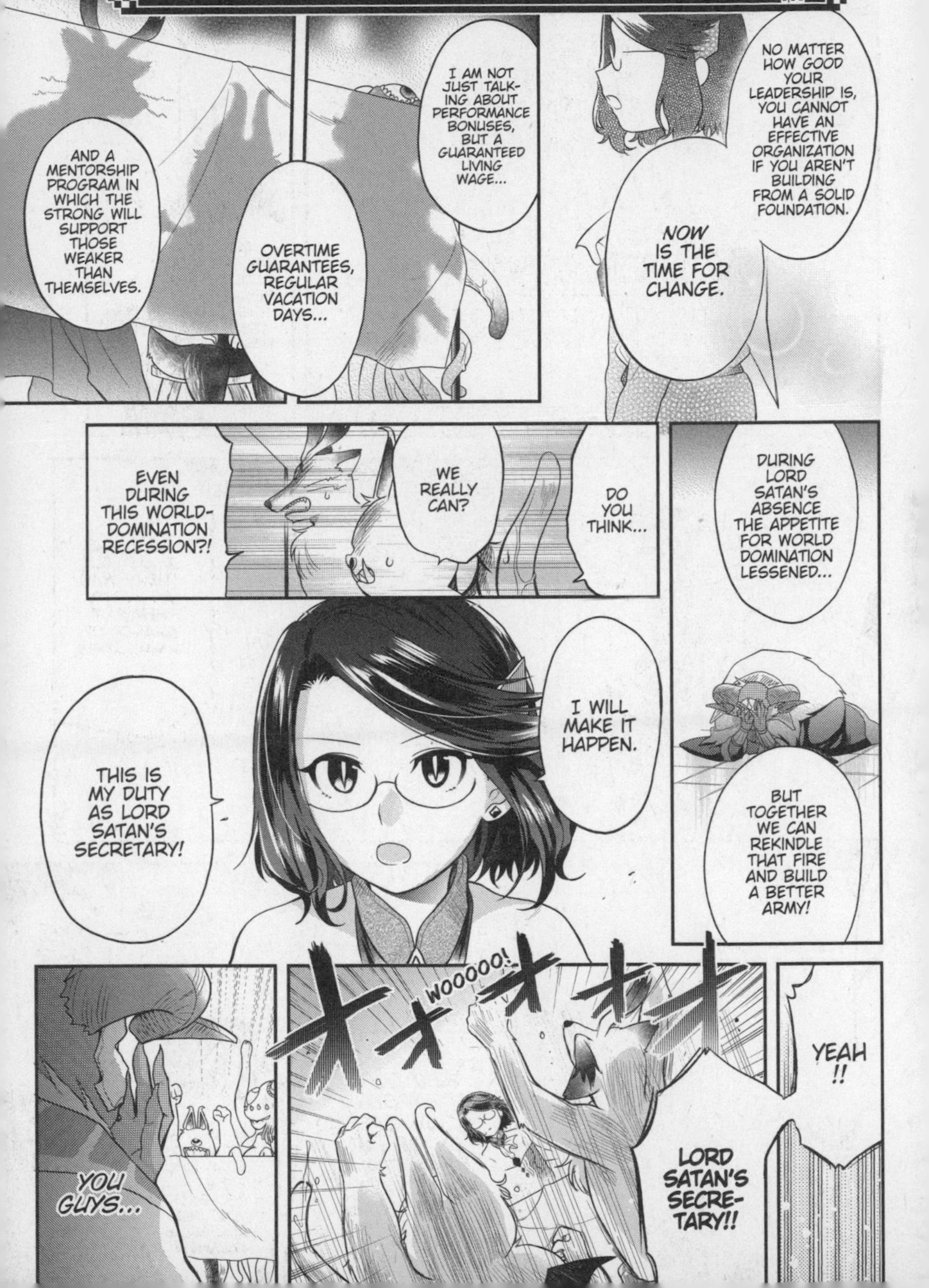
NO MATTER HOW GOOD YOUR LEADERSHIP IS, YOU CANNOT HAVE AN EFFECTIVE ORGANIZATION IF YOU AREN'T BUILDING FROM A SOLID FOUNDATION.
*NOW* IS THE TIME FOR CHANGE.
I AM NOT JUST TALKING ABOUT PERFORMANCE BONUSES, BUT A GUARANTEED LIVING WAGE...
OVERTIME GUARANTEES, REGULAR VACATION DAYS...
AND A MENTORSHIP PROGRAM IN WHICH THE STRONG WILL SUPPORT THOSE WEAKER THAN THEMSELVES.
DURING LORD SATAN'S ABSENCE THE APPETITE FOR WORLD DOMINATION LESSENED...
BUT TOGETHER WE CAN REKINDLE THAT FIRE AND BUILD A BETTER ARMY!
DO YOU THINK...
WE REALLY CAN?
EVEN DURING THIS WORLD-DOMINATION RECESSION?!
I WILL MAKE IT HAPPEN.
THIS IS MY DUTY AS LORD SATAN'S SECRETARY!
YEAH!!
WOOOOO!
LORD SATAN'S SECRE-TARY!!
YOU GUYS...

# WANTED: A DEMON WITH A BRAIN!

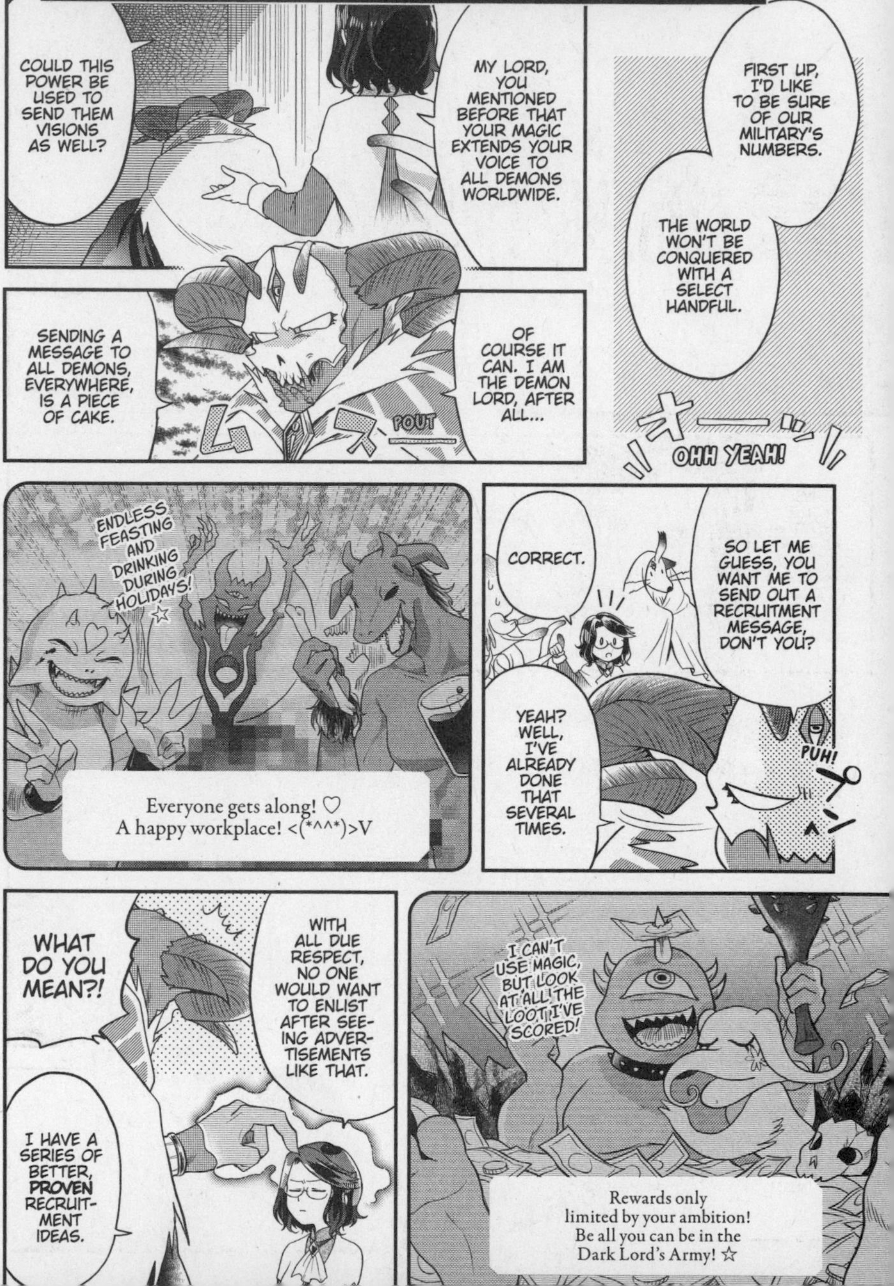

FIRST UP, I'D LIKE TO BE SURE OF OUR MILITARY'S NUMBERS.
THE WORLD WON'T BE CONQUERED WITH A SELECT HANDFUL.
OHH YEAH!
MY LORD, YOU MENTIONED BEFORE THAT YOUR MAGIC EXTENDS YOUR VOICE TO ALL DEMONS WORLDWIDE.
COULD THIS POWER BE USED TO SEND THEM VISIONS AS WELL?
OF COURSE IT CAN. I AM THE DEMON LORD, AFTER ALL...
SENDING A MESSAGE TO ALL DEMONS, EVERYWHERE, IS A PIECE OF CAKE.
POUT
SO LET ME GUESS, YOU WANT ME TO SEND OUT A RECRUITMENT MESSAGE, DON'T YOU?
CORRECT.
YEAH? WELL, I'VE ALREADY DONE THAT SEVERAL TIMES.
PUH!
ENDLESS FEASTING AND DRINKING DURING HOLIDAYS! ☆
Everyone gets along! ♡
A happy workplace! <(*^^*)>V
I CAN'T USE MAGIC, BUT LOOK AT ALL THE LOOT I'VE SCORED!
Rewards only limited by your ambition!
Be all you can be in the Dark Lord's Army! ☆
WITH ALL DUE RESPECT, NO ONE WOULD WANT TO ENLIST AFTER SEEING ADVERTISEMENTS LIKE THAT.
WHAT DO YOU MEAN?!
I HAVE A SERIES OF BETTER, **PROVEN** RECRUITMENT IDEAS.

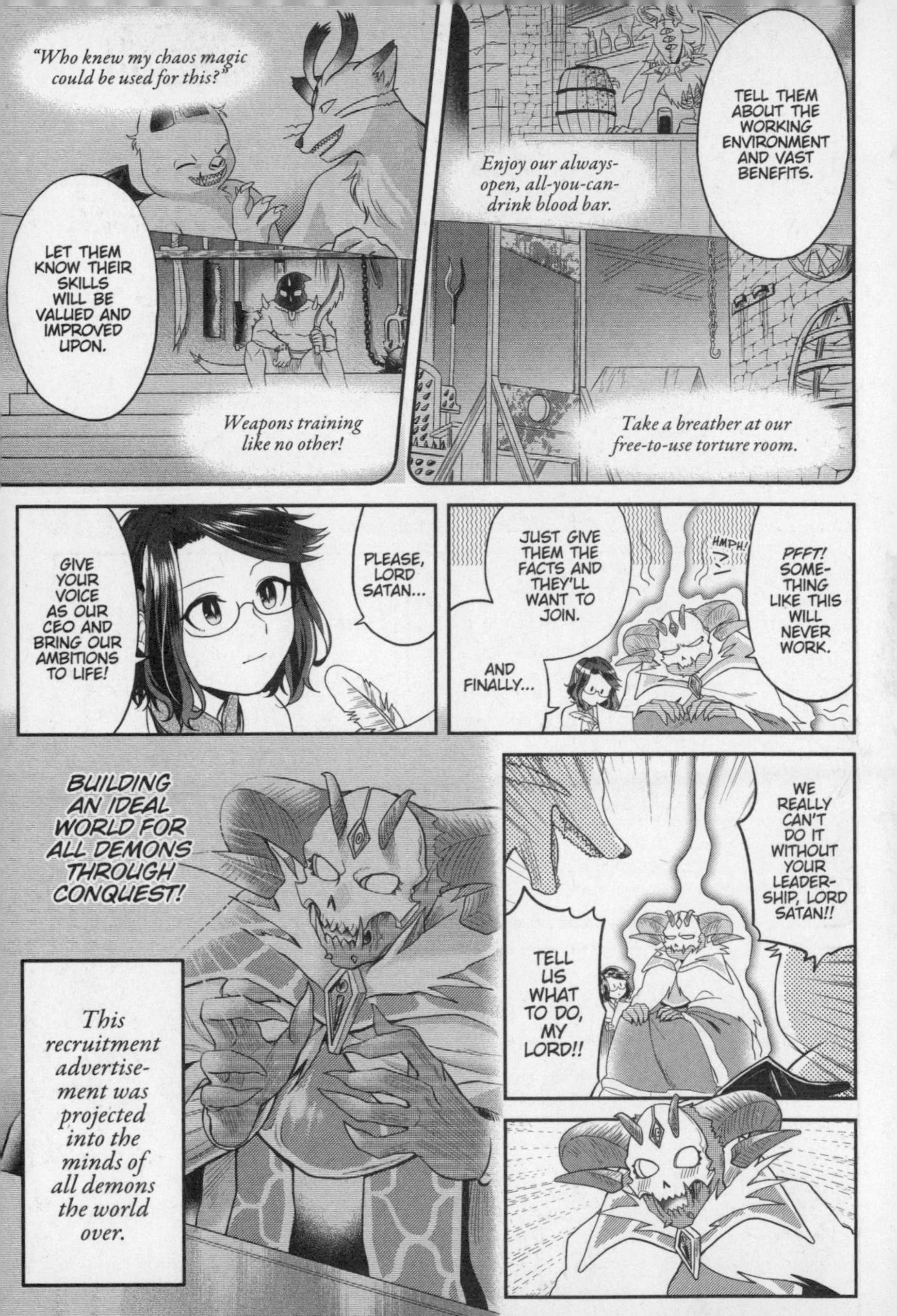
TELL THEM ABOUT THE WORKING ENVIRONMENT AND VAST BENEFITS.
Enjoy our always-open, all-you-can-drink blood bar.
Take a breather at our free-to-use torture room.
"Who knew my chaos magic could be used for this?"
LET THEM KNOW THEIR SKILLS WILL BE VALUED AND IMPROVED UPON.
Weapons training like no other!
PFFT! SOMETHING LIKE THIS WILL NEVER WORK.
HMPH!
JUST GIVE THEM THE FACTS AND THEY'LL WANT TO JOIN.
AND FINALLY...
PLEASE, LORD SATAN...
GIVE YOUR VOICE AS OUR CEO AND BRING OUR AMBITIONS TO LIFE!
WE REALLY CAN'T DO IT WITHOUT YOUR LEADERSHIP, LORD SATAN!!
TELL US WHAT TO DO, MY LORD!!
BUILDING AN IDEAL WORLD FOR ALL DEMONS THROUGH CONQUEST!
This recruitment advertisement was projected into the minds of all demons the world over.

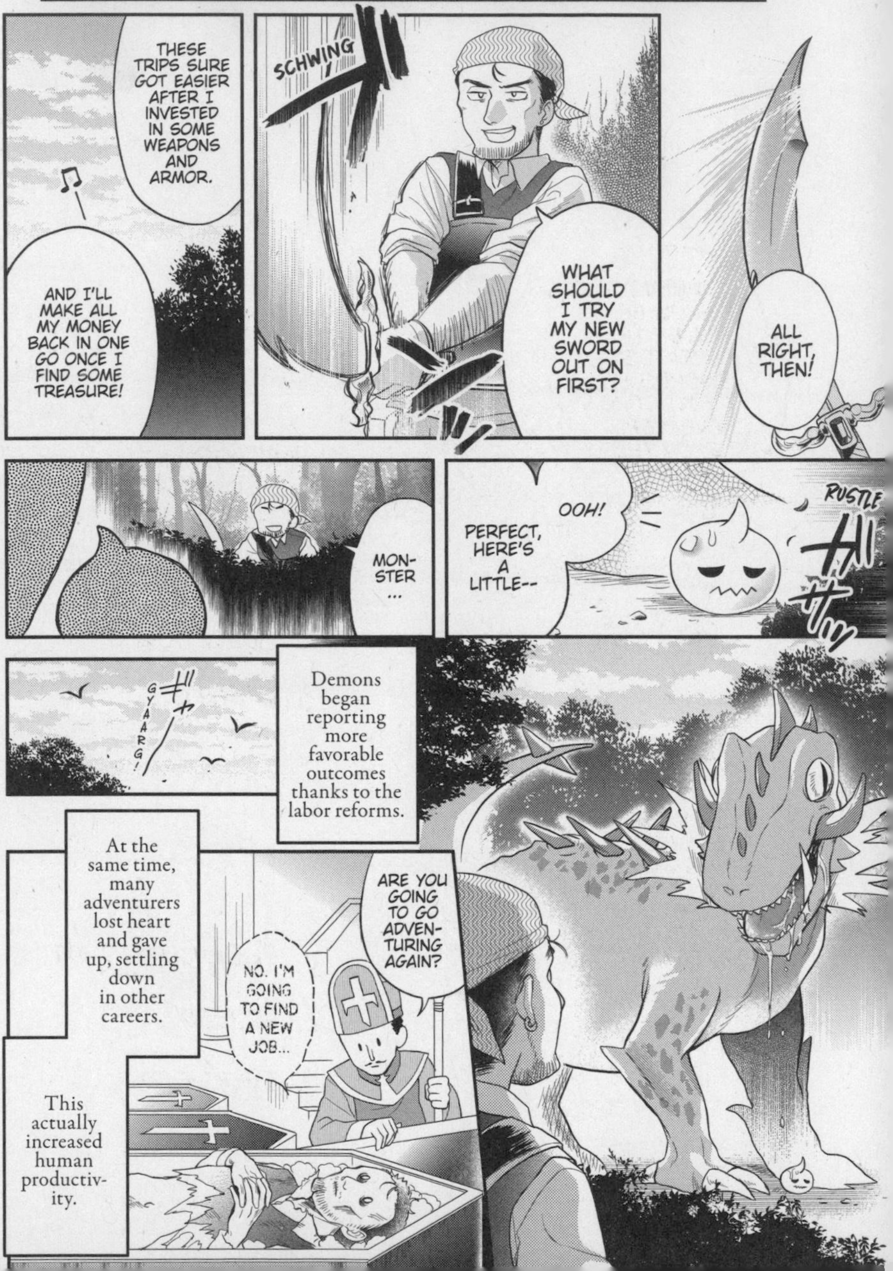
SCHWING
ALL RIGHT, THEN!
WHAT SHOULD I TRY MY NEW SWORD OUT ON FIRST?
THESE TRIPS SURE GOT EASIER AFTER I INVESTED IN SOME WEAPONS AND ARMOR.
♪
AND I'LL MAKE ALL MY MONEY BACK IN ONE GO ONCE I FIND SOME TREASURE!
RUSTLE
OOH!
PERFECT, HERE'S A LITTLE--
MON-STER...
Demons began reporting more favorable outcomes thanks to the labor reforms.
GYAARG!
At the same time, many adventurers lost heart and gave up, settling down in other careers.
ARE YOU GOING TO GO ADVEN-TURING AGAIN?
NO. I'M GOING TO FIND A NEW JOB...
This actually increased human productiv-ity.

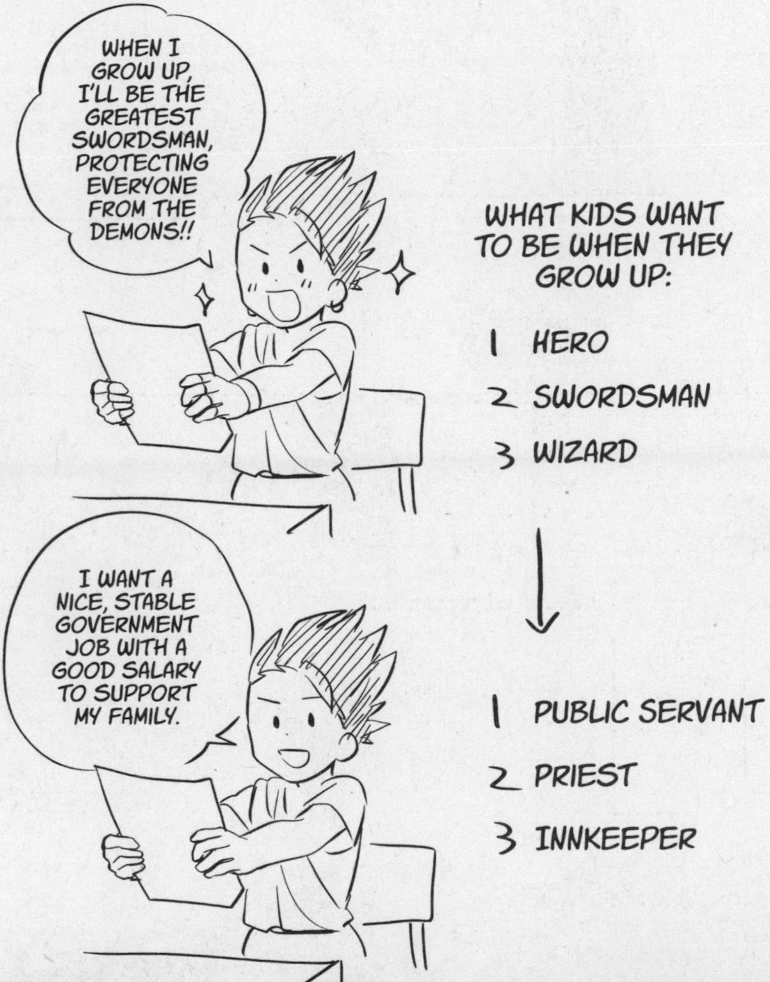
WHAT KIDS WANT TO BE WHEN THEY GROW UP:
1 HERO
2 SWORDSMAN
3 WIZARD
WHEN I GROW UP, I'LL BE THE GREATEST SWORDSMAN, PROTECTING EVERYONE FROM THE DEMONS!!
1 PUBLIC SERVANT
2 PRIEST
3 INNKEEPER
I WANT A NICE, STABLE GOVERNMENT JOB WITH A GOOD SALARY TO SUPPORT MY FAMILY.

# SATAN'S SECRETARY

## A KING WITH A DREAM (ONCE)

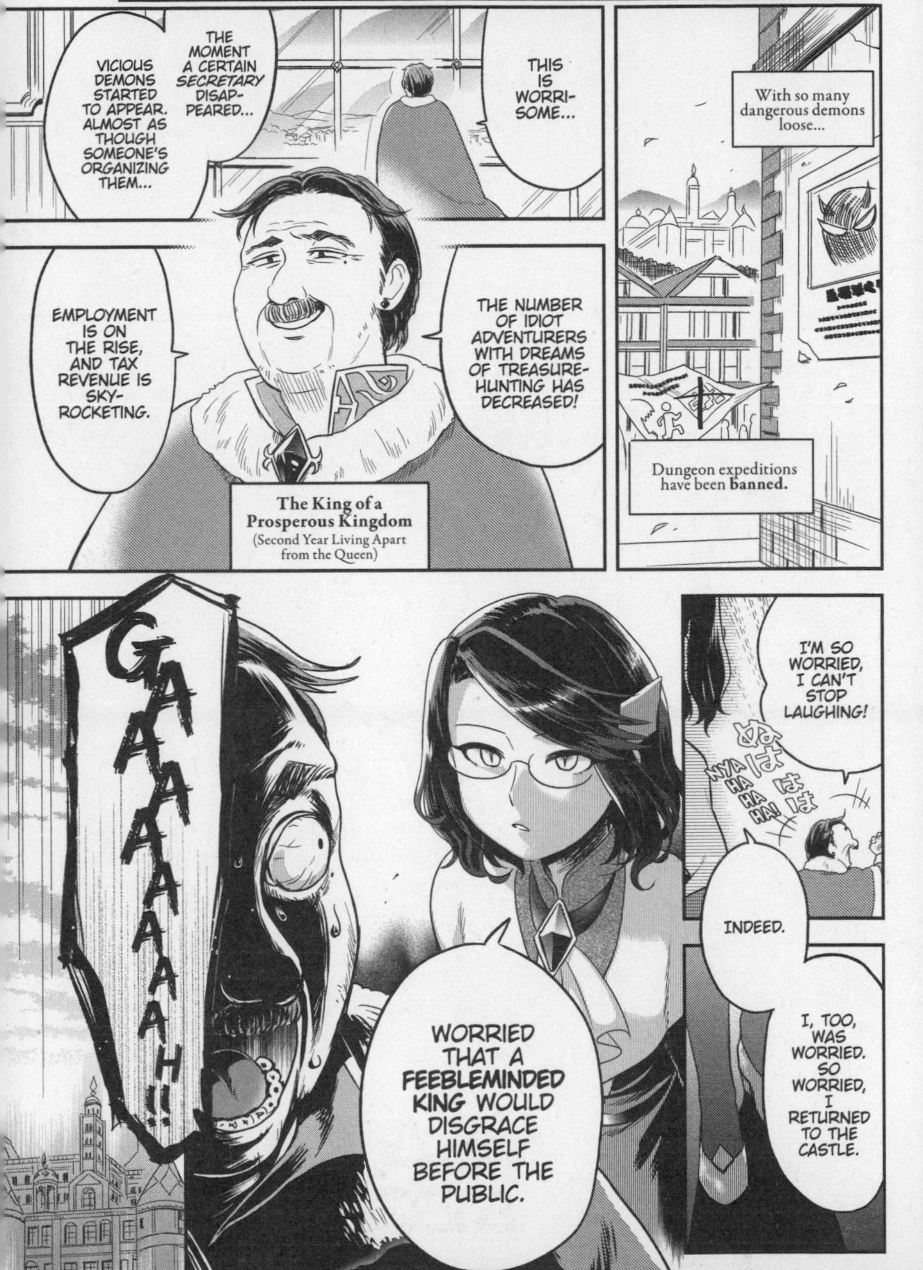
With so many dangerous demons loose...
Dungeon expeditions have been **banned.**
THIS IS WORRI-SOME...
THE MOMENT A CERTAIN SECRETARY DISAP-PEARED...
VICIOUS DEMONS STARTED TO APPEAR. ALMOST AS THOUGH SOMEONE'S ORGANIZING THEM...
THE NUMBER OF IDIOT ADVENTURERS WITH DREAMS OF TREASURE-HUNTING HAS DECREASED!
EMPLOYMENT IS ON THE RISE, AND TAX REVENUE IS SKY-ROCKETING.
**The King of a Prosperous Kingdom**
(Second Year Living Apart from the Queen)
I'M SO WORRIED, I CAN'T STOP LAUGHING!
ぬははは
NYA HA HA HA!
INDEED.
I, TOO, WAS WORRIED. SO WORRIED, I RETURNED TO THE CASTLE.
WORRIED THAT A FEEBLEMINDED KING WOULD DISGRACE HIMSELF BEFORE THE PUBLIC.
GAAAAAAAAH!!

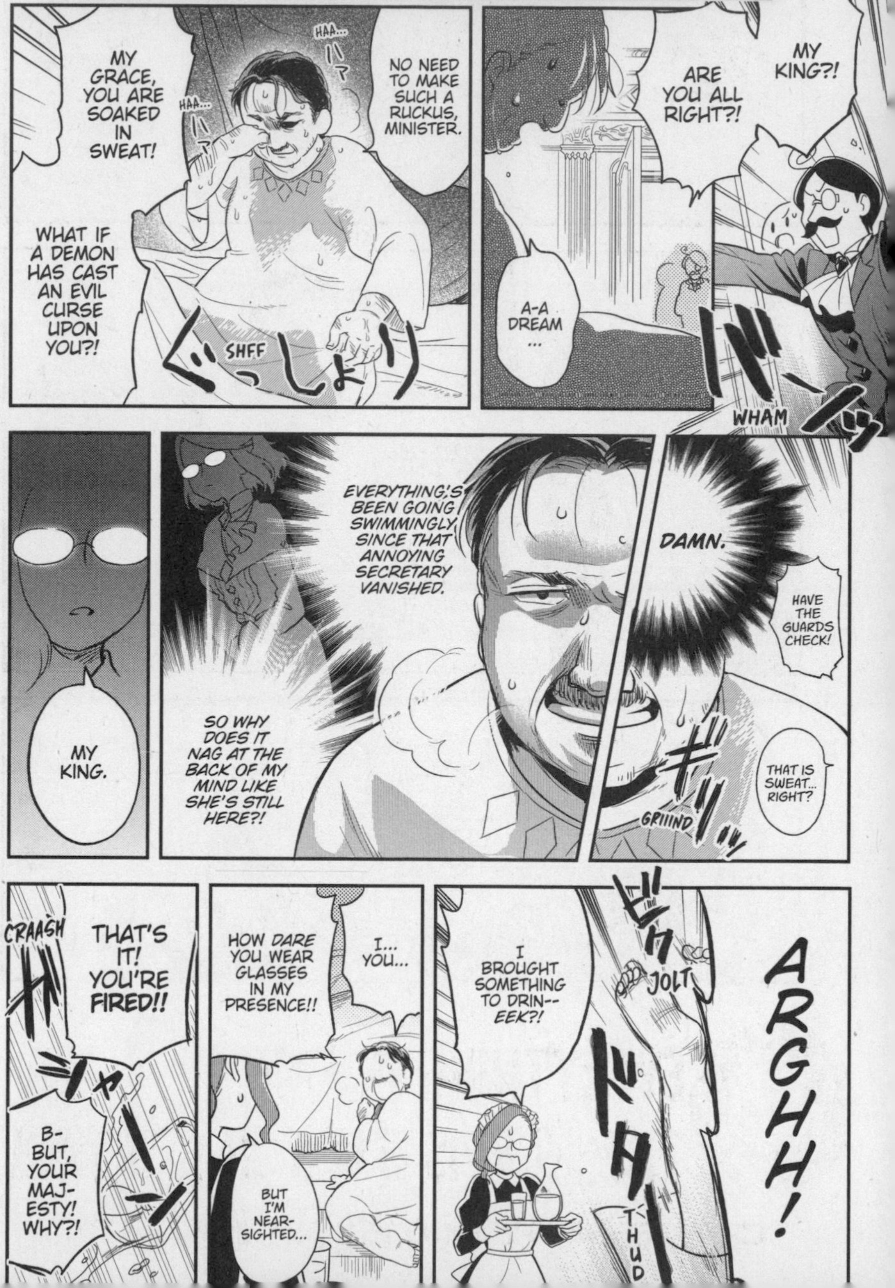
MY KING?!
ARE YOU ALL RIGHT?!
WHAM
A-A DREAM...
NO NEED TO MAKE SUCH A RUCKUS, MINISTER.
HAA...
HAA...
MY GRACE, YOU ARE SOAKED IN SWEAT!
SHFF
WHAT IF A DEMON HAS CAST AN EVIL CURSE UPON YOU?!
DAMN.
HAVE THE GUARDS CHECK!
GRIIIND
THAT IS SWEAT... RIGHT?
EVERYTHING'S BEEN GOING SWIMMINGLY SINCE THAT ANNOYING SECRETARY VANISHED.
SO WHY DOES IT NAG AT THE BACK OF MY MIND LIKE SHE'S STILL HERE?!
MY KING.
ARGHH!
I BROUGHT SOMETHING TO DRIN-- EEK?!
JOLT
THUD
I... YOU...
HOW DARE YOU WEAR GLASSES IN MY PRESENCE!!
BUT I'M NEAR-SIGHTED...
THAT'S IT! YOU'RE FIRED!!
CRAASH
B-BUT, YOUR MAJESTY! WHY?!

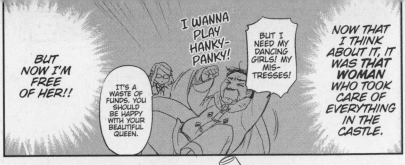

NOW THAT I THINK ABOUT IT, IT WAS THAT WOMAN WHO TOOK CARE OF EVERYTHING IN THE CASTLE.
BUT I NEED MY DANCING GIRLS! MY MIS-TRESSES!
I WANNA PLAY HANKY-PANKY!
IT'S A WASTE OF FUNDS. YOU SHOULD BE HAPPY WITH YOUR BEAUTIFUL QUEEN.
BUT NOW I'M FREE OF HER!!
ANY WOMAN WHO WEARS GLASSES IN MY COURT IS TO BE FIRED!!
FROM NOW ON, CASTLE EMPLOY-MENT DECISIONS COME STRAIGHT FROM ME!!
RUMBLE
AND ALL WOMEN WITH SPEC-TACLES ARE BAN-ISHED!!
BUT, YOUR MAJ-ESTY...
STOMP
STOMP
THE KING'S OUT-BURSTS ARE GETTING WORSE EVERY DAY...
IF ONLY THAT SECRETARY WERE HERE... SHE WAS THE ONLY ONE WHO COULD KEEP THE KING UNDER CONTROL.
THAT'S IT! YOU'RE FIRED, TOO!!
WHAAAAT?!

# EVERYTHING IS FINE. THE KING IS BACK IN CONTROL!

## CHAPTER 4: THE KING IS LOST IN A DREAM

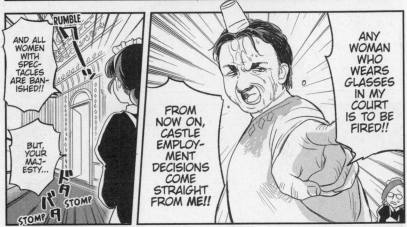

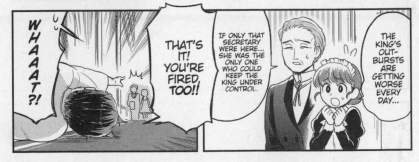

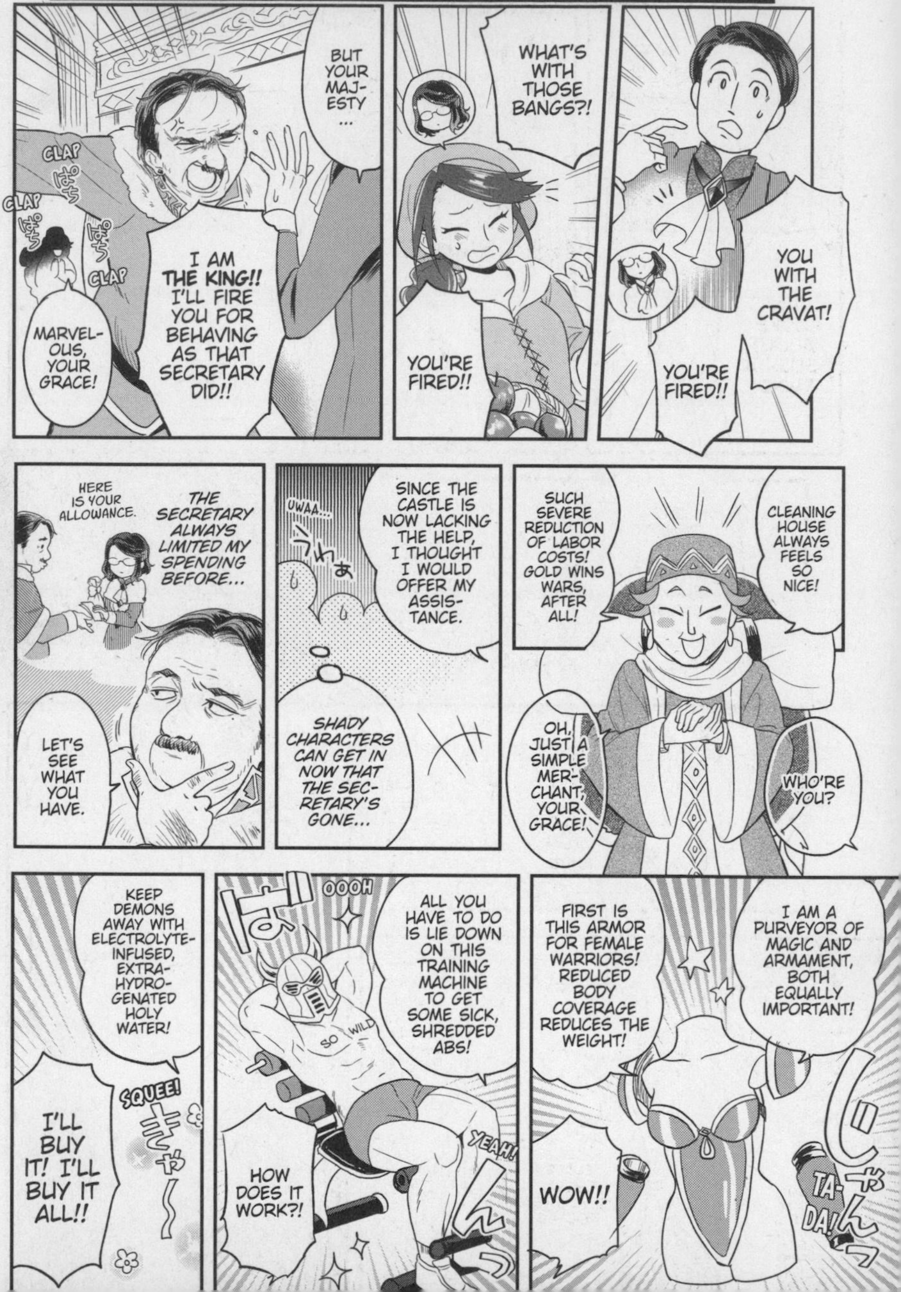
YOU WITH THE CRAVAT!
YOU'RE FIRED!!
WHAT'S WITH THOSE BANGS?!
YOU'RE FIRED!!
BUT YOUR MAJ-ESTY ...
I AM THE KING!! I'LL FIRE YOU FOR BEHAVING AS THAT SECRETARY DID!!
CLAP
CLAP
CLAP
MARVEL-OUS, YOUR GRACE!
CLEANING HOUSE ALWAYS FEELS SO NICE!
SUCH SEVERE REDUCTION OF LABOR COSTS! GOLD WINS WARS, AFTER ALL!
WHO'RE YOU?
OH, JUST A SIMPLE MER-CHANT, YOUR GRACE!
SINCE THE CASTLE IS NOW LACKING THE HELP, I THOUGHT I WOULD OFFER MY ASSIS-TANCE.
UWAA...
SHADY CHARACTERS CAN GET IN NOW THAT THE SEC-RETARY'S GONE...
THE SECRETARY ALWAYS LIMITED MY SPENDING BEFORE...
HERE IS YOUR ALLOWANCE.
LET'S SEE WHAT YOU HAVE.
I AM A PURVEYOR OF MAGIC AND ARMAMENT, BOTH EQUALLY IMPORTANT!
FIRST IS THIS ARMOR FOR FEMALE WARRIORS! REDUCED BODY COVERAGE REDUCES THE WEIGHT!
TA-DA!
WOW!!
ALL YOU HAVE TO DO IS LIE DOWN ON THIS TRAINING MACHINE TO GET SOME SICK, SHREDDED ABS!
OOOH
SO WILD
YEAH!
HOW DOES IT WORK?!
KEEP DEMONS AWAY WITH ELECTROLYTE-INFUSED, EXTRA-HYDRO-GENATED HOLY WATER!
SQUEE!
I'LL BUY IT! I'LL BUY IT ALL!!

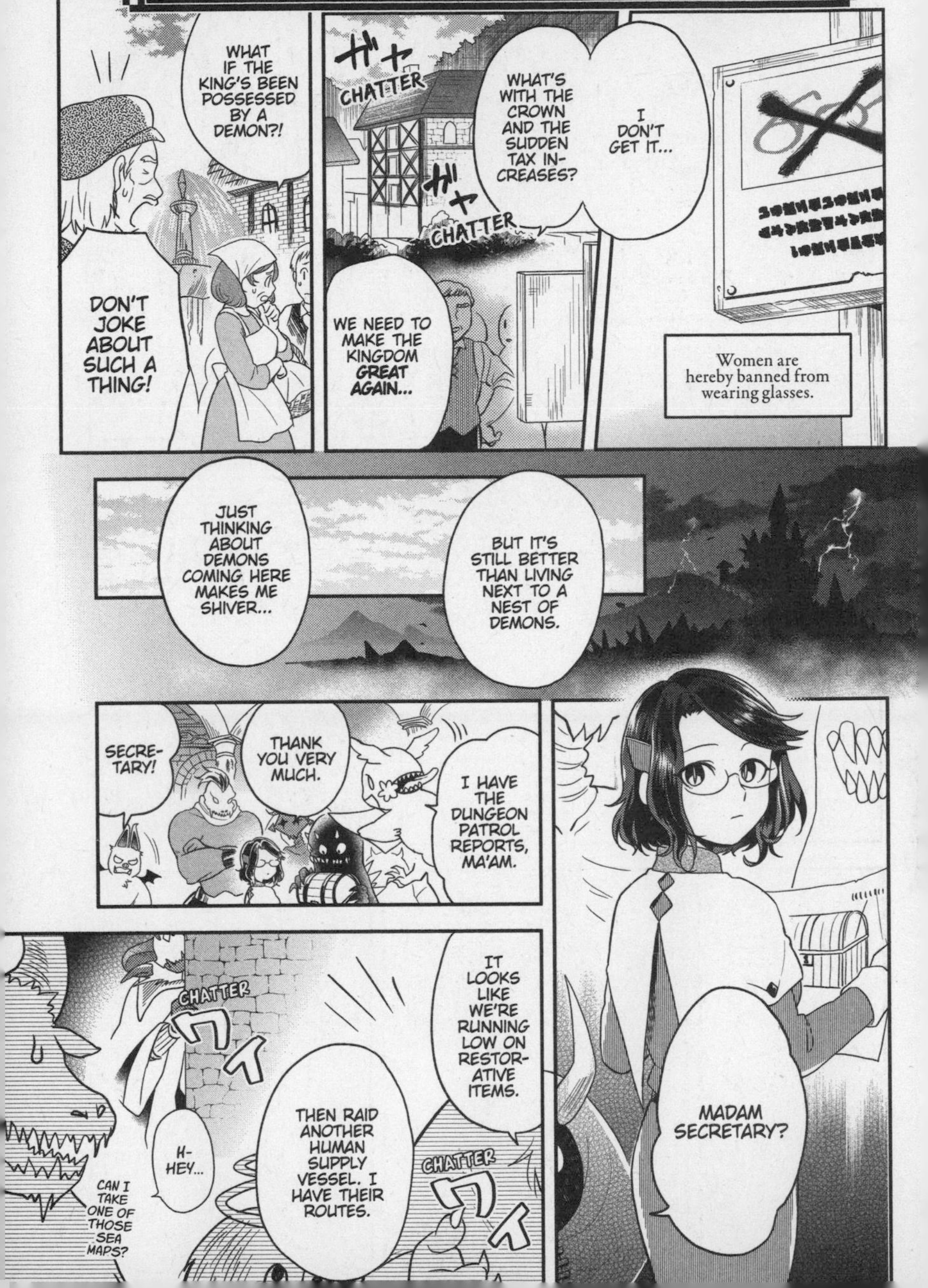
Women are hereby banned from wearing glasses.
I DON'T GET IT...
WHAT'S WITH THE CROWN AND THE SUDDEN TAX IN-CREASES?
ガヤ CHATTER
ガヤ CHATTER
WE NEED TO MAKE THE KINGDOM **GREAT AGAIN...**
WHAT IF THE KING'S BEEN POSSESSED BY A DEMON?!
DON'T JOKE ABOUT SUCH A THING!
BUT IT'S STILL BETTER THAN LIVING NEXT TO A NEST OF DEMONS.
JUST THINKING ABOUT DEMONS COMING HERE MAKES ME SHIVER...
MADAM SECRETARY?
I HAVE THE DUNGEON PATROL REPORTS, MA'AM.
THANK YOU VERY MUCH.
SECRE-TARY!
IT LOOKS LIKE WE'RE RUNNING LOW ON RESTOR-ATIVE ITEMS.
THEN RAID ANOTHER HUMAN SUPPLY VESSEL. I HAVE THEIR ROUTES.
ワイ CHATTER
ワイ CHATTER
H-HEY...
CAN I TAKE ONE OF THOSE SEA MAPS?

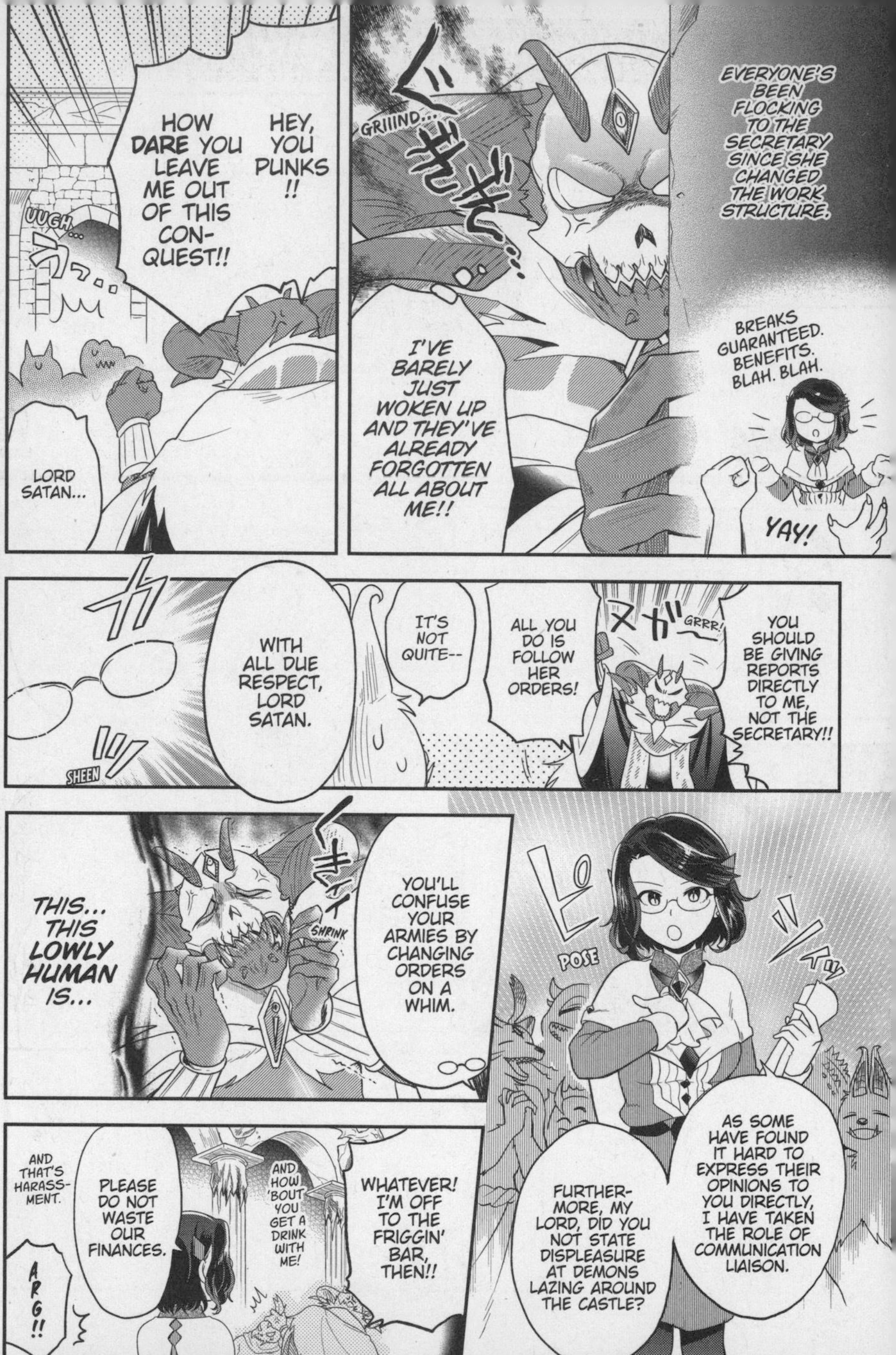
EVERYONE'S BEEN FLOCKING TO THE SECRETARY SINCE SHE CHANGED THE WORK STRUCTURE.
BREAKS GUARANTEED. BENEFITS. BLAH. BLAH.
YAY!
GRIIIND...
I'VE BARELY JUST WOKEN UP AND THEY'VE ALREADY FORGOTTEN ALL ABOUT ME!!
HEY, YOU PUNKS!!
HOW DARE YOU LEAVE ME OUT OF THIS CON-QUEST!!
UUGH...
LORD SATAN...
YOU SHOULD BE GIVING REPORTS DIRECTLY TO ME, NOT THE SECRETARY!!
GRRR!
ALL YOU DO IS FOLLOW HER ORDERS!
IT'S NOT QUITE--
WITH ALL DUE RESPECT, LORD SATAN.
SHEEN
POSE
AS SOME HAVE FOUND IT HARD TO EXPRESS THEIR OPINIONS TO YOU DIRECTLY, I HAVE TAKEN THE ROLE OF COMMUNICATION LIAISON.
FURTHER-MORE, MY LORD, DID YOU NOT STATE DISPLEASURE AT DEMONS LAZING AROUND THE CASTLE?
YOU'LL CONFUSE YOUR ARMIES BY CHANGING ORDERS ON A WHIM.
SHRINK
THIS... THIS LOWLY HUMAN IS...
WHATEVER! I'M OFF TO THE FRIGGIN' BAR, THEN!!
AND HOW 'BOUT YOU GET A DRINK WITH ME!
PLEASE DO NOT WASTE OUR FINANCES.
AND THAT'S HARASS-MENT.
ARG!!

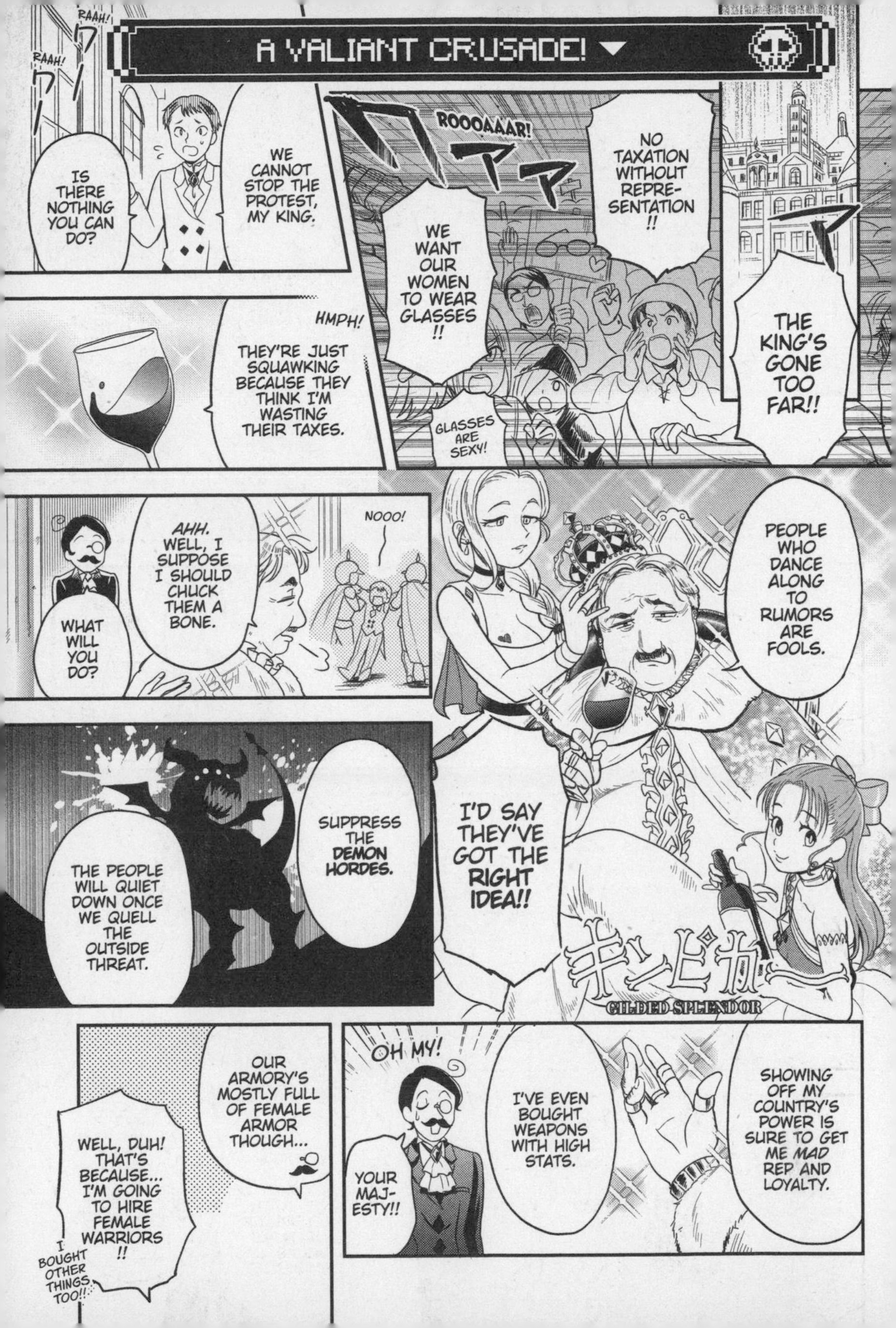
A VALIANT CRUSADE!
THE KING'S GONE TOO FAR!!
ROOOAAAR!
NO TAXATION WITHOUT REPRESENTATION!!
WE WANT OUR WOMEN TO WEAR GLASSES!!
GLASSES ARE SEXY!
RAAH!
RAAH!
WE CANNOT STOP THE PROTEST, MY KING.
IS THERE NOTHING YOU CAN DO?
HMPH!
THEY'RE JUST SQUAWKING BECAUSE THEY THINK I'M WASTING THEIR TAXES.
PEOPLE WHO DANCE ALONG TO RUMORS ARE FOOLS.
I'D SAY THEY'VE GOT THE RIGHT IDEA!!
GILDED SPLENDOR
AHH. WELL, I SUPPOSE I SHOULD CHUCK THEM A BONE.
NOOO!
WHAT WILL YOU DO?
SUPPRESS THE DEMON HORDES.
THE PEOPLE WILL QUIET DOWN ONCE WE QUELL THE OUTSIDE THREAT.
SHOWING OFF MY COUNTRY'S POWER IS SURE TO GET ME MAD REP AND LOYALTY.
I'VE EVEN BOUGHT WEAPONS WITH HIGH STATS.
OH MY!
YOUR MAJESTY!!
OUR ARMORY'S MOSTLY FULL OF FEMALE ARMOR THOUGH...
WELL, DUH! THAT'S BECAUSE... I'M GOING TO HIRE FEMALE WARRIORS!!
I BOUGHT OTHER THINGS TOO!!

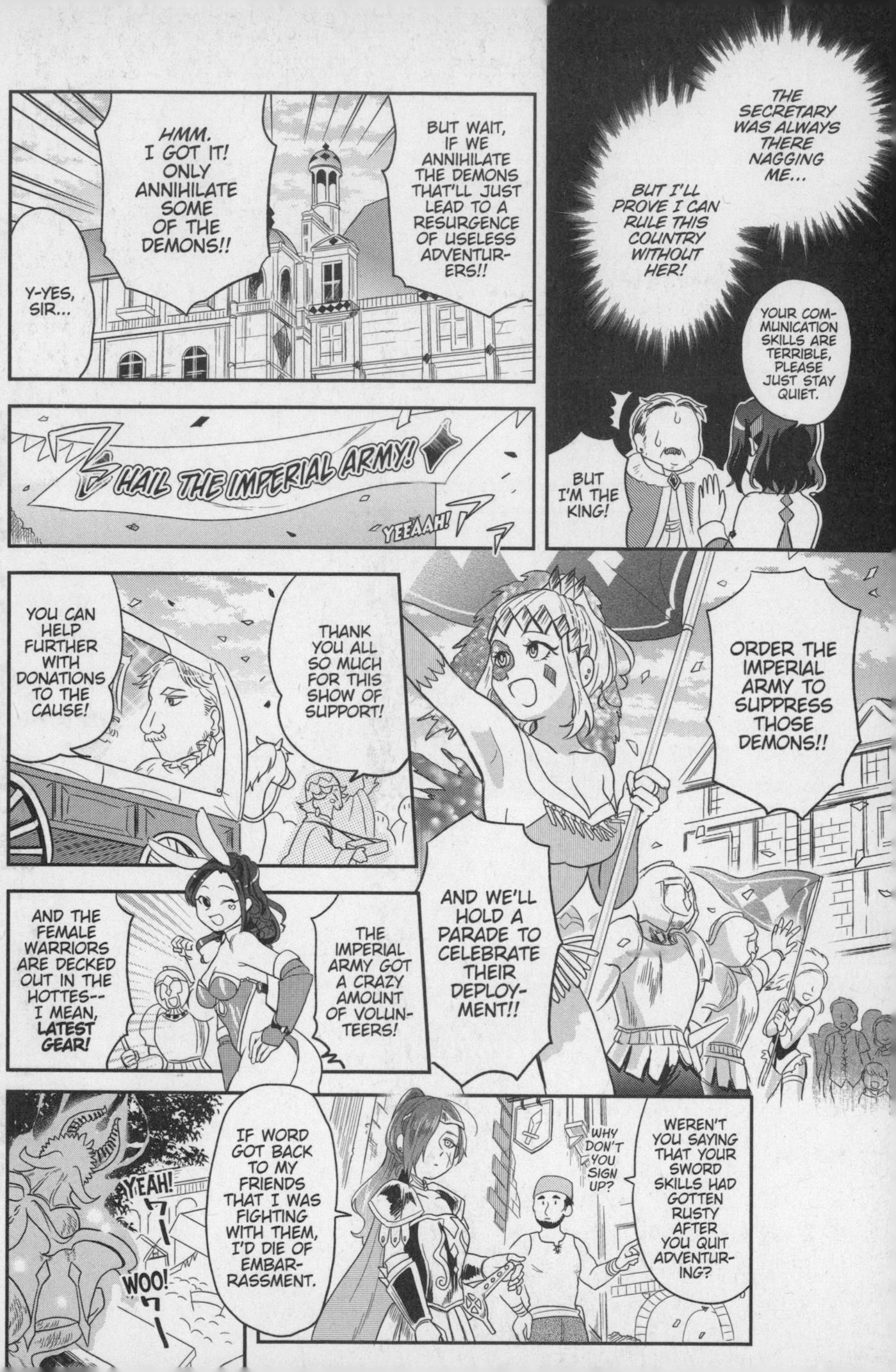

THE SECRETARY WAS ALWAYS THERE NAGGING ME...
BUT I'LL PROVE I CAN RULE THIS COUNTRY WITHOUT HER!
YOUR COMMUNICATION SKILLS ARE TERRIBLE, PLEASE JUST STAY QUIET.
BUT I'M THE KING!
BUT WAIT, IF WE ANNIHILATE THE DEMONS THAT'LL JUST LEAD TO A RESURGENCE OF USELESS ADVENTURERS!!
HMM. I GOT IT! ONLY ANNIHILATE SOME OF THE DEMONS!!
Y-YES, SIR...
HAIL THE IMPERIAL ARMY!
YEEAAH!
ORDER THE IMPERIAL ARMY TO SUPPRESS THOSE DEMONS!!
AND WE'LL HOLD A PARADE TO CELEBRATE THEIR DEPLOYMENT!!
THANK YOU ALL SO MUCH FOR THIS SHOW OF SUPPORT!
YOU CAN HELP FURTHER WITH DONATIONS TO THE CAUSE!
THE IMPERIAL ARMY GOT A CRAZY AMOUNT OF VOLUNTEERS!
AND THE FEMALE WARRIORS ARE DECKED OUT IN THE HOTTES-- I MEAN, LATEST GEAR!
WEREN'T YOU SAYING THAT YOUR SWORD SKILLS HAD GOTTEN RUSTY AFTER YOU QUIT ADVENTURING?
WHY DON'T YOU SIGN UP?
IF WORD GOT BACK TO MY FRIENDS THAT I WAS FIGHTING WITH THEM, I'D DIE OF EMBARRASSMENT.
YEAH!
WOO!

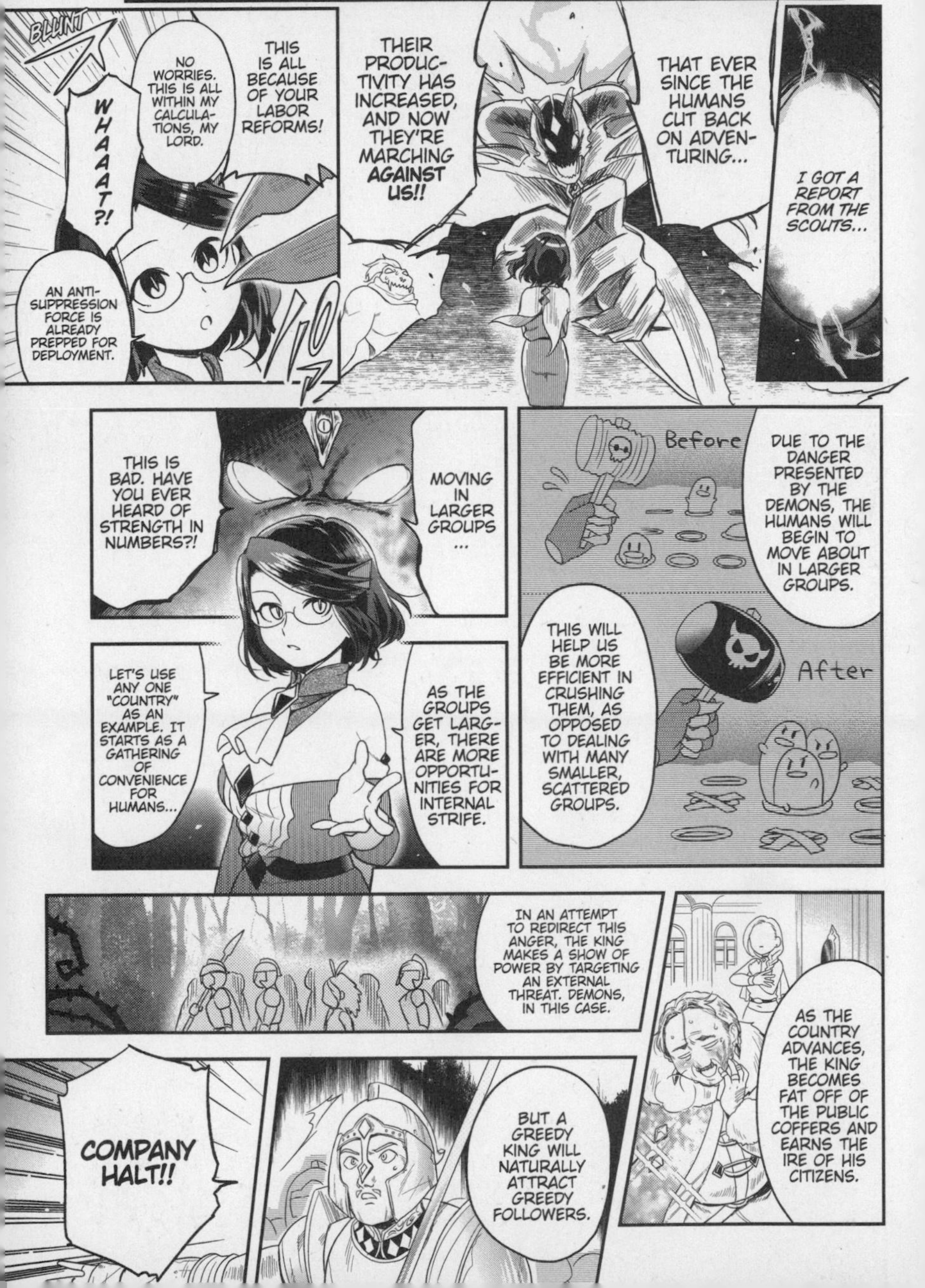
I GOT A REPORT FROM THE SCOUTS...
THAT EVER SINCE THE HUMANS CUT BACK ON ADVENTURING...
THEIR PRODUCTIVITY HAS INCREASED, AND NOW THEY'RE MARCHING AGAINST US!!
THIS IS ALL BECAUSE OF YOUR LABOR REFORMS!
BLUNT
WHAAAAT?!
NO WORRIES. THIS IS ALL WITHIN MY CALCULATIONS, MY LORD.
AN ANTI-SUPPRESSION FORCE IS ALREADY PREPPED FOR DEPLOYMENT.
Before
DUE TO THE DANGER PRESENTED BY THE DEMONS, THE HUMANS WILL BEGIN TO MOVE ABOUT IN LARGER GROUPS.
After
THIS WILL HELP US BE MORE EFFICIENT IN CRUSHING THEM, AS OPPOSED TO DEALING WITH MANY SMALLER, SCATTERED GROUPS.
MOVING IN LARGER GROUPS ...
THIS IS BAD. HAVE YOU EVER HEARD OF STRENGTH IN NUMBERS?!
AS THE GROUPS GET LARGER, THERE ARE MORE OPPORTUNITIES FOR INTERNAL STRIFE.
LET'S USE ANY ONE "COUNTRY" AS AN EXAMPLE. IT STARTS AS A GATHERING OF CONVENIENCE FOR HUMANS...
AS THE COUNTRY ADVANCES, THE KING BECOMES FAT OFF OF THE PUBLIC COFFERS AND EARNS THE IRE OF HIS CITIZENS.
IN AN ATTEMPT TO REDIRECT THIS ANGER, THE KING MAKES A SHOW OF POWER BY TARGETING AN EXTERNAL THREAT. DEMONS, IN THIS CASE.
BUT A GREEDY KING WILL NATURALLY ATTRACT GREEDY FOLLOWERS.
COMPANY HALT!!

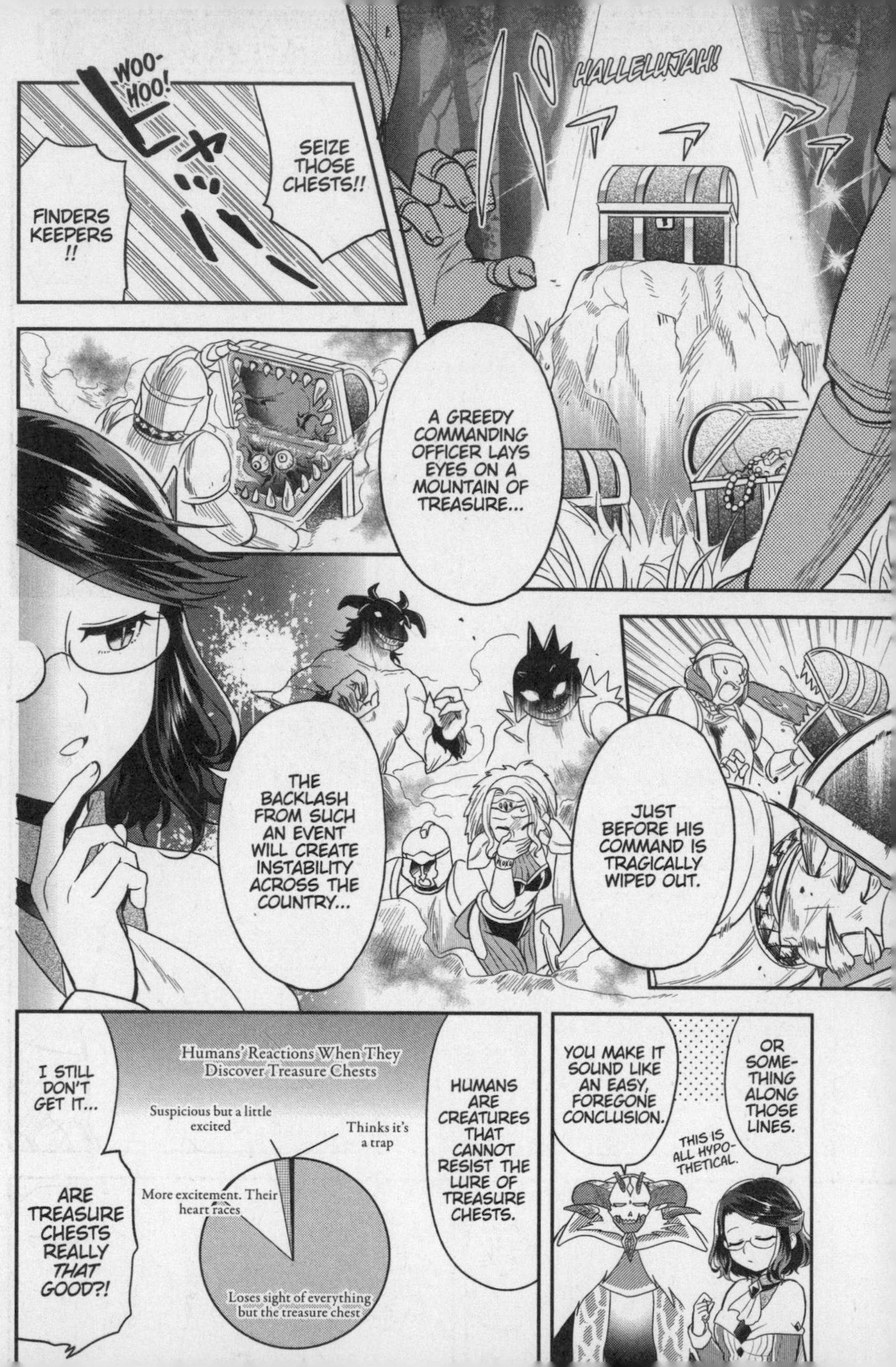
HALLELUJAH!
WOO-HOO!
SEIZE THOSE CHESTS!!
FINDERS KEEPERS!!
A GREEDY COMMANDING OFFICER LAYS EYES ON A MOUNTAIN OF TREASURE...
JUST BEFORE HIS COMMAND IS TRAGICALLY WIPED OUT.
THE BACKLASH FROM SUCH AN EVENT WILL CREATE INSTABILITY ACROSS THE COUNTRY...
OR SOMETHING ALONG THOSE LINES.
YOU MAKE IT SOUND LIKE AN EASY, FOREGONE CONCLUSION.
THIS IS ALL HYPOTHETICAL.
HUMANS ARE CREATURES THAT CANNOT RESIST THE LURE OF TREASURE CHESTS.
Humans' Reactions When They Discover Treasure Chests
Suspicious but a little excited
Thinks it's a trap
More excitement. Their heart races
Loses sight of everything but the treasure chest
I STILL DON'T GET IT...
ARE TREASURE CHESTS REALLY *THAT* GOOD?!

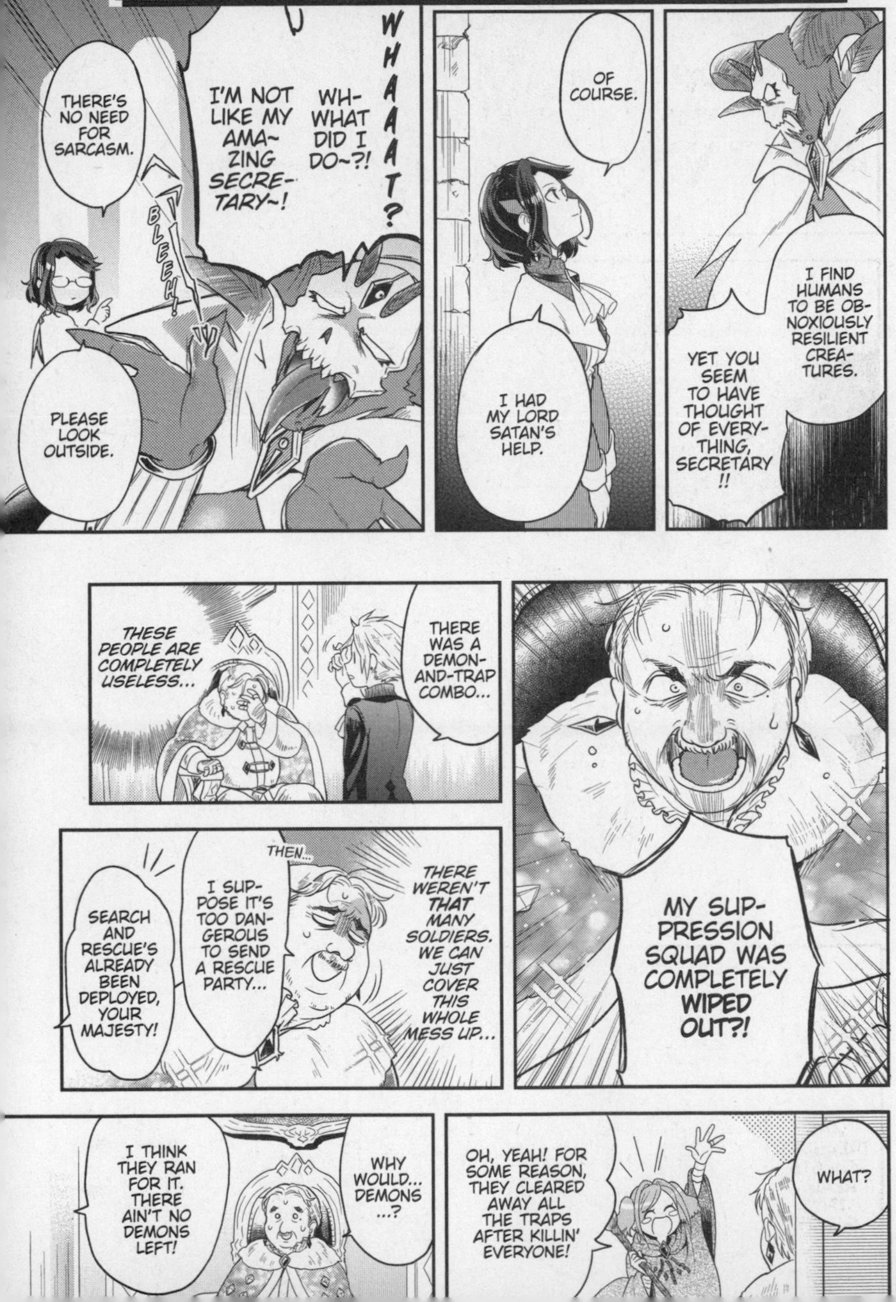
I FIND HUMANS TO BE OBNOXIOUSLY RESILIENT CREATURES.
YET YOU SEEM TO HAVE THOUGHT OF EVERYTHING, SECRETARY!!
OF COURSE.
I HAD MY LORD SATAN'S HELP.
WHAAAAAT?
WH-WHAT DID I DO~?!
I'M NOT LIKE MY AMAZING SECRETARY~!
THERE'S NO NEED FOR SARCASM.
BLEEH!
PLEASE LOOK OUTSIDE.
MY SUPPRESSION SQUAD WAS COMPLETELY WIPED OUT?!
THERE WAS A DEMON-AND-TRAP COMBO...
THESE PEOPLE ARE COMPLETELY USELESS...
THERE WEREN'T THAT MANY SOLDIERS. WE CAN JUST COVER THIS WHOLE MESS UP...
THEN...
I SUPPOSE IT'S TOO DANGEROUS TO SEND A RESCUE PARTY...
SEARCH AND RESCUE'S ALREADY BEEN DEPLOYED, YOUR MAJESTY!
WHAT?
OH, YEAH! FOR SOME REASON, THEY CLEARED AWAY ALL THE TRAPS AFTER KILLIN' EVERYONE!
WHY WOULD... DEMONS ...?
I THINK THEY RAN FOR IT. THERE AIN'T NO DEMONS LEFT!

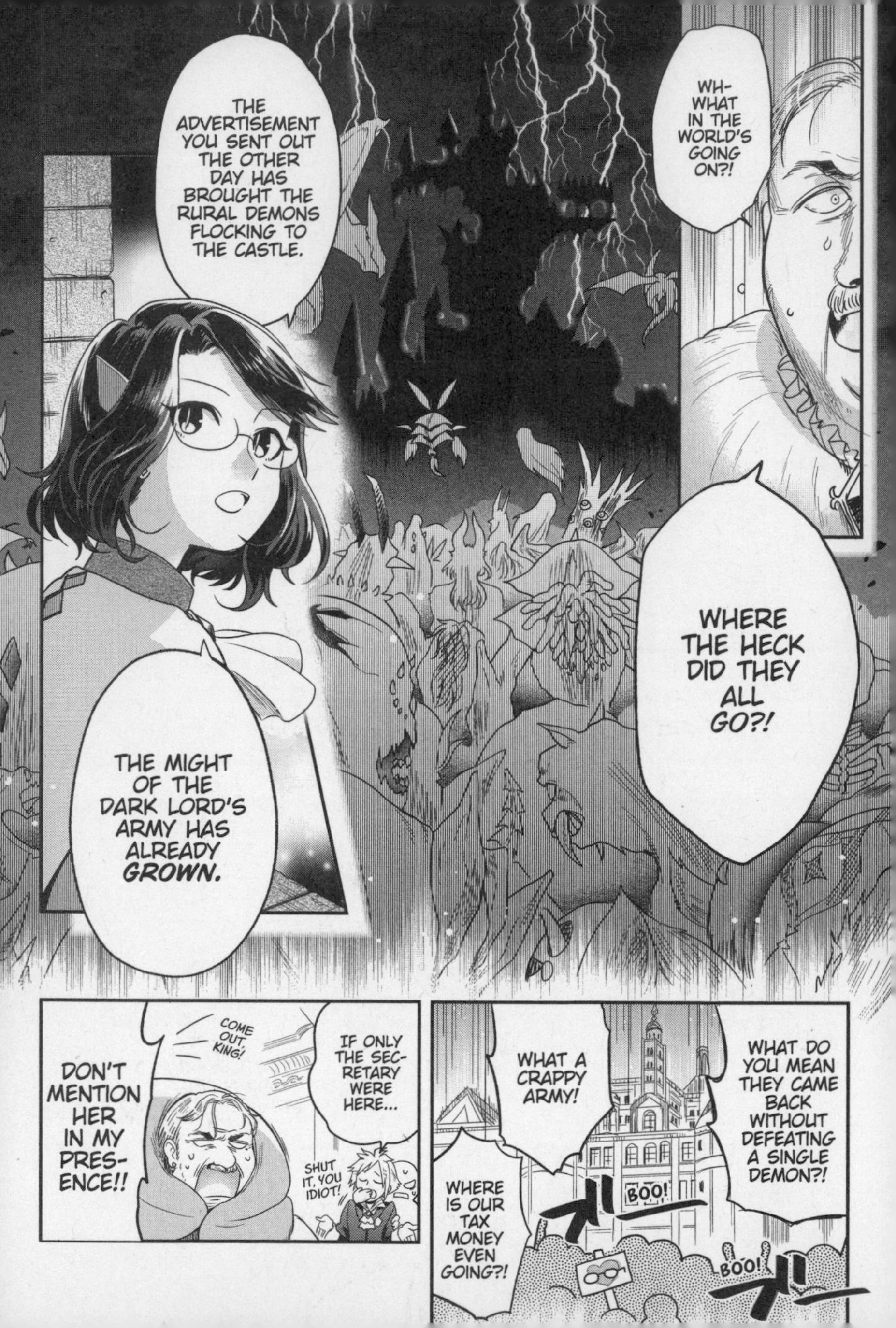
WH- WHAT IN THE WORLD'S GOING ON?!
THE ADVERTISEMENT YOU SENT OUT THE OTHER DAY HAS BROUGHT THE RURAL DEMONS FLOCKING TO THE CASTLE.
WHERE THE HECK DID THEY ALL GO?!
THE MIGHT OF THE DARK LORD'S ARMY HAS ALREADY GROWN.
WHAT DO YOU MEAN THEY CAME BACK WITHOUT DEFEATING A SINGLE DEMON?!
WHAT A CRAPPY ARMY!
BOO!
WHERE IS OUR TAX MONEY EVEN GOING?!
BOO!
IF ONLY THE SEC- RETARY WERE HERE...
COME OUT, KING!
DON'T MENTION HER IN MY PRES- ENCE!!
SHUT IT, YOU IDIOT!

I HAVE ASSIGNED ALL COUNTRIES
THROUGHOUT THE WORLD A SYMBOL.

♡ ♧ ◇ ♤ ⊖⋈

ONE
PARTICULARLY
ADVANCED
COUNTRY IS THE
DIAMOND.

**SATAN'S SECRETARY**

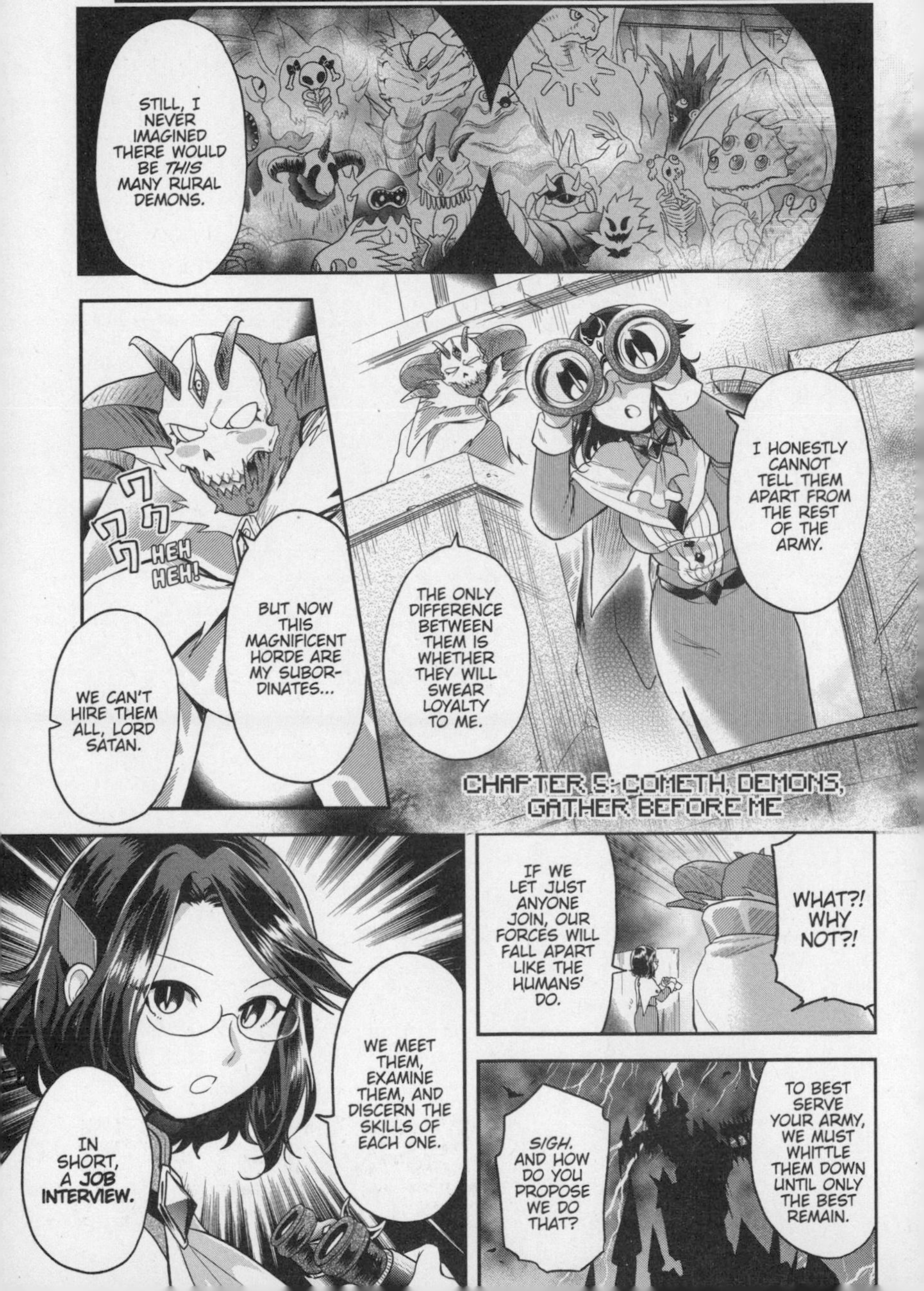
STILL, I NEVER IMAGINED THERE WOULD BE *THIS* MANY RURAL DEMONS.
I HONESTLY CANNOT TELL THEM APART FROM THE REST OF THE ARMY.
THE ONLY DIFFERENCE BETWEEN THEM IS WHETHER THEY WILL SWEAR LOYALTY TO ME.
HEH HEH!
BUT NOW THIS MAGNIFICENT HORDE ARE MY SUBOR-DINATES...
WE CAN'T HIRE THEM ALL, LORD SATAN.
CHAPTER 5: COMETH, DEMONS, GATHER BEFORE ME
WHAT?! WHY NOT?!
IF WE LET JUST ANYONE JOIN, OUR FORCES WILL FALL APART LIKE THE HUMANS' DO.
TO BEST SERVE YOUR ARMY, WE MUST WHITTLE THEM DOWN UNTIL ONLY THE BEST REMAIN.
*SIGH.* AND HOW DO YOU PROPOSE WE DO THAT?
WE MEET THEM, EXAMINE THEM, AND DISCERN THE SKILLS OF EACH ONE.
IN SHORT, A **JOB INTERVIEW.**

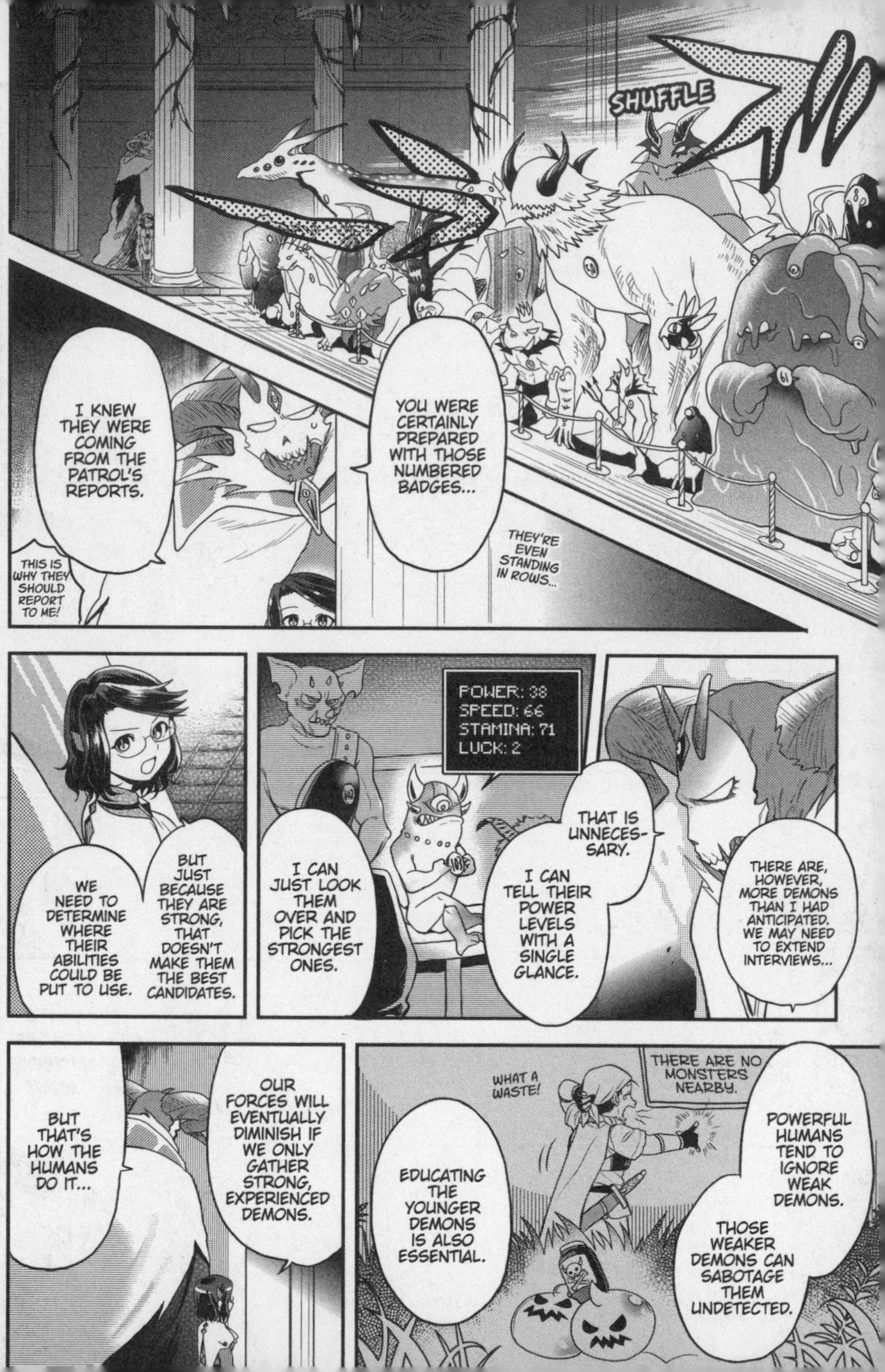
SHUFFLE
YOU WERE CERTAINLY PREPARED WITH THOSE NUMBERED BADGES...
THEY'RE EVEN STANDING IN ROWS...
I KNEW THEY WERE COMING FROM THE PATROL'S REPORTS.
THIS IS WHY THEY SHOULD REPORT TO ME!
THERE ARE, HOWEVER, MORE DEMONS THAN I HAD ANTICIPATED. WE MAY NEED TO EXTEND INTERVIEWS...
THAT IS UNNECES-SARY.
I CAN TELL THEIR POWER LEVELS WITH A SINGLE GLANCE.
POWER: 38
SPEED: 66
STAMINA: 71
LUCK: 2
I CAN JUST LOOK THEM OVER AND PICK THE STRONGEST ONES.
BUT JUST BECAUSE THEY ARE STRONG, THAT DOESN'T MAKE THEM THE BEST CANDIDATES.
WE NEED TO DETERMINE WHERE THEIR ABILITIES COULD BE PUT TO USE.
THERE ARE NO MONSTERS NEARBY.
WHAT A WASTE!
POWERFUL HUMANS TEND TO IGNORE WEAK DEMONS.
THOSE WEAKER DEMONS CAN SABOTAGE THEM UNDETECTED.
EDUCATING THE YOUNGER DEMONS IS ALSO ESSENTIAL.
OUR FORCES WILL EVENTUALLY DIMINISH IF WE ONLY GATHER STRONG, EXPERIENCED DEMONS.
BUT THAT'S HOW THE HUMANS DO IT...

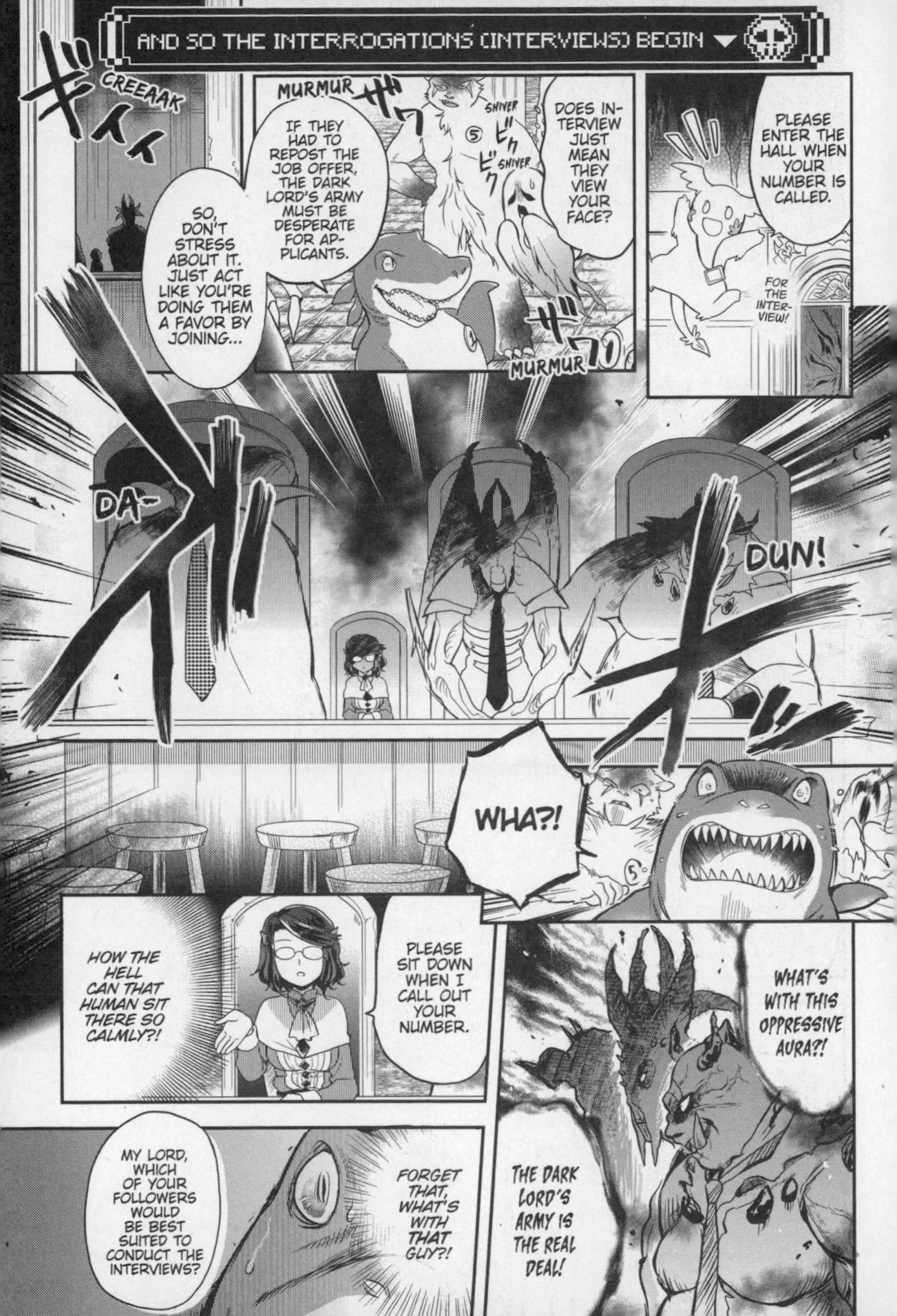
AND SO THE INTERROGATIONS (INTERVIEWS) BEGIN
PLEASE ENTER THE HALL WHEN YOUR NUMBER IS CALLED.
FOR THE INTERVIEW!
DOES INTERVIEW JUST MEAN THEY VIEW YOUR FACE?
SHIVER
SHIVER
MURMUR
IF THEY HAD TO REPOST THE JOB OFFER, THE DARK LORD'S ARMY MUST BE DESPERATE FOR APPLICANTS.
SO, DON'T STRESS ABOUT IT. JUST ACT LIKE YOU'RE DOING THEM A FAVOR BY JOINING...
MURMUR
CREEAAK
DA-
DUN!
WHA?!
WHAT'S WITH THIS OPPRESSIVE AURA?!
THE DARK LORD'S ARMY IS THE REAL DEAL!
PLEASE SIT DOWN WHEN I CALL OUT YOUR NUMBER.
HOW THE HELL CAN THAT HUMAN SIT THERE SO CALMLY?!
FORGET THAT, WHAT'S WITH THAT GUY?!
MY LORD, WHICH OF YOUR FOLLOWERS WOULD BE BEST SUITED TO CONDUCT THE INTERVIEWS?

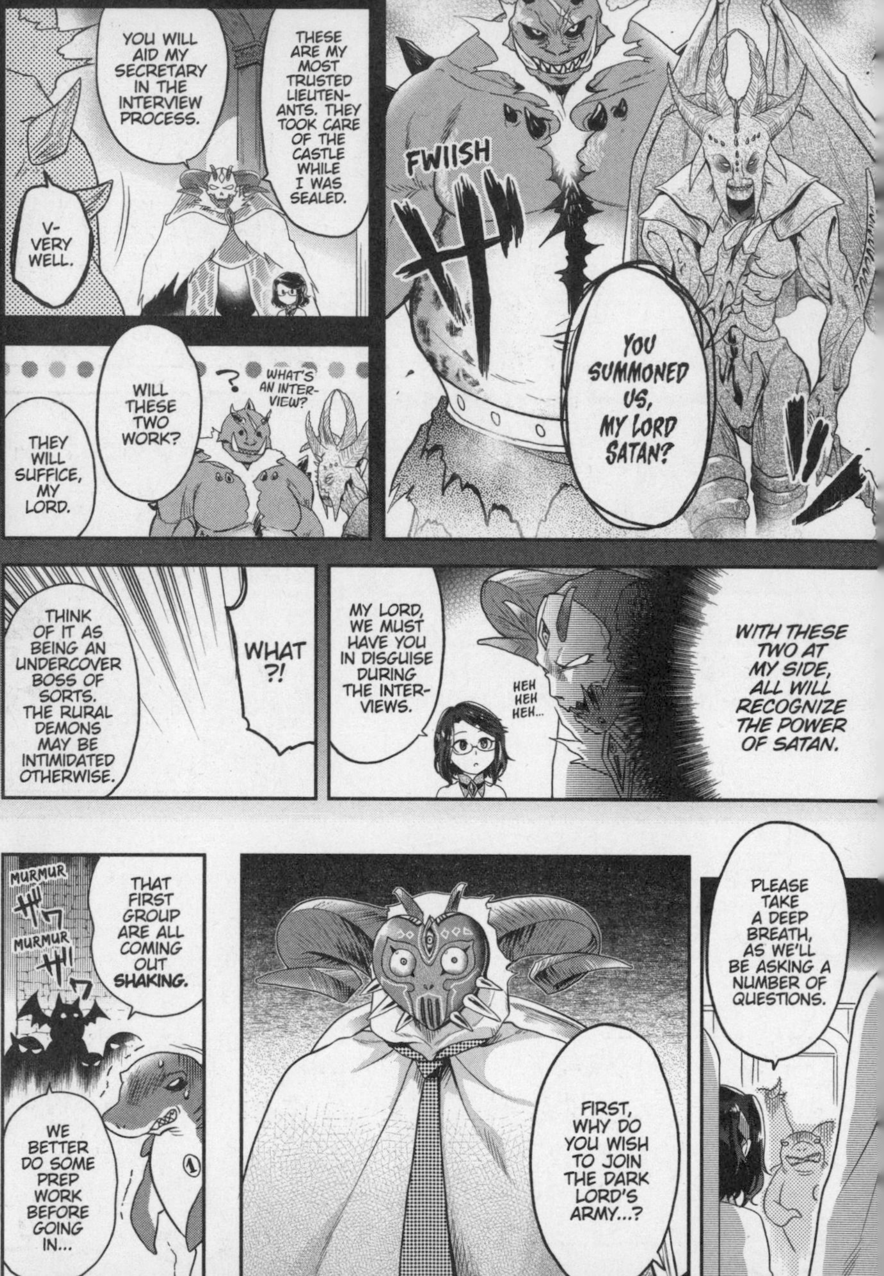
FWIISH
YOU SUMMONED US, MY LORD SATAN?
THESE ARE MY MOST TRUSTED LIEUTEN-ANTS. THEY TOOK CARE OF THE CASTLE WHILE I WAS SEALED.
YOU WILL AID MY SECRETARY IN THE INTERVIEW PROCESS.
V- VERY WELL.
WHAT'S AN INTER-VIEW?
?
WILL THESE TWO WORK?
THEY WILL SUFFICE, MY LORD.
WITH THESE TWO AT MY SIDE, ALL WILL RECOGNIZE THE POWER OF SATAN.
HEH HEH HEH...
MY LORD, WE MUST HAVE YOU IN DISGUISE DURING THE INTER-VIEWS.
WHAT ?!
THINK OF IT AS BEING AN UNDERCOVER BOSS OF SORTS. THE RURAL DEMONS MAY BE INTIMIDATED OTHERWISE.
PLEASE TAKE A DEEP BREATH, AS WE'LL BE ASKING A NUMBER OF QUESTIONS.
FIRST, WHY DO YOU WISH TO JOIN THE DARK LORD'S ARMY...?
MURMUR
MURMUR
THAT FIRST GROUP ARE ALL COMING OUT SHAKING.
WE BETTER DO SOME PREP WORK BEFORE GOING IN...

# SO THESE ARE THE MILLENNIAL DEMONS

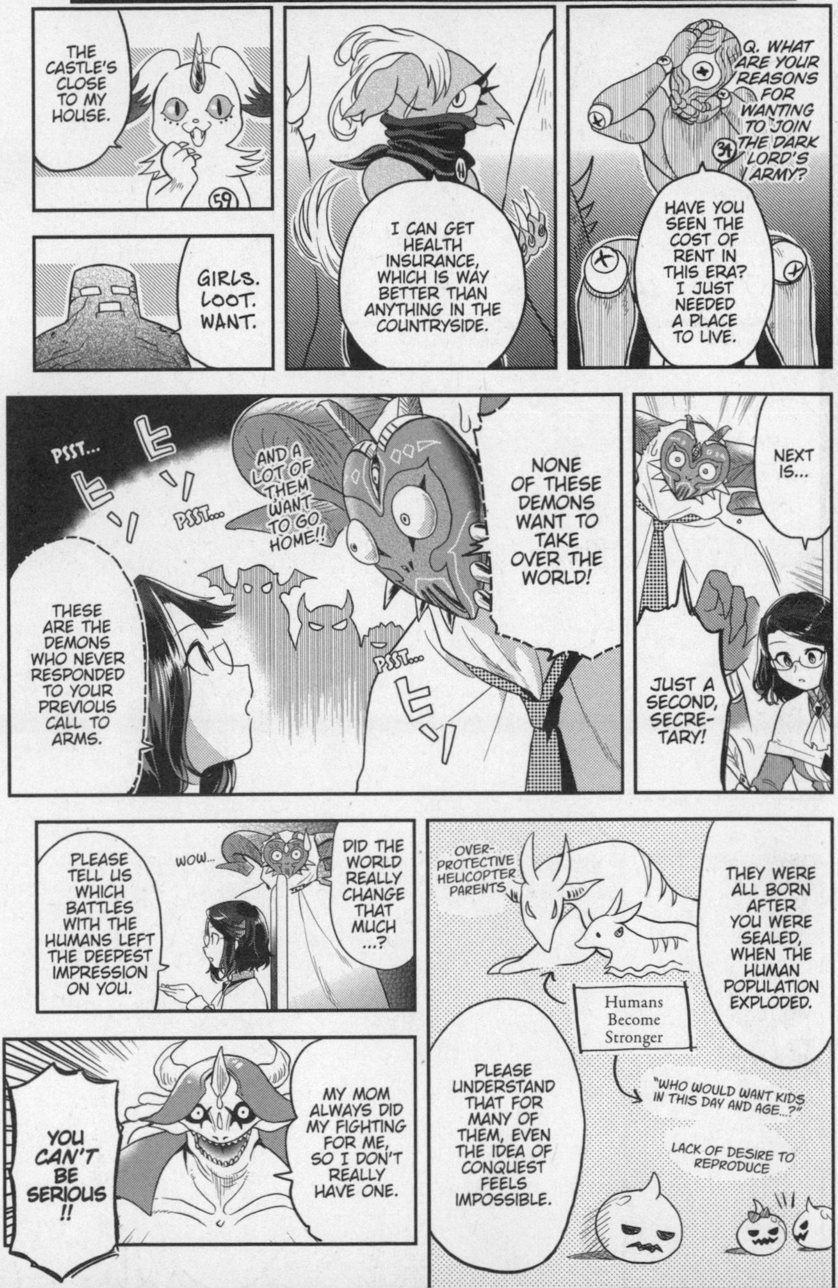
Q. WHAT ARE YOUR REASONS FOR WANTING TO JOIN THE DARK LORD'S ARMY?
HAVE YOU SEEN THE COST OF RENT IN THIS ERA? I JUST NEEDED A PLACE TO LIVE.
I CAN GET HEALTH INSURANCE, WHICH IS WAY BETTER THAN ANYTHING IN THE COUNTRYSIDE.
THE CASTLE'S CLOSE TO MY HOUSE.
GIRLS. LOOT. WANT.
NEXT IS...
JUST A SECOND, SECRETARY!
NONE OF THESE DEMONS WANT TO TAKE OVER THE WORLD!
AND A LOT OF THEM WANT TO GO HOME!!
PSST...
PSST...
PSST...
THESE ARE THE DEMONS WHO NEVER RESPONDED TO YOUR PREVIOUS CALL TO ARMS.
THEY WERE ALL BORN AFTER YOU WERE SEALED, WHEN THE HUMAN POPULATION EXPLODED.
OVER-PROTECTIVE HELICOPTER PARENTS
Humans Become Stronger
PLEASE UNDERSTAND THAT FOR MANY OF THEM, EVEN THE IDEA OF CONQUEST FEELS IMPOSSIBLE.
"WHO WOULD WANT KIDS IN THIS DAY AND AGE...?"
LACK OF DESIRE TO REPRODUCE
DID THE WORLD REALLY CHANGE THAT MUCH ...?
WOW...
PLEASE TELL US WHICH BATTLES WITH THE HUMANS LEFT THE DEEPEST IMPRESSION ON YOU.
MY MOM ALWAYS DID MY FIGHTING FOR ME, SO I DON'T REALLY HAVE ONE.
YOU CAN'T BE SERIOUS!!

THERE ARE A LOT OF DEMONS HERE WITH POTENTIAL!

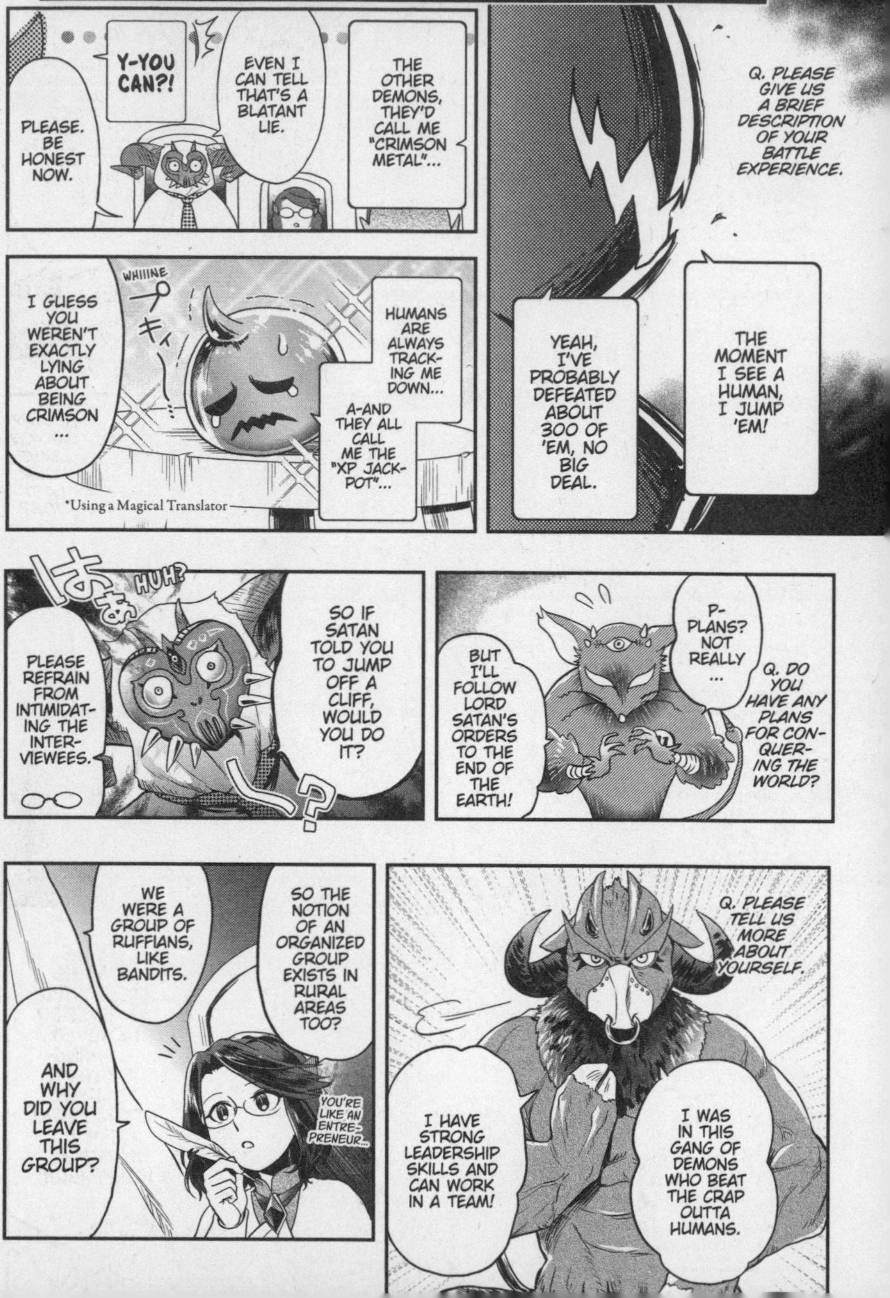
Q. PLEASE GIVE US A BRIEF DESCRIPTION OF YOUR BATTLE EXPERIENCE.
THE MOMENT I SEE A HUMAN, I JUMP 'EM!
YEAH, I'VE PROBABLY DEFEATED ABOUT 300 OF 'EM, NO BIG DEAL.
THE OTHER DEMONS, THEY'D CALL ME "CRIMSON METAL"...
EVEN I CAN TELL THAT'S A BLATANT LIE.
Y-YOU CAN?!
PLEASE. BE HONEST NOW.
HUMANS ARE ALWAYS TRACKING ME DOWN...
A-AND THEY ALL CALL ME THE "XP JACKPOT"...
WHIIINE
I GUESS YOU WEREN'T EXACTLY LYING ABOUT BEING CRIMSON ...
Q. DO YOU HAVE ANY PLANS FOR CONQUERING THE WORLD?
P-PLANS? NOT REALLY ...
BUT I'LL FOLLOW LORD SATAN'S ORDERS TO THE END OF THE EARTH!
SO IF SATAN TOLD YOU TO JUMP OFF A CLIFF, WOULD YOU DO IT?
HUH?
PLEASE REFRAIN FROM INTIMIDATING THE INTERVIEWEES.
Q. PLEASE TELL US MORE ABOUT YOURSELF.
I WAS IN THIS GANG OF DEMONS WHO BEAT THE CRAP OUTTA HUMANS.
I HAVE STRONG LEADERSHIP SKILLS AND CAN WORK IN A TEAM!
SO THE NOTION OF AN ORGANIZED GROUP EXISTS IN RURAL AREAS TOO?
WE WERE A GROUP OF RUFFIANS, LIKE BANDITS.
YOU'RE LIKE AN ENTREPRENEUR...
AND WHY DID YOU LEAVE THIS GROUP?
*Using a Magical Translator

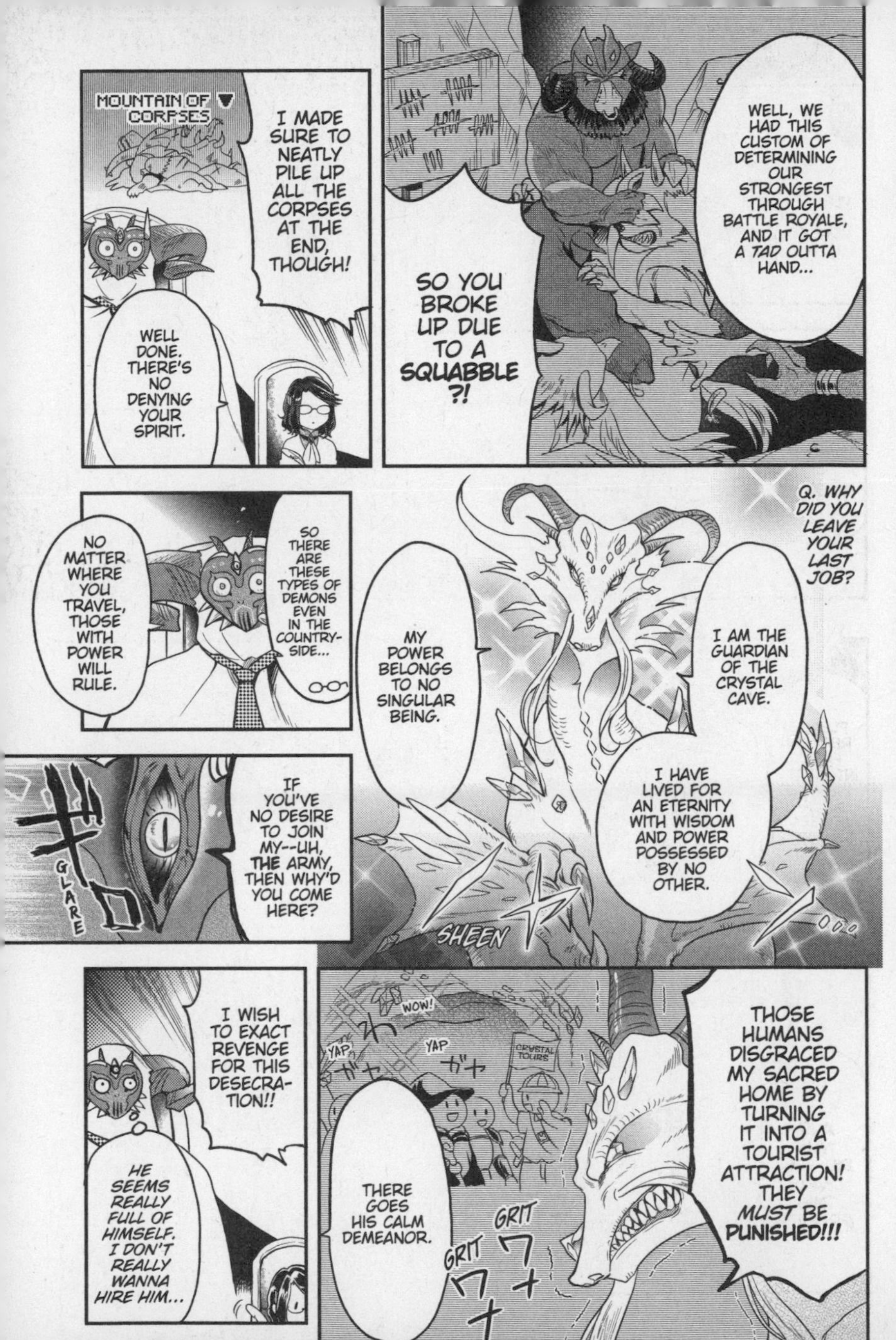
WELL, WE HAD THIS CUSTOM OF DETERMINING OUR STRONGEST THROUGH BATTLE ROYALE, AND IT GOT A *TAD* OUTTA HAND...
SO YOU BROKE UP DUE TO A **SQUABBLE**?!
MOUNTAIN OF CORPSES
I MADE SURE TO NEATLY PILE UP ALL THE CORPSES AT THE END, THOUGH!
WELL DONE. THERE'S NO DENYING YOUR SPIRIT.
Q. WHY DID YOU LEAVE YOUR LAST JOB?
I AM THE GUARDIAN OF THE CRYSTAL CAVE.
MY POWER BELONGS TO NO SINGULAR BEING.
I HAVE LIVED FOR AN ETERNITY WITH WISDOM AND POWER POSSESSED BY NO OTHER.
SHEEN
SO THERE ARE THESE TYPES OF DEMONS EVEN IN THE COUNTRYSIDE...
NO MATTER WHERE YOU TRAVEL, THOSE WITH POWER WILL RULE.
IF YOU'VE NO DESIRE TO JOIN MY--UH, **THE** ARMY, THEN WHY'D YOU COME HERE?
GLARE
THOSE HUMANS DISGRACED MY SACRED HOME BY TURNING IT INTO A TOURIST ATTRACTION! THEY *MUST* BE **PUNISHED!!!**
WOW!
YAP
YAP
CRYSTAL TOURS
GRIT
GRIT
THERE GOES HIS CALM DEMEANOR.
I WISH TO EXACT REVENGE FOR THIS DESECRATION!!
*HE SEEMS REALLY FULL OF HIMSELF. I DON'T REALLY WANNA HIRE HIM...*

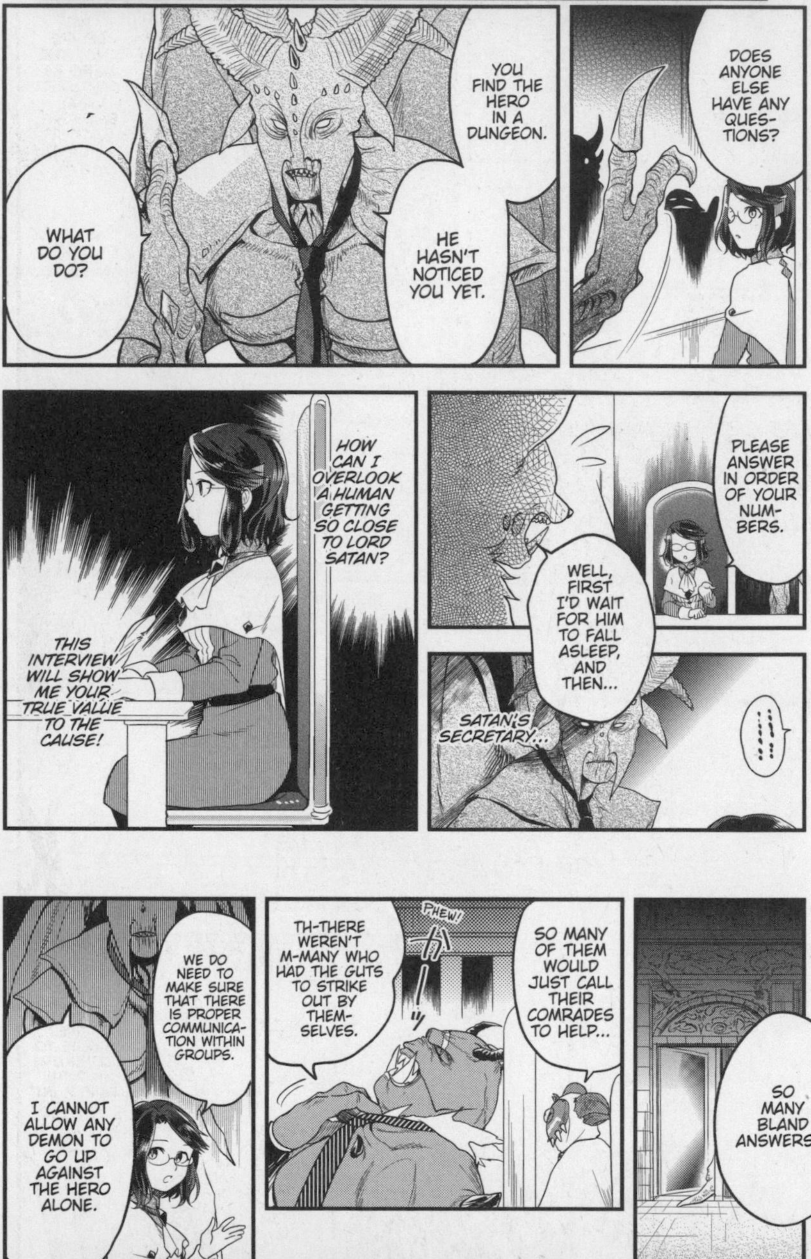
DOES ANYONE ELSE HAVE ANY QUES-TIONS?
YOU FIND THE HERO IN A DUNGEON.
HE HASN'T NOTICED YOU YET.
WHAT DO YOU DO?
PLEASE ANSWER IN ORDER OF YOUR NUM-BERS.
WELL, FIRST I'D WAIT FOR HIM TO FALL ASLEEP, AND THEN...
SATAN'S SECRETARY...
HOW CAN I OVERLOOK A HUMAN GETTING SO CLOSE TO LORD SATAN?
THIS INTERVIEW WILL SHOW ME YOUR TRUE VALUE TO THE CAUSE!
SO MANY BLAND ANSWERS...
SO MANY OF THEM WOULD JUST CALL THEIR COMRADES TO HELP...
TH-THERE WEREN'T M-MANY WHO HAD THE GUTS TO STRIKE OUT BY THEM-SELVES.
WE DO NEED TO MAKE SURE THAT THERE IS PROPER COMMUNICA-TION WITHIN GROUPS.
I CANNOT ALLOW ANY DEMON TO GO UP AGAINST THE HERO ALONE.

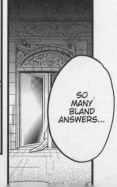

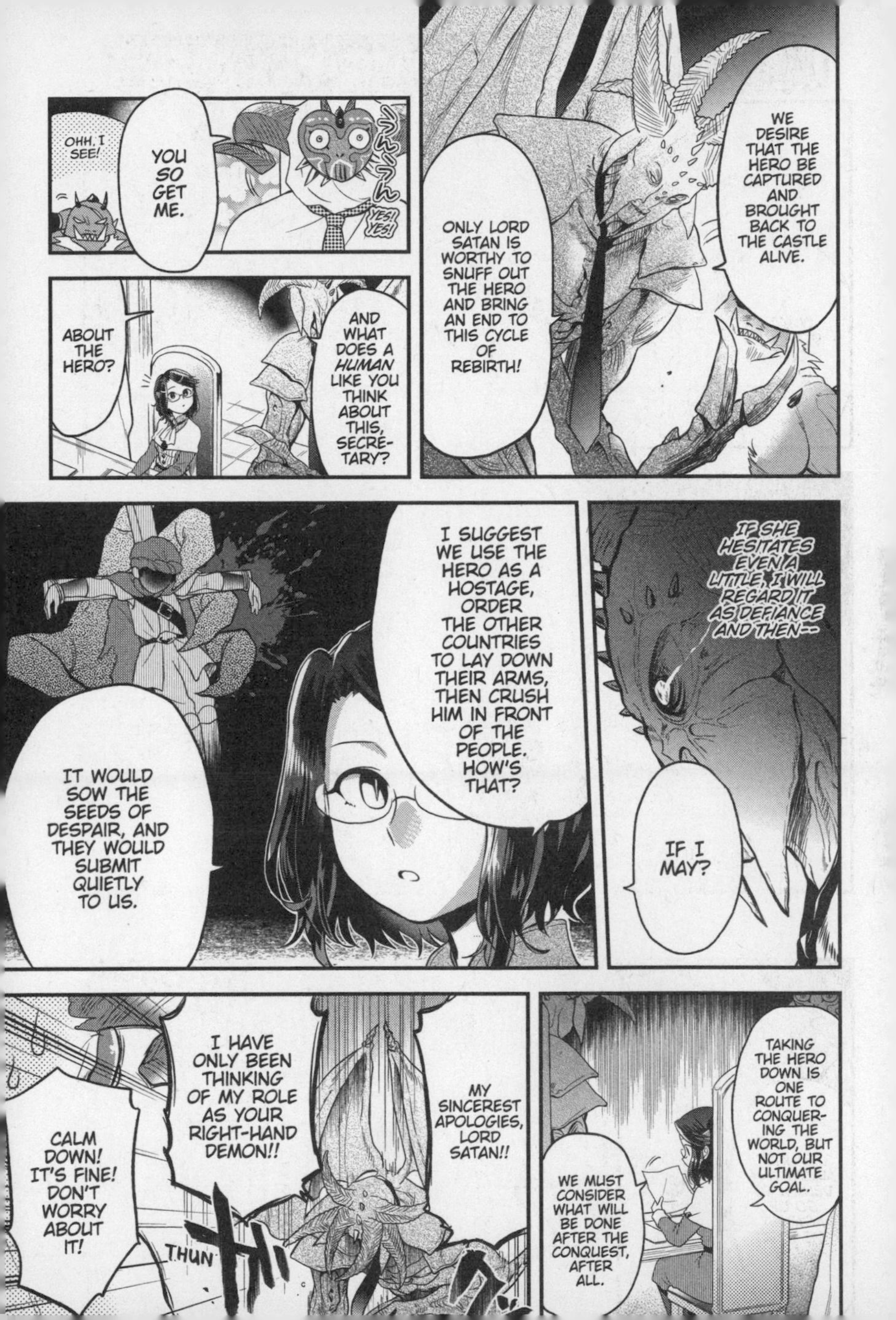
WE DESIRE THAT THE HERO BE CAPTURED AND BROUGHT BACK TO THE CASTLE ALIVE.
ONLY LORD SATAN IS WORTHY TO SNUFF OUT THE HERO AND BRING AN END TO THIS CYCLE OF REBIRTH!
YOU SO GET ME.
YES! YES!
OHH, I SEE!
AND WHAT DOES A *HUMAN* LIKE YOU THINK ABOUT THIS, SECRETARY?
ABOUT THE HERO?
IF SHE HESITATES EVEN A LITTLE, I WILL REGARD IT AS DEFIANCE AND THEN--
IF I MAY?
I SUGGEST WE USE THE HERO AS A HOSTAGE, ORDER THE OTHER COUNTRIES TO LAY DOWN THEIR ARMS, THEN CRUSH HIM IN FRONT OF THE PEOPLE. HOW'S THAT?
IT WOULD SOW THE SEEDS OF DESPAIR, AND THEY WOULD SUBMIT QUIETLY TO US.
TAKING THE HERO DOWN IS ONE ROUTE TO CONQUERING THE WORLD, BUT NOT OUR ULTIMATE GOAL.
WE MUST CONSIDER WHAT WILL BE DONE AFTER THE CONQUEST, AFTER ALL.
MY SINCEREST APOLOGIES, LORD SATAN!!
I HAVE ONLY BEEN THINKING OF MY ROLE AS YOUR RIGHT-HAND DEMON!!
THUN
CALM DOWN! IT'S FINE! DON'T WORRY ABOUT IT!

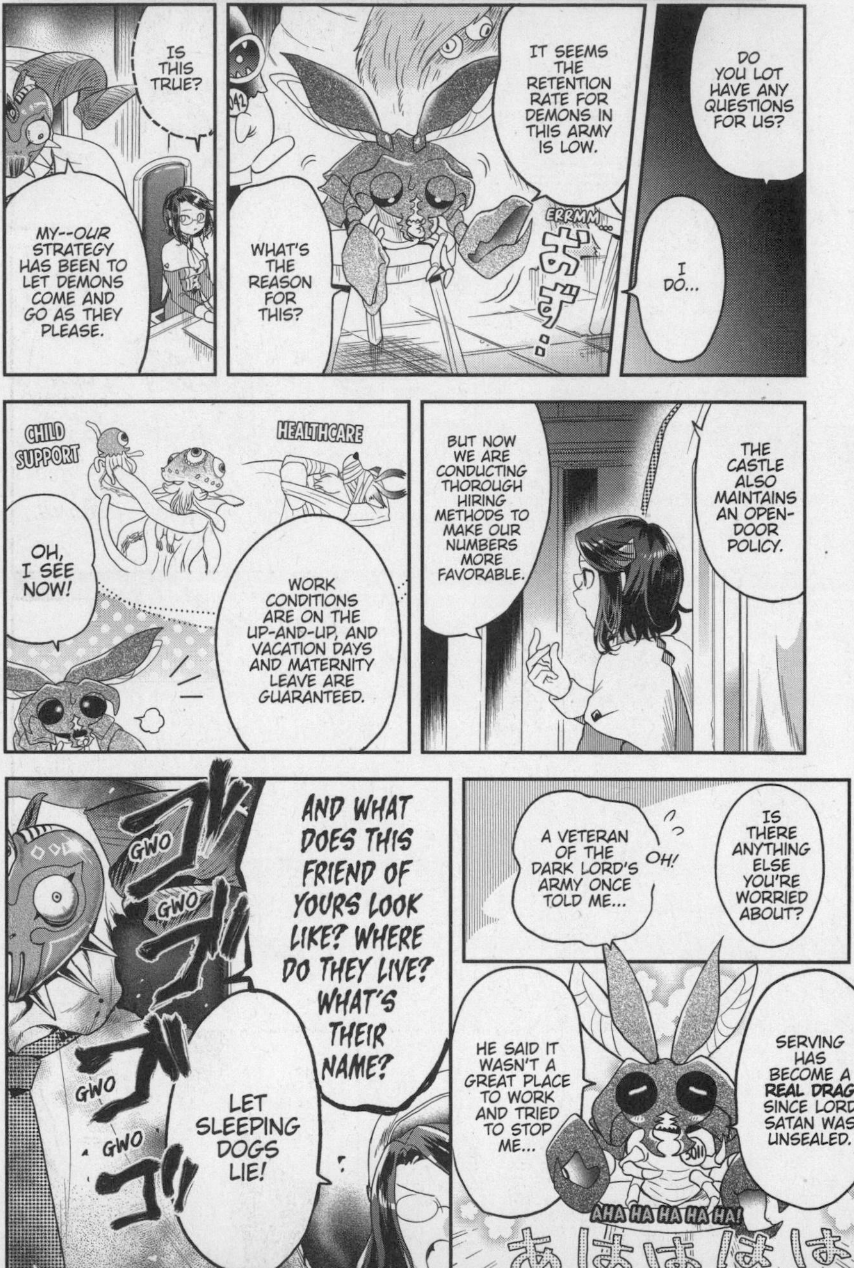
DO YOU LOT HAVE ANY QUESTIONS FOR US?
I DO...
IT SEEMS THE RETENTION RATE FOR DEMONS IN THIS ARMY IS LOW.
ERRMM...
おず…
WHAT'S THE REASON FOR THIS?
IS THIS TRUE?
MY--OUR STRATEGY HAS BEEN TO LET DEMONS COME AND GO AS THEY PLEASE.
THE CASTLE ALSO MAINTAINS AN OPEN-DOOR POLICY.
BUT NOW WE ARE CONDUCTING THOROUGH HIRING METHODS TO MAKE OUR NUMBERS MORE FAVORABLE.
HEALTHCARE
CHILD SUPPORT
WORK CONDITIONS ARE ON THE UP-AND-UP, AND VACATION DAYS AND MATERNITY LEAVE ARE GUARANTEED.
OH, I SEE NOW!
IS THERE ANYTHING ELSE YOU'RE WORRIED ABOUT?
OH!
A VETERAN OF THE DARK LORD'S ARMY ONCE TOLD ME...
SERVING HAS BECOME A **REAL DRAG** SINCE LORD SATAN WAS UNSEALED.
HE SAID IT WASN'T A GREAT PLACE TO WORK AND TRIED TO STOP ME...
AHA HA HA HA HA!
あははははは
AND WHAT DOES THIS FRIEND OF YOURS LOOK LIKE? WHERE DO THEY LIVE? WHAT'S THEIR NAME?
GWO
GWO
GWO
GWO
LET SLEEPING DOGS LIE!

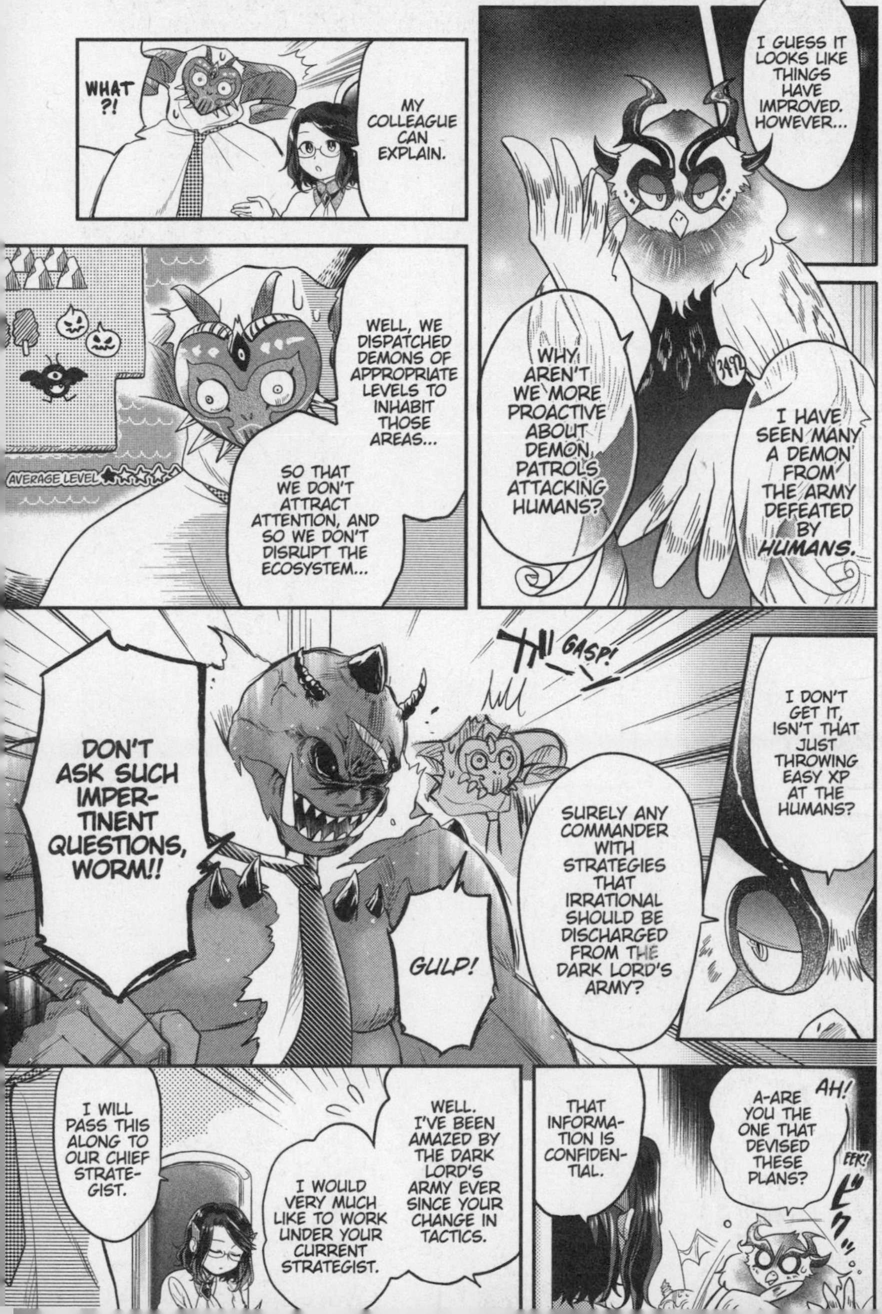

I GUESS IT LOOKS LIKE THINGS HAVE IMPROVED. HOWEVER...
I HAVE SEEN MANY A DEMON FROM THE ARMY DEFEATED BY HUMANS.
WHY AREN'T WE MORE PROACTIVE ABOUT DEMON PATROLS ATTACKING HUMANS?
3492
MY COLLEAGUE CAN EXPLAIN.
WHAT?!
WELL, WE DISPATCHED DEMONS OF APPROPRIATE LEVELS TO INHABIT THOSE AREAS...
SO THAT WE DON'T ATTRACT ATTENTION, AND SO WE DON'T DISRUPT THE ECOSYSTEM...
AVERAGE LEVEL
I DON'T GET IT, ISN'T THAT JUST THROWING EASY XP AT THE HUMANS?
SURELY ANY COMMANDER WITH STRATEGIES THAT IRRATIONAL SHOULD BE DISCHARGED FROM THE DARK LORD'S ARMY?
GASP!
DON'T ASK SUCH IMPER-TINENT QUESTIONS, WORM!!
GULP!
AH!
A-ARE YOU THE ONE THAT DEVISED THESE PLANS?
EEK!
THAT INFORMA-TION IS CONFIDEN-TIAL.
WELL. I'VE BEEN AMAZED BY THE DARK LORD'S ARMY EVER SINCE YOUR CHANGE IN TACTICS.
I WOULD VERY MUCH LIKE TO WORK UNDER YOUR CURRENT STRATEGIST.
I WILL PASS THIS ALONG TO OUR CHIEF STRATE-GIST.

# IF IT WERE ME, IF IT WERE ME

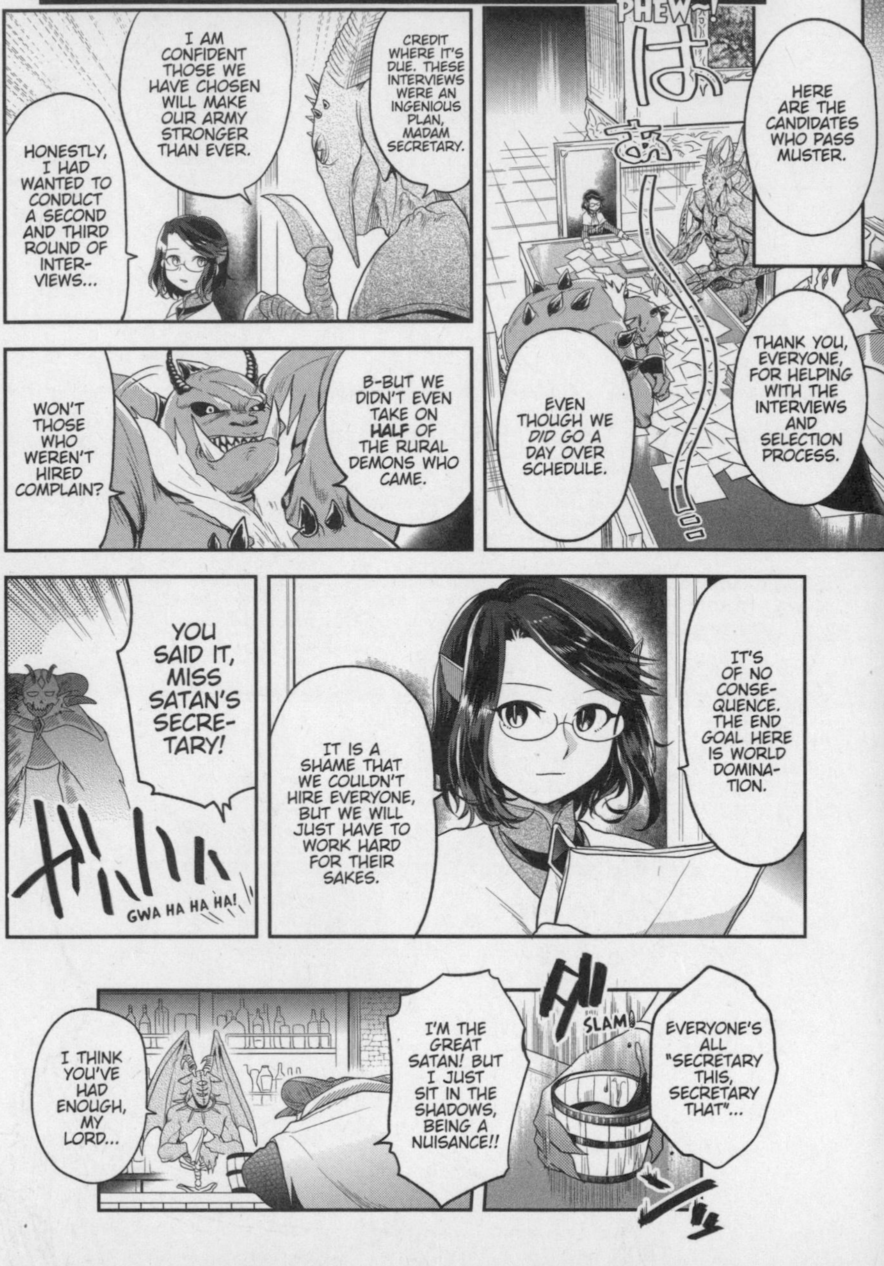
PHEW~!
HERE ARE THE CANDIDATES WHO PASS MUSTER.
THANK YOU, EVERYONE, FOR HELPING WITH THE INTERVIEWS AND SELECTION PROCESS.
EVEN THOUGH WE *DID* GO A DAY OVER SCHEDULE.
CREDIT WHERE IT'S DUE. THESE INTERVIEWS WERE AN INGENIOUS PLAN, MADAM SECRETARY.
I AM CONFIDENT THOSE WE HAVE CHOSEN WILL MAKE OUR ARMY STRONGER THAN EVER.
HONESTLY, I HAD WANTED TO CONDUCT A SECOND AND THIRD ROUND OF INTER-VIEWS...
B-BUT WE DIDN'T EVEN TAKE ON **HALF** OF THE RURAL DEMONS WHO CAME.
WON'T THOSE WHO WEREN'T HIRED COMPLAIN?
IT'S OF NO CONSE-QUENCE. THE END GOAL HERE IS WORLD DOMINA-TION.
IT IS A SHAME THAT WE COULDN'T HIRE EVERYONE, BUT WE WILL JUST HAVE TO WORK HARD FOR THEIR SAKES.
YOU SAID IT, MISS SATAN'S SECRE-TARY!
GWA HA HA HA!
EVERYONE'S ALL "SECRETARY THIS, SECRETARY THAT"...
SLAM
I'M THE GREAT SATAN! BUT I JUST SIT IN THE SHADOWS, BEING A NUISANCE!!
I THINK YOU'VE HAD ENOUGH, MY LORD...

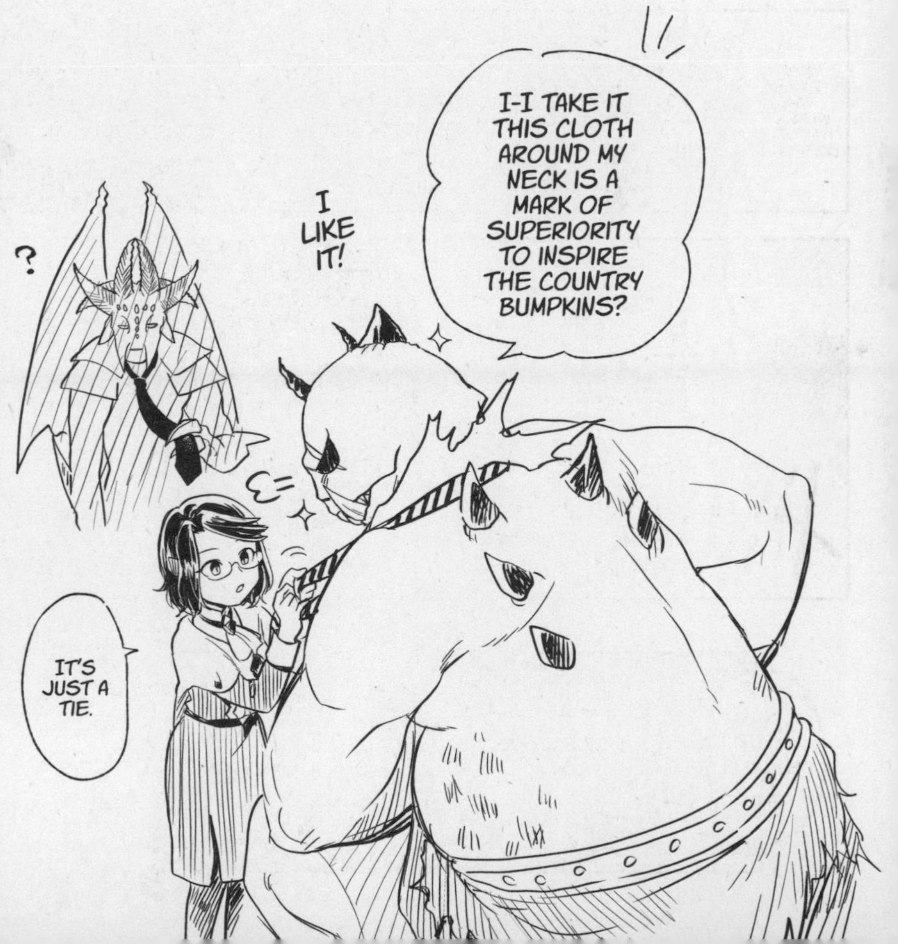
I-I TAKE IT THIS CLOTH AROUND MY NECK IS A MARK OF SUPERIORITY TO INSPIRE THE COUNTRY BUMPKINS?
I LIKE IT!
?
IT'S JUST A TIE.

# SATAN'S SECRETARY

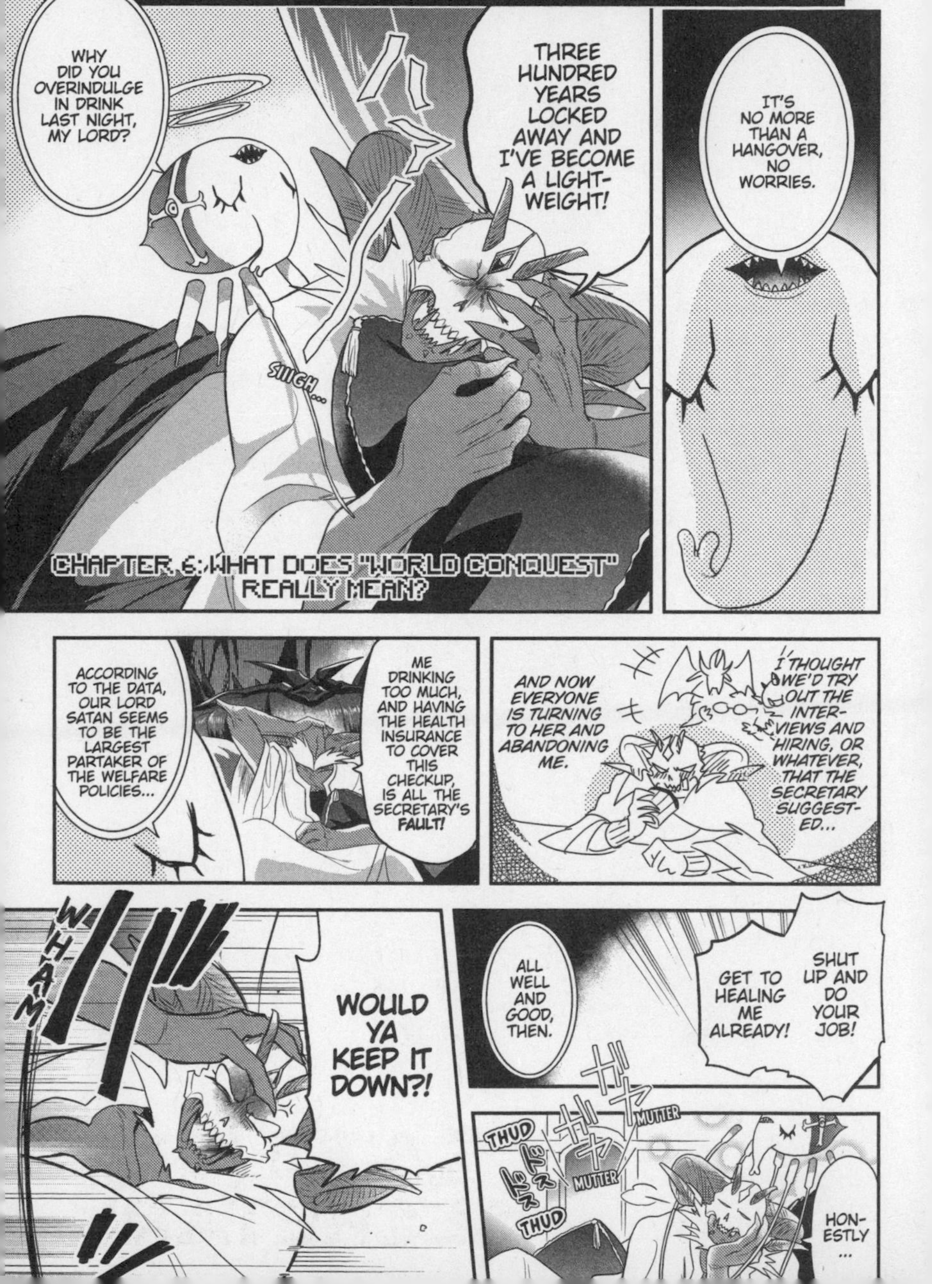
IT'S NO MORE THAN A HANGOVER, NO WORRIES.
THREE HUNDRED YEARS LOCKED AWAY AND I'VE BECOME A LIGHT-WEIGHT!
WHY DID YOU OVERINDULGE IN DRINK LAST NIGHT, MY LORD?
SIIIGH...
CHAPTER 6: WHAT DOES "WORLD CONQUEST" REALLY MEAN?
I THOUGHT WE'D TRY OUT THE INTER-VIEWS AND HIRING, OR WHATEVER, THAT THE SECRETARY SUGGEST-ED...
AND NOW EVERYONE IS TURNING TO HER AND ABANDONING ME.
ME DRINKING TOO MUCH, AND HAVING THE HEALTH INSURANCE TO COVER THIS CHECKUP, IS ALL THE SECRETARY'S FAULT!
ACCORDING TO THE DATA, OUR LORD SATAN SEEMS TO BE THE LARGEST PARTAKER OF THE WELFARE POLICIES...
SHUT UP AND DO YOUR JOB!
GET TO HEALING ME ALREADY!
ALL WELL AND GOOD, THEN.
MUTTER
THUD
MUTTER
THUD
HON-ESTLY...
WOULD YA KEEP IT DOWN?!
WHAM

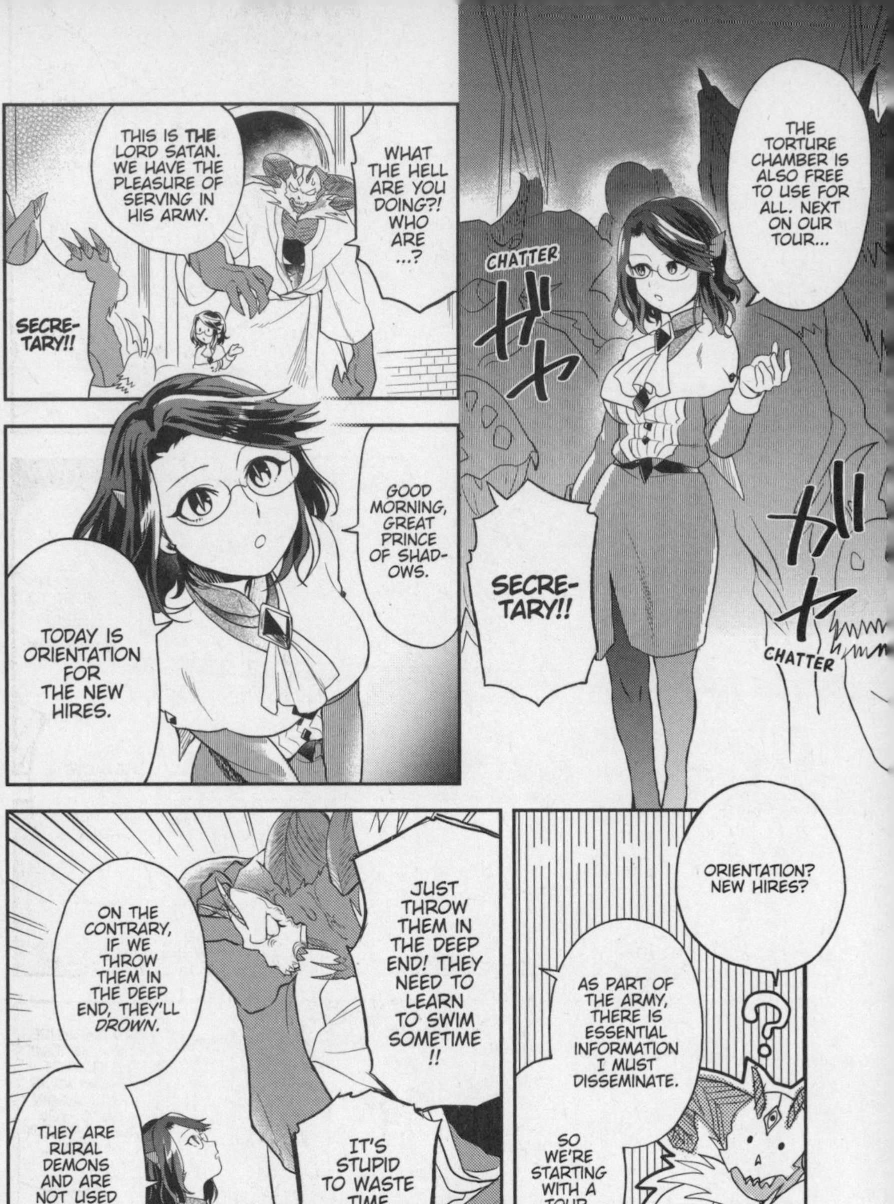
THE TORTURE CHAMBER IS ALSO FREE TO USE FOR ALL. NEXT ON OUR TOUR...
CHATTER
SECRETARY!!
CHATTER
WHAT THE HELL ARE YOU DOING?! WHO ARE ...?
THIS IS THE LORD SATAN. WE HAVE THE PLEASURE OF SERVING IN HIS ARMY.
SECRETARY!!
GOOD MORNING, GREAT PRINCE OF SHADOWS.
TODAY IS ORIENTATION FOR THE NEW HIRES.
ORIENTATION? NEW HIRES?
AS PART OF THE ARMY, THERE IS ESSENTIAL INFORMATION I MUST DISSEMINATE.
SO WE'RE STARTING WITH A TOUR.
JUST THROW THEM IN THE DEEP END! THEY NEED TO LEARN TO SWIM SOMETIME!!
ON THE CONTRARY, IF WE THROW THEM IN THE DEEP END, THEY'LL *DROWN*.
IT'S STUPID TO WASTE TIME **CODDLING** THEM!!
THEY ARE RURAL DEMONS AND ARE NOT USED TO THIS KIND OF ENVIRONMENT.

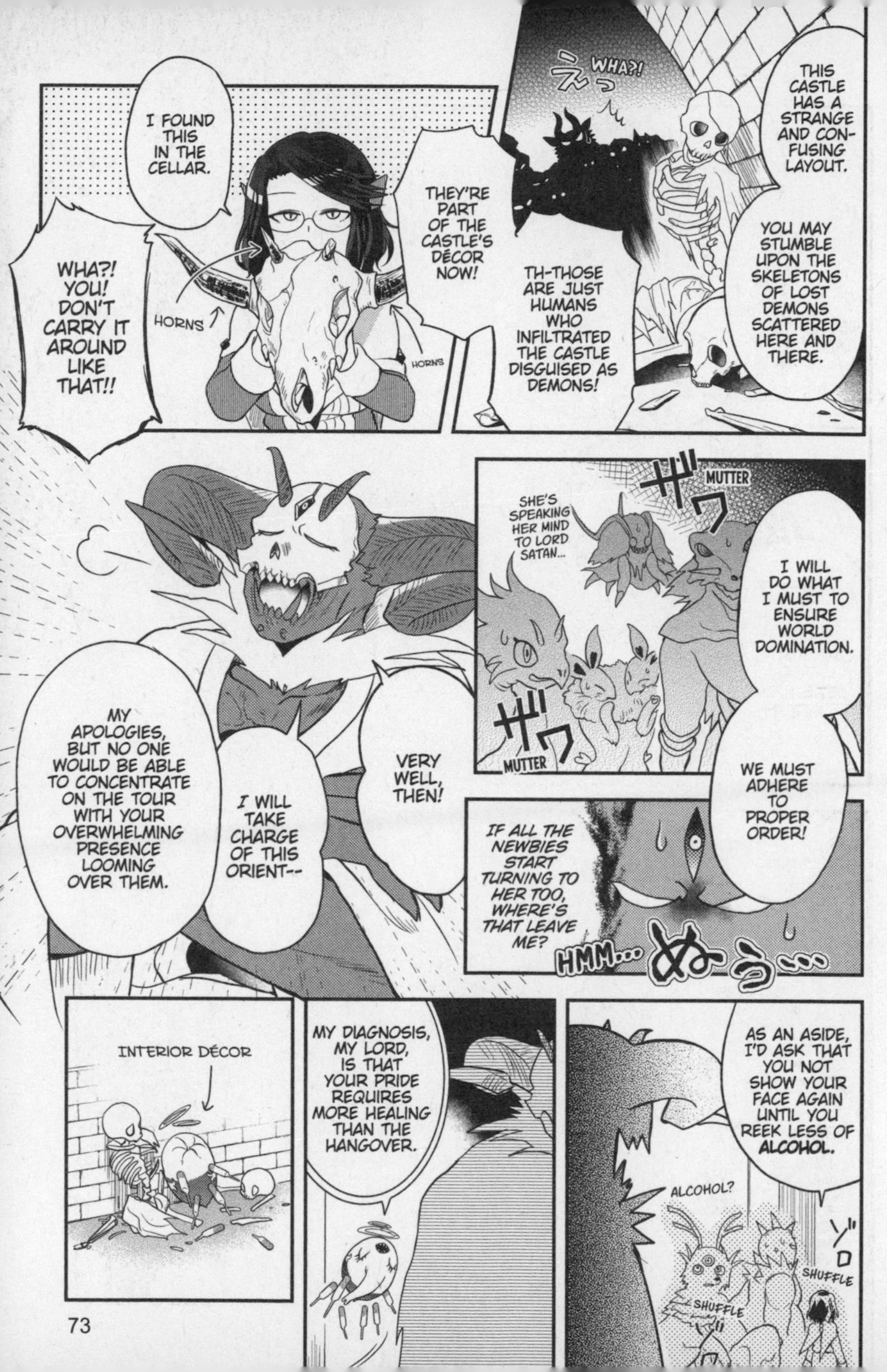

えっ
WHA?!
THIS CASTLE HAS A STRANGE AND CONFUSING LAYOUT.
YOU MAY STUMBLE UPON THE SKELETONS OF LOST DEMONS SCATTERED HERE AND THERE.
TH-THOSE ARE JUST HUMANS WHO INFILTRATED THE CASTLE DISGUISED AS DEMONS!
THEY'RE PART OF THE CASTLE'S DÉCOR NOW!
I FOUND THIS IN THE CELLAR.
HORNS
HORNS
WHA?! YOU! DON'T CARRY IT AROUND LIKE THAT!!
ザワ
MUTTER
SHE'S SPEAKING HER MIND TO LORD SATAN...
ザワ
MUTTER
I WILL DO WHAT I MUST TO ENSURE WORLD DOMINATION.
WE MUST ADHERE TO PROPER ORDER!
IF ALL THE NEWBIES START TURNING TO HER TOO, WHERE'S THAT LEAVE ME?
ぬう...
HMM...
VERY WELL, THEN!
I WILL TAKE CHARGE OF THIS ORIENT--
MY APOLOGIES, BUT NO ONE WOULD BE ABLE TO CONCENTRATE ON THE TOUR WITH YOUR OVERWHELMING PRESENCE LOOMING OVER THEM.
AS AN ASIDE, I'D ASK THAT YOU NOT SHOW YOUR FACE AGAIN UNTIL YOU REEK LESS OF **ALCOHOL.**
ALCOHOL?
ゾロ
SHUFFLE
SHUFFLE
MY DIAGNOSIS, MY LORD, IS THAT YOUR PRIDE REQUIRES MORE HEALING THAN THE HANGOVER.
INTERIOR DÉCOR

## VIOLENCE BREEDS MONEY

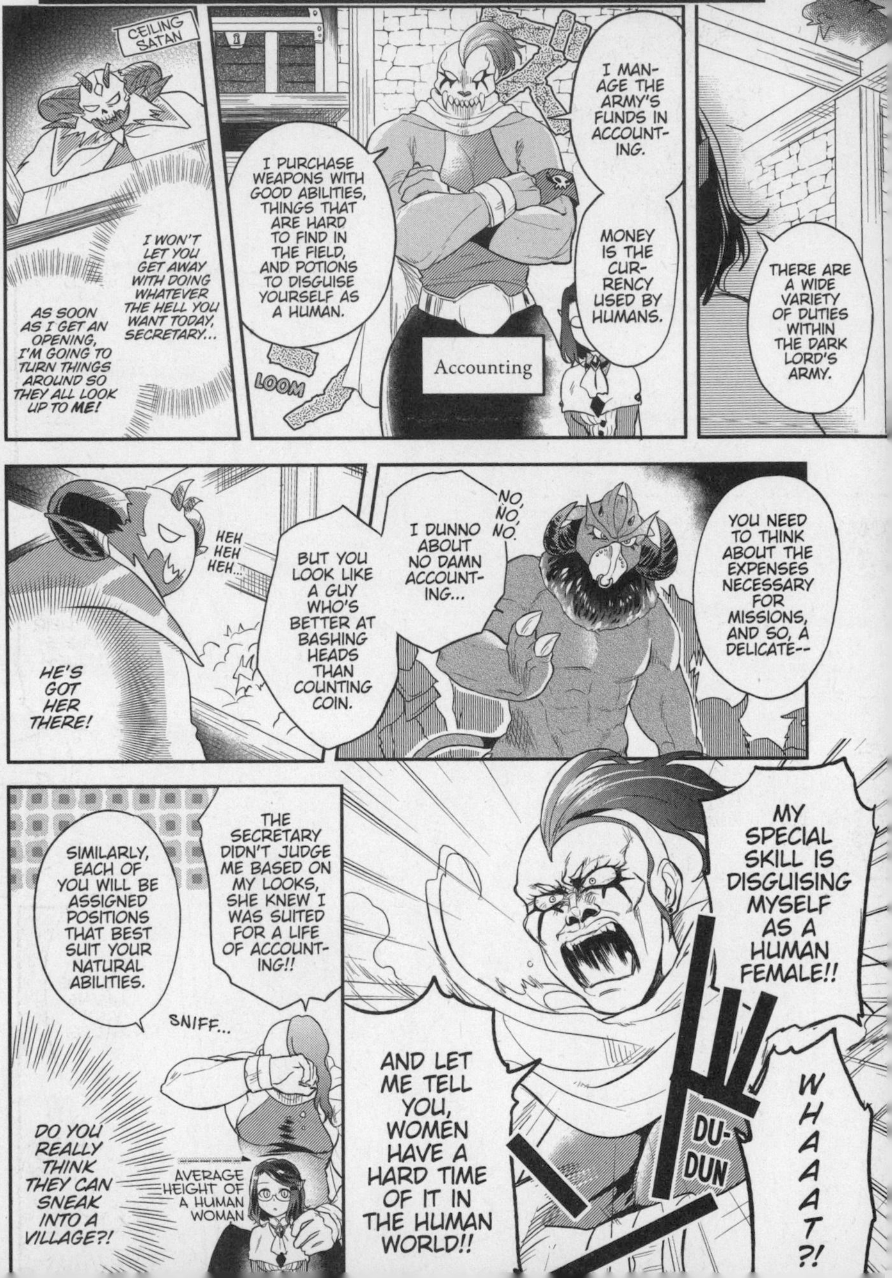
THERE ARE A WIDE VARIETY OF DUTIES WITHIN THE DARK LORD'S ARMY.
I MAN-AGE THE ARMY'S FUNDS IN ACCOUNT-ING.
MONEY IS THE CUR-RENCY USED BY HUMANS.
I PURCHASE WEAPONS WITH GOOD ABILITIES, THINGS THAT ARE HARD TO FIND IN THE FIELD, AND POTIONS TO DISGUISE YOURSELF AS A HUMAN.
Accounting
LOOM
CEILING SATAN
I WON'T LET YOU GET AWAY WITH DOING WHATEVER THE HELL YOU WANT TODAY, SECRETARY...
AS SOON AS I GET AN OPENING, I'M GOING TO TURN THINGS AROUND SO THEY ALL LOOK UP TO ME!
YOU NEED TO THINK ABOUT THE EXPENSES NECESSARY FOR MISSIONS, AND SO, A DELICATE--
NO, NO, NO.
I DUNNO ABOUT NO DAMN ACCOUNT-ING...
BUT YOU LOOK LIKE A GUY WHO'S BETTER AT BASHING HEADS THAN COUNTING COIN.
HEH HEH HEH...
HE'S GOT HER THERE!
MY SPECIAL SKILL IS DISGUISING MYSELF AS A HUMAN FEMALE!!
WHAAAT?!
DU-DUN
AND LET ME TELL YOU, WOMEN HAVE A HARD TIME OF IT IN THE HUMAN WORLD!!
THE SECRETARY DIDN'T JUDGE ME BASED ON MY LOOKS, SHE KNEW I WAS SUITED FOR A LIFE OF ACCOUNT-ING!!
SIMILARLY, EACH OF YOU WILL BE ASSIGNED POSITIONS THAT BEST SUIT YOUR NATURAL ABILITIES.
SNIFF...
AVERAGE HEIGHT OF A HUMAN WOMAN
DO YOU REALLY THINK THEY CAN SNEAK INTO A VILLAGE?!

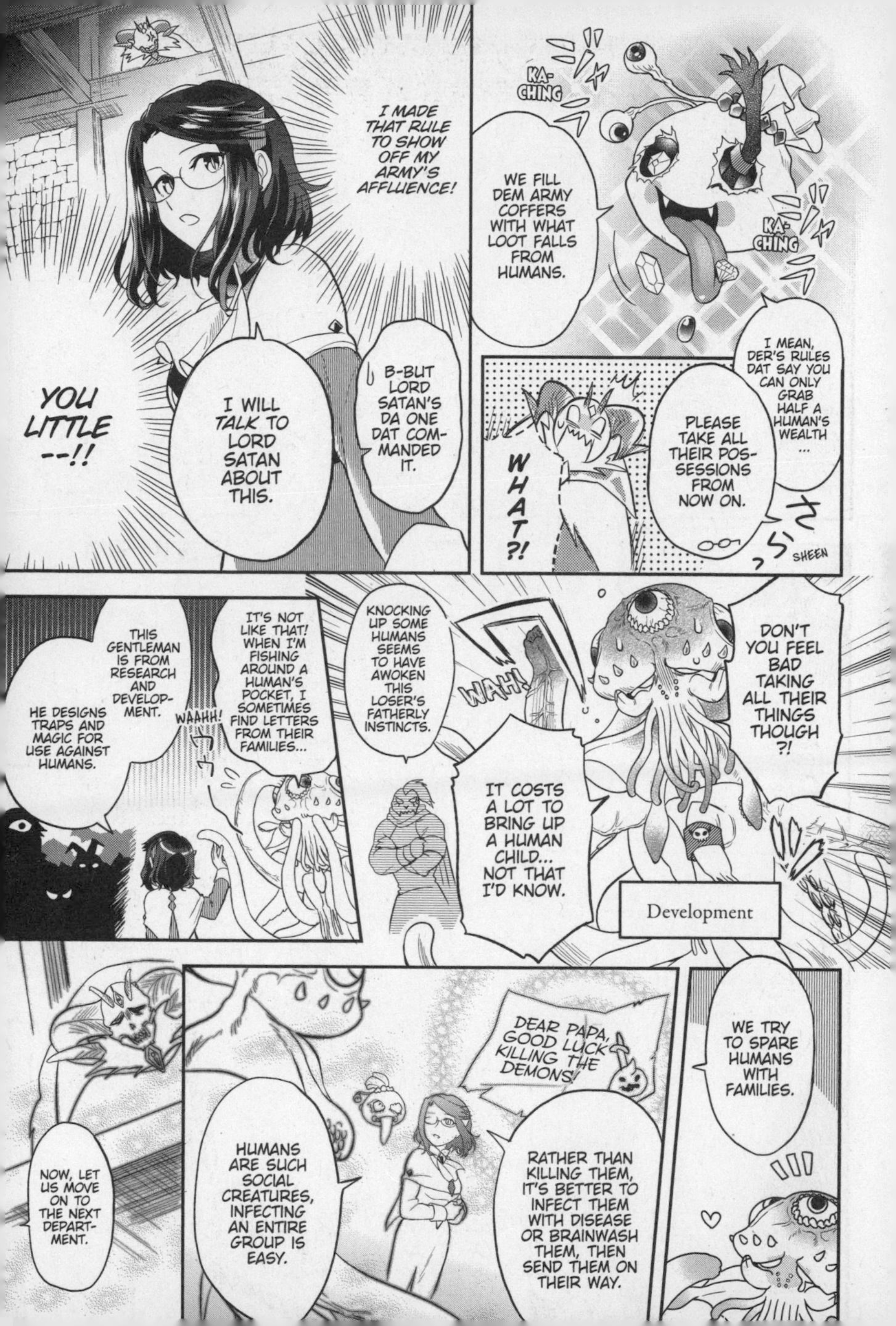
KA-CHING
WE FILL DEM ARMY COFFERS WITH WHAT LOOT FALLS FROM HUMANS.
KA-CHING
I MEAN, DER'S RULES DAT SAY YOU CAN ONLY GRAB HALF A HUMAN'S WEALTH ...
PLEASE TAKE ALL THEIR POSSESSIONS FROM NOW ON.
WHAT?!
SHEEN
B-BUT LORD SATAN'S DA ONE DAT COMMANDED IT.
I WILL TALK TO LORD SATAN ABOUT THIS.
I MADE THAT RULE TO SHOW OFF MY ARMY'S AFFLUENCE!
YOU LITTLE--!!
Development
DON'T YOU FEEL BAD TAKING ALL THEIR THINGS THOUGH?!
IT COSTS A LOT TO BRING UP A HUMAN CHILD... NOT THAT I'D KNOW.
WAH!
KNOCKING UP SOME HUMANS SEEMS TO HAVE AWOKEN THIS LOSER'S FATHERLY INSTINCTS.
IT'S NOT LIKE THAT! WHEN I'M FISHING AROUND A HUMAN'S POCKET, I SOMETIMES FIND LETTERS FROM THEIR FAMILIES...
WAAHH!
THIS GENTLEMAN IS FROM RESEARCH AND DEVELOPMENT.
HE DESIGNS TRAPS AND MAGIC FOR USE AGAINST HUMANS.
WE TRY TO SPARE HUMANS WITH FAMILIES.
DEAR PAPA, GOOD LUCK KILLING THE DEMONS!
RATHER THAN KILLING THEM, IT'S BETTER TO INFECT THEM WITH DISEASE OR BRAINWASH THEM, THEN SEND THEM ON THEIR WAY.
HUMANS ARE SUCH SOCIAL CREATURES, INFECTING AN ENTIRE GROUP IS EASY.
NOW, LET US MOVE ON TO THE NEXT DEPARTMENT.

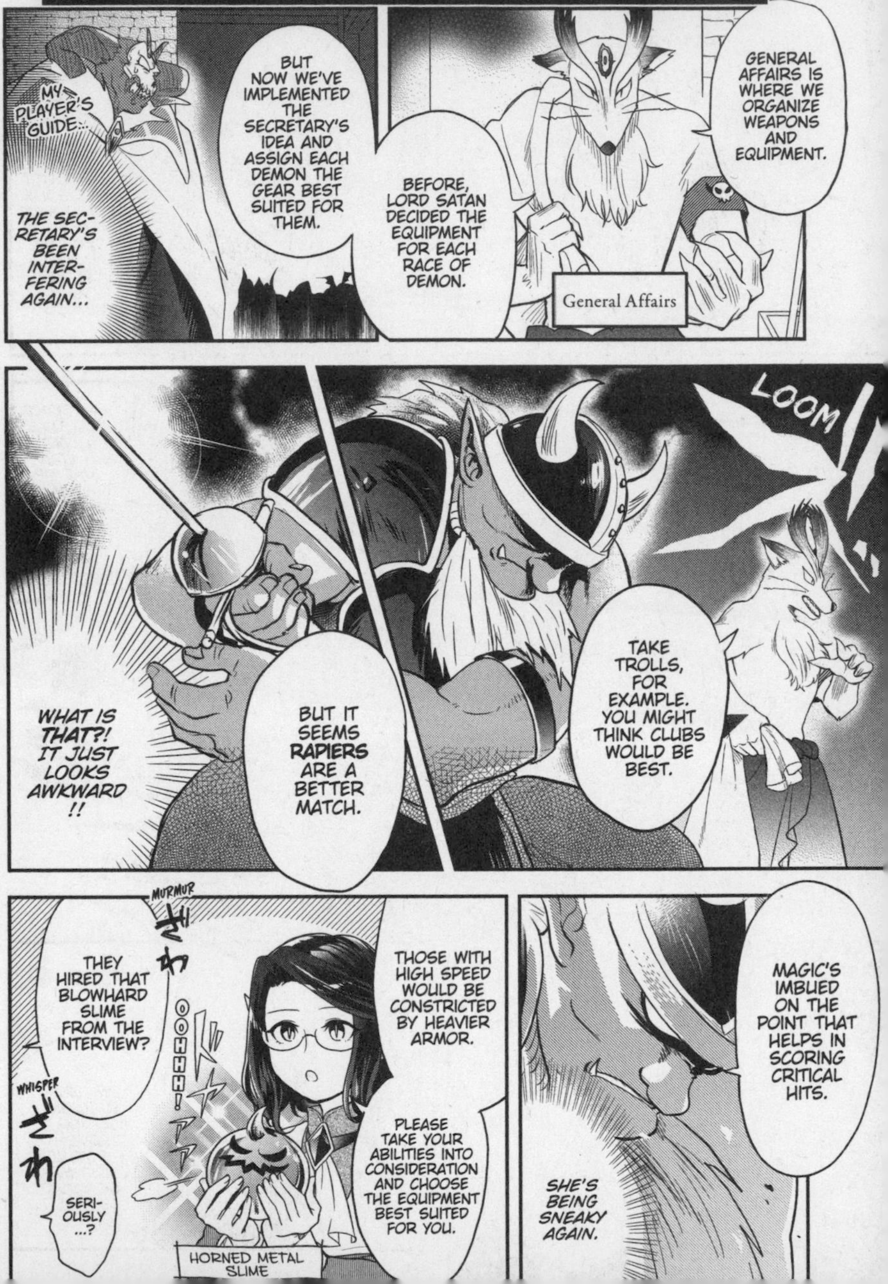
GENERAL AFFAIRS IS WHERE WE ORGANIZE WEAPONS AND EQUIPMENT.
BEFORE, LORD SATAN DECIDED THE EQUIPMENT FOR EACH RACE OF DEMON.
General Affairs
BUT NOW WE'VE IMPLEMENTED THE SECRETARY'S IDEA AND ASSIGN EACH DEMON THE GEAR BEST SUITED FOR THEM.
MY PLAYER'S GUIDE...
THE SECRETARY'S BEEN INTERFERING AGAIN...
LOOM
TAKE TROLLS, FOR EXAMPLE. YOU MIGHT THINK CLUBS WOULD BE BEST.
BUT IT SEEMS **RAPIERS** ARE A BETTER MATCH.
WHAT IS **THAT?!** IT JUST LOOKS AWKWARD !!
MAGIC'S IMBUED ON THE POINT THAT HELPS IN SCORING CRITICAL HITS.
SHE'S BEING SNEAKY AGAIN.
THOSE WITH HIGH SPEED WOULD BE CONSTRICTED BY HEAVIER ARMOR.
PLEASE TAKE YOUR ABILITIES INTO CONSIDERATION AND CHOOSE THE EQUIPMENT BEST SUITED FOR YOU.
OOHHHH!
MURMUR
THEY HIRED THAT BLOWHARD SLIME FROM THE INTERVIEW?
WHISPER
SERIOUSLY ...?
HORNED METAL SLIME

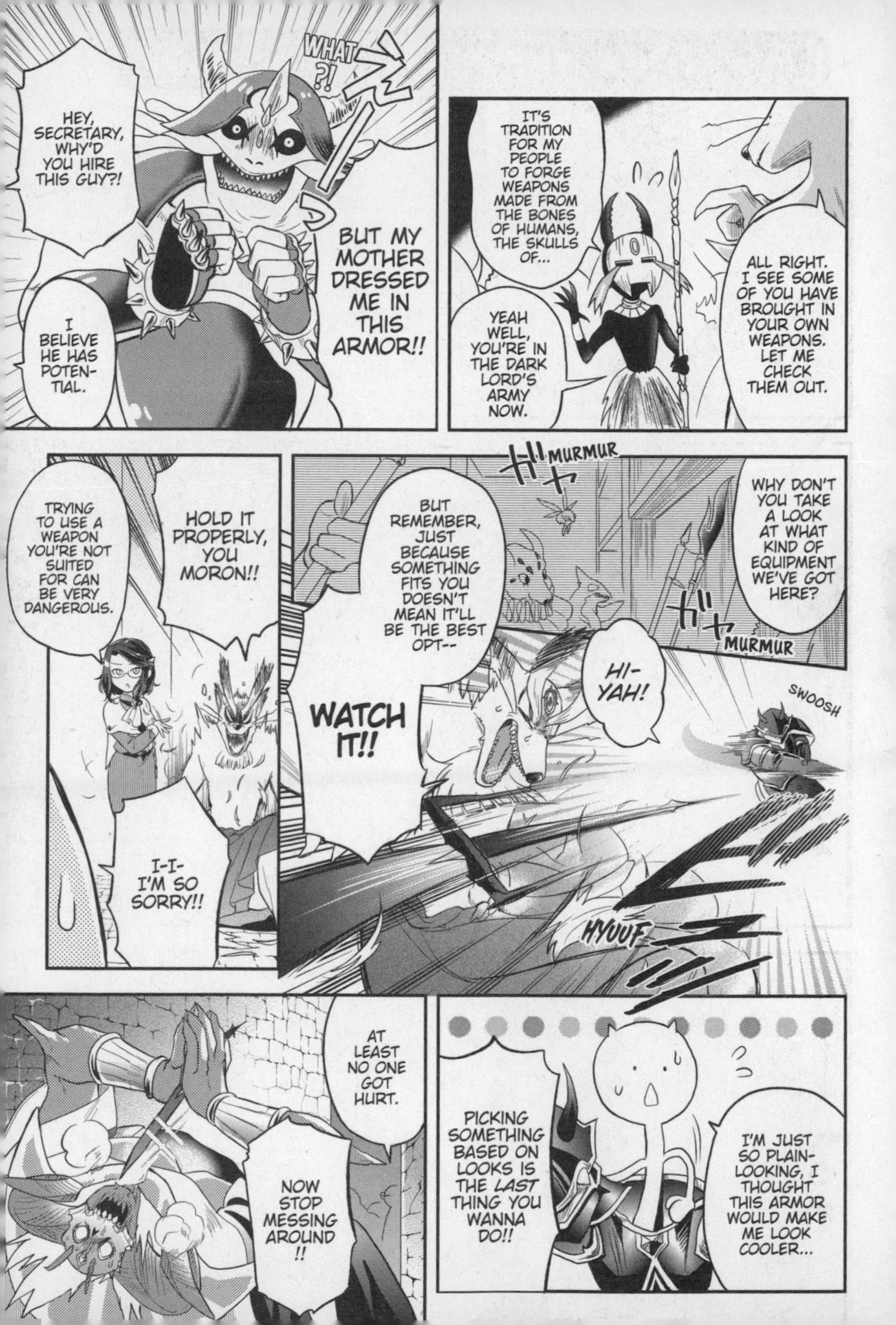
ALL RIGHT. I SEE SOME OF YOU HAVE BROUGHT IN YOUR OWN WEAPONS. LET ME CHECK THEM OUT.
IT'S TRADITION FOR MY PEOPLE TO FORGE WEAPONS MADE FROM THE BONES OF HUMANS, THE SKULLS OF...
YEAH WELL, YOU'RE IN THE DARK LORD'S ARMY NOW.
WHAT ?!
BUT MY MOTHER DRESSED ME IN THIS ARMOR!!
HEY, SECRETARY, WHY'D YOU HIRE THIS GUY?!
I BELIEVE HE HAS POTEN-TIAL.
WHY DON'T YOU TAKE A LOOK AT WHAT KIND OF EQUIPMENT WE'VE GOT HERE?
MURMUR
MURMUR
SWOOSH
HI-YAH!
BUT REMEMBER, JUST BECAUSE SOMETHING FITS YOU DOESN'T MEAN IT'LL BE THE BEST OPT--
WATCH IT!!
HYUUF
HOLD IT PROPERLY, YOU MORON!!
TRYING TO USE A WEAPON YOU'RE NOT SUITED FOR CAN BE VERY DANGEROUS.
I-I-I'M SO SORRY!!
I'M JUST SO PLAIN-LOOKING, I THOUGHT THIS ARMOR WOULD MAKE ME LOOK COOLER...
PICKING SOMETHING BASED ON LOOKS IS THE LAST THING YOU WANNA DO!!
AT LEAST NO ONE GOT HURT.
NOW STOP MESSING AROUND!!

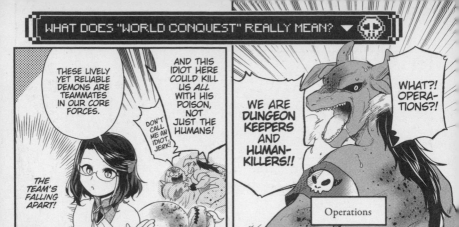

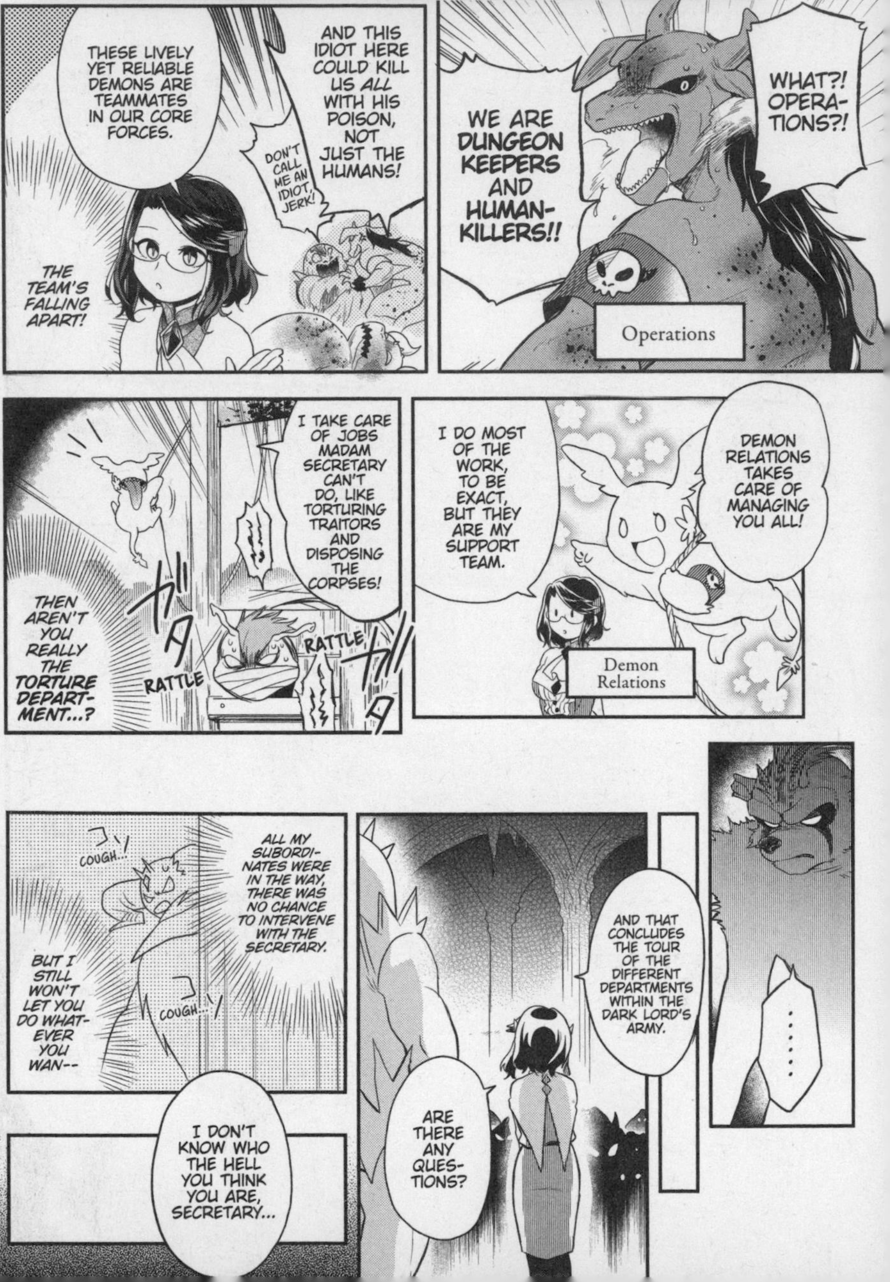
WHAT?! OPERATIONS?!
WE ARE DUNGEON KEEPERS AND HUMAN-KILLERS!!
Operations
AND THIS IDIOT HERE COULD KILL US ALL WITH HIS POISON, NOT JUST THE HUMANS!
DON'T CALL ME AN IDIOT, JERK!
THESE LIVELY YET RELIABLE DEMONS ARE TEAMMATES IN OUR CORE FORCES.
THE TEAM'S FALLING APART!
DEMON RELATIONS TAKES CARE OF MANAGING YOU ALL!
I DO MOST OF THE WORK, TO BE EXACT, BUT THEY ARE MY SUPPORT TEAM.
Demon Relations
I TAKE CARE OF JOBS MADAM SECRETARY CAN'T DO, LIKE TORTURING TRAITORS AND DISPOSING THE CORPSES!
RATTLE
RATTLE
THEN AREN'T YOU REALLY THE TORTURE DEPARTMENT...?
......
AND THAT CONCLUDES THE TOUR OF THE DIFFERENT DEPARTMENTS WITHIN THE DARK LORD'S ARMY.
ARE THERE ANY QUESTIONS?
ALL MY SUBORDINATES WERE IN THE WAY, THERE WAS NO CHANCE TO INTERVENE WITH THE SECRETARY.
COUGH...!
BUT I STILL WON'T LET YOU DO WHATEVER YOU WAN--
COUGH...!
I DON'T KNOW WHO THE HELL YOU THINK YOU ARE, SECRETARY...

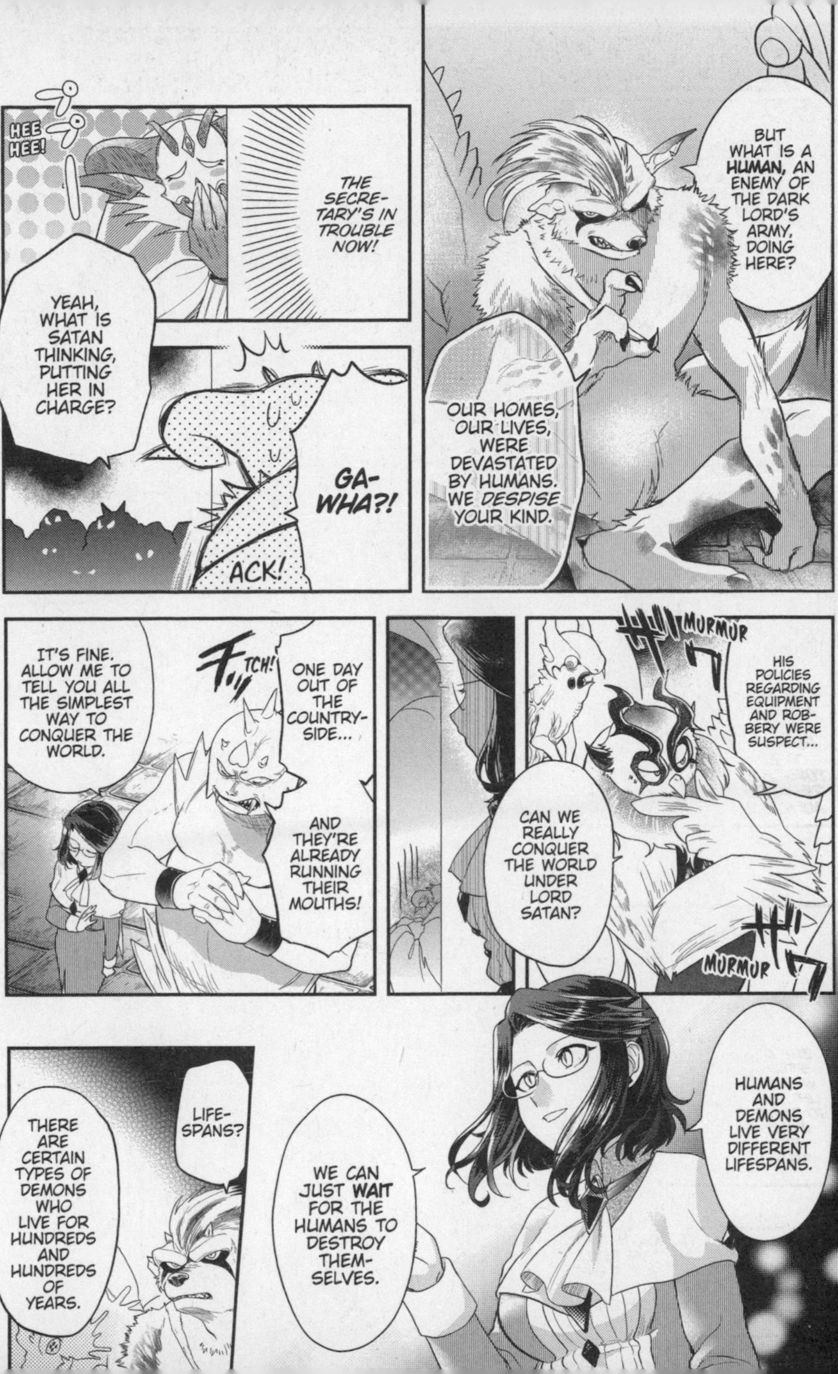
BUT WHAT IS A HUMAN, AN ENEMY OF THE DARK LORD'S ARMY, DOING HERE?
OUR HOMES, OUR LIVES, WERE DEVASTATED BY HUMANS. WE DESPISE YOUR KIND.
THE SECRE-TARY'S IN TROUBLE NOW!
HEE HEE!
YEAH, WHAT IS SATAN THINKING, PUTTING HER IN CHARGE?
GA-WHA?!
ACK!
MURMUR
HIS POLICIES REGARDING EQUIPMENT AND ROB-BERY WERE SUSPECT...
CAN WE REALLY CONQUER THE WORLD UNDER LORD SATAN?
MURMUR
ONE DAY OUT OF THE COUNTRY-SIDE...
TCH!
AND THEY'RE ALREADY RUNNING THEIR MOUTHS!
IT'S FINE. ALLOW ME TO TELL YOU ALL THE SIMPLEST WAY TO CONQUER THE WORLD.
HUMANS AND DEMONS LIVE VERY DIFFERENT LIFESPANS.
WE CAN JUST WAIT FOR THE HUMANS TO DESTROY THEM-SELVES.
LIFE-SPANS?
THERE ARE CERTAIN TYPES OF DEMONS WHO LIVE FOR HUNDREDS AND HUNDREDS OF YEARS.

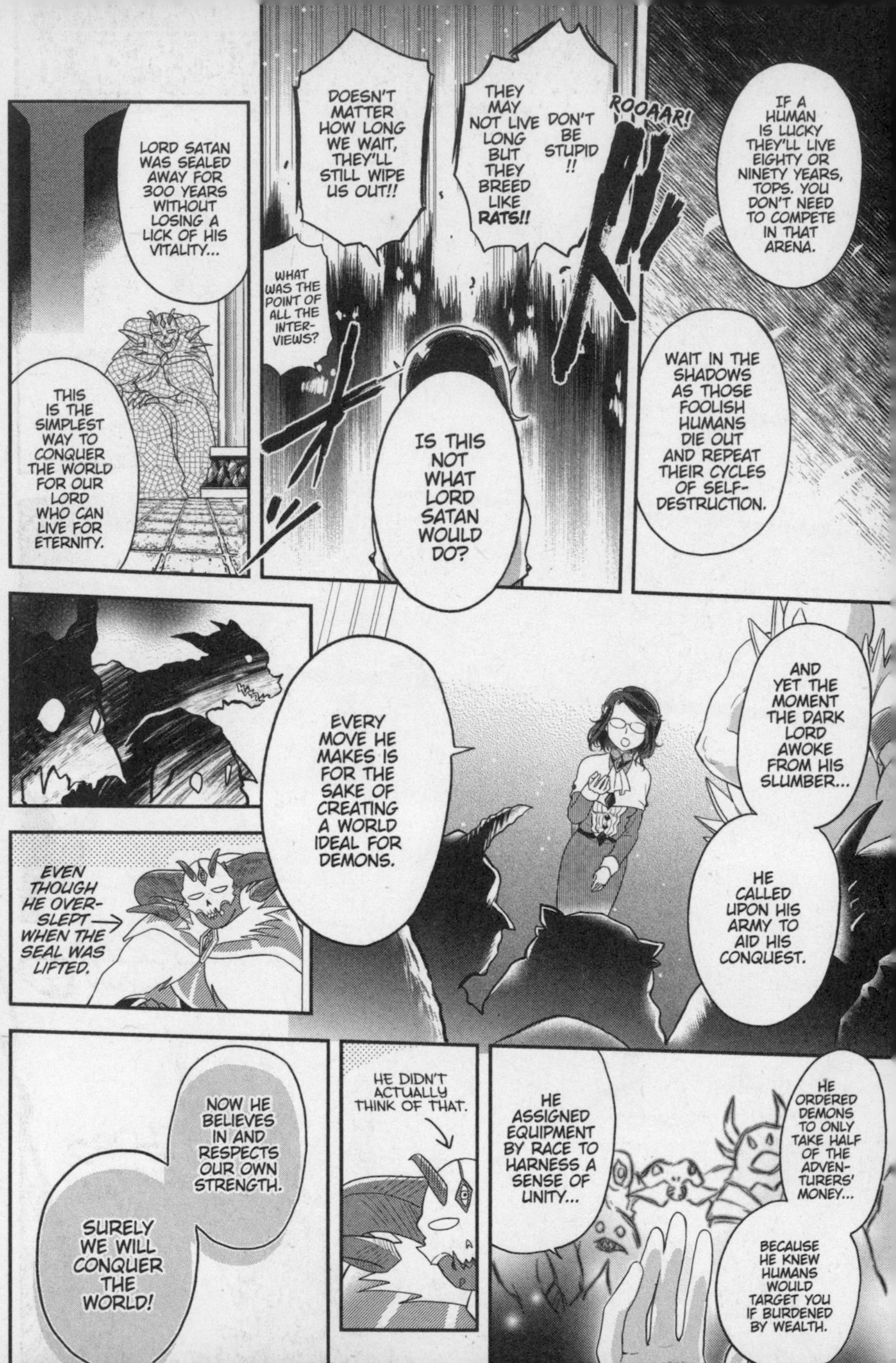
IF A HUMAN IS LUCKY THEY'LL LIVE EIGHTY OR NINETY YEARS, TOPS. YOU DON'T NEED TO COMPETE IN THAT ARENA.
WAIT IN THE SHADOWS AS THOSE FOOLISH HUMANS DIE OUT AND REPEAT THEIR CYCLES OF SELF-DESTRUCTION.
ROOAAR!
DON'T BE STUPID !!
THEY MAY NOT LIVE LONG BUT THEY BREED LIKE RATS!!
DOESN'T MATTER HOW LONG WE WAIT, THEY'LL STILL WIPE US OUT!!
WHAT WAS THE POINT OF ALL THE INTERVIEWS?
IS THIS NOT WHAT LORD SATAN WOULD DO?
LORD SATAN WAS SEALED AWAY FOR 300 YEARS WITHOUT LOSING A LICK OF HIS VITALITY...
THIS IS THE SIMPLEST WAY TO CONQUER THE WORLD FOR OUR LORD WHO CAN LIVE FOR ETERNITY.
AND YET THE MOMENT THE DARK LORD AWOKE FROM HIS SLUMBER...
HE CALLED UPON HIS ARMY TO AID HIS CONQUEST.
EVERY MOVE HE MAKES IS FOR THE SAKE OF CREATING A WORLD IDEAL FOR DEMONS.
EVEN THOUGH HE OVER-SLEPT WHEN THE SEAL WAS LIFTED.
HE ORDERED DEMONS TO ONLY TAKE HALF OF THE ADVEN-TURERS' MONEY...
BECAUSE HE KNEW HUMANS WOULD TARGET YOU IF BURDENED BY WEALTH.
HE ASSIGNED EQUIPMENT BY RACE TO HARNESS A SENSE OF UNITY...
HE DIDN'T ACTUALLY THINK OF THAT.
NOW HE BELIEVES IN AND RESPECTS OUR OWN STRENGTH.
SURELY WE WILL CONQUER THE WORLD!

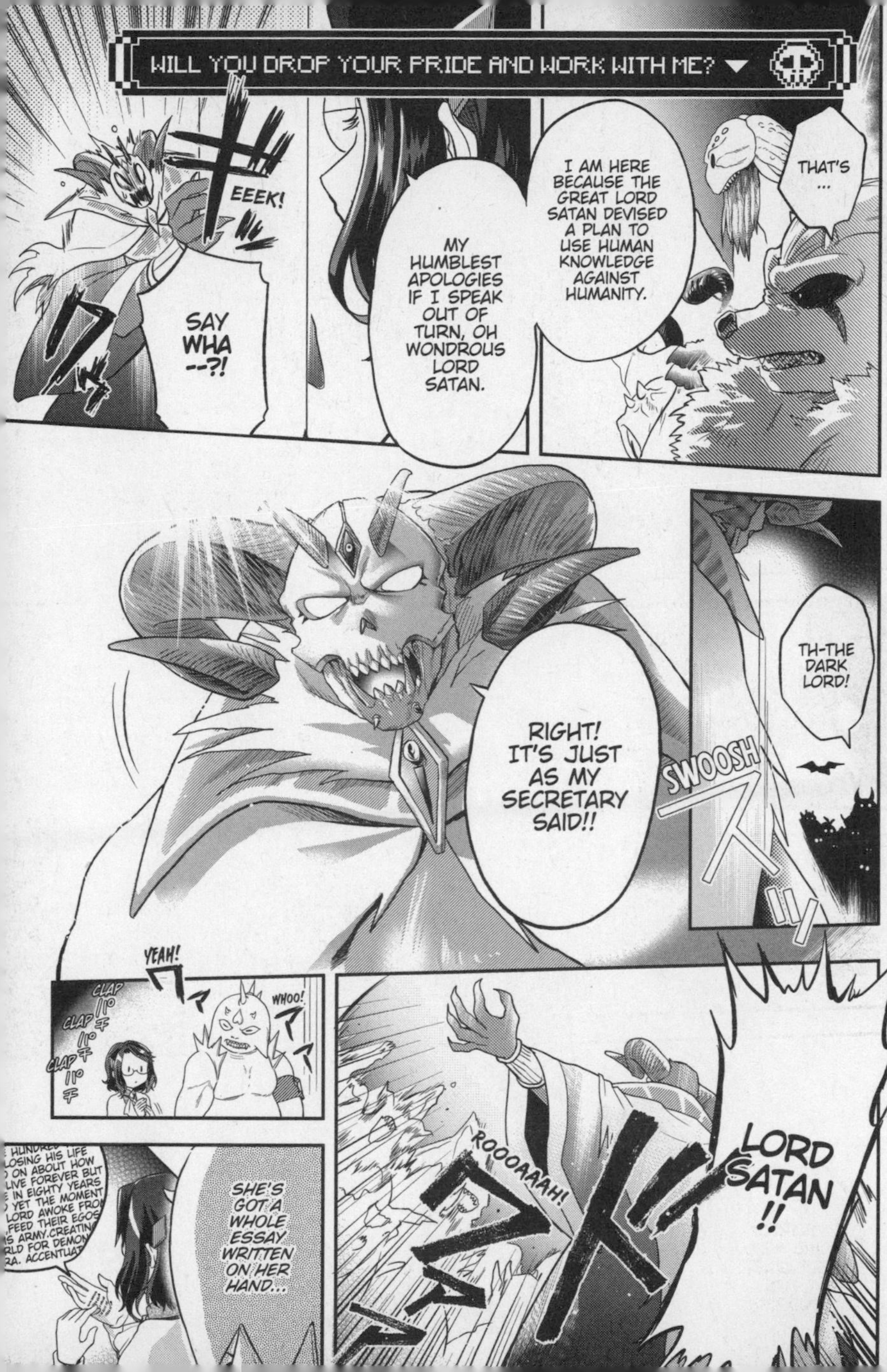
WILL YOU DROP YOUR PRIDE AND WORK WITH ME?
THAT'S ...
I AM HERE BECAUSE THE GREAT LORD SATAN DEVISED A PLAN TO USE HUMAN KNOWLEDGE AGAINST HUMANITY.
MY HUMBLEST APOLOGIES IF I SPEAK OUT OF TURN, OH WONDROUS LORD SATAN.
EEEK!
SAY WHA--?!
TH-THE DARK LORD!
SWOOSH
RIGHT! IT'S JUST AS MY SECRETARY SAID!!
LORD SATAN!!
ROOOAAAH!
YEAH!
WHOO!
CLAP
CLAP
CLAP
SHE'S GOT A WHOLE ESSAY WRITTEN ON HER HAND...

# BROKEN VOW

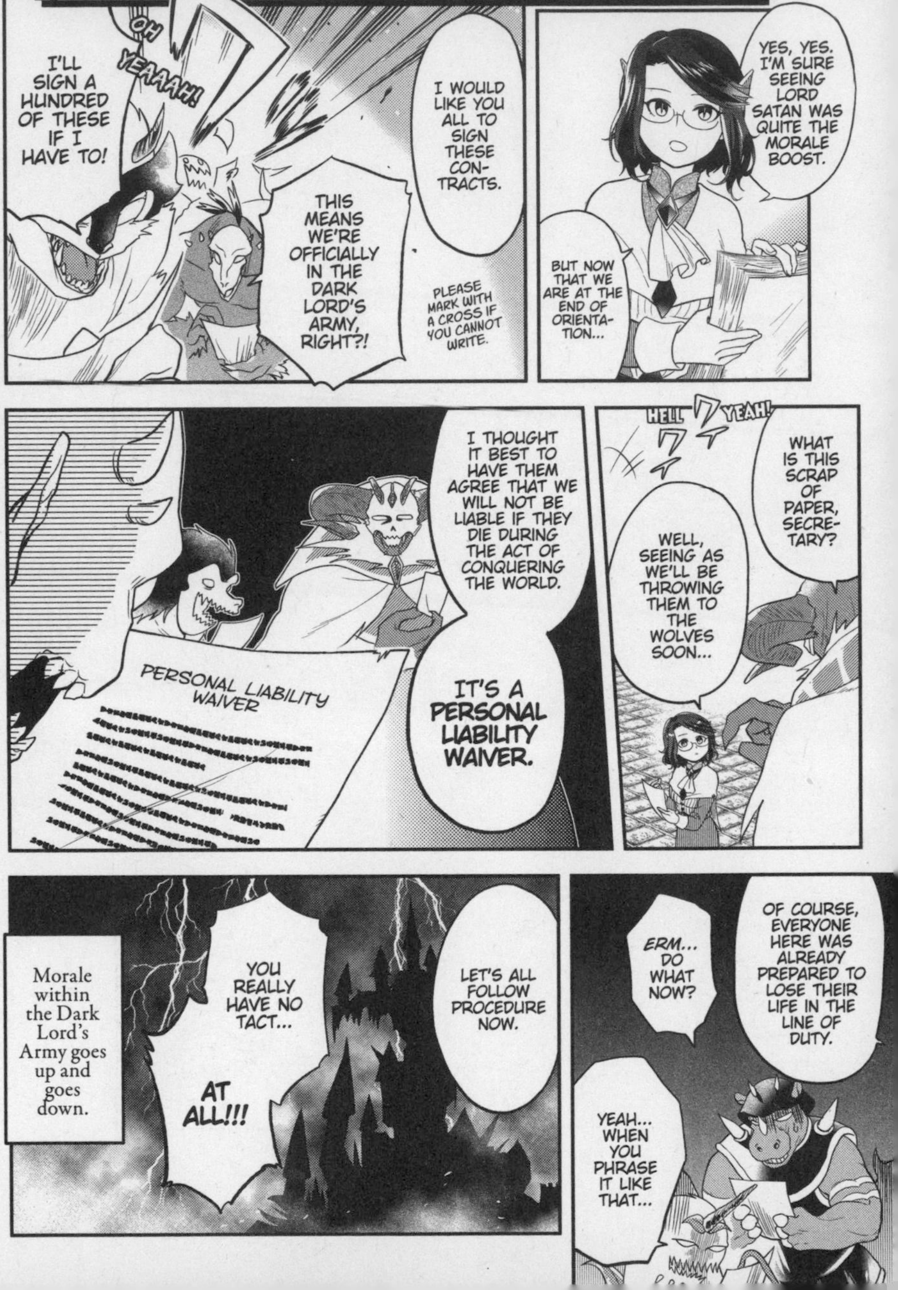
YES, YES. I'M SURE SEEING LORD SATAN WAS QUITE THE MORALE BOOST.
BUT NOW THAT WE ARE AT THE END OF ORIENTATION...
I WOULD LIKE YOU ALL TO SIGN THESE CONTRACTS.
PLEASE MARK WITH A CROSS IF YOU CANNOT WRITE.
THIS MEANS WE'RE OFFICIALLY IN THE DARK LORD'S ARMY, RIGHT?!
OH YEAAAH!
I'LL SIGN A HUNDRED OF THESE IF I HAVE TO!
HELL YEAH!
WHAT IS THIS SCRAP OF PAPER, SECRETARY?
WELL, SEEING AS WE'LL BE THROWING THEM TO THE WOLVES SOON...
I THOUGHT IT BEST TO HAVE THEM AGREE THAT WE WILL NOT BE LIABLE IF THEY DIE DURING THE ACT OF CONQUERING THE WORLD.
IT'S A PERSONAL LIABILITY WAIVER.
PERSONAL LIABILITY WAIVER
OF COURSE, EVERYONE HERE WAS ALREADY PREPARED TO LOSE THEIR LIFE IN THE LINE OF DUTY.
ERM... DO WHAT NOW?
YEAH... WHEN YOU PHRASE IT LIKE THAT...
LET'S ALL FOLLOW PROCEDURE NOW.
YOU REALLY HAVE NO TACT...
AT ALL!!!
Morale within the Dark Lord's Army goes up and goes down.

## ALL ACCORDING TO PLAN

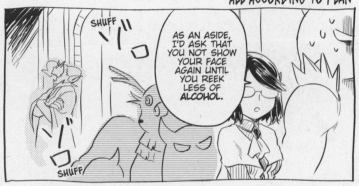

AS AN ASIDE, I'D ASK THAT YOU NOT SHOW YOUR FACE AGAIN UNTIL YOU REEK LESS OF ALCOHOL.
SHUFF
SHUFF
HEY, SECRETARY! WHY THE HELL DID YOU TAKE THIS HUGE DETOUR PAST LORD SATAN'S ROOM?!
DO YOU WANT TO GET KILLED?!
I ASKED YOU TO COME ALONG PRECISELY SO THAT WOULDN'T HAPPEN.
IF YOU MAKE A BAD FIRST IMPRESSION, THE ONLY WAY IT CAN GO FROM THERE IS UP.

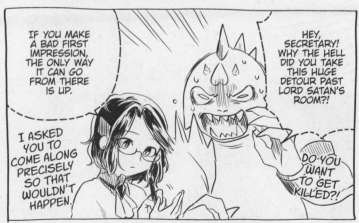

# SATAN'S SECRETARY

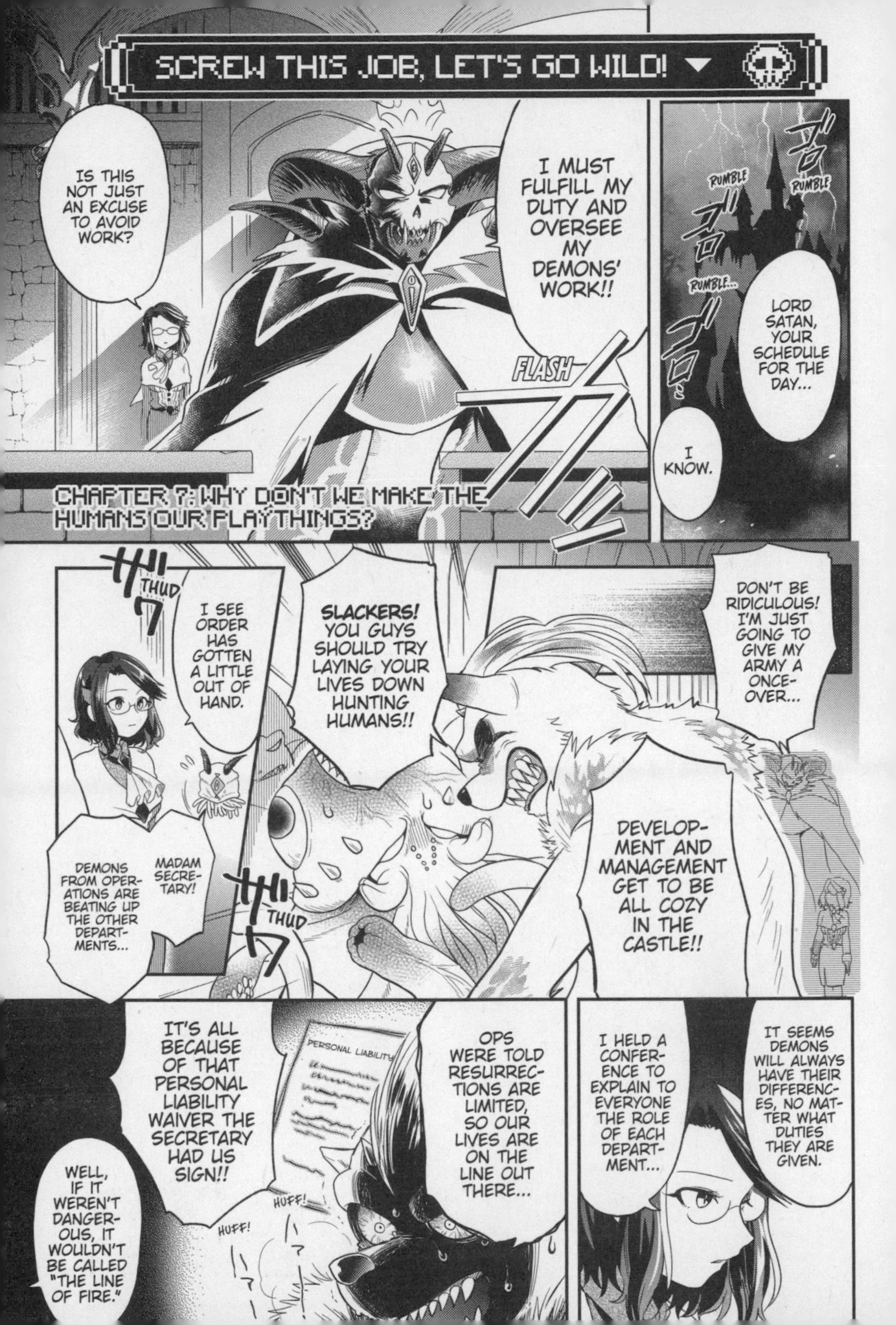
SCREW THIS JOB, LET'S GO WILD!
RUMBLE
RUMBLE
RUMBLE...
LORD SATAN, YOUR SCHEDULE FOR THE DAY...
I KNOW.
I MUST FULFILL MY DUTY AND OVERSEE MY DEMONS' WORK!!
FLASH
IS THIS NOT JUST AN EXCUSE TO AVOID WORK?
CHAPTER 7: WHY DON'T WE MAKE THE HUMANS OUR PLAYTHINGS?
DON'T BE RIDICULOUS! I'M JUST GOING TO GIVE MY ARMY A ONCE-OVER...
DEVELOPMENT AND MANAGEMENT GET TO BE ALL COZY IN THE CASTLE!!
SLACKERS! YOU GUYS SHOULD TRY LAYING YOUR LIVES DOWN HUNTING HUMANS!!
THUD
I SEE ORDER HAS GOTTEN A LITTLE OUT OF HAND.
MADAM SECRETARY!
DEMONS FROM OPERATIONS ARE BEATING UP THE OTHER DEPARTMENTS...
THUD
IT SEEMS DEMONS WILL ALWAYS HAVE THEIR DIFFERENCES, NO MATTER WHAT DUTIES THEY ARE GIVEN.
I HELD A CONFERENCE TO EXPLAIN TO EVERYONE THE ROLE OF EACH DEPARTMENT...
OPS WERE TOLD RESURRECTIONS ARE LIMITED, SO OUR LIVES ARE ON THE LINE OUT THERE...
IT'S ALL BECAUSE OF THAT PERSONAL LIABILITY WAIVER THE SECRETARY HAD US SIGN!!
PERSONAL LIABILITY
HUFF!
HUFF!
WELL, IF IT WEREN'T DANGEROUS, IT WOULDN'T BE CALLED "THE LINE OF FIRE."

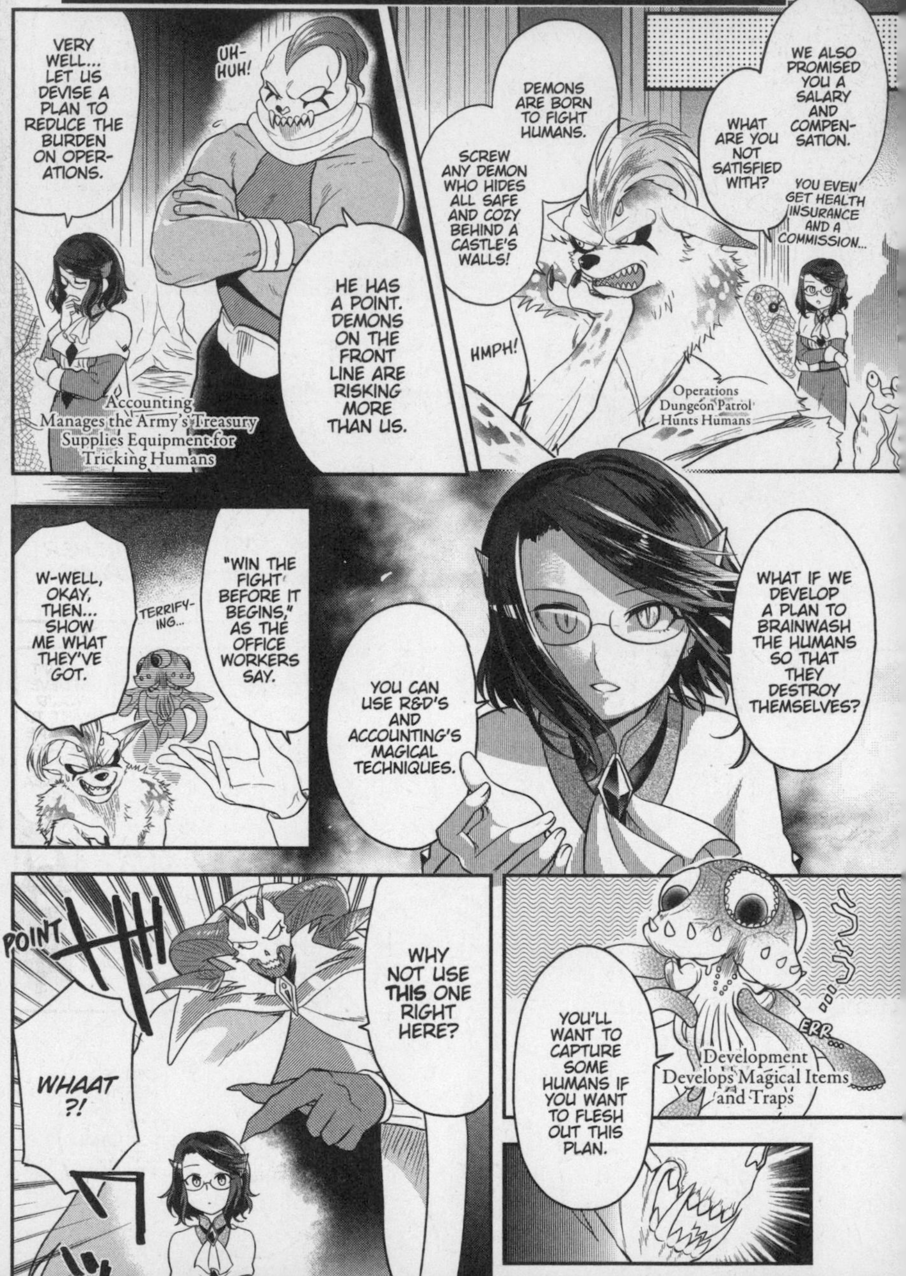
WE ALSO PROMISED YOU A SALARY AND COMPENSATION.
WHAT ARE YOU NOT SATISFIED WITH?
YOU EVEN GET HEALTH INSURANCE AND A COMMISSION...
DEMONS ARE BORN TO FIGHT HUMANS.
SCREW ANY DEMON WHO HIDES ALL SAFE AND COZY BEHIND A CASTLE'S WALLS!
HMPH!
Operations
Dungeon Patrol
Hunts Humans
UH-HUH!
VERY WELL... LET US DEVISE A PLAN TO REDUCE THE BURDEN ON OPERATIONS.
HE HAS A POINT. DEMONS ON THE FRONT LINE ARE RISKING MORE THAN US.
Accounting
Manages the Army's Treasury
Supplies Equipment for Tricking Humans
WHAT IF WE DEVELOP A PLAN TO BRAINWASH THE HUMANS SO THAT THEY DESTROY THEMSELVES?
YOU CAN USE R&D'S AND ACCOUNTING'S MAGICAL TECHNIQUES.
"WIN THE FIGHT BEFORE IT BEGINS," AS THE OFFICE WORKERS SAY.
TERRIFYING...
W-WELL, OKAY, THEN... SHOW ME WHAT THEY'VE GOT.
YOU'LL WANT TO CAPTURE SOME HUMANS IF YOU WANT TO FLESH OUT THIS PLAN.
ERR...
Development
Develops Magical Items and Traps
WHY NOT USE THIS ONE RIGHT HERE?
POINT
WHAAT ?!

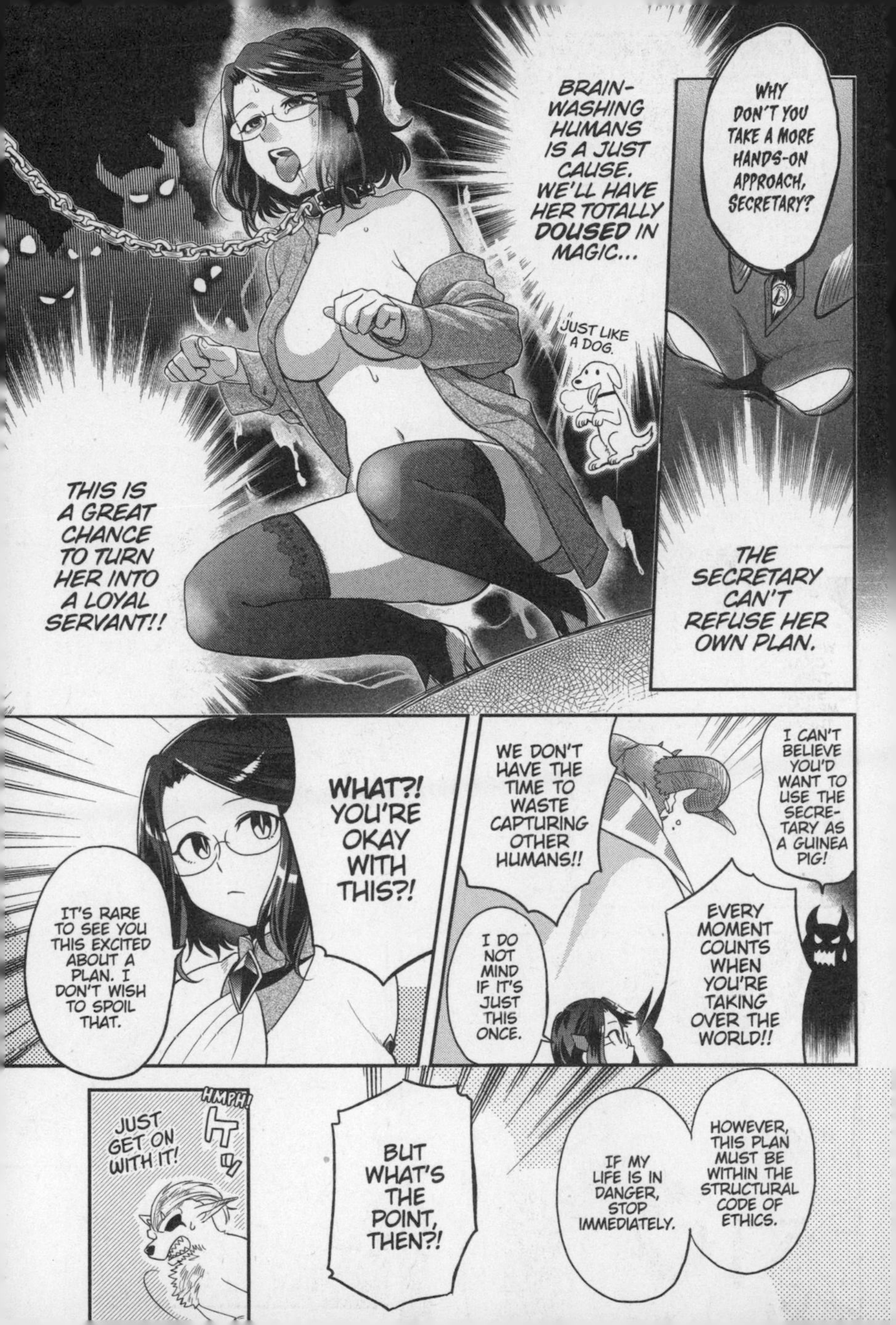
WHY DON'T YOU TAKE A MORE HANDS-ON APPROACH, SECRETARY?
THE SECRETARY CAN'T REFUSE HER OWN PLAN.
BRAIN-WASHING HUMANS IS A JUST CAUSE. WE'LL HAVE HER TOTALLY DOUSED IN MAGIC...
JUST LIKE A DOG.
THIS IS A GREAT CHANCE TO TURN HER INTO A LOYAL SERVANT!!
I CAN'T BELIEVE YOU'D WANT TO USE THE SECRETARY AS A GUINEA PIG!
WE DON'T HAVE THE TIME TO WASTE CAPTURING OTHER HUMANS!!
EVERY MOMENT COUNTS WHEN YOU'RE TAKING OVER THE WORLD!!
I DO NOT MIND IF IT'S JUST THIS ONCE.
WHAT?! YOU'RE OKAY WITH THIS?!
IT'S RARE TO SEE YOU THIS EXCITED ABOUT A PLAN. I DON'T WISH TO SPOIL THAT.
HOWEVER, THIS PLAN MUST BE WITHIN THE STRUCTURAL CODE OF ETHICS.
IF MY LIFE IS IN DANGER, STOP IMMEDIATELY.
BUT WHAT'S THE POINT, THEN?!
HMPH!
JUST GET ON WITH IT!

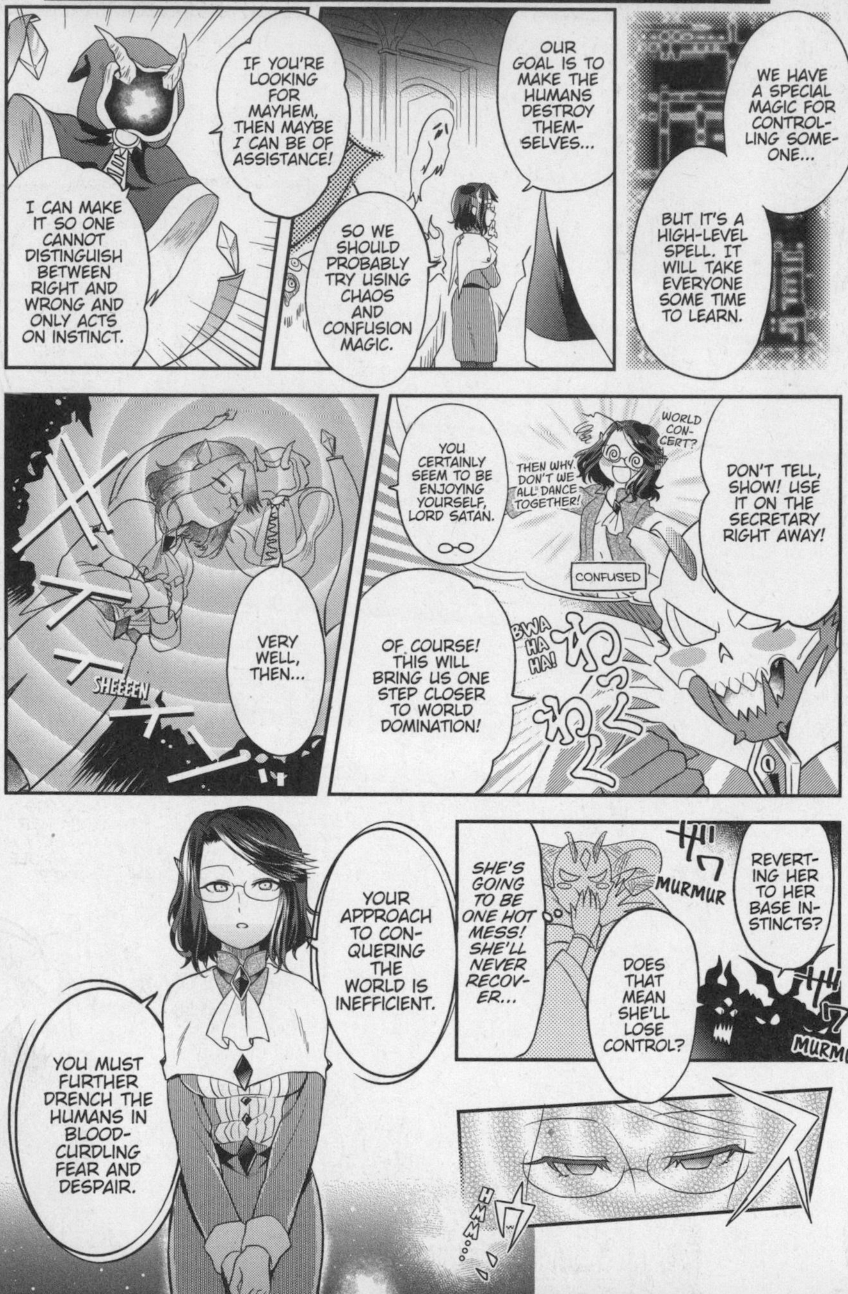
WE HAVE A SPECIAL MAGIC FOR CONTROLLING SOMEONE...
BUT IT'S A HIGH-LEVEL SPELL. IT WILL TAKE EVERYONE SOME TIME TO LEARN.
OUR GOAL IS TO MAKE THE HUMANS DESTROY THEMSELVES...
SO WE SHOULD PROBABLY TRY USING CHAOS AND CONFUSION MAGIC.
IF YOU'RE LOOKING FOR MAYHEM, THEN MAYBE *I* CAN BE OF ASSISTANCE!
I CAN MAKE IT SO ONE CANNOT DISTINGUISH BETWEEN RIGHT AND WRONG AND ONLY ACTS ON INSTINCT.
DON'T TELL, SHOW! USE IT ON THE SECRETARY RIGHT AWAY!
WORLD CONCERT?
THEN WHY DON'T WE ALL DANCE TOGETHER!
YOU CERTAINLY SEEM TO BE ENJOYING YOURSELF, LORD SATAN.
CONFUSED
BWA HA HA!
OF COURSE! THIS WILL BRING US ONE STEP CLOSER TO WORLD DOMINATION!
VERY WELL, THEN...
SHEEEEN
REVERTING HER TO HER BASE INSTINCTS?
MURMUR
SHE'S GOING TO BE ONE HOT MESS! SHE'LL NEVER RECOVER...
DOES THAT MEAN SHE'LL LOSE CONTROL?
MURMUR
HMM...
YOUR APPROACH TO CONQUERING THE WORLD IS INEFFICIENT.
YOU MUST FURTHER DRENCH THE HUMANS IN BLOODCURDLING FEAR AND DESPAIR.

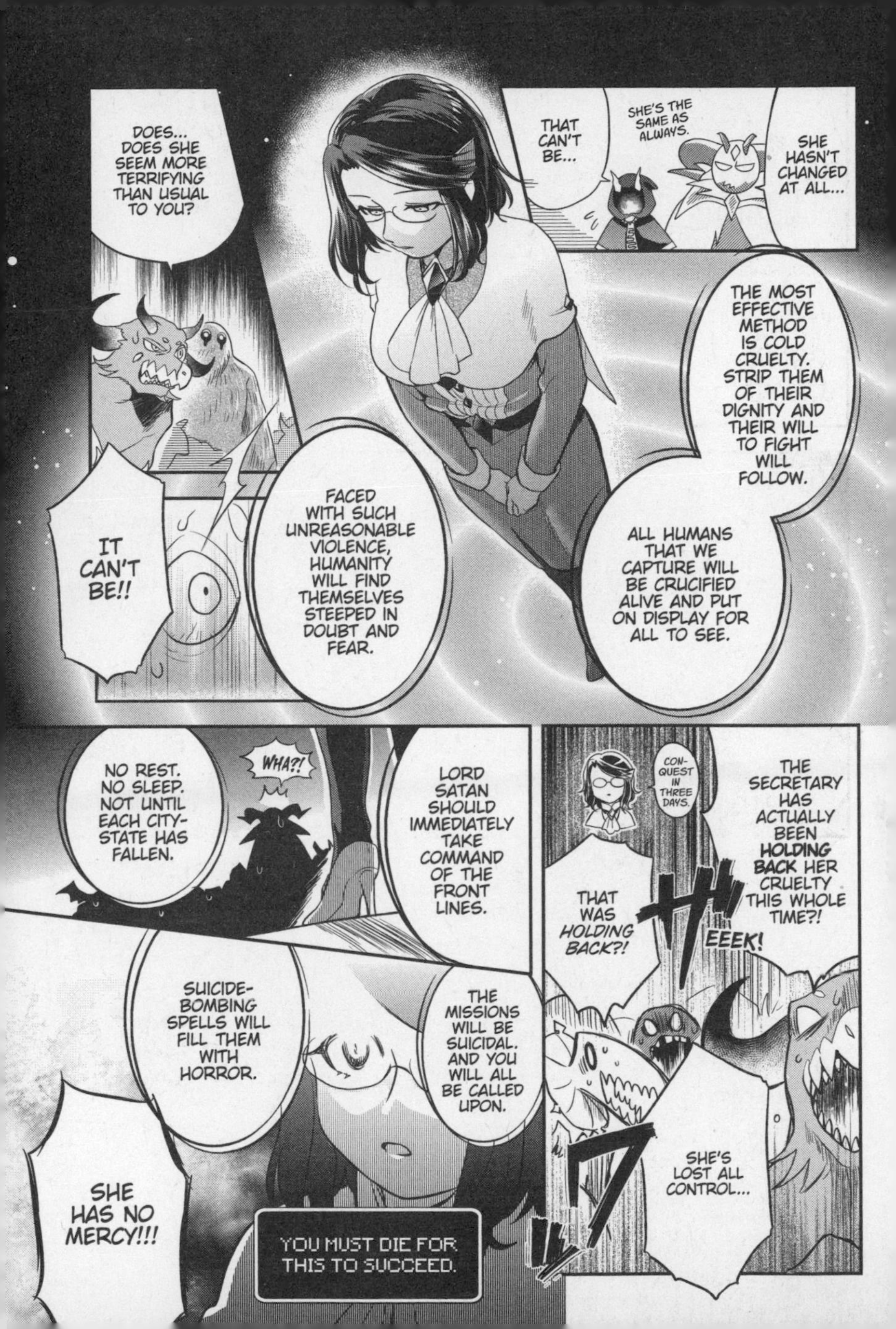
SHE HASN'T CHANGED AT ALL...
SHE'S THE SAME AS ALWAYS.
THAT CAN'T BE...
THE MOST EFFECTIVE METHOD IS COLD CRUELTY. STRIP THEM OF THEIR DIGNITY AND THEIR WILL TO FIGHT WILL FOLLOW.
ALL HUMANS THAT WE CAPTURE WILL BE CRUCIFIED ALIVE AND PUT ON DISPLAY FOR ALL TO SEE.
FACED WITH SUCH UNREASONABLE VIOLENCE, HUMANITY WILL FIND THEMSELVES STEEPED IN DOUBT AND FEAR.
DOES... DOES SHE SEEM MORE TERRIFYING THAN USUAL TO YOU?
IT CAN'T BE!!
THE SECRETARY HAS ACTUALLY BEEN HOLDING BACK HER CRUELTY THIS WHOLE TIME?!
CONQUEST IN THREE DAYS.
EEEK!
THAT WAS HOLDING BACK?!
SHE'S LOST ALL CONTROL...
LORD SATAN SHOULD IMMEDIATELY TAKE COMMAND OF THE FRONT LINES.
WHA?!
NO REST. NO SLEEP. NOT UNTIL EACH CITY-STATE HAS FALLEN.
THE MISSIONS WILL BE SUICIDAL. AND YOU WILL ALL BE CALLED UPON.
SUICIDE-BOMBING SPELLS WILL FILL THEM WITH HORROR.
SHE HAS NO MERCY!!!
YOU MUST DIE FOR THIS TO SUCCEED.

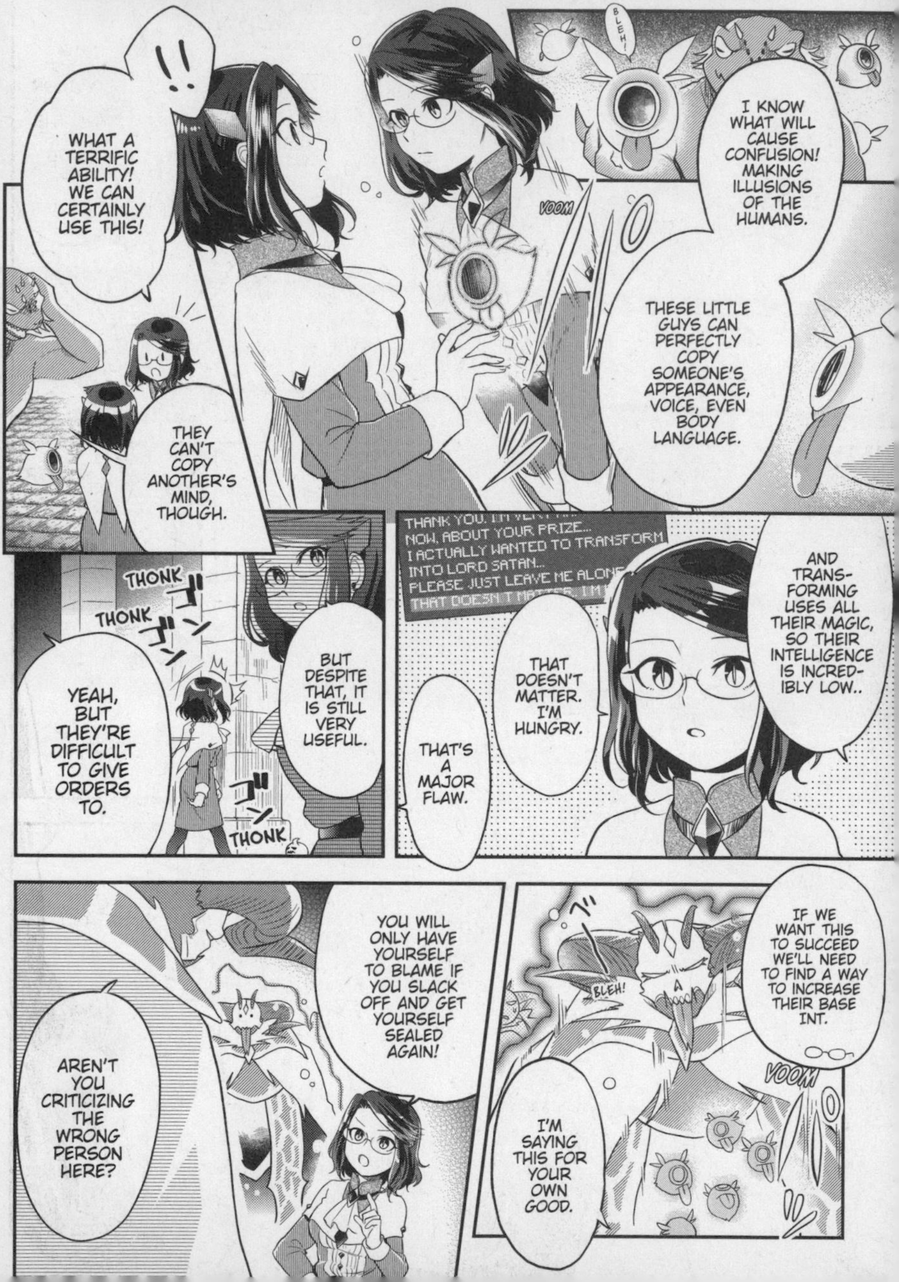
BLEH!
I KNOW WHAT WILL CAUSE CONFUSION! MAKING ILLUSIONS OF THE HUMANS.
!!
WHAT A TERRIFIC ABILITY! WE CAN CERTAINLY USE THIS!
VOOM
THESE LITTLE GUYS CAN PERFECTLY COPY SOMEONE'S APPEARANCE, VOICE, EVEN BODY LANGUAGE.
THEY CAN'T COPY ANOTHER'S MIND, THOUGH.
NOW, ABOUT YOUR PRIZE...
I ACTUALLY WANTED TO TRANSFORM
INTO LORD SATAN...
PLEASE JUST LEAVE ME ALONE
AND TRANSFORMING USES ALL THEIR MAGIC, SO THEIR INTELLIGENCE IS INCREDIBLY LOW..
THAT DOESN'T MATTER. I'M HUNGRY.
THAT'S A MAJOR FLAW.
BUT DESPITE THAT, IT IS STILL VERY USEFUL.
THONK
THONK
YEAH, BUT THEY'RE DIFFICULT TO GIVE ORDERS TO.
THONK
IF WE WANT THIS TO SUCCEED WE'LL NEED TO FIND A WAY TO INCREASE THEIR BASE INT.
BLEH!
VOOM
I'M SAYING THIS FOR YOUR OWN GOOD.
YOU WILL ONLY HAVE YOURSELF TO BLAME IF YOU SLACK OFF AND GET YOURSELF SEALED AGAIN!
AREN'T YOU CRITICIZING THE WRONG PERSON HERE?

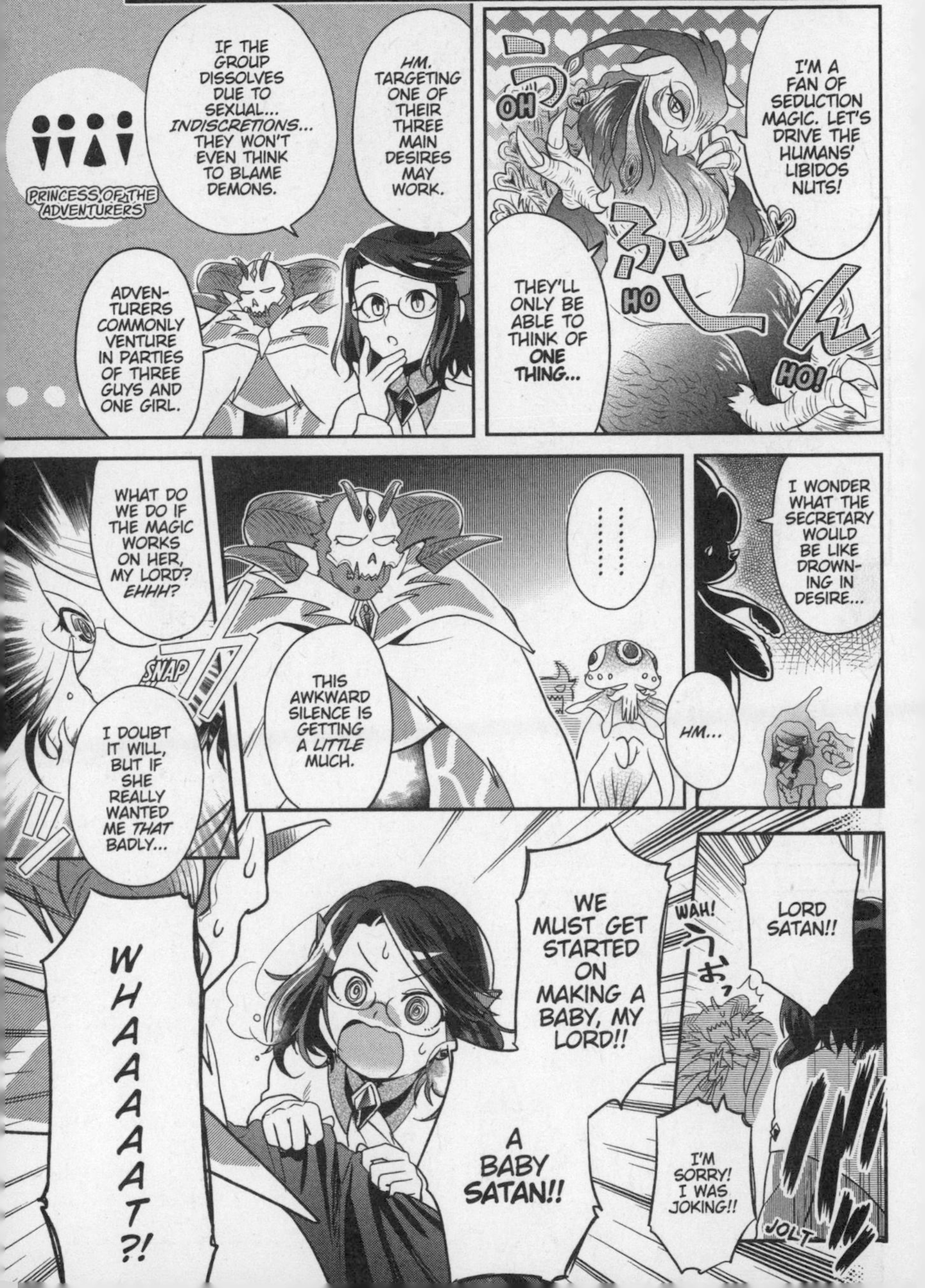
I'M A FAN OF SEDUCTION MAGIC. LET'S DRIVE THE HUMANS' LIBIDOS NUTS!
OH
HO
HO!
THEY'LL ONLY BE ABLE TO THINK OF ONE THING...
*HM.* TARGETING ONE OF THEIR THREE MAIN DESIRES MAY WORK.
IF THE GROUP DISSOLVES DUE TO SEXUAL... *INDISCRETIONS*... THEY WON'T EVEN THINK TO BLAME DEMONS.
PRINCESS OF THE ADVENTURERS
ADVEN-TURERS COMMONLY VENTURE IN PARTIES OF THREE GUYS AND ONE GIRL.
...
I WONDER WHAT THE SECRETARY WOULD BE LIKE DROWN-ING IN DESIRE...
HM...
......
THIS AWKWARD SILENCE IS GETTING A *LITTLE* MUCH.
WHAT DO WE DO IF THE MAGIC WORKS ON HER, MY LORD? *EHHH?*
SNAP
I DOUBT IT WILL, BUT IF SHE REALLY WANTED ME *THAT* BADLY...
LORD SATAN!!
WAH!
I'M SORRY! I WAS JOKING!!
JOLT
WE MUST GET STARTED ON MAKING A BABY, MY LORD!!
A BABY SATAN!!
WHAAAAAAAT?!

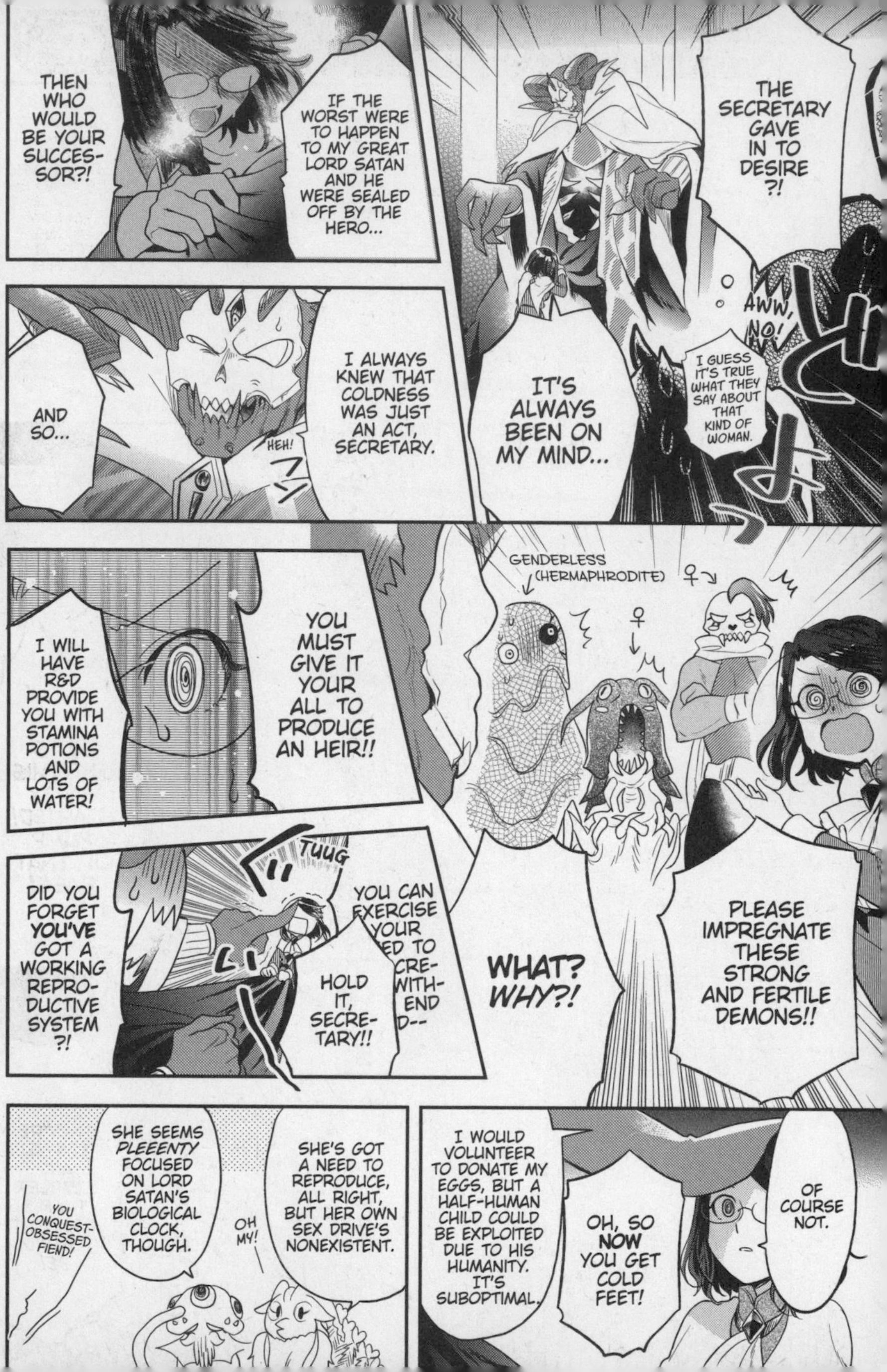
THE SECRETARY GAVE IN TO DESIRE ?!
AWW, NO!
I GUESS IT'S TRUE WHAT THEY SAY ABOUT THAT KIND OF WOMAN.
IT'S ALWAYS BEEN ON MY MIND...
IF THE WORST WERE TO HAPPEN TO MY GREAT LORD SATAN AND HE WERE SEALED OFF BY THE HERO...
THEN WHO WOULD BE YOUR SUCCES-SOR?!
I ALWAYS KNEW THAT COLDNESS WAS JUST AN ACT, SECRETARY.
HEH!
AND SO...
♀
GENDERLESS (HERMAPHRODITE)
♀
PLEASE IMPREGNATE THESE STRONG AND FERTILE DEMONS!!
WHAT? WHY?!
YOU MUST GIVE IT YOUR ALL TO PRODUCE AN HEIR!!
I WILL HAVE R&D PROVIDE YOU WITH STAMINA POTIONS AND LOTS OF WATER!
TUUG
YOU CAN EXERCISE YOUR ED TO CRE- WITH- END D--
HOLD IT, SECRE-TARY!!
DID YOU FORGET YOU'VE GOT A WORKING REPRO-DUCTIVE SYSTEM ?!
OF COURSE NOT.
I WOULD VOLUNTEER TO DONATE MY EGGS, BUT A HALF-HUMAN CHILD COULD BE EXPLOITED DUE TO HIS HUMANITY. IT'S SUBOPTIMAL.
OH, SO NOW YOU GET COLD FEET!
SHE'S GOT A NEED TO REPRODUCE, ALL RIGHT, BUT HER OWN SEX DRIVE'S NONEXISTENT.
OH MY!
SHE SEEMS PLEEENTY FOCUSED ON LORD SATAN'S BIOLOGICAL CLOCK, THOUGH.
YOU CONQUEST-OBSESSED FIEND!

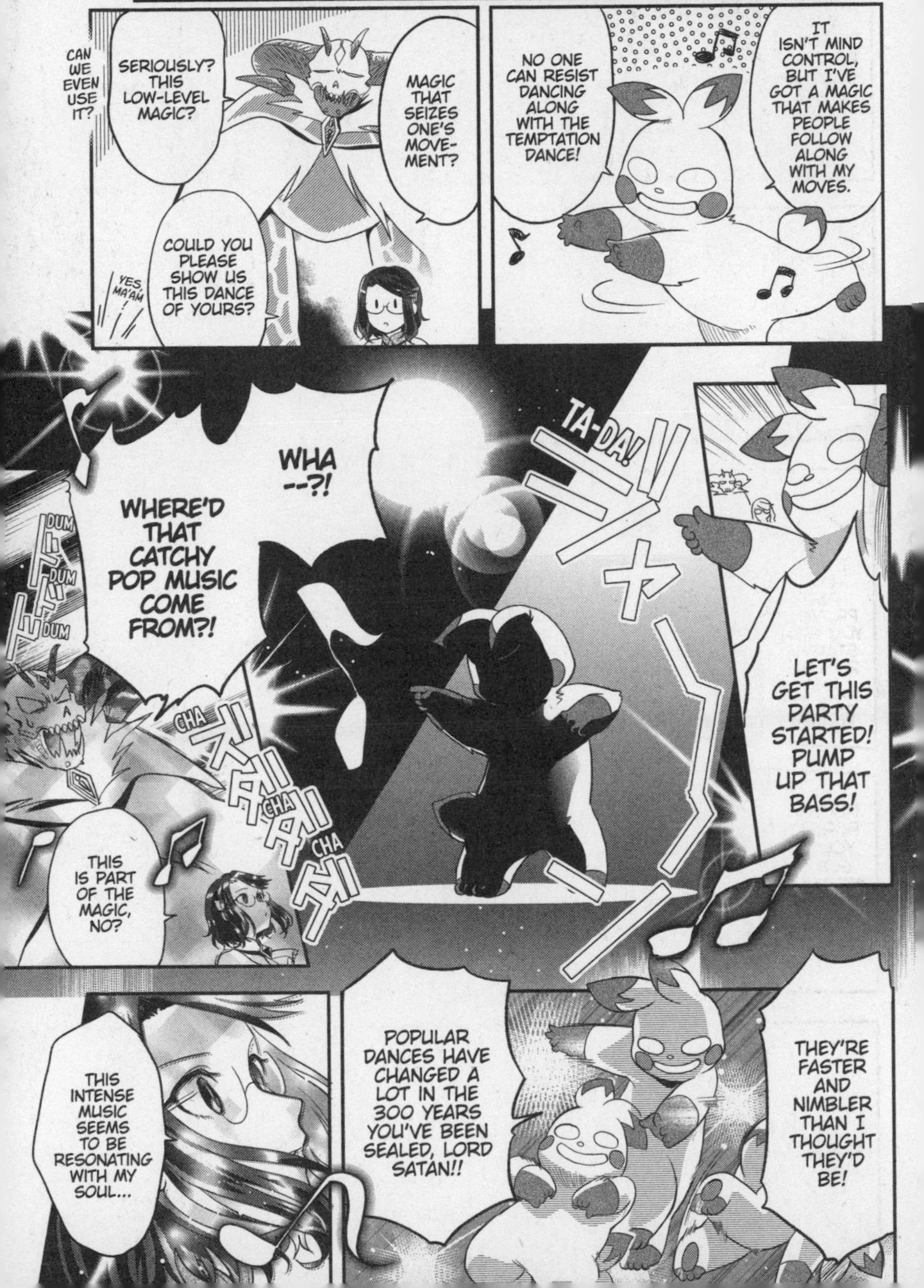
IT ISN'T MIND CONTROL, BUT I'VE GOT A MAGIC THAT MAKES PEOPLE FOLLOW ALONG WITH MY MOVES.
NO ONE CAN RESIST DANCING ALONG WITH THE TEMPTATION DANCE!
MAGIC THAT SEIZES ONE'S MOVE-MENT?
SERIOUSLY? THIS LOW-LEVEL MAGIC?
CAN WE EVEN USE IT?
COULD YOU PLEASE SHOW US THIS DANCE OF YOURS?
YES, MA'AM!
LET'S GET THIS PARTY STARTED! PUMP UP THAT BASS!
TA-DA!
WHA--?!
WHERE'D THAT CATCHY POP MUSIC COME FROM?!
DUM DUM DUM
CHA CHA CHA
THIS IS PART OF THE MAGIC, NO?
THEY'RE FASTER AND NIMBLER THAN I THOUGHT THEY'D BE!
POPULAR DANCES HAVE CHANGED A LOT IN THE 300 YEARS YOU'VE BEEN SEALED, LORD SATAN!!
THIS INTENSE MUSIC SEEMS TO BE RESONATING WITH MY SOUL...

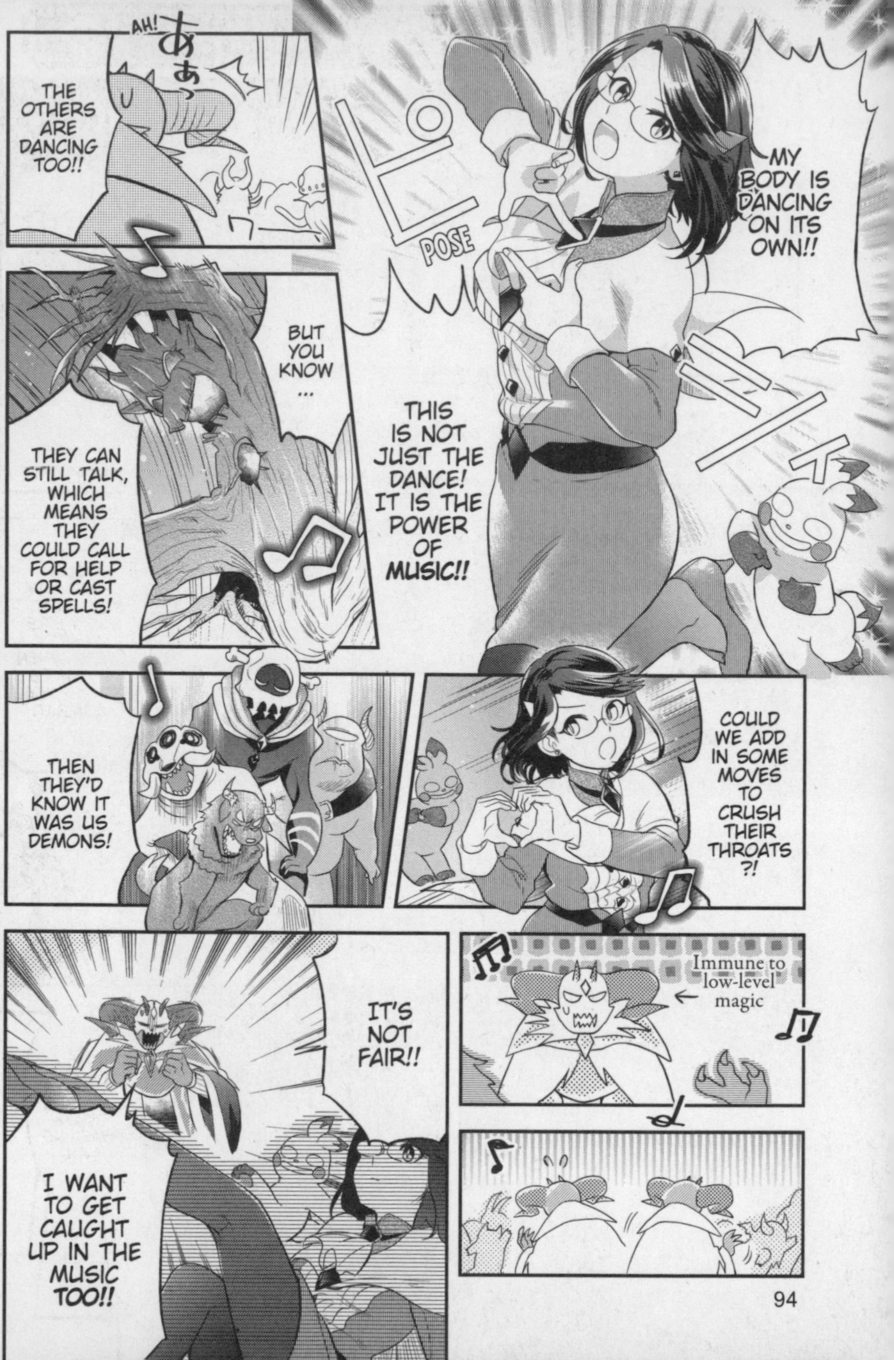
ピ
POSE
MY BODY IS DANCING ON ITS OWN!!
ミ ィ
AH! あぁっ
THE OTHERS ARE DANCING TOO!!
THIS IS NOT JUST THE DANCE! IT IS THE POWER OF MUSIC!!
BUT YOU KNOW ...
THEY CAN STILL TALK, WHICH MEANS THEY COULD CALL FOR HELP OR CAST SPELLS!
THEN THEY'D KNOW IT WAS US DEMONS!
COULD WE ADD IN SOME MOVES TO CRUSH THEIR THROATS?!
Immune to low-level magic
IT'S NOT FAIR!!
I WANT TO GET CAUGHT UP IN THE MUSIC TOO!!

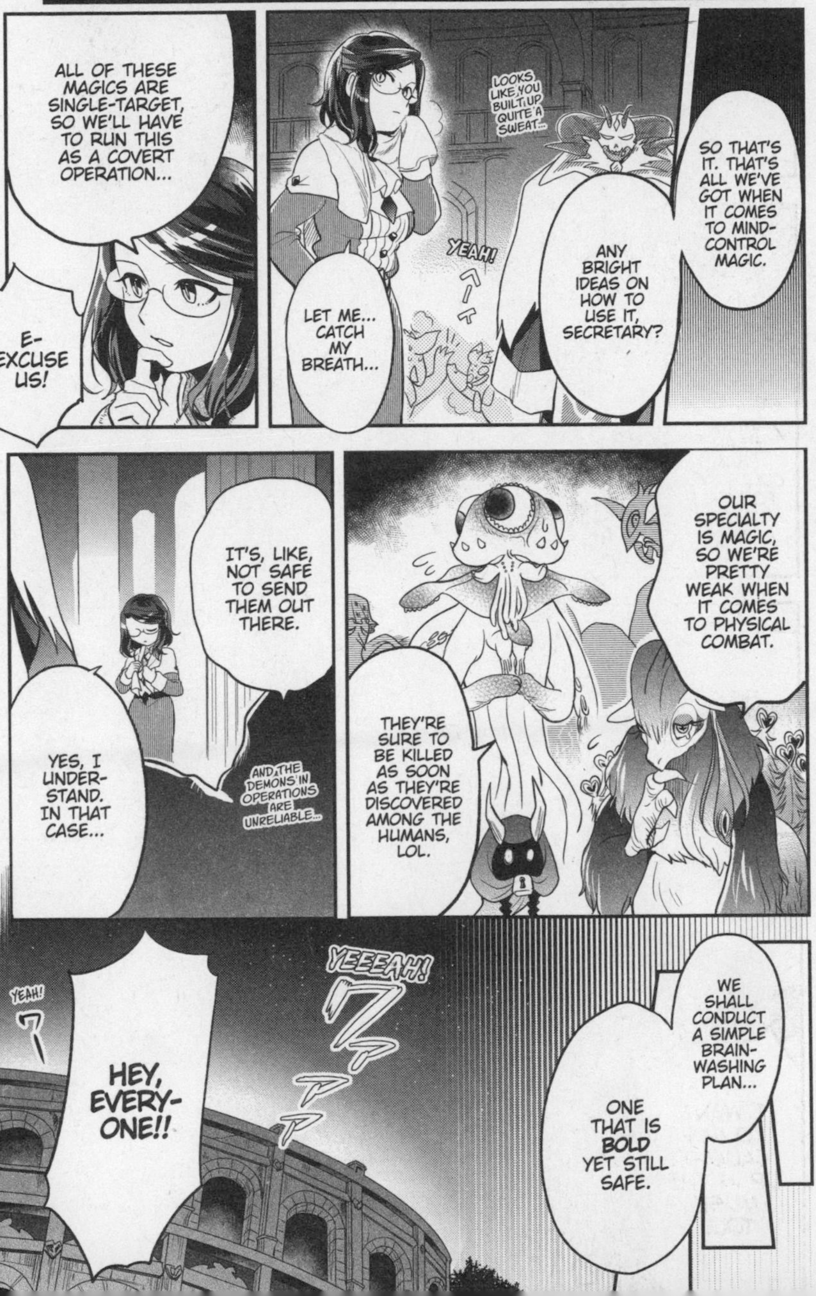
SO THAT'S IT. THAT'S ALL WE'VE GOT WHEN IT COMES TO MIND-CONTROL MAGIC.
ANY BRIGHT IDEAS ON HOW TO USE IT, SECRETARY?
LOOKS LIKE YOU BUILT UP QUITE A SWEAT...
YEAH!
LET ME... CATCH MY BREATH...
ALL OF THESE MAGICS ARE SINGLE-TARGET, SO WE'LL HAVE TO RUN THIS AS A COVERT OPERATION...
E-EXCUSE US!
OUR SPECIALTY IS MAGIC, SO WE'RE PRETTY WEAK WHEN IT COMES TO PHYSICAL COMBAT.
THEY'RE SURE TO BE KILLED AS SOON AS THEY'RE DISCOVERED AMONG THE HUMANS, LOL.
IT'S, LIKE, NOT SAFE TO SEND THEM OUT THERE.
AND THE DEMONS IN OPERATIONS ARE UNRELIABLE...
YES, I UNDERSTAND. IN THAT CASE...
WE SHALL CONDUCT A SIMPLE BRAIN-WASHING PLAN...
ONE THAT IS **BOLD** YET STILL SAFE.
YEEEEAH!
HEY, EVERY-ONE!!
YEAH!
WHOO!

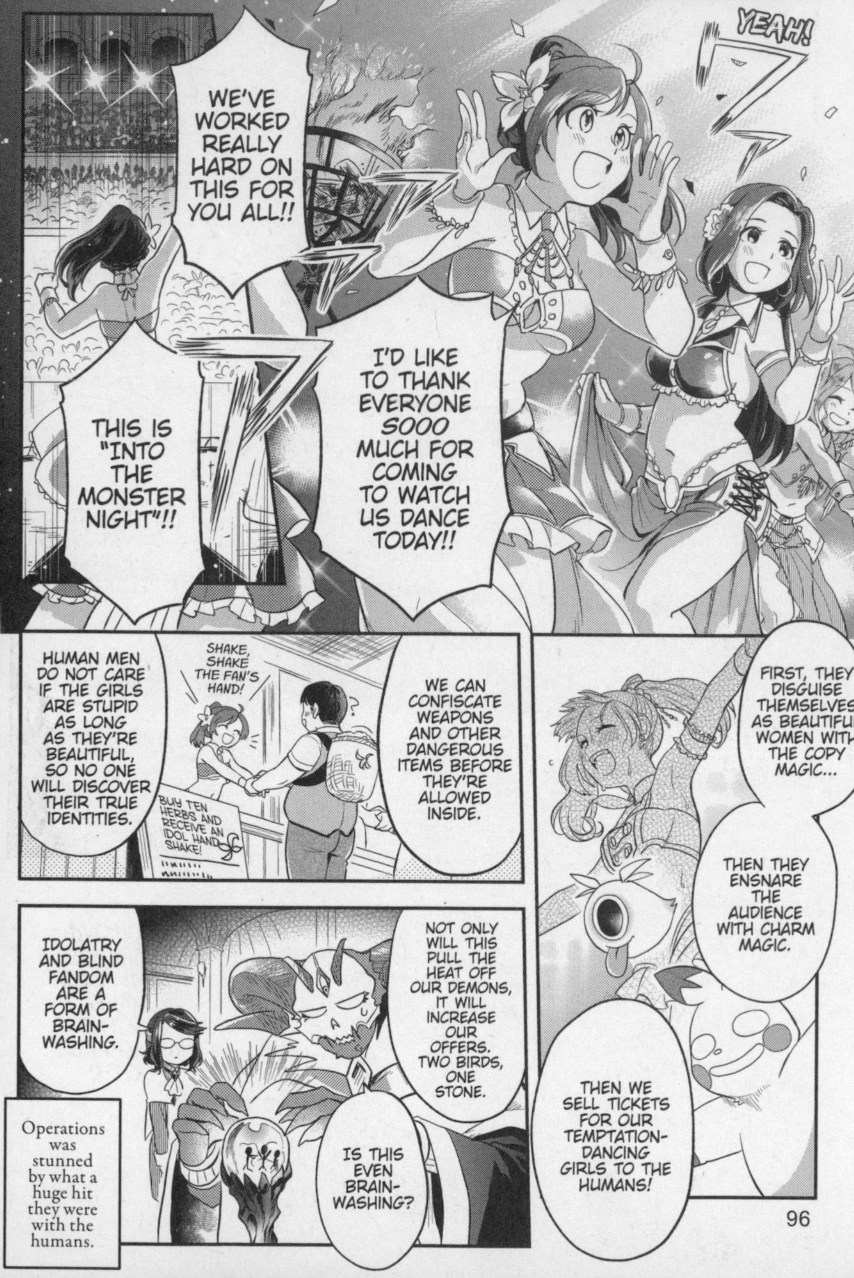
YEAH!
WE'VE WORKED REALLY HARD ON THIS FOR YOU ALL!!
I'D LIKE TO THANK EVERYONE *SOOO* MUCH FOR COMING TO WATCH US DANCE TODAY!!
THIS IS "INTO THE MONSTER NIGHT"!!
FIRST, THEY DISGUISE THEMSELVES AS BEAUTIFUL WOMEN WITH THE COPY MAGIC...
THEN THEY ENSNARE THE AUDIENCE WITH CHARM MAGIC.
THEN WE SELL TICKETS FOR OUR TEMPTATION-DANCING GIRLS TO THE HUMANS!
WE CAN CONFISCATE WEAPONS AND OTHER DANGEROUS ITEMS BEFORE THEY'RE ALLOWED INSIDE.
SHAKE, SHAKE THE FAN'S HAND!
BUY TEN HERBS AND RECEIVE AN IDOL HAND SHAKE!
HUMAN MEN DO NOT CARE IF THE GIRLS ARE STUPID AS LONG AS THEY'RE BEAUTIFUL, SO NO ONE WILL DISCOVER THEIR TRUE IDENTITIES.
NOT ONLY WILL THIS PULL THE HEAT OFF OUR DEMONS, IT WILL INCREASE OUR OFFERS. TWO BIRDS, ONE STONE.
IDOLATRY AND BLIND FANDOM ARE A FORM OF BRAIN-WASHING.
IS THIS EVEN BRAIN-WASHING?
Operations was stunned by what a huge hit they were with the humans.

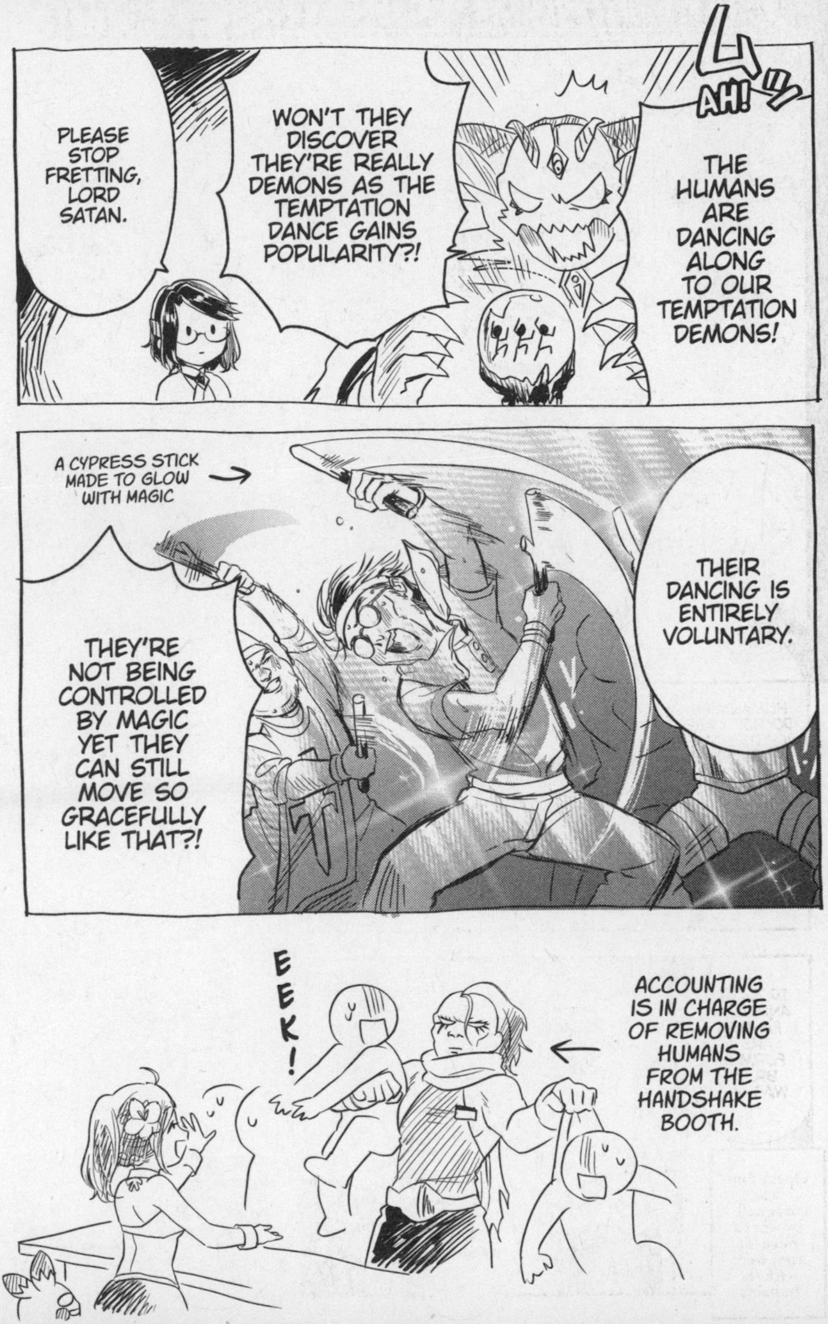
AH!
THE HUMANS ARE DANCING ALONG TO OUR TEMPTATION DEMONS!
WON'T THEY DISCOVER THEY'RE REALLY DEMONS AS THE TEMPTATION DANCE GAINS POPULARITY?!
PLEASE STOP FRETTING, LORD SATAN.
THEIR DANCING IS ENTIRELY VOLUNTARY.
A CYPRESS STICK MADE TO GLOW WITH MAGIC
THEY'RE NOT BEING CONTROLLED BY MAGIC YET THEY CAN STILL MOVE SO GRACEFULLY LIKE THAT?!
ACCOUNTING IS IN CHARGE OF REMOVING HUMANS FROM THE HANDSHAKE BOOTH.
EEK!

# SATAN'S SECRETARY

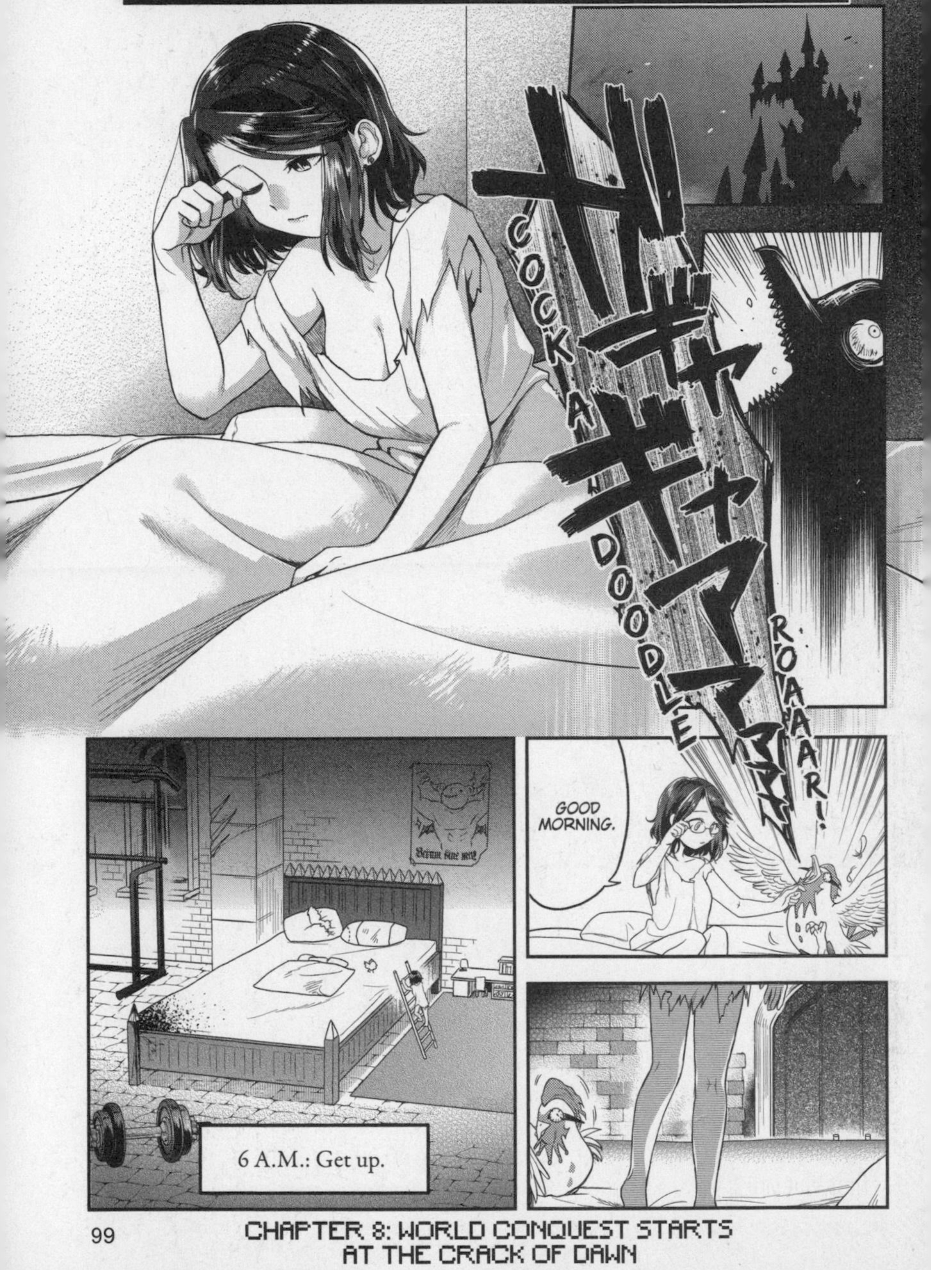
COCK A DOODLE
ROAAAR!
GOOD MORNING.
6 A.M.: Get up.



## CHAPTER 8: WORLD CONQUEST STARTS AT THE CRACK OF DAWN

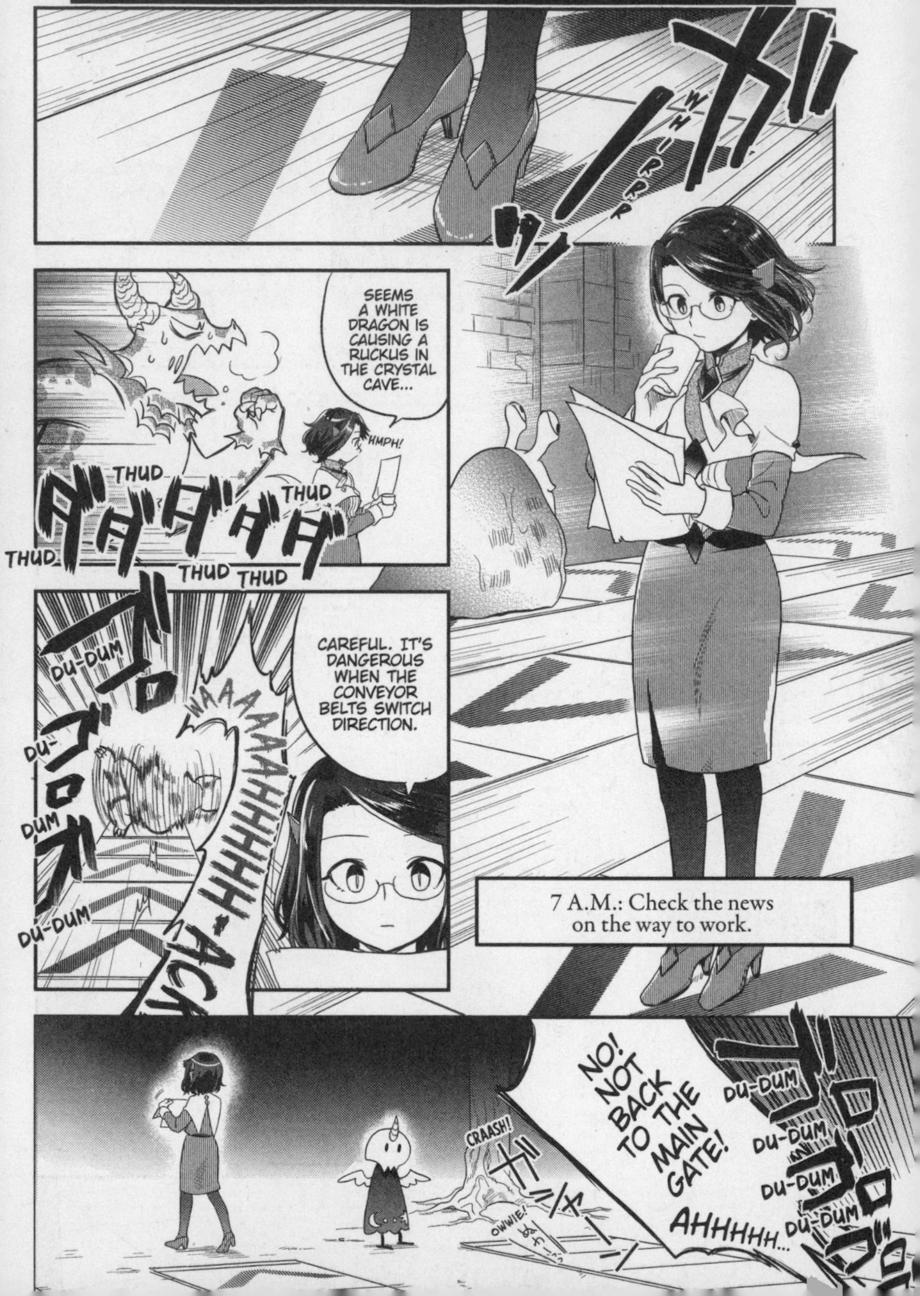
WHIRRRR
7 A.M.: Check the news on the way to work.
SEEMS A WHITE DRAGON IS CAUSING A RUCKUS IN THE CRYSTAL CAVE...
HMPH!
THUD THUD THUD THUD THUD
CAREFUL. IT'S DANGEROUS WHEN THE CONVEYOR BELTS SWITCH DIRECTION.
WAAAAAAAHHHHHHH-ACK
DU-DUM DU-DUM DU-DUM
NO! NOT BACK TO THE MAIN GATE!
DU-DUM DU-DUM DU-DUM DU-DUM
AHHHHH...
CRAASH!
OWWIE!

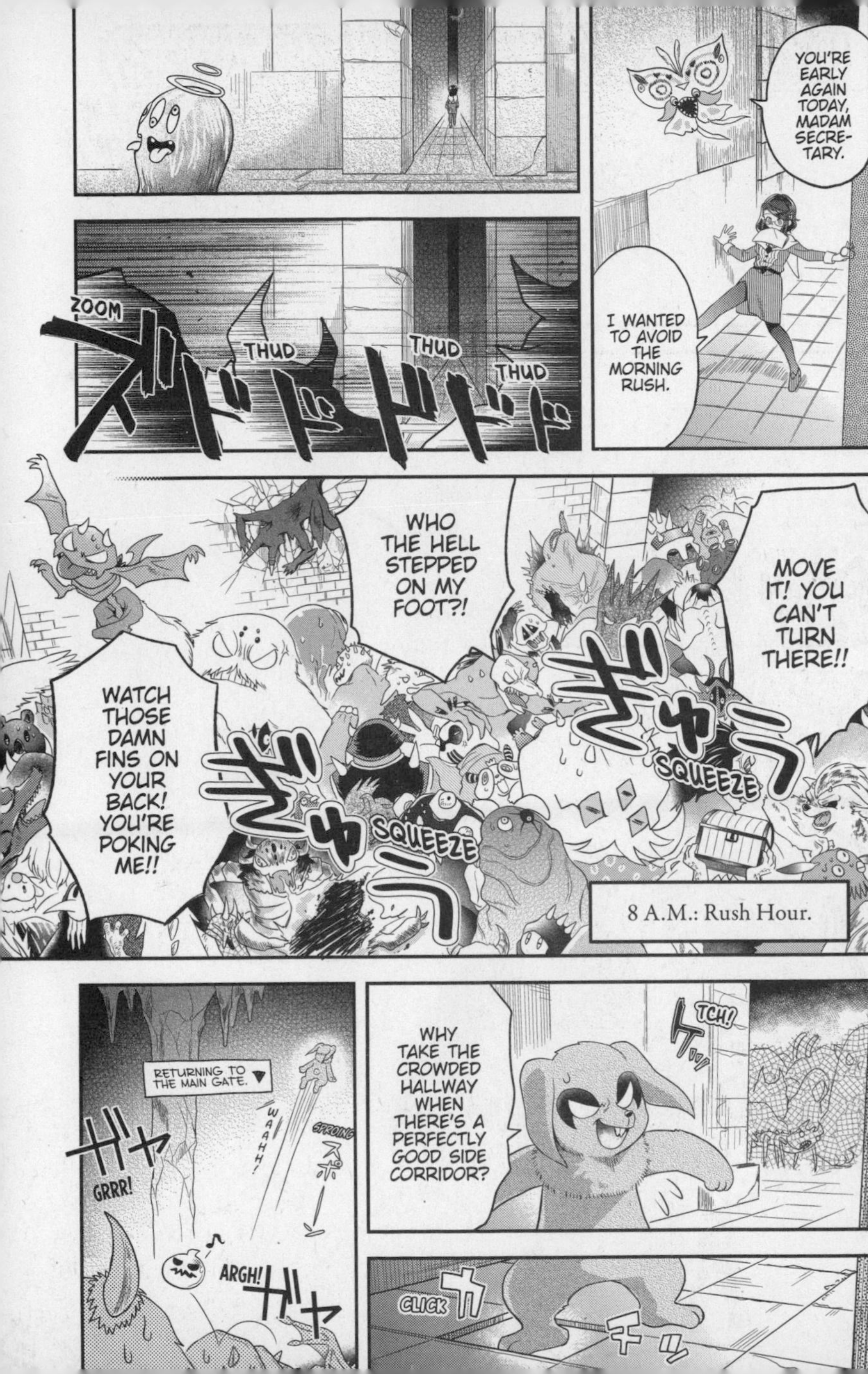
YOU'RE EARLY AGAIN TODAY, MADAM SECRETARY.
I WANTED TO AVOID THE MORNING RUSH.
ZOOM
THUD
THUD
THUD
MOVE IT! YOU CAN'T TURN THERE!!
WHO THE HELL STEPPED ON MY FOOT?!
SQUEEZE
SQUEEZE
WATCH THOSE DAMN FINS ON YOUR BACK! YOU'RE POKING ME!!
8 A.M.: Rush Hour.
TCH!
WHY TAKE THE CROWDED HALLWAY WHEN THERE'S A PERFECTLY GOOD SIDE CORRIDOR?
CLICK
RETURNING TO THE MAIN GATE.
SPROING
WAAHH!
GRRR!
ARGH!

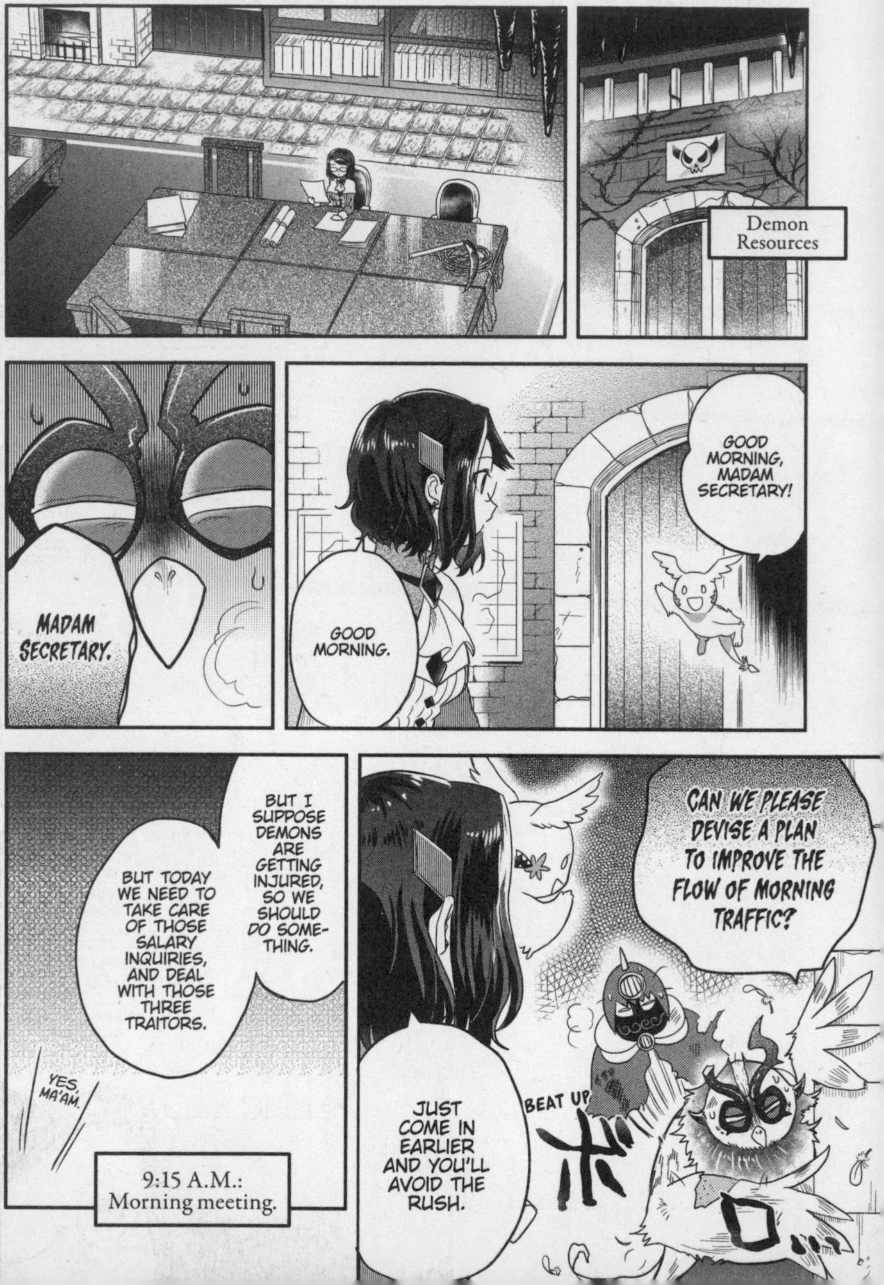
Demon Resources
GOOD MORNING, MADAM SECRETARY!
GOOD MORNING.
MADAM SECRETARY.
CAN WE PLEASE DEVISE A PLAN TO IMPROVE THE FLOW OF MORNING TRAFFIC?
BEAT UP
JUST COME IN EARLIER AND YOU'LL AVOID THE RUSH.
BUT I SUPPOSE DEMONS ARE GETTING INJURED, SO WE SHOULD DO SOME-THING.
BUT TODAY WE NEED TO TAKE CARE OF THOSE SALARY INQUIRIES, AND DEAL WITH THOSE THREE TRAITORS.
YES, MA'AM.
9:15 A.M.: Morning meeting.

# CREATING A "WORKPLACE"

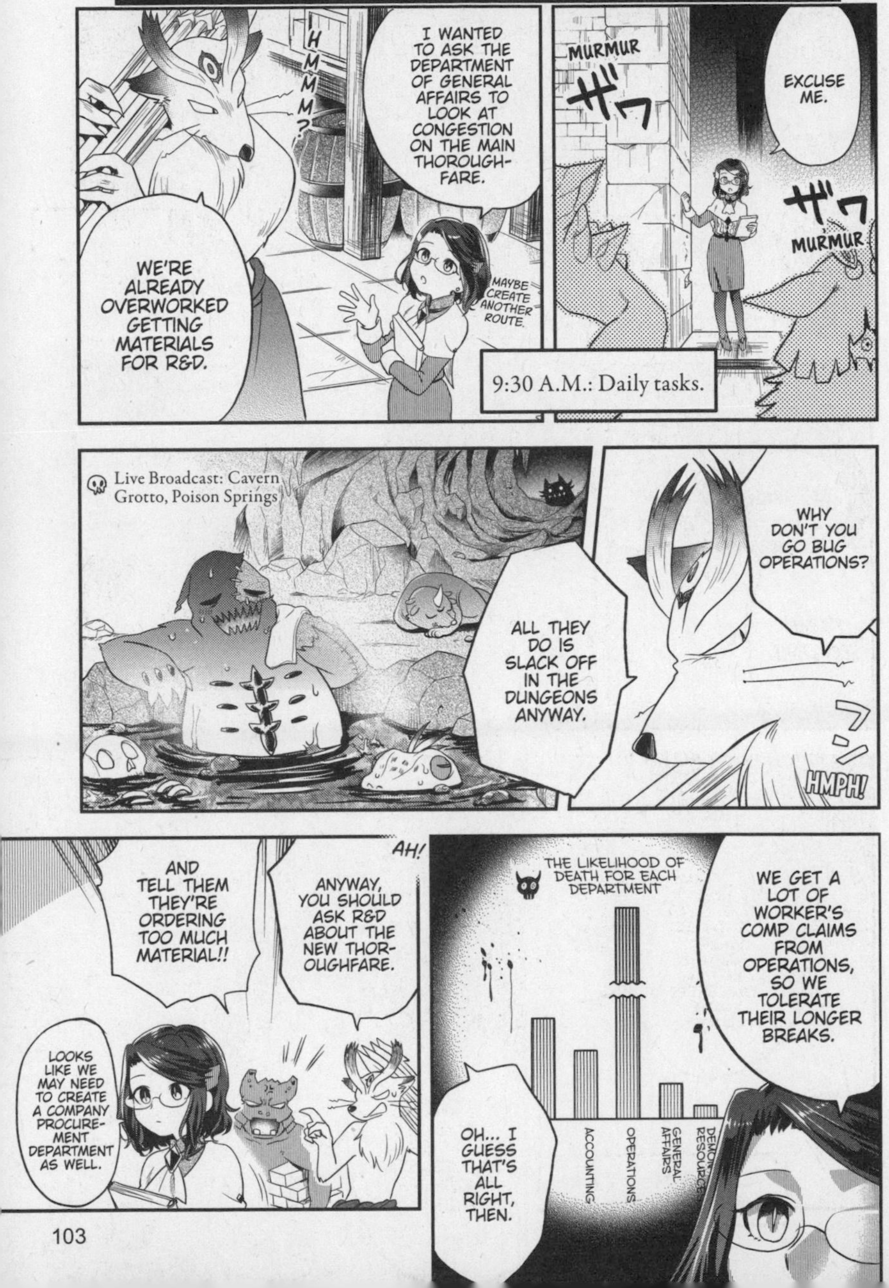
MURMUR
ザワ
EXCUSE ME.
ザワ
MURMUR
9:30 A.M.: Daily tasks.
I WANTED TO ASK THE DEPARTMENT OF GENERAL AFFAIRS TO LOOK AT CONGESTION ON THE MAIN THOROUGH-FARE.
HMMMM?
WE'RE ALREADY OVERWORKED GETTING MATERIALS FOR R&D.
MAYBE CREATE ANOTHER ROUTE.
WHY DON'T YOU GO BUG OPERATIONS?
ALL THEY DO IS SLACK OFF IN THE DUNGEONS ANYWAY.
フン
HMPH!
Live Broadcast: Cavern Grotto, Poison Springs
THE LIKELIHOOD OF DEATH FOR EACH DEPARTMENT
DEMON RESOURCES
GENERAL AFFAIRS
OPERATIONS
ACCOUNTING
WE GET A LOT OF WORKER'S COMP CLAIMS FROM OPERATIONS, SO WE TOLERATE THEIR LONGER BREAKS.
OH... I GUESS THAT'S ALL RIGHT, THEN.
AH!
ANYWAY, YOU SHOULD ASK R&D ABOUT THE NEW THOR-OUGHFARE.
AND TELL THEM THEY'RE ORDERING TOO MUCH MATERIAL!!
LOOKS LIKE WE MAY NEED TO CREATE A COMPANY PROCURE-MENT DEPARTMENT AS WELL.

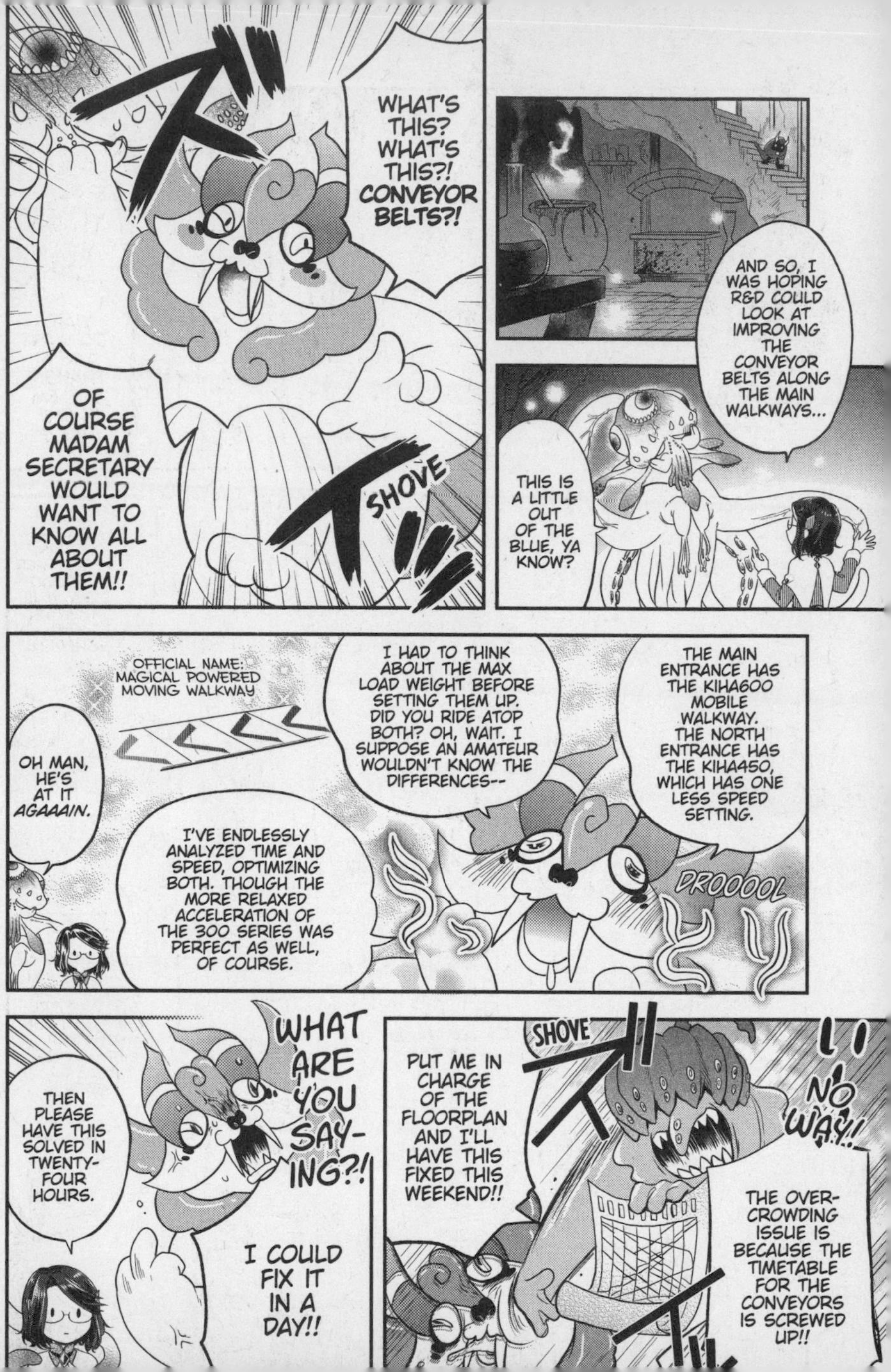
AND SO, I WAS HOPING R&D COULD LOOK AT IMPROVING THE CONVEYOR BELTS ALONG THE MAIN WALKWAYS...
THIS IS A LITTLE OUT OF THE BLUE, YA KNOW?
WHAT'S THIS? WHAT'S THIS?! CONVEYOR BELTS?!
OF COURSE MADAM SECRETARY WOULD WANT TO KNOW ALL ABOUT THEM!!
SHOVE
THE MAIN ENTRANCE HAS THE KIHA600 MOBILE WALKWAY. THE NORTH ENTRANCE HAS THE KIHA450, WHICH HAS ONE LESS SPEED SETTING.
I HAD TO THINK ABOUT THE MAX LOAD WEIGHT BEFORE SETTING THEM UP. DID YOU RIDE ATOP BOTH? OH, WAIT. I SUPPOSE AN AMATEUR WOULDN'T KNOW THE DIFFERENCES--
OFFICIAL NAME: MAGICAL POWERED MOVING WALKWAY
OH MAN, HE'S AT IT AGAAAIN.
I'VE ENDLESSLY ANALYZED TIME AND SPEED, OPTIMIZING BOTH. THOUGH THE MORE RELAXED ACCELERATION OF THE 300 SERIES WAS PERFECT AS WELL, OF COURSE.
DROOOOL
NO WAY!!
THE OVER-CROWDING ISSUE IS BECAUSE THE TIMETABLE FOR THE CONVEYORS IS SCREWED UP!!
SHOVE
PUT ME IN CHARGE OF THE FLOORPLAN AND I'LL HAVE THIS FIXED THIS WEEKEND!!
WHAT ARE YOU SAY-ING?!
THEN PLEASE HAVE THIS SOLVED IN TWENTY-FOUR HOURS.
I COULD FIX IT IN A DAY!!

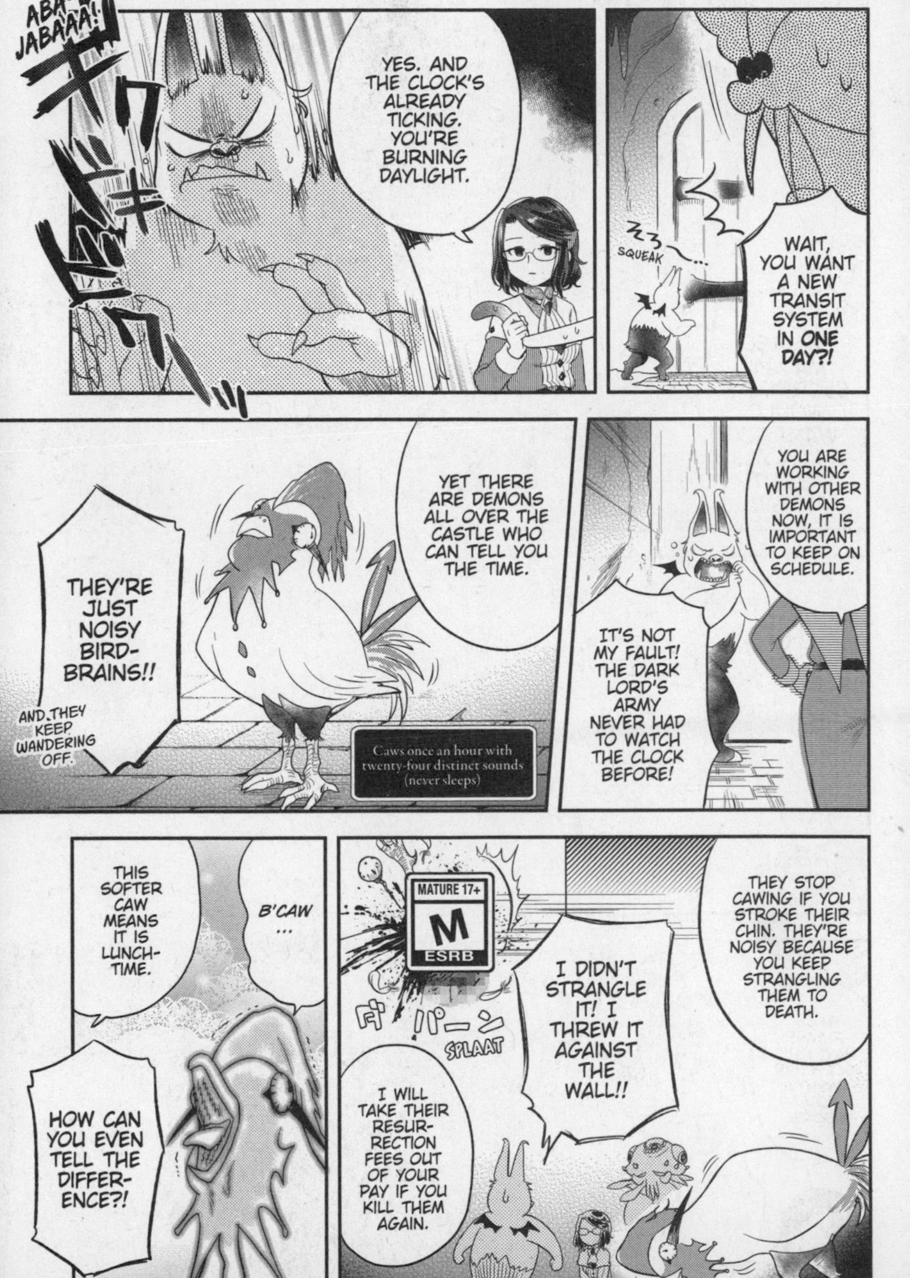
WAIT, YOU WANT A NEW TRANSIT SYSTEM IN ONE DAY?!
SQUEAK
YES. AND THE CLOCK'S ALREADY TICKING. YOU'RE BURNING DAYLIGHT.
ABA-JABAAA!!
YOU ARE WORKING WITH OTHER DEMONS NOW, IT IS IMPORTANT TO KEEP ON SCHEDULE.
IT'S NOT MY FAULT! THE DARK LORD'S ARMY NEVER HAD TO WATCH THE CLOCK BEFORE!
YET THERE ARE DEMONS ALL OVER THE CASTLE WHO CAN TELL YOU THE TIME.
THEY'RE JUST NOISY BIRD-BRAINS!!
AND THEY KEEP WANDERING OFF.
Caws once an hour with twenty-four distinct sounds (never sleeps)
THEY STOP CAWING IF YOU STROKE THEIR CHIN. THEY'RE NOISY BECAUSE YOU KEEP STRANGLING THEM TO DEATH.
MATURE 17+ M ESRB
SPLAAT
I DIDN'T STRANGLE IT! I THREW IT AGAINST THE WALL!!
I WILL TAKE THEIR RESURRECTION FEES OUT OF YOUR PAY IF YOU KILL THEM AGAIN.
B'CAW ...
THIS SOFTER CAW MEANS IT IS LUNCH-TIME.
HOW CAN YOU EVEN TELL THE DIFFERENCE?!

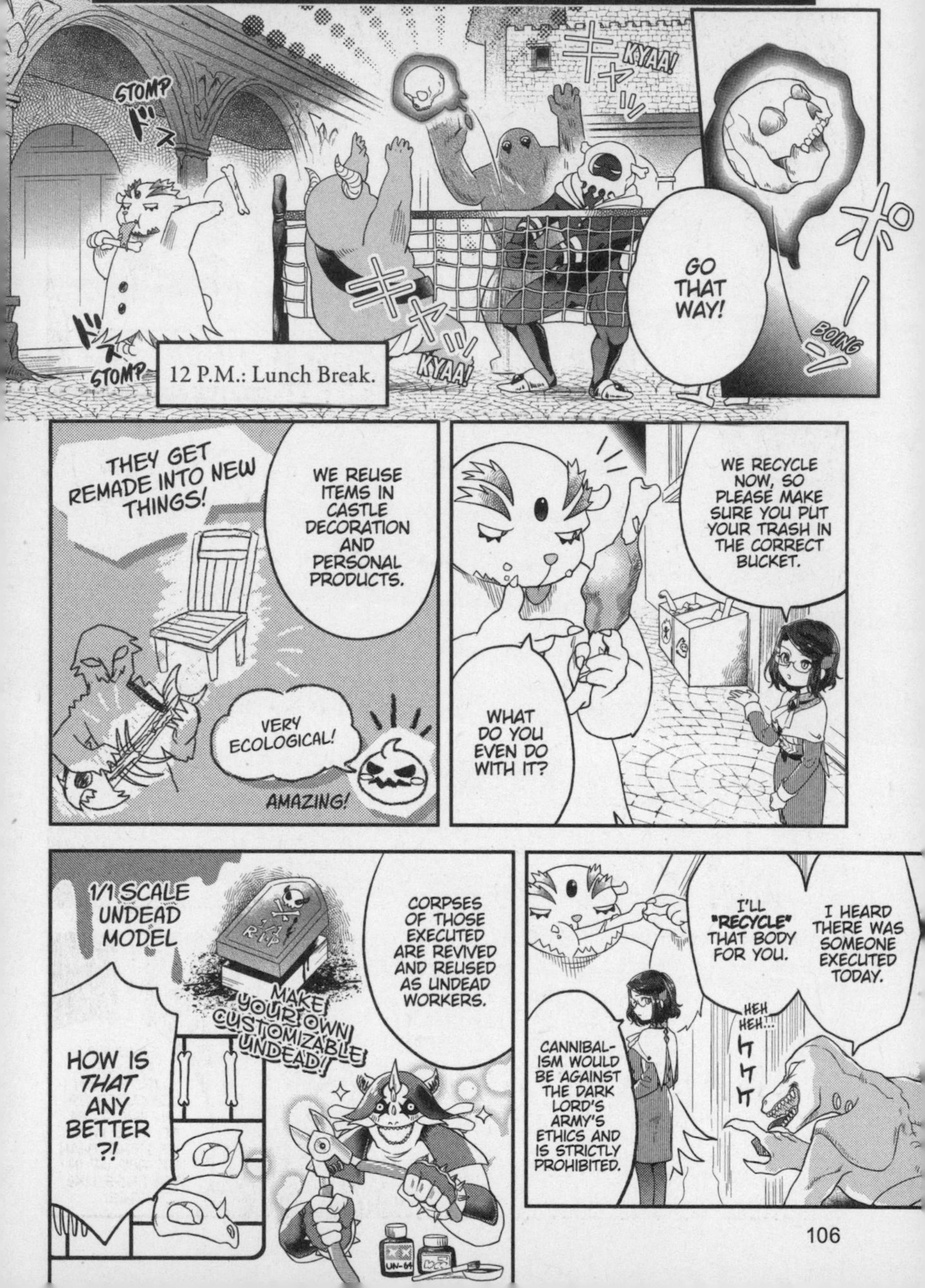
GO THAT WAY!
BOING
KYAA!
STOMP
STOMP
KYAA!
12 P.M.: Lunch Break.
WE RECYCLE NOW, SO PLEASE MAKE SURE YOU PUT YOUR TRASH IN THE CORRECT BUCKET.
WHAT DO YOU EVEN DO WITH IT?
WE REUSE ITEMS IN CASTLE DECORATION AND PERSONAL PRODUCTS.
THEY GET REMADE INTO NEW THINGS!
VERY ECOLOGICAL!
AMAZING!
I HEARD THERE WAS SOMEONE EXECUTED TODAY.
I'LL "RECYCLE" THAT BODY FOR YOU.
HEH HEH...
CANNIBAL-ISM WOULD BE AGAINST THE DARK LORD'S ARMY'S ETHICS AND IS STRICTLY PROHIBITED.
CORPSES OF THOSE EXECUTED ARE REVIVED AND REUSED AS UNDEAD WORKERS.
1/1 SCALE UNDEAD MODEL
RIP
MAKE YOUR OWN CUSTOMIZABLE UNDEAD!
HOW IS *THAT* ANY BETTER ?!
UN-04

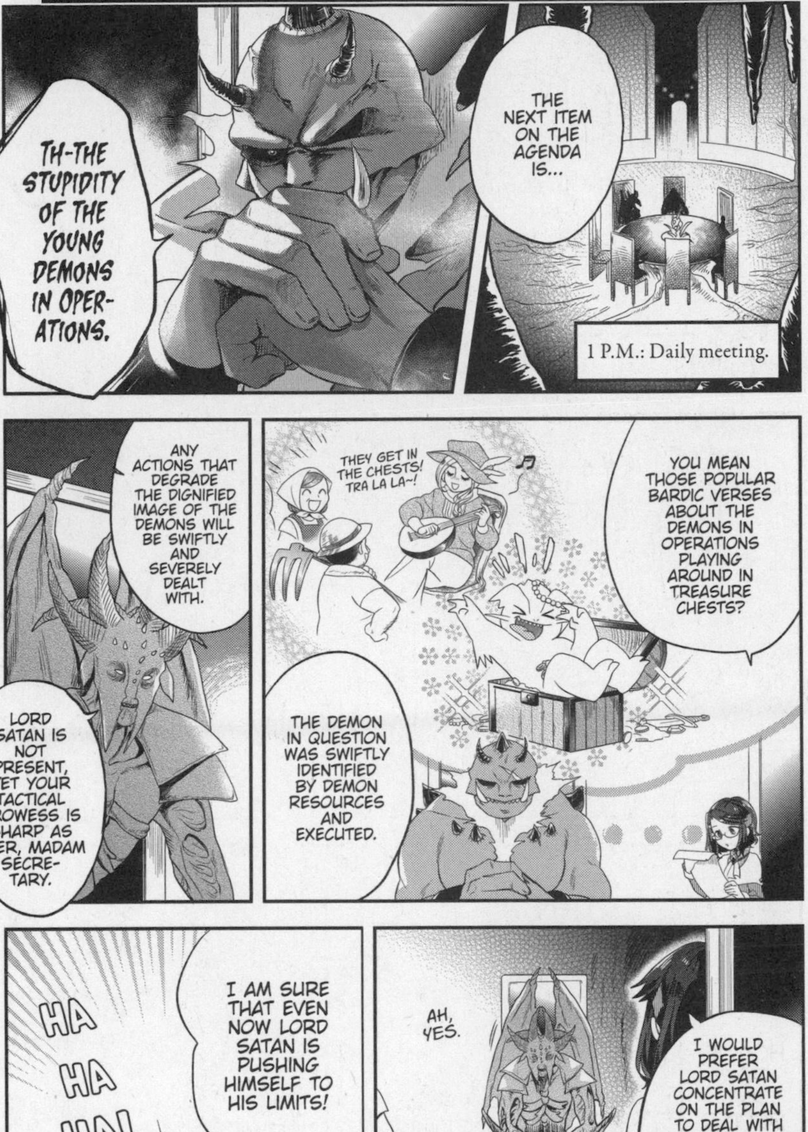
THE NEXT ITEM ON THE AGENDA IS...
1 P.M.: Daily meeting.
TH-THE STUPIDITY OF THE YOUNG DEMONS IN OPERATIONS.
YOU MEAN THOSE POPULAR BARDIC VERSES ABOUT THE DEMONS IN OPERATIONS PLAYING AROUND IN TREASURE CHESTS?
THEY GET IN THE CHESTS! TRA LA LA~!
THE DEMON IN QUESTION WAS SWIFTLY IDENTIFIED BY DEMON RESOURCES AND EXECUTED.
ANY ACTIONS THAT DEGRADE THE DIGNIFIED IMAGE OF THE DEMONS WILL BE SWIFTLY AND SEVERELY DEALT WITH.
LORD SATAN IS NOT PRESENT, YET YOUR TACTICAL PROWESS IS SHARP AS EVER, MADAM SECRETARY.
I WOULD PREFER LORD SATAN CONCENTRATE ON THE PLAN TO DEAL WITH THE HERO THAN BE TIED UP IN MEETINGS LIKE THIS.
AH, YES.
I AM SURE THAT EVEN NOW LORD SATAN IS PUSHING HIMSELF TO HIS LIMITS!
HA HA HA!

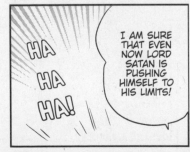

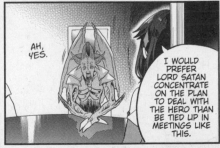

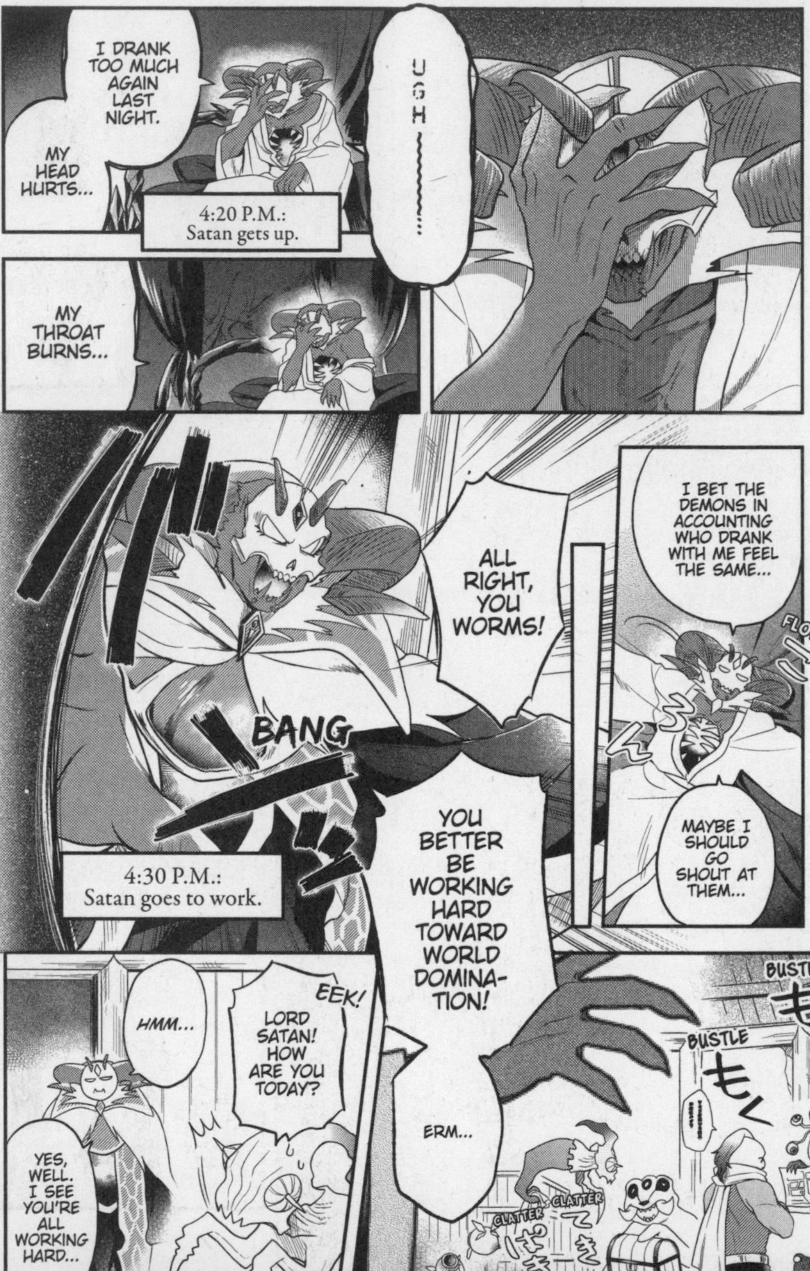
UGH......
I DRANK TOO MUCH AGAIN LAST NIGHT.
MY HEAD HURTS...
4:20 P.M.: Satan gets up.
MY THROAT BURNS...
I BET THE DEMONS IN ACCOUNTING WHO DRANK WITH ME FEEL THE SAME...
FLOP
MAYBE I SHOULD GO SHOUT AT THEM...
BANG
ALL RIGHT, YOU WORMS!
YOU BETTER BE WORKING HARD TOWARD WORLD DOMINATION!
4:30 P.M.: Satan goes to work.
BUSTLE
BUSTLE
ERM...
CLATTER
CLATTER
EEK!
LORD SATAN! HOW ARE YOU TODAY?
HMM...
YES, WELL. I SEE YOU'RE ALL WORKING HARD...

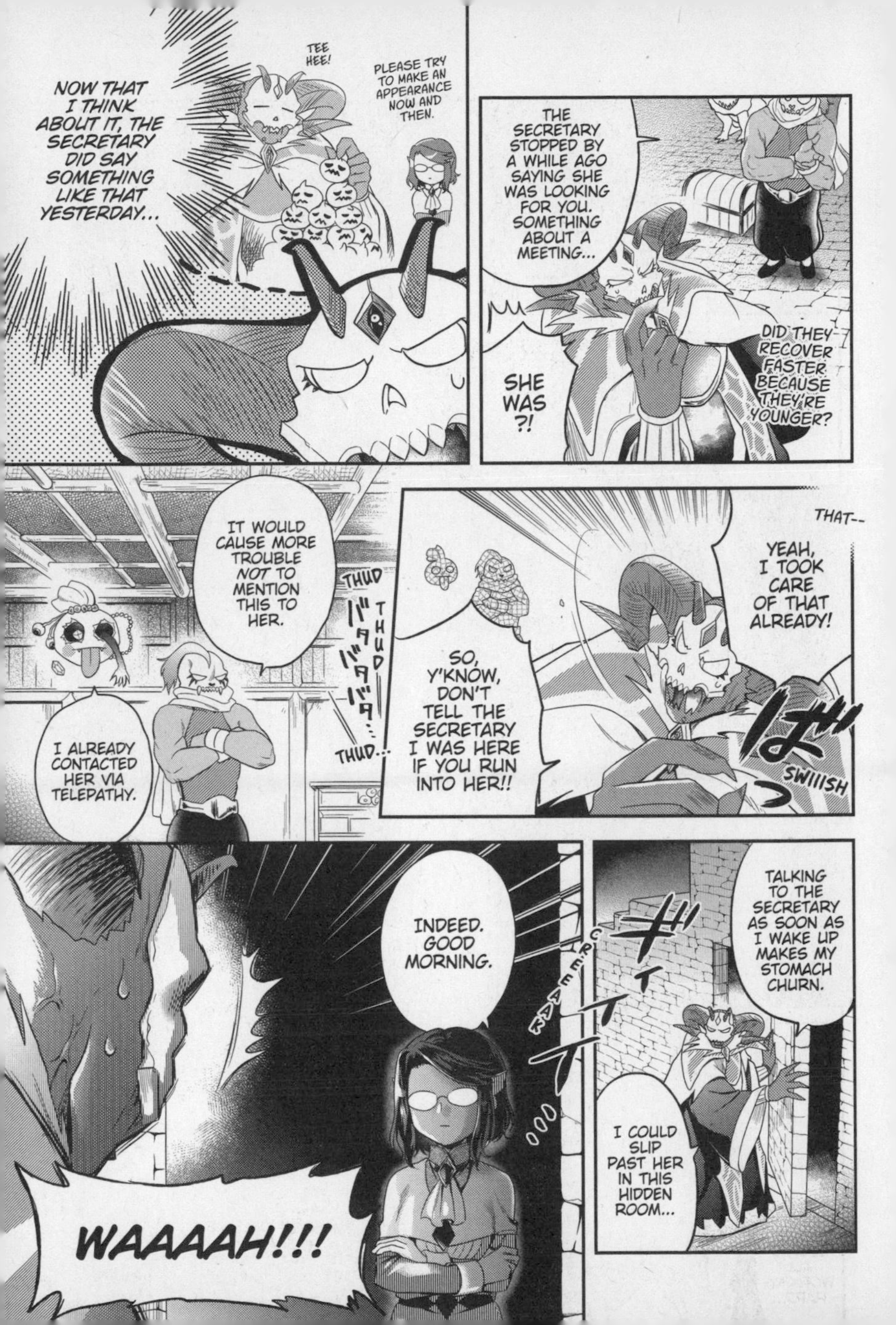

THE SECRETARY STOPPED BY A WHILE AGO SAYING SHE WAS LOOKING FOR YOU. SOMETHING ABOUT A MEETING...
SHE WAS?!
DID THEY RECOVER FASTER BECAUSE THEY'RE YOUNGER?
PLEASE TRY TO MAKE AN APPEARANCE NOW AND THEN.
TEE HEE!
NOW THAT I THINK ABOUT IT, THE SECRETARY DID SAY SOMETHING LIKE THAT YESTERDAY...
THAT--
YEAH, I TOOK CARE OF THAT ALREADY!
SO, Y'KNOW, DON'T TELL THE SECRETARY I WAS HERE IF YOU RUN INTO HER!!
SWIIISH
IT WOULD CAUSE MORE TROUBLE *NOT* TO MENTION THIS TO HER.
THUD THUD THUD...
I ALREADY CONTACTED HER VIA TELEPATHY.
TALKING TO THE SECRETARY AS SOON AS I WAKE UP MAKES MY STOMACH CHURN.
CREEEAK
I COULD SLIP PAST HER IN THIS HIDDEN ROOM...
INDEED. GOOD MORNING.
WAAAAH!!!

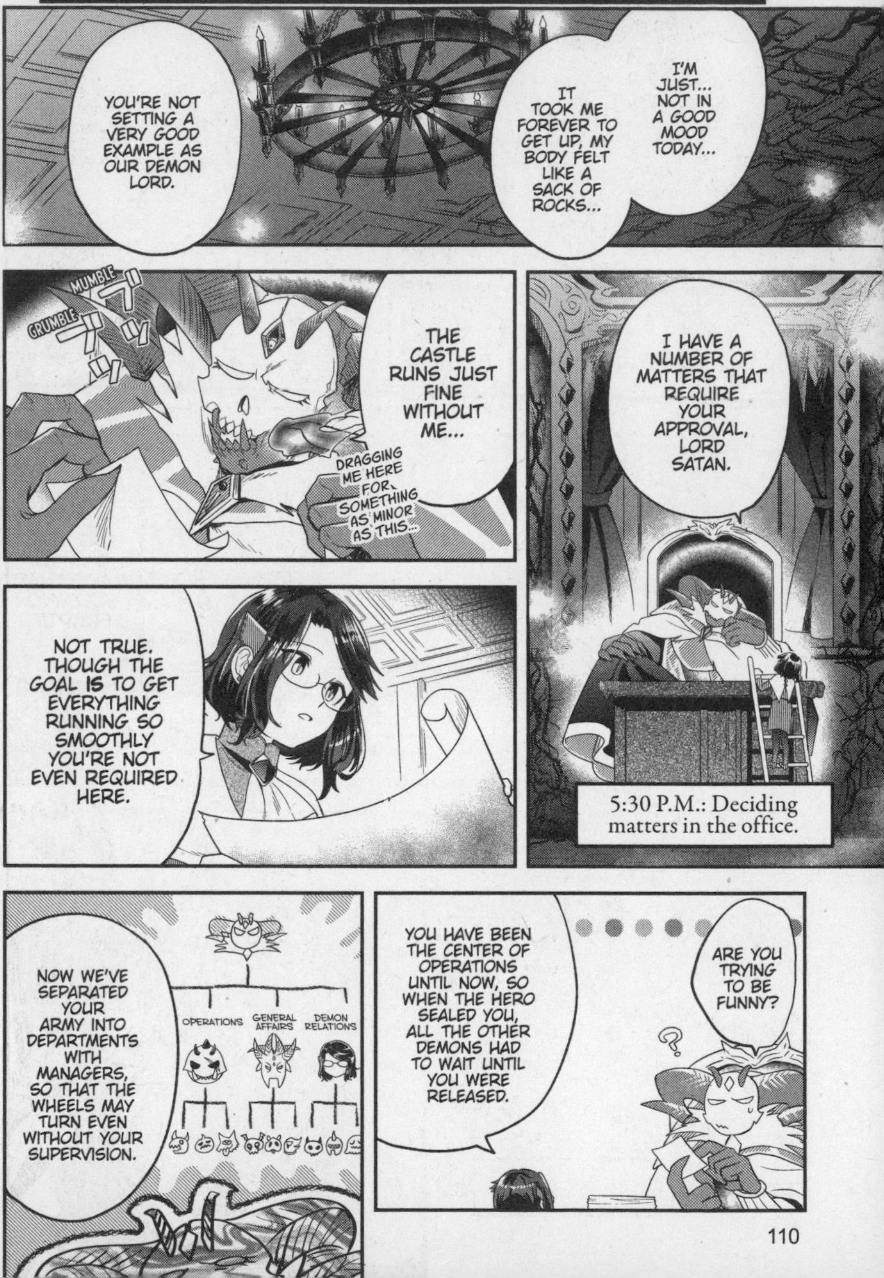
I'M JUST... NOT IN A GOOD MOOD TODAY...
IT TOOK ME FOREVER TO GET UP, MY BODY FELT LIKE A SACK OF ROCKS...
YOU'RE NOT SETTING A VERY GOOD EXAMPLE AS OUR DEMON LORD.
I HAVE A NUMBER OF MATTERS THAT REQUIRE YOUR APPROVAL, LORD SATAN.
5:30 P.M.: Deciding matters in the office.
THE CASTLE RUNS JUST FINE WITHOUT ME...
DRAGGING ME HERE FOR SOMETHING AS MINOR AS THIS...
MUMBLE
GRUMBLE
NOT TRUE. THOUGH THE GOAL IS TO GET EVERYTHING RUNNING SO SMOOTHLY YOU'RE NOT EVEN REQUIRED HERE.
ARE YOU TRYING TO BE FUNNY?
?
YOU HAVE BEEN THE CENTER OF OPERATIONS UNTIL NOW, SO WHEN THE HERO SEALED YOU, ALL THE OTHER DEMONS HAD TO WAIT UNTIL YOU WERE RELEASED.
NOW WE'VE SEPARATED YOUR ARMY INTO DEPARTMENTS WITH MANAGERS, SO THAT THE WHEELS MAY TURN EVEN WITHOUT YOUR SUPERVISION.
OPERATIONS
GENERAL AFFAIRS
DEMON RELATIONS

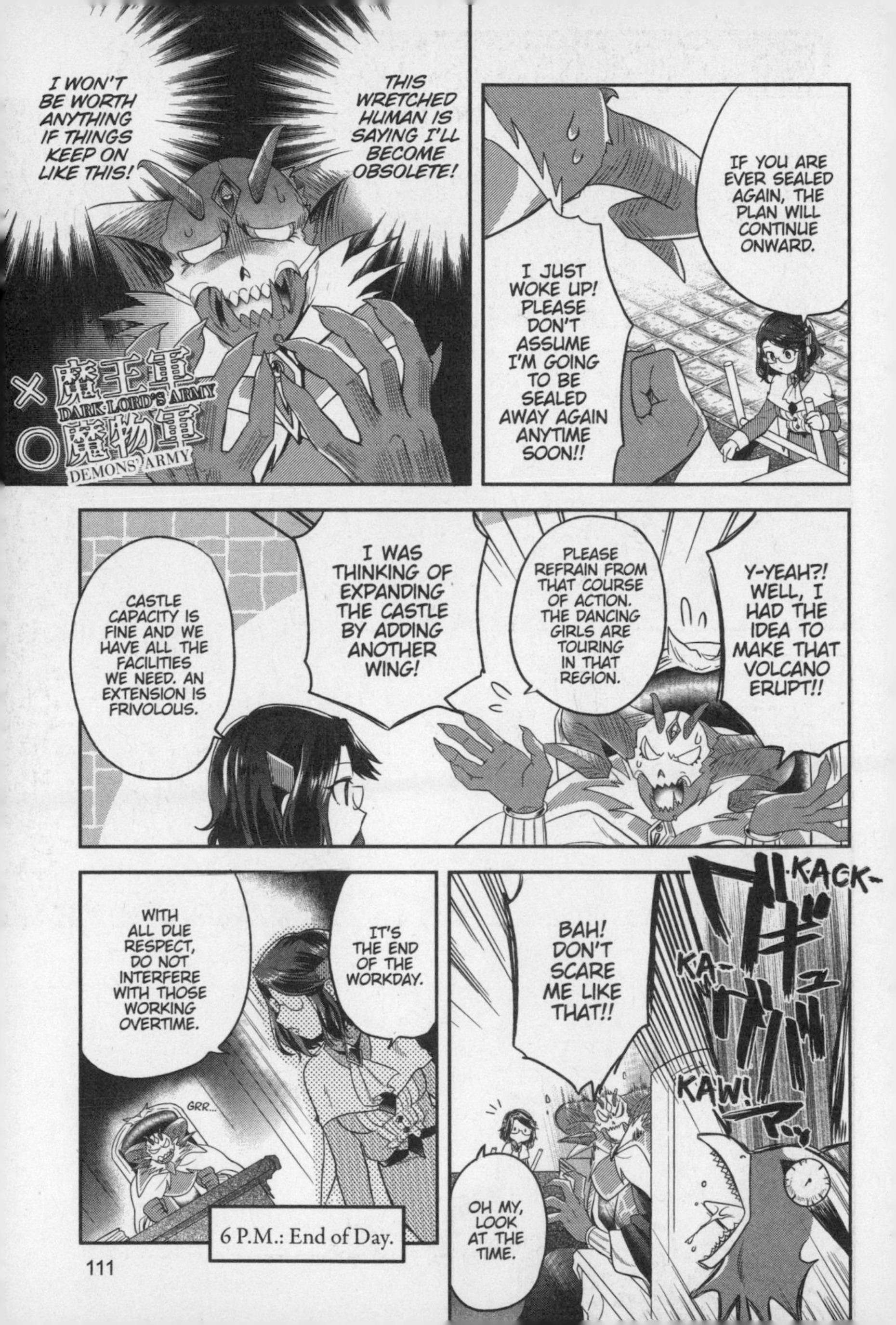
IF YOU ARE EVER SEALED AGAIN, THE PLAN WILL CONTINUE ONWARD.
I JUST WOKE UP! PLEASE DON'T ASSUME I'M GOING TO BE SEALED AWAY AGAIN ANYTIME SOON!!
THIS WRETCHED HUMAN IS SAYING I'LL BECOME OBSOLETE!
I WON'T BE WORTH ANYTHING IF THINGS KEEP ON LIKE THIS!
×魔王軍 DARK LORD'S ARMY
○魔物軍 DEMONS' ARMY
Y-YEAH?! WELL, I HAD THE IDEA TO MAKE THAT VOLCANO ERUPT!!
PLEASE REFRAIN FROM THAT COURSE OF ACTION. THE DANCING GIRLS ARE TOURING IN THAT REGION.
I WAS THINKING OF EXPANDING THE CASTLE BY ADDING ANOTHER WING!
CASTLE CAPACITY IS FINE AND WE HAVE ALL THE FACILITIES WE NEED. AN EXTENSION IS FRIVOLOUS.
-KACK-
KA-
KAW!
OH MY, LOOK AT THE TIME.
BAH! DON'T SCARE ME LIKE THAT!!
IT'S THE END OF THE WORKDAY.
WITH ALL DUE RESPECT, DO NOT INTERFERE WITH THOSE WORKING OVERTIME.
GRR...
6 P.M.: End of Day.

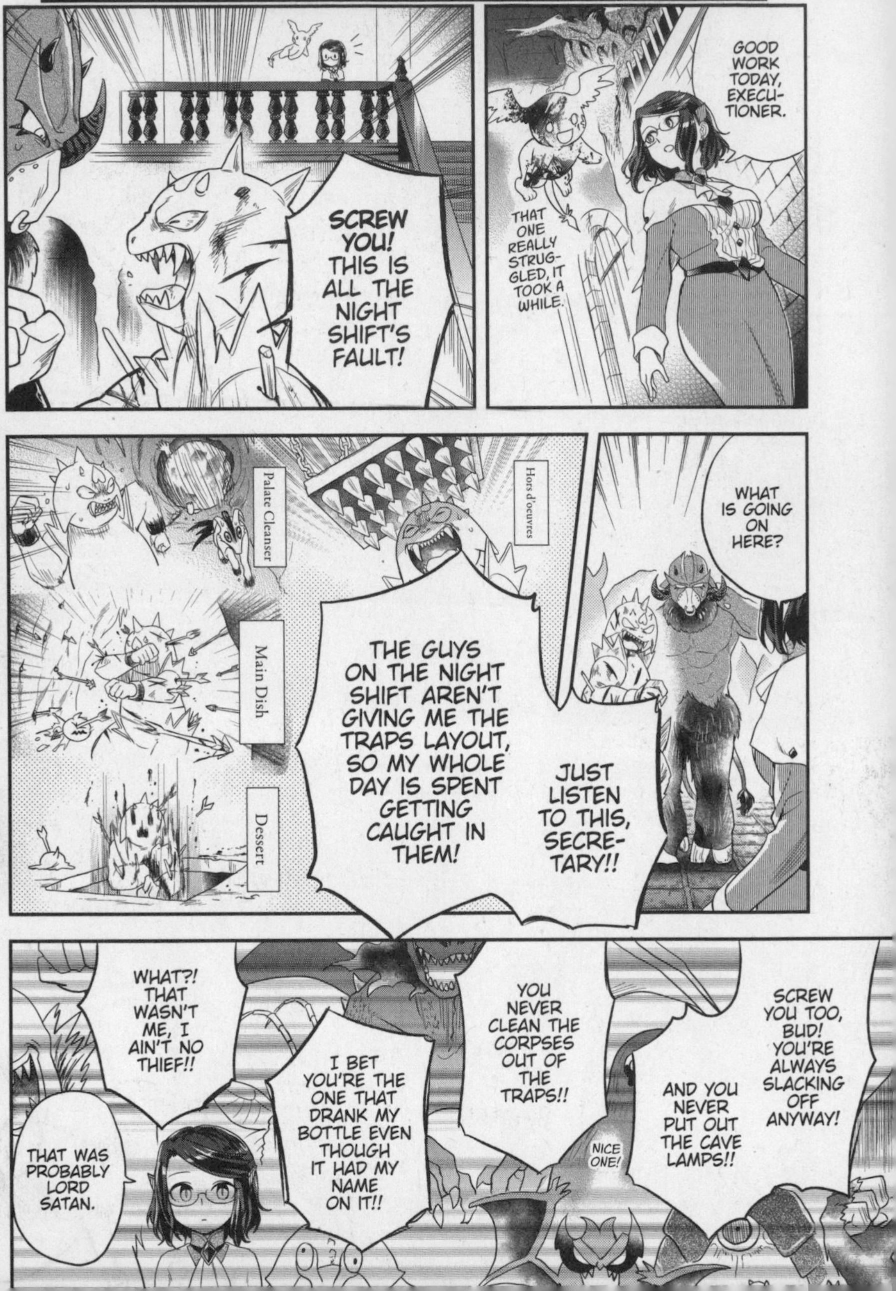
GOOD WORK TODAY, EXECUTIONER.
THAT ONE REALLY STRUGGLED, IT TOOK A WHILE.
SCREW YOU! THIS IS ALL THE NIGHT SHIFT'S FAULT!
WHAT IS GOING ON HERE?
JUST LISTEN TO THIS, SECRETARY!!
THE GUYS ON THE NIGHT SHIFT AREN'T GIVING ME THE TRAPS LAYOUT, SO MY WHOLE DAY IS SPENT GETTING CAUGHT IN THEM!
Hors d'oeuvres
Palate Cleanser
Main Dish
Dessert
SCREW YOU TOO, BUD! YOU'RE ALWAYS SLACKING OFF ANYWAY!
AND YOU NEVER PUT OUT THE CAVE LAMPS!!
NICE ONE!
YOU NEVER CLEAN THE CORPSES OUT OF THE TRAPS!!
I BET YOU'RE THE ONE THAT DRANK MY BOTTLE EVEN THOUGH IT HAD MY NAME ON IT!!
WHAT?! THAT WASN'T ME, I AIN'T NO THIEF!!
THAT WAS PROBABLY LORD SATAN.

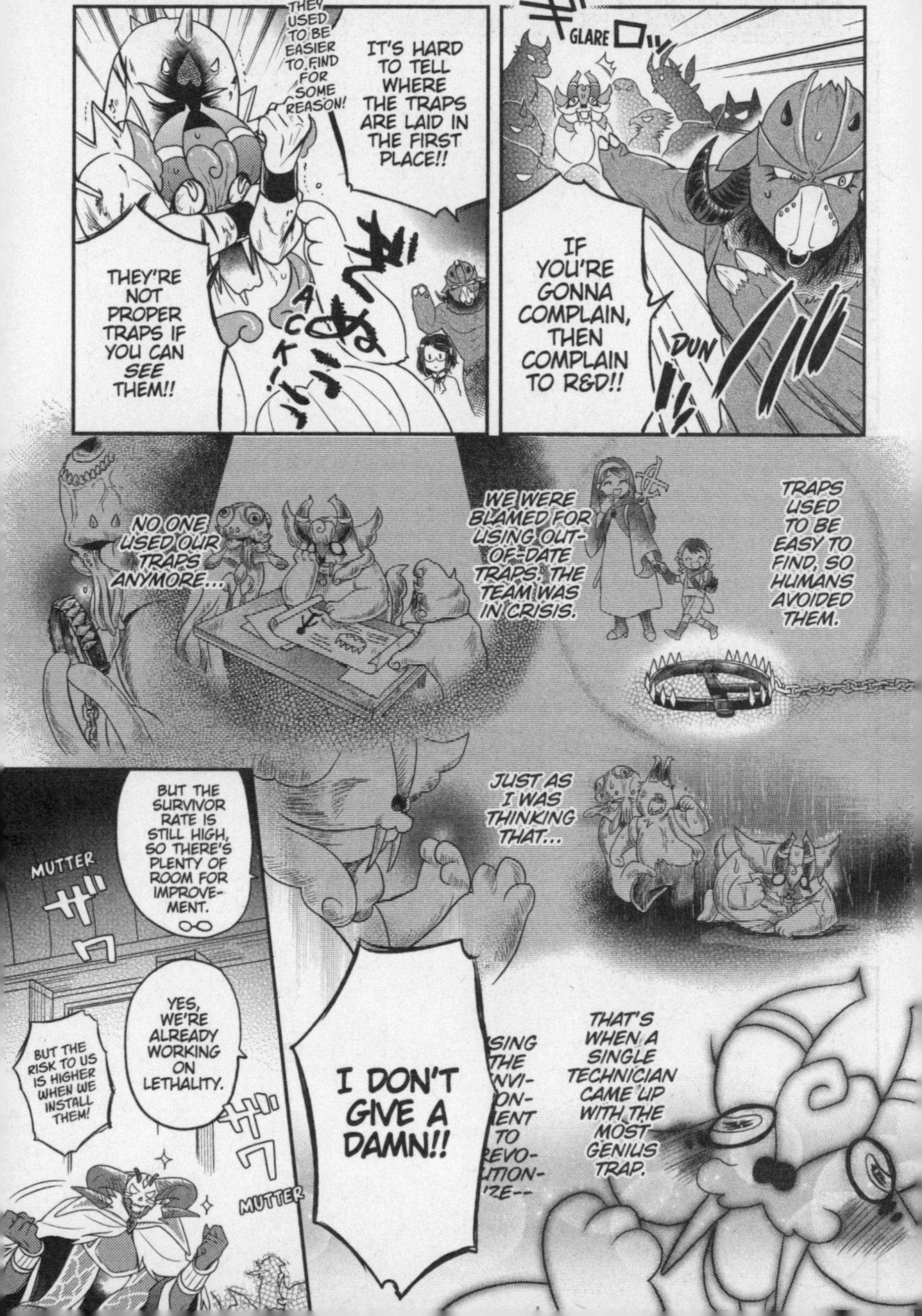
GLARE
IF YOU'RE GONNA COMPLAIN, THEN COMPLAIN TO R&D!!
DUN
IT'S HARD TO TELL WHERE THE TRAPS ARE LAID IN THE FIRST PLACE!!
THEY USED TO BE EASIER TO FIND FOR SOME REASON!
THEY'RE NOT PROPER TRAPS IF YOU CAN SEE THEM!!
ACK!!
TRAPS USED TO BE EASY TO FIND, SO HUMANS AVOIDED THEM.
WE WERE BLAMED FOR USING OUT-OF-DATE TRAPS. THE TEAM WAS IN CRISIS.
NO ONE USED OUR TRAPS ANYMORE...
JUST AS I WAS THINKING THAT...
THAT'S WHEN A SINGLE TECHNICIAN CAME UP WITH THE MOST GENIUS TRAP.
SING THE NVI- ON- IENT TO REVO- UTION- IZE--
I DON'T GIVE A DAMN!!
BUT THE SURVIVOR RATE IS STILL HIGH, SO THERE'S PLENTY OF ROOM FOR IMPROVEMENT.
MUTTER
YES, WE'RE ALREADY WORKING ON LETHALITY.
BUT THE RISK TO US IS HIGHER WHEN WE INSTALL THEM!
MUTTER

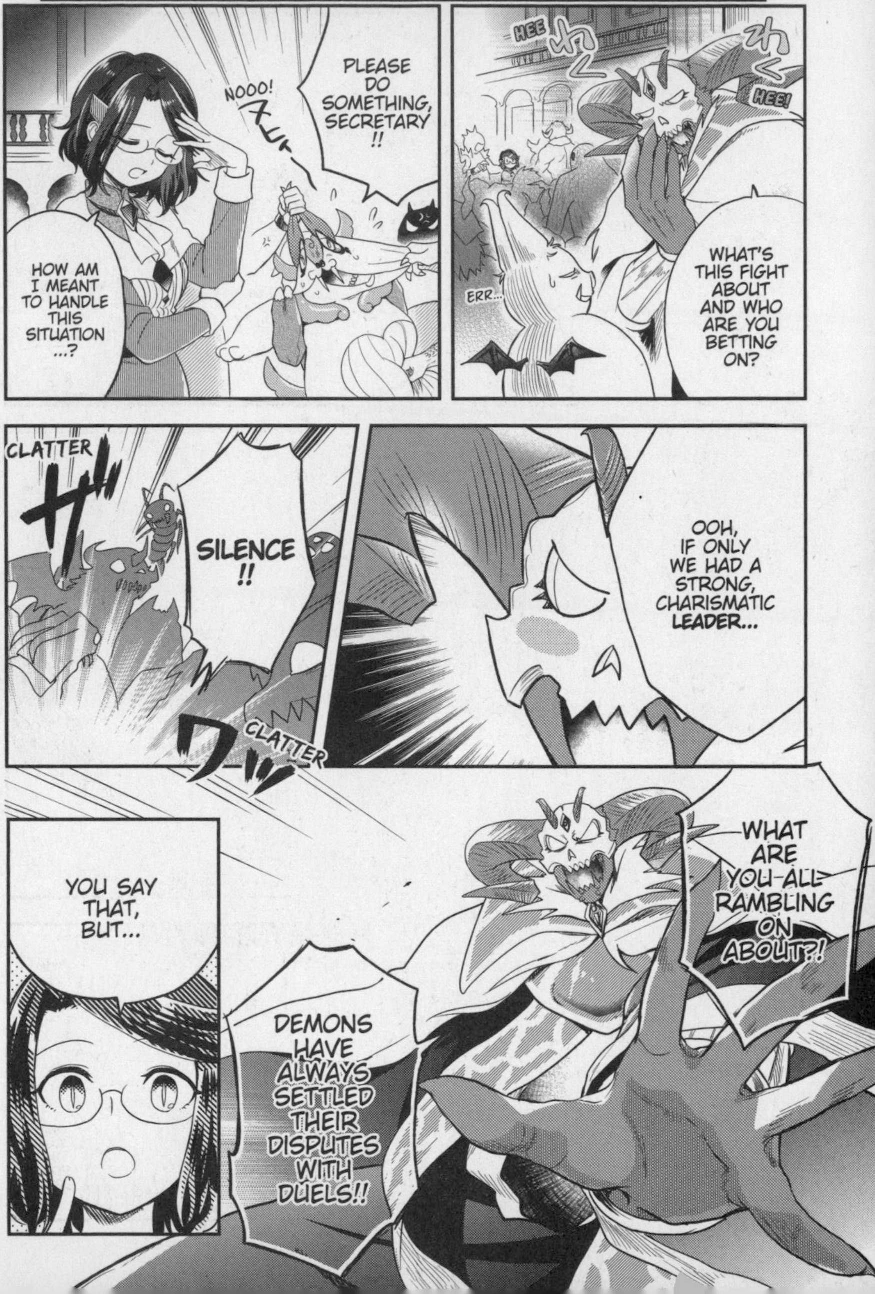
HEE
HEE!
WHAT'S THIS FIGHT ABOUT AND WHO ARE YOU BETTING ON?
ERR...
PLEASE DO SOMETHING, SECRETARY!!
NOOO!
HOW AM I MEANT TO HANDLE THIS SITUATION...?
OOH, IF ONLY WE HAD A STRONG, CHARISMATIC LEADER...
CLATTER
SILENCE!!
CLATTER
WHAT ARE YOU ALL RAMBLING ON ABOUT?!
DEMONS HAVE ALWAYS SETTLED THEIR DISPUTES WITH DUELS!!
YOU SAY THAT, BUT...

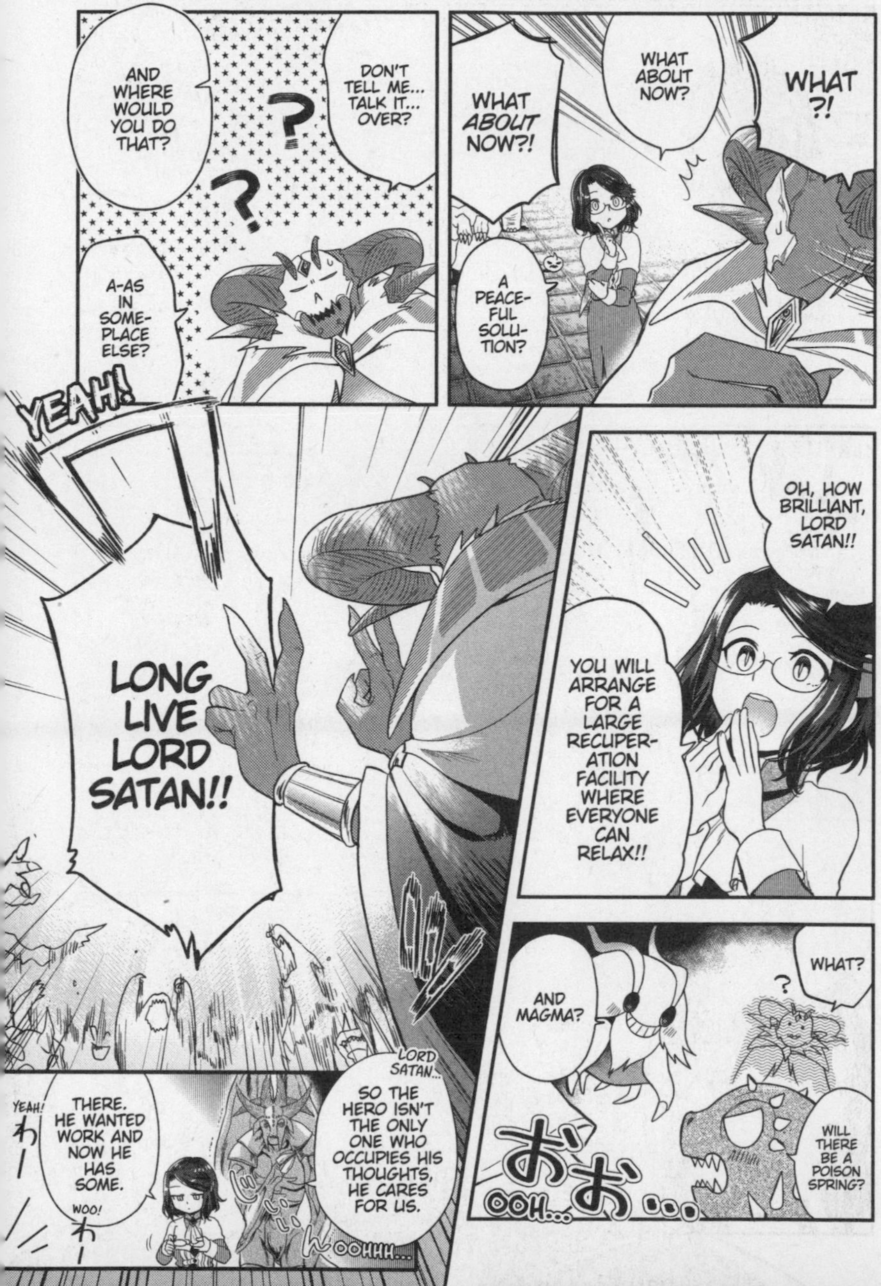
WHAT ?!
WHAT ABOUT NOW?
WHAT ABOUT NOW?!
A PEACEFUL SOLUTION?
DON'T TELL ME... TALK IT... OVER?
AND WHERE WOULD YOU DO THAT?
A-AS IN SOMEPLACE ELSE?
OH, HOW BRILLIANT, LORD SATAN!!
YOU WILL ARRANGE FOR A LARGE RECUPERATION FACILITY WHERE EVERYONE CAN RELAX!!
WHAT?
AND MAGMA?
WILL THERE BE A POISON SPRING?
おお...
OOH...
YEAH!
LONG LIVE LORD SATAN!!
LORD SATAN...
SO THE HERO ISN'T THE ONLY ONE WHO OCCUPIES HIS THOUGHTS, HE CARES FOR US.
じーん
OOHHH...
THERE. HE WANTED WORK AND NOW HE HAS SOME.
YEAH!
わー
WOO!
わー

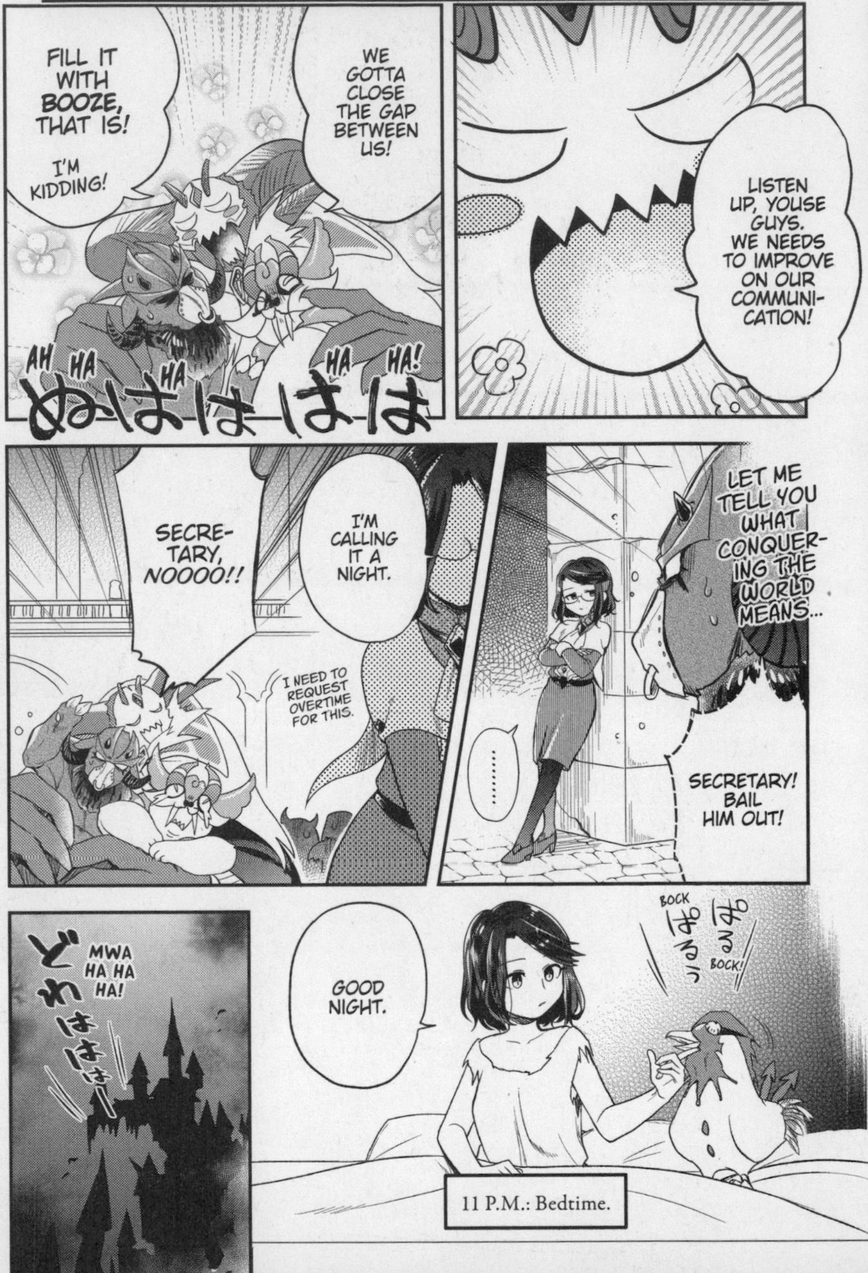
LISTEN UP, YOUSE GUYS. WE NEEDS TO IMPROVE ON OUR COMMUNI-CATION!
WE GOTTA CLOSE THE GAP BETWEEN US!
FILL IT WITH BOOZE, THAT IS!
I'M KIDDING!
AH HA HA HA HA!
ぬははははは
LET ME TELL YOU WHAT CONQUER-ING THE WORLD MEANS...
......
SECRETARY! BAIL HIM OUT!
I'M CALLING IT A NIGHT.
SECRE-TARY, NOOOO!!
I NEED TO REQUEST OVERTIME FOR THIS.
BOCK BOCK!
ぽるぽるっ
GOOD NIGHT.
11 P.M.: Bedtime.
MWA HA HA HA!
どわはははー

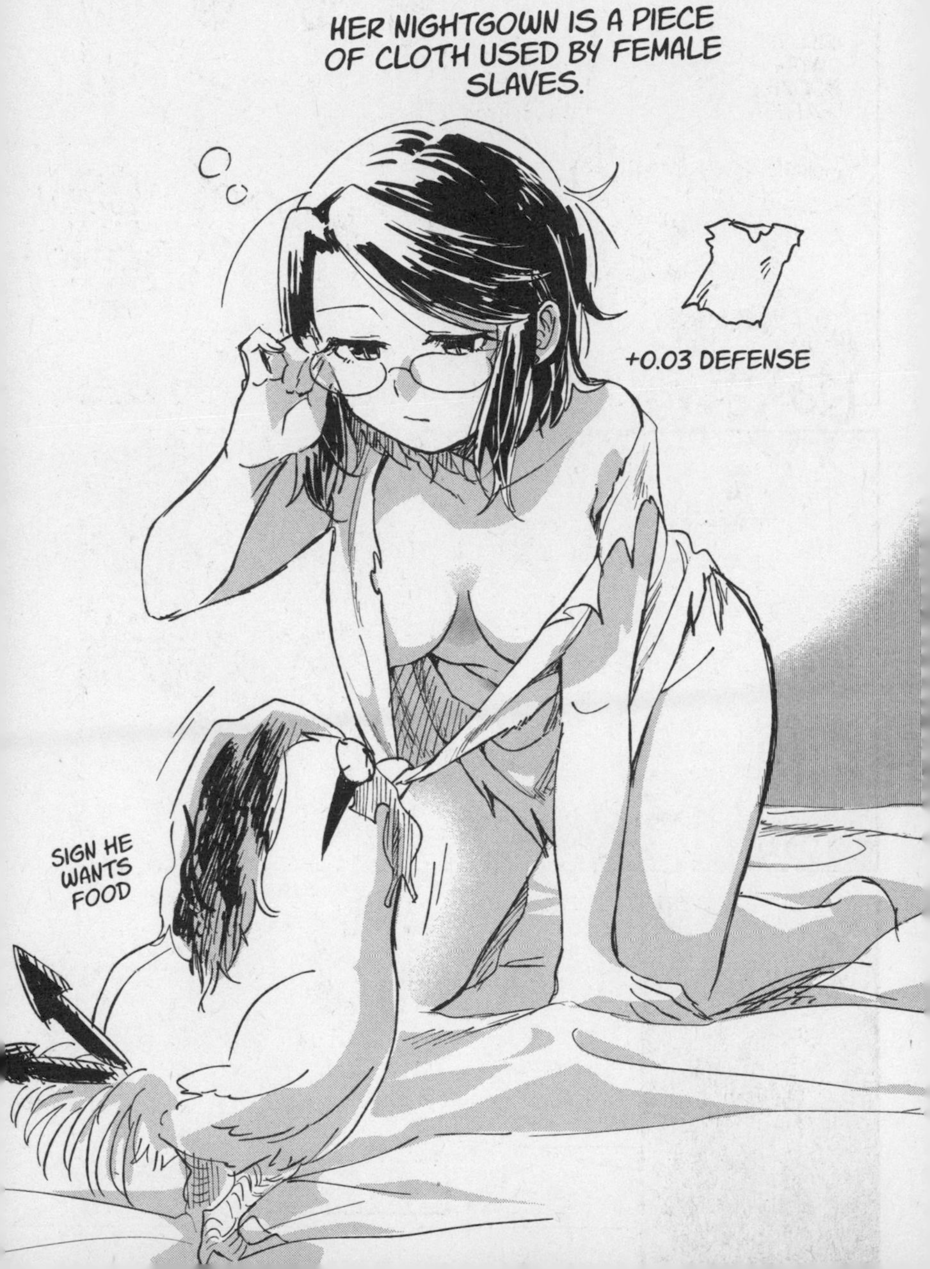
HER NIGHTGOWN IS A PIECE OF CLOTH USED BY FEMALE SLAVES.
+0.03 DEFENSE
SIGN HE WANTS FOOD

# SATAN'S SECRETARY

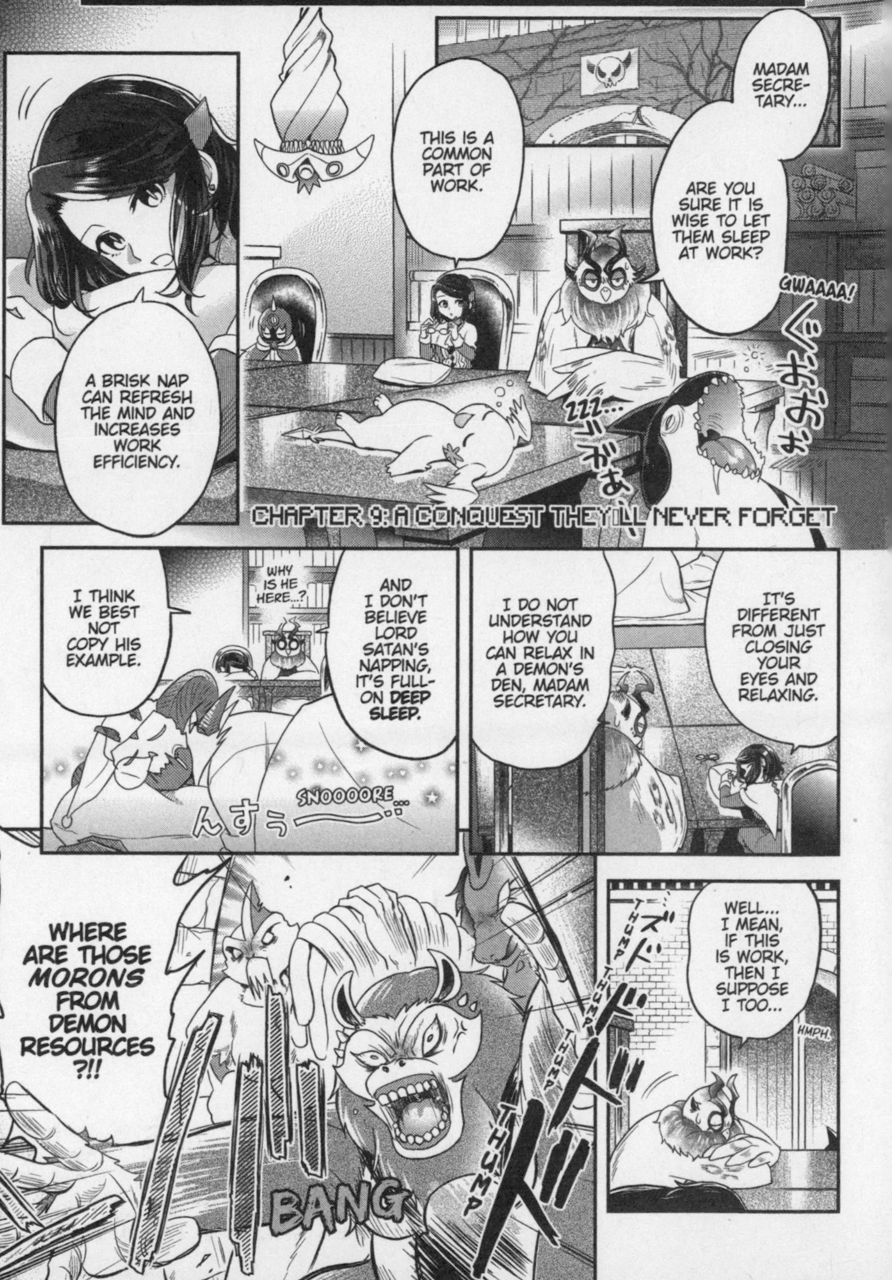
MADAM SECRETARY...
ARE YOU SURE IT IS WISE TO LET THEM SLEEP AT WORK?
GWAAAA!
ZZZ...
THIS IS A COMMON PART OF WORK.
CHAPTER 9: A CONQUEST THEY'LL NEVER FORGET
A BRISK NAP CAN REFRESH THE MIND AND INCREASES WORK EFFICIENCY.
IT'S DIFFERENT FROM JUST CLOSING YOUR EYES AND RELAXING.
I DO NOT UNDERSTAND HOW YOU CAN RELAX IN A DEMON'S DEN, MADAM SECRETARY.
AND I DON'T BELIEVE LORD SATAN'S NAPPING, IT'S FULL-ON **DEEP SLEEP.**
WHY IS HE HERE...?
I THINK WE BEST NOT COPY HIS EXAMPLE.
SNOOOORE...
WELL... I MEAN, IF THIS IS WORK, THEN I SUPPOSE I TOO...
HMPH.
THUMP THUMP THUMP THUMP
WHERE ARE THOSE *MORONS* FROM DEMON RESOURCES?!!
BANG

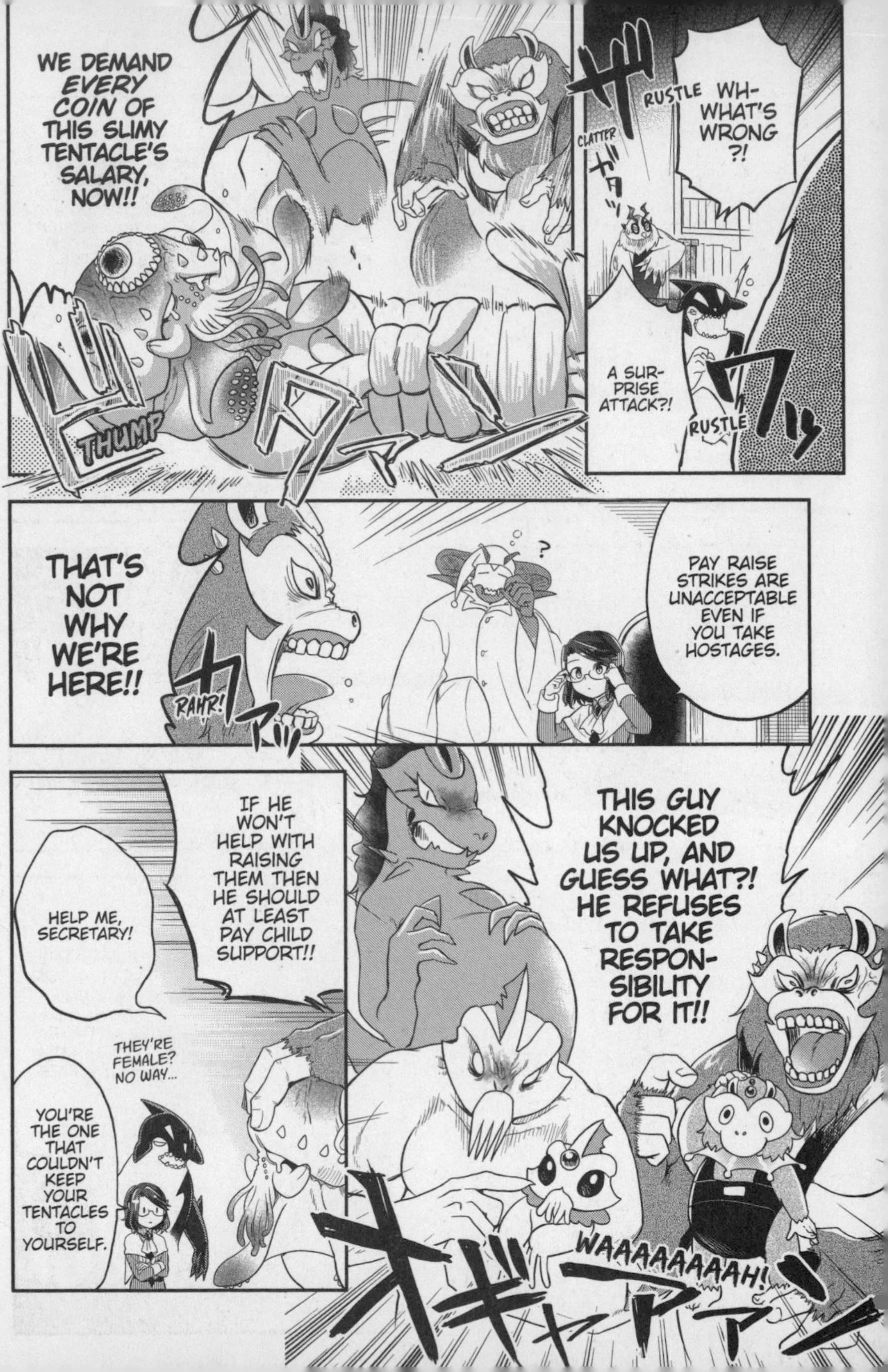
RUSTLE
WH-WHAT'S WRONG?!
CLATTER
A SUR-PRISE ATTACK?!
RUSTLE
WE DEMAND EVERY COIN OF THIS SLIMY TENTACLE'S SALARY, NOW!!
THUMP
PAY RAISE STRIKES ARE UNACCEPTABLE EVEN IF YOU TAKE HOSTAGES.
?
THAT'S NOT WHY WE'RE HERE!!
RAHR!
THIS GUY KNOCKED US UP, AND GUESS WHAT?! HE REFUSES TO TAKE RESPON-SIBILITY FOR IT!!
IF HE WON'T HELP WITH RAISING THEM THEN HE SHOULD AT LEAST PAY CHILD SUPPORT!!
WAAAAAAAAAH!
HELP ME, SECRETARY!
THEY'RE FEMALE? NO WAY...
YOU'RE THE ONE THAT COULDN'T KEEP YOUR TENTACLES TO YOURSELF.

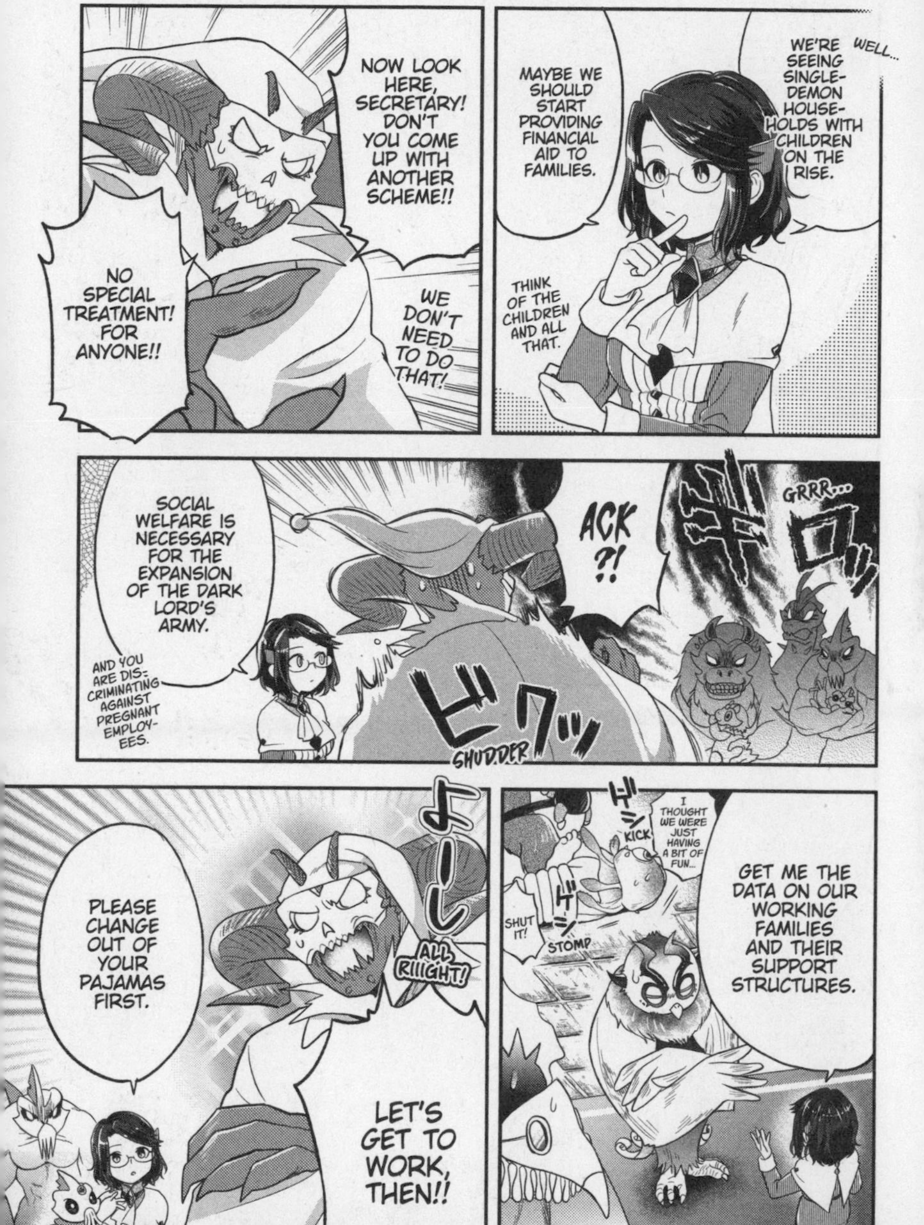
WELL...
WE'RE SEEING SINGLE-DEMON HOUSEHOLDS WITH CHILDREN ON THE RISE.
MAYBE WE SHOULD START PROVIDING FINANCIAL AID TO FAMILIES.
THINK OF THE CHILDREN AND ALL THAT.
NOW LOOK HERE, SECRETARY! DON'T YOU COME UP WITH ANOTHER SCHEME!!
WE DON'T NEED TO DO THAT!
NO SPECIAL TREATMENT! FOR ANYONE!!
GRRR...
ギロッ
ACK ?!
SOCIAL WELFARE IS NECESSARY FOR THE EXPANSION OF THE DARK LORD'S ARMY.
AND YOU ARE DIS-CRIMINATING AGAINST PREGNANT EMPLOY-EES.
ビクッ
SHUDDER
ゲシ
KICK
I THOUGHT WE WERE JUST HAVING A BIT OF FUN...
ゲシ
STOMP
SHUT IT!
GET ME THE DATA ON OUR WORKING FAMILIES AND THEIR SUPPORT STRUCTURES.
よーし
ALL RIIIGHT!
PLEASE CHANGE OUT OF YOUR PAJAMAS FIRST.
LET'S GET TO WORK, THEN!!

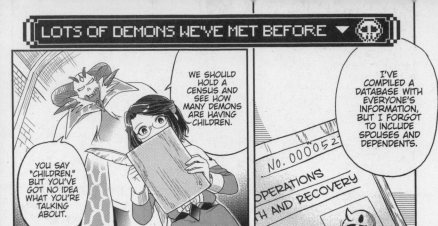

# LOTS OF DEMONS WE'VE MET BEFORE

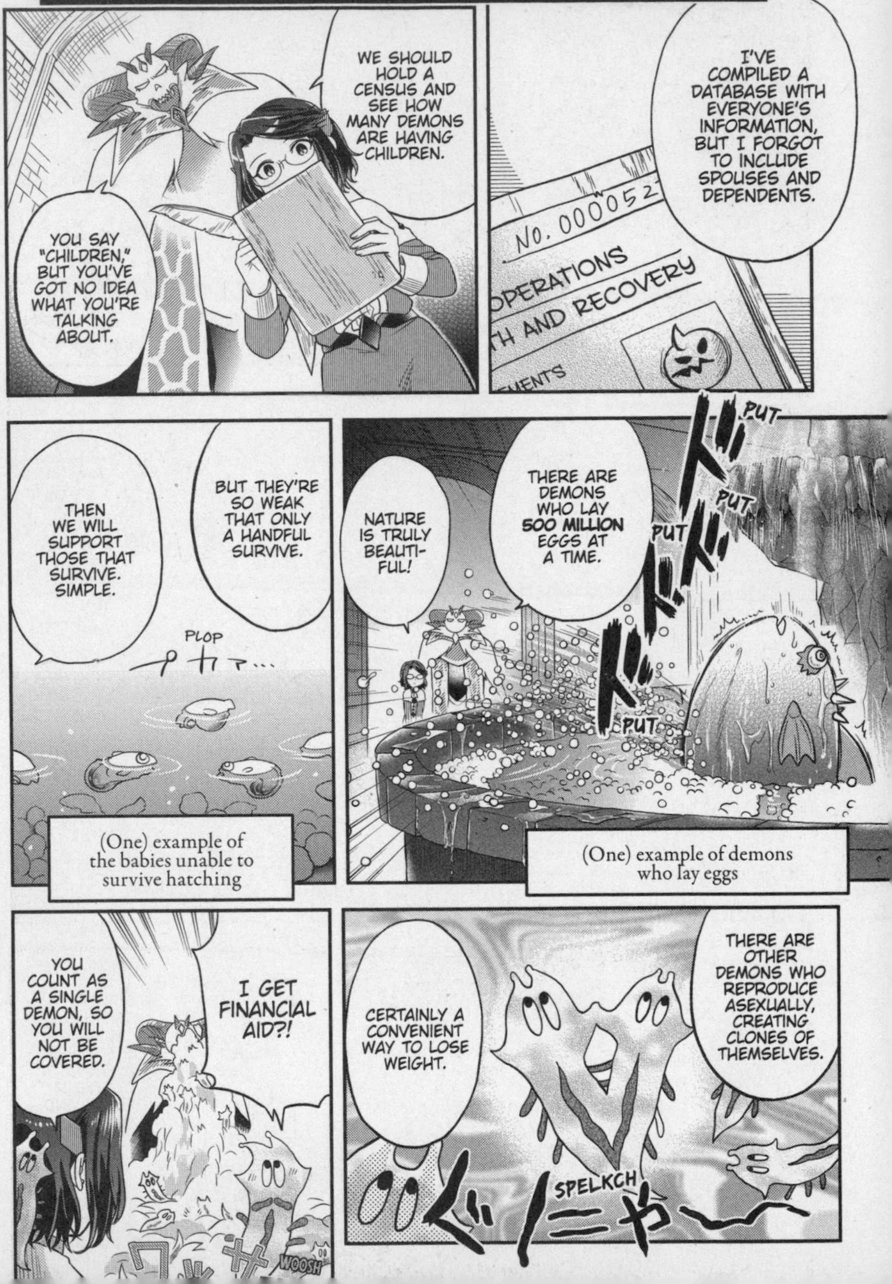

I'VE COMPILED A DATABASE WITH EVERYONE'S INFORMATION, BUT I FORGOT TO INCLUDE SPOUSES AND DEPENDENTS.
NO. 000052
WE SHOULD HOLD A CENSUS AND SEE HOW MANY DEMONS ARE HAVING CHILDREN.
YOU SAY "CHILDREN," BUT YOU'VE GOT NO IDEA WHAT YOU'RE TALKING ABOUT.
PUT
PUT
PUT
PUT
THERE ARE DEMONS WHO LAY **500 MILLION** EGGS AT A TIME.
NATURE IS TRULY BEAUTIFUL!
(One) example of demons who lay eggs
BUT THEY'RE SO WEAK THAT ONLY A HANDFUL SURVIVE.
THEN WE WILL SUPPORT THOSE THAT SURVIVE. SIMPLE.
PLOP
(One) example of the babies unable to survive hatching
THERE ARE OTHER DEMONS WHO REPRODUCE ASEXUALLY, CREATING CLONES OF THEMSELVES.
CERTAINLY A CONVENIENT WAY TO LOSE WEIGHT.
SPELKCH
I GET FINANCIAL AID?!
YOU COUNT AS A SINGLE DEMON, SO YOU WILL NOT BE COVERED.
WOOSH

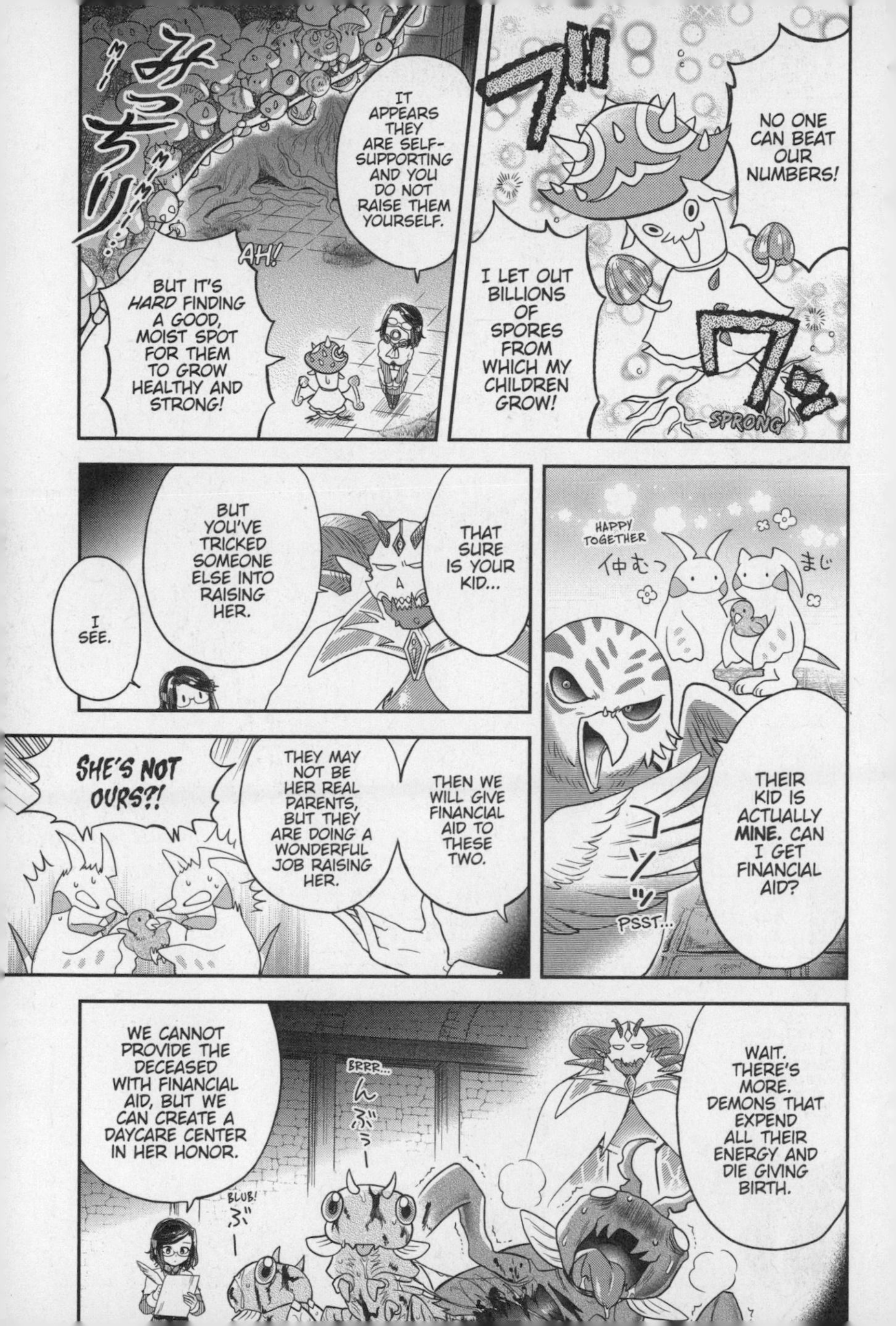

ブ
NO ONE CAN BEAT OUR NUMBERS!
I LET OUT BILLIONS OF SPORES FROM WHICH MY CHILDREN GROW!
ワ
SPRONG
IT APPEARS THEY ARE SELF-SUPPORTING AND YOU DO NOT RAISE THEM YOURSELF.
AH!
BUT IT'S *HARD* FINDING A GOOD, MOIST SPOT FOR THEM TO GROW HEALTHY AND STRONG!
みっちり
M-M-M...
HAPPY TOGETHER
仲むつ
まじ
THEIR KID IS ACTUALLY **MINE**. CAN I GET FINANCIAL AID?
コソッ
PSST...
THAT SURE IS YOUR KID...
BUT YOU'VE TRICKED SOMEONE ELSE INTO RAISING HER.
I SEE.
THEN WE WILL GIVE FINANCIAL AID TO THESE TWO.
THEY MAY NOT BE HER REAL PARENTS, BUT THEY ARE DOING A WONDERFUL JOB RAISING HER.
SHE'S NOT OURS?!
WAIT. THERE'S MORE. DEMONS THAT EXPEND ALL THEIR ENERGY AND DIE GIVING BIRTH.
BRRR...
んぶぅー
WE CANNOT PROVIDE THE DECEASED WITH FINANCIAL AID, BUT WE CAN CREATE A DAYCARE CENTER IN HER HONOR.
BLUB!
ぶー

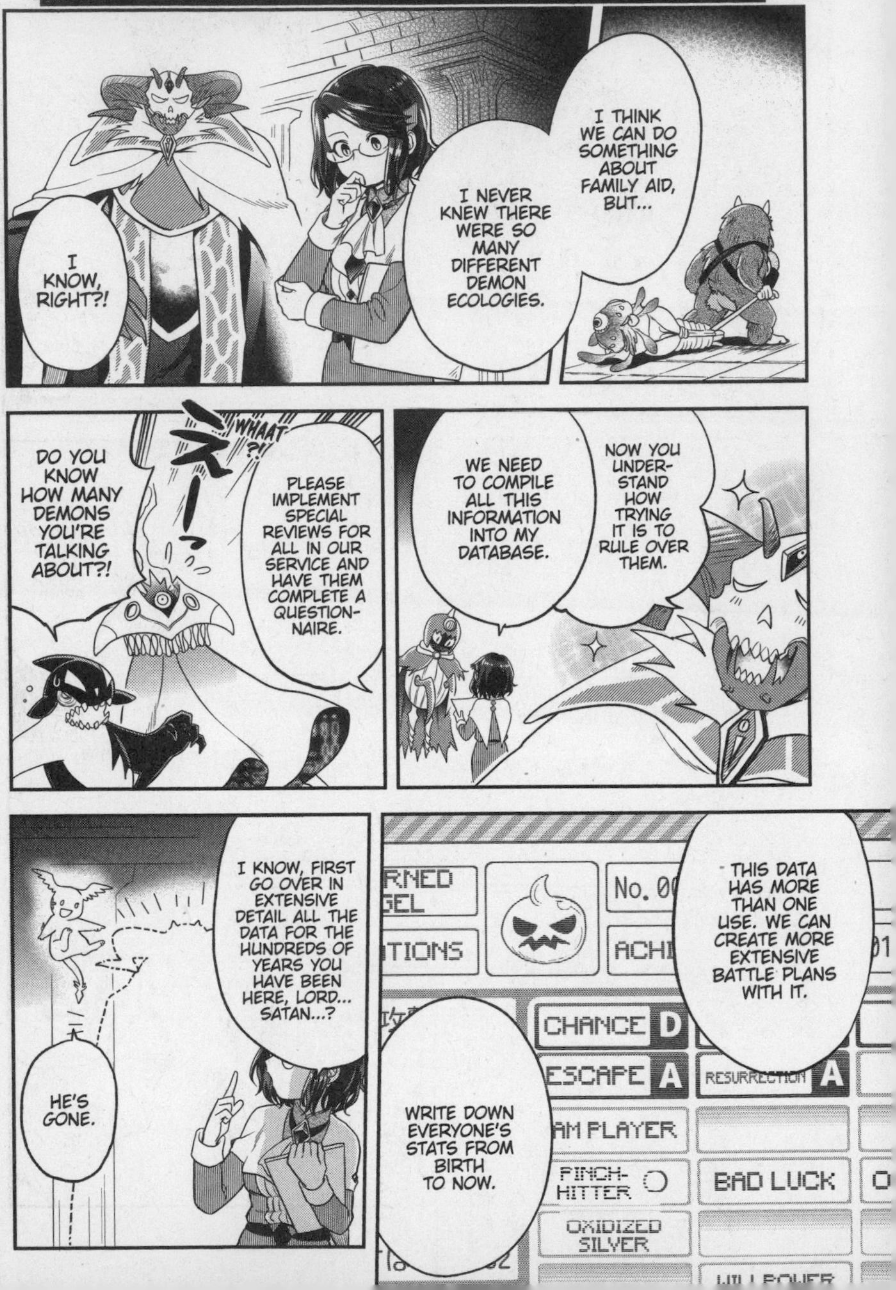
I THINK WE CAN DO SOMETHING ABOUT FAMILY AID, BUT...
I NEVER KNEW THERE WERE SO MANY DIFFERENT DEMON ECOLOGIES.
I KNOW, RIGHT?!
NOW YOU UNDERSTAND HOW TRYING IT IS TO RULE OVER THEM.
WE NEED TO COMPILE ALL THIS INFORMATION INTO MY DATABASE.
PLEASE IMPLEMENT SPECIAL REVIEWS FOR ALL IN OUR SERVICE AND HAVE THEM COMPLETE A QUESTIONNAIRE.
WHAAT?!
DO YOU KNOW HOW MANY DEMONS YOU'RE TALKING ABOUT?!
THIS DATA HAS MORE THAN ONE USE. WE CAN CREATE MORE EXTENSIVE BATTLE PLANS WITH IT.
CHANCE D
ESCAPE A
RESURRECTION A
PINCH-HITTER ○
BAD LUCK
OXIDIZED SILVER
WRITE DOWN EVERYONE'S STATS FROM BIRTH TO NOW.
I KNOW, FIRST GO OVER IN EXTENSIVE DETAIL ALL THE DATA FOR THE HUNDREDS OF YEARS YOU HAVE BEEN HERE, LORD... SATAN...?
HE'S GONE.

# NAMING THE DEMONS

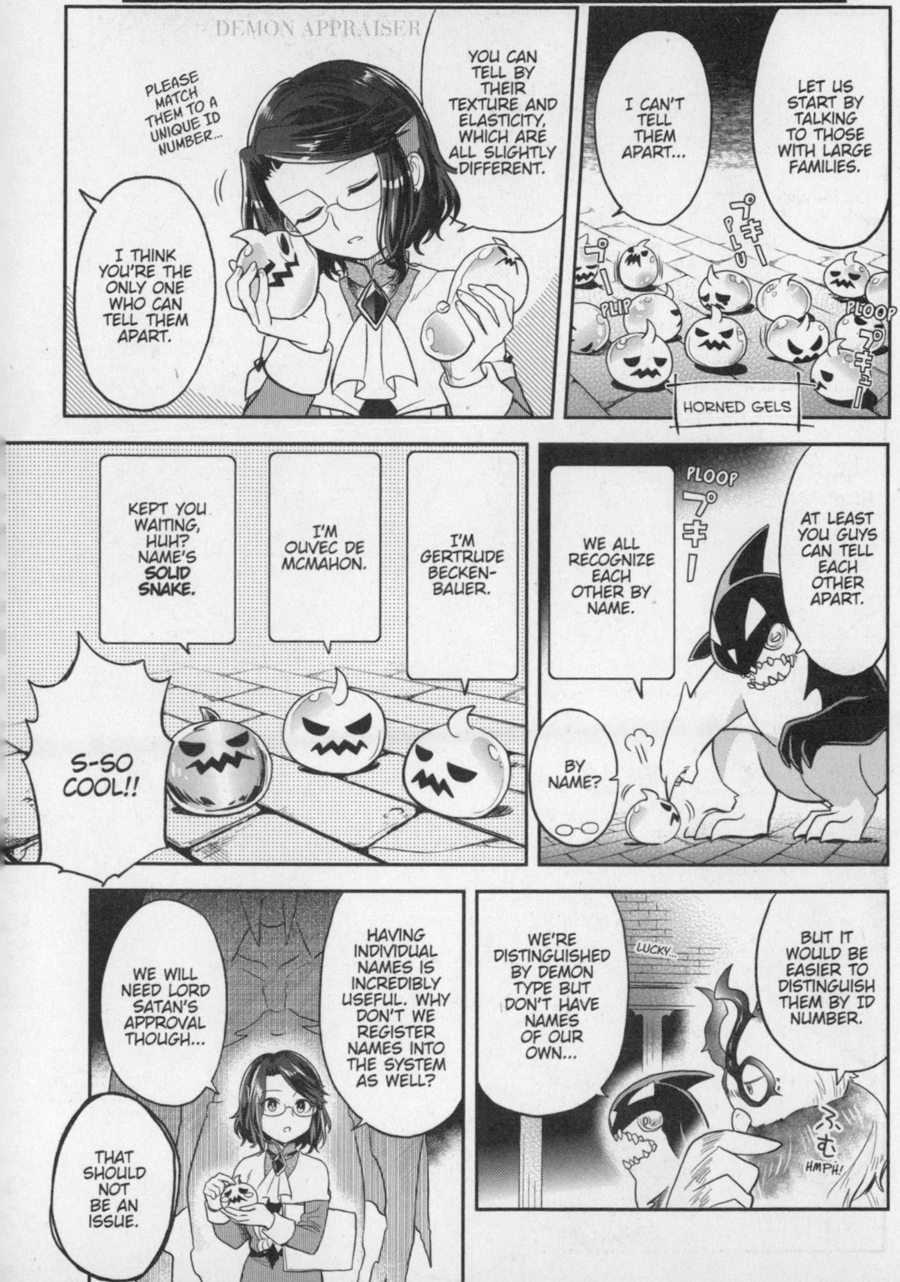
LET US START BY TALKING TO THOSE WITH LARGE FAMILIES.
I CAN'T TELL THEM APART...
プキー
PLU
プー
PLIP
PLOOP
プキュー
HORNED GELS
DEMON APPRAISER
YOU CAN TELL BY THEIR TEXTURE AND ELASTICITY, WHICH ARE ALL SLIGHTLY DIFFERENT.
PLEASE MATCH THEM TO A UNIQUE ID NUMBER...
I THINK YOU'RE THE ONLY ONE WHO CAN TELL THEM APART.
AT LEAST YOU GUYS CAN TELL EACH OTHER APART.
PLOOP
プキー
WE ALL RECOGNIZE EACH OTHER BY NAME.
BY NAME?
I'M GERTRUDE BECKENBAUER.
I'M OUVEC DE MCMAHON.
KEPT YOU WAITING, HUH? NAME'S **SOLID SNAKE.**
S-SO COOL!!
BUT IT WOULD BE EASIER TO DISTINGUISH THEM BY ID NUMBER.
LUCKY...
WE'RE DISTINGUISHED BY DEMON TYPE BUT DON'T HAVE NAMES OF OUR OWN...
ふむ
HMPH!
HAVING INDIVIDUAL NAMES IS INCREDIBLY USEFUL. WHY DON'T WE REGISTER NAMES INTO THE SYSTEM AS WELL?
WE WILL NEED LORD SATAN'S APPROVAL THOUGH...
THAT SHOULD NOT BE AN ISSUE.

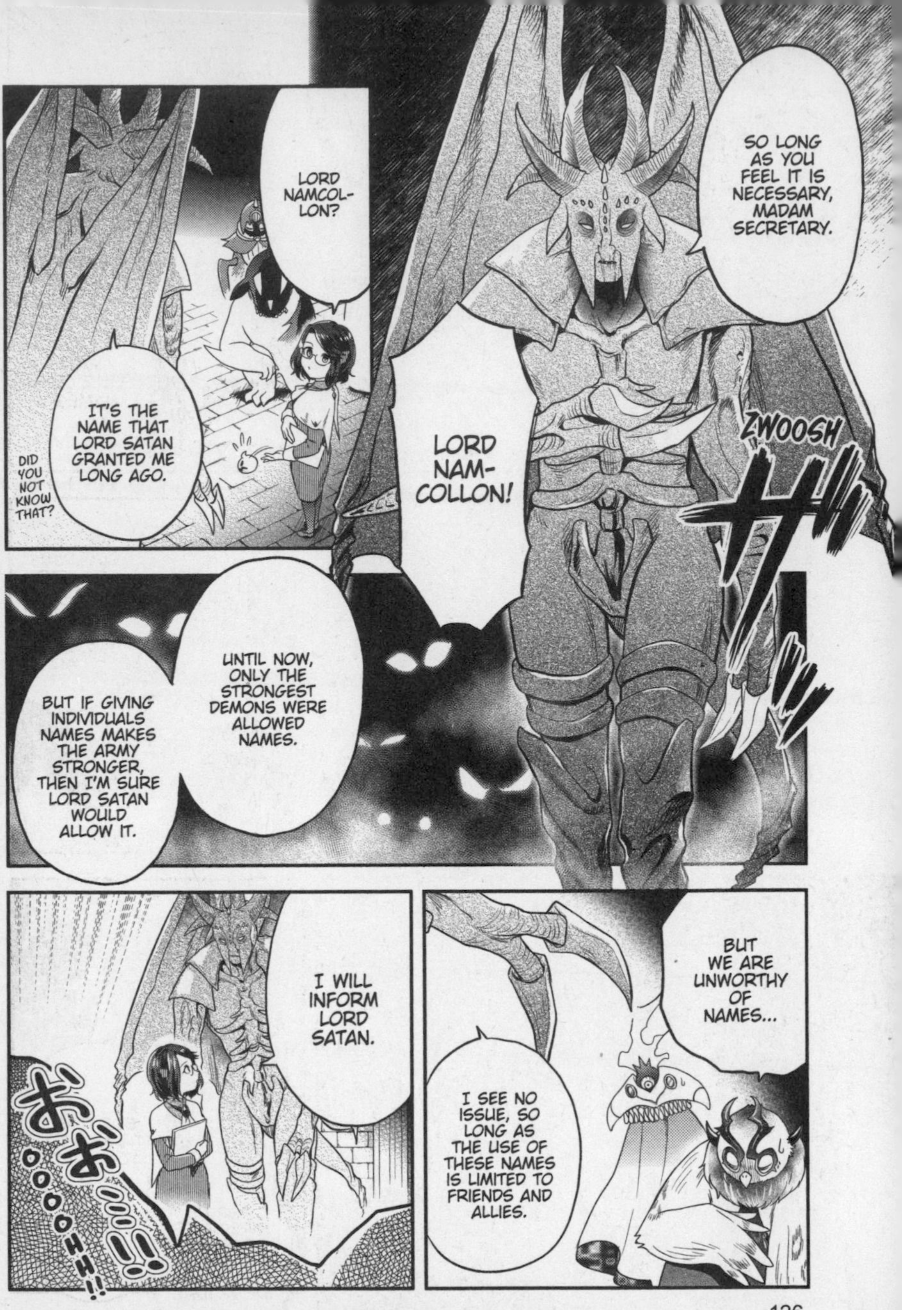
SO LONG AS YOU FEEL IT IS NECESSARY, MADAM SECRETARY.
LORD NAM-COLLON!
ZWOOSH
LORD NAMCOL-LON?
IT'S THE NAME THAT LORD SATAN GRANTED ME LONG AGO.
DID YOU NOT KNOW THAT?
UNTIL NOW, ONLY THE STRONGEST DEMONS WERE ALLOWED NAMES.
BUT IF GIVING INDIVIDUALS NAMES MAKES THE ARMY STRONGER, THEN I'M SURE LORD SATAN WOULD ALLOW IT.
BUT WE ARE UNWORTHY OF NAMES...
I SEE NO ISSUE, SO LONG AS THE USE OF THESE NAMES IS LIMITED TO FRIENDS AND ALLIES.
I WILL INFORM LORD SATAN.
おお
OOOOOHH!!

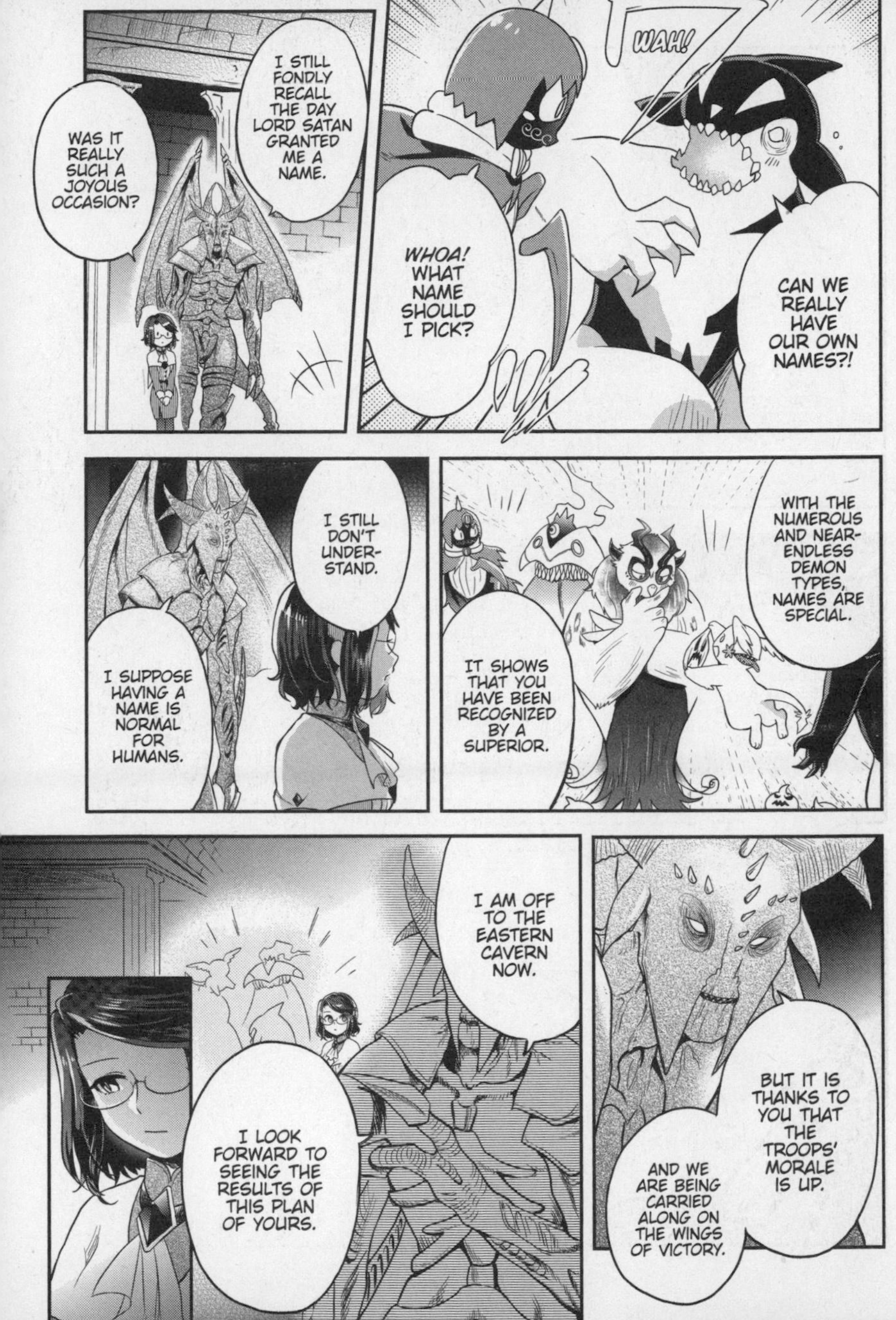
WAH!
CAN WE REALLY HAVE OUR OWN NAMES?!
WHOA! WHAT NAME SHOULD I PICK?
I STILL FONDLY RECALL THE DAY LORD SATAN GRANTED ME A NAME.
WAS IT REALLY SUCH A JOYOUS OCCASION?
WITH THE NUMEROUS AND NEAR-ENDLESS DEMON TYPES, NAMES ARE SPECIAL.
IT SHOWS THAT YOU HAVE BEEN RECOGNIZED BY A SUPERIOR.
I STILL DON'T UNDER-STAND.
I SUPPOSE HAVING A NAME IS NORMAL FOR HUMANS.
BUT IT IS THANKS TO YOU THAT THE TROOPS' MORALE IS UP.
AND WE ARE BEING CARRIED ALONG ON THE WINGS OF VICTORY.
I AM OFF TO THE EASTERN CAVERN NOW.
I LOOK FORWARD TO SEEING THE RESULTS OF THIS PLAN OF YOURS.

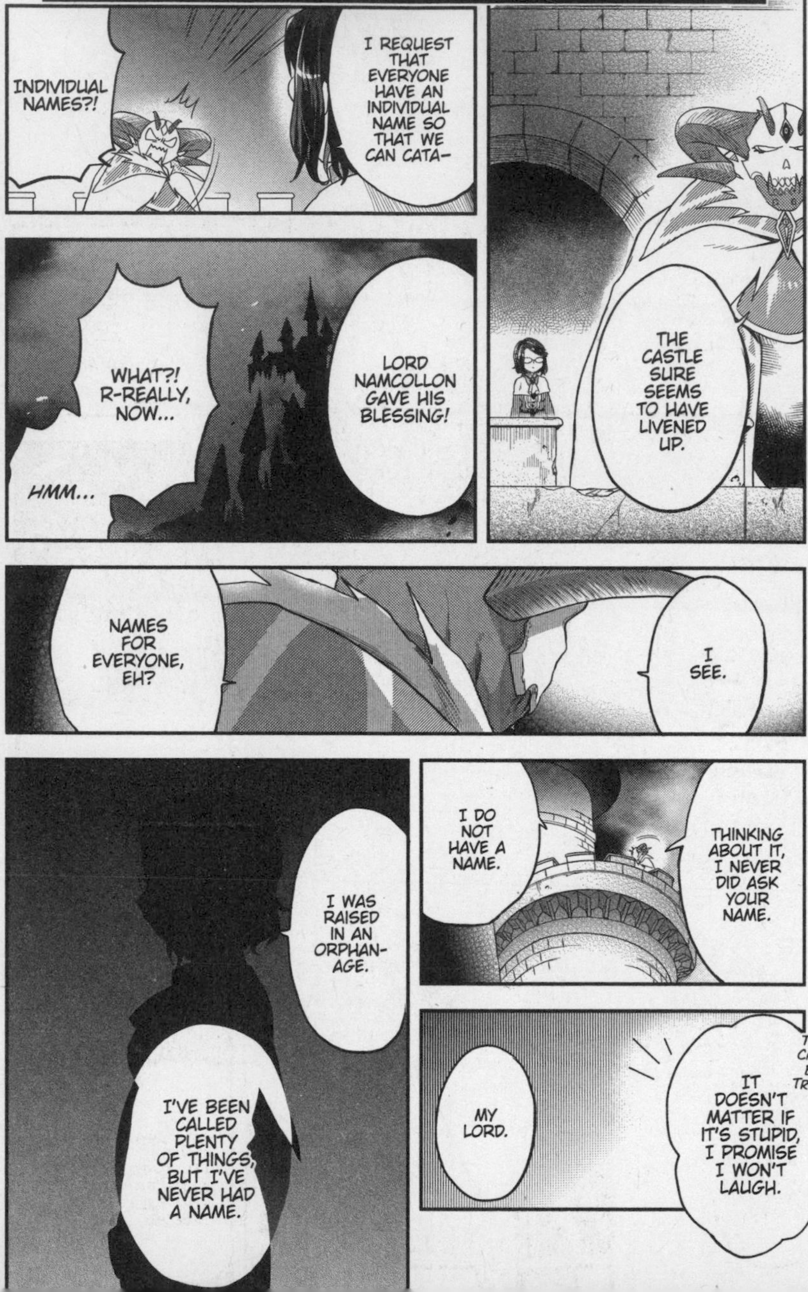
THE CASTLE SURE SEEMS TO HAVE LIVENED UP.
I REQUEST THAT EVERYONE HAVE AN INDIVIDUAL NAME SO THAT WE CAN CATA-
INDIVIDUAL NAMES?!
LORD NAMCOLLON GAVE HIS BLESSING!
WHAT?! R-REALLY, NOW...
HMM...
I SEE.
NAMES FOR EVERYONE, EH?
THINKING ABOUT IT, I NEVER DID ASK YOUR NAME.
I DO NOT HAVE A NAME.
THAT CAN'T BE TRUE!
IT DOESN'T MATTER IF IT'S STUPID, I PROMISE I WON'T LAUGH.
MY LORD.
I WAS RAISED IN AN ORPHAN-AGE.
I'VE BEEN CALLED PLENTY OF THINGS, BUT I'VE NEVER HAD A NAME.

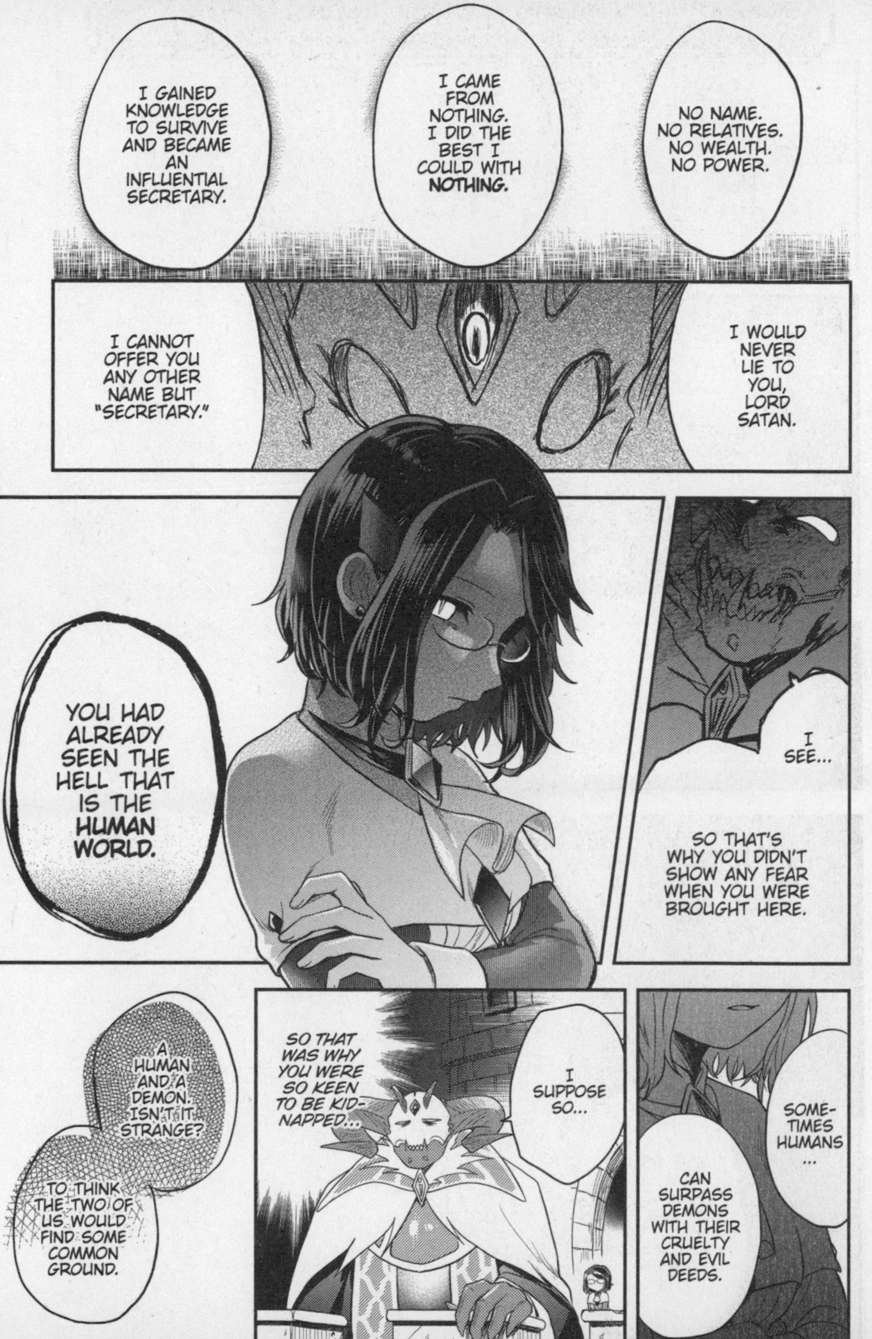
NO NAME. NO RELATIVES. NO WEALTH. NO POWER.
I CAME FROM NOTHING. I DID THE BEST I COULD WITH NOTHING.
I GAINED KNOWLEDGE TO SURVIVE AND BECAME AN INFLUENTIAL SECRETARY.
I WOULD NEVER LIE TO YOU, LORD SATAN.
I CANNOT OFFER YOU ANY OTHER NAME BUT "SECRETARY."
I SEE...
SO THAT'S WHY YOU DIDN'T SHOW ANY FEAR WHEN YOU WERE BROUGHT HERE.
YOU HAD ALREADY SEEN THE HELL THAT IS THE HUMAN WORLD.
SOME-TIMES HUMANS...
CAN SURPASS DEMONS WITH THEIR CRUELTY AND EVIL DEEDS.
I SUPPOSE SO...
SO THAT WAS WHY YOU WERE SO KEEN TO BE KID-NAPPED...
A HUMAN AND A DEMON. ISN'T IT STRANGE?
TO THINK THE TWO OF US WOULD FIND SOME COMMON GROUND.

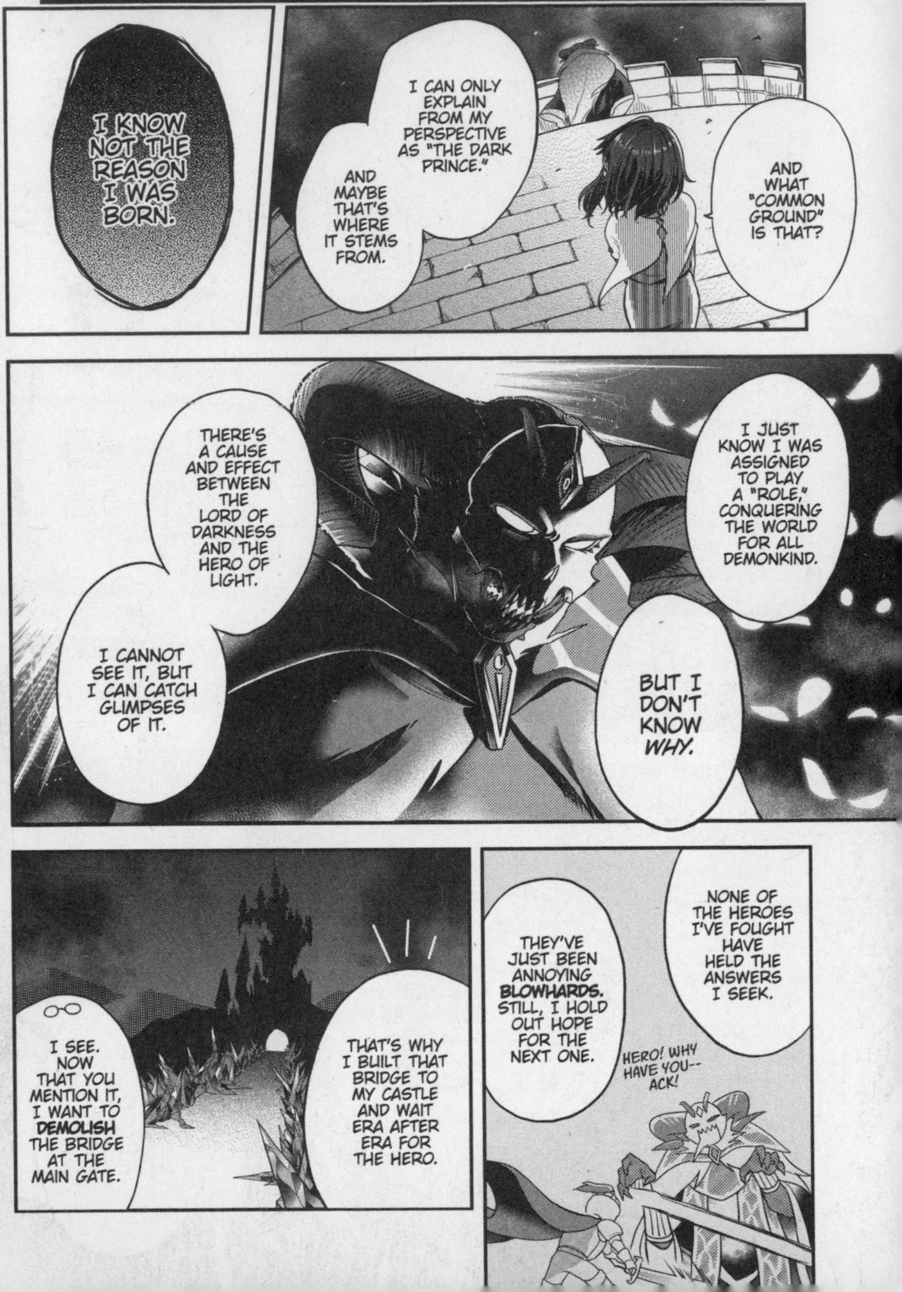
AND WHAT "COMMON GROUND" IS THAT?
I CAN ONLY EXPLAIN FROM MY PERSPECTIVE AS "THE DARK PRINCE."
AND MAYBE THAT'S WHERE IT STEMS FROM.
I KNOW NOT THE REASON I WAS BORN.
I JUST KNOW I WAS ASSIGNED TO PLAY A "ROLE," CONQUERING THE WORLD FOR ALL DEMONKIND.
BUT I DON'T KNOW *WHY.*
THERE'S A CAUSE AND EFFECT BETWEEN THE LORD OF DARKNESS AND THE HERO OF LIGHT.
I CANNOT SEE IT, BUT I CAN CATCH GLIMPSES OF IT.
NONE OF THE HEROES I'VE FOUGHT HAVE HELD THE ANSWERS I SEEK.
THEY'VE JUST BEEN ANNOYING **BLOWHARDS.** STILL, I HOLD OUT HOPE FOR THE NEXT ONE.
HERO! WHY HAVE YOU-- ACK!
THAT'S WHY I BUILT THAT BRIDGE TO MY CASTLE AND WAIT ERA AFTER ERA FOR THE HERO.
I SEE. NOW THAT YOU MENTION IT, I WANT TO **DEMOLISH** THE BRIDGE AT THE MAIN GATE.

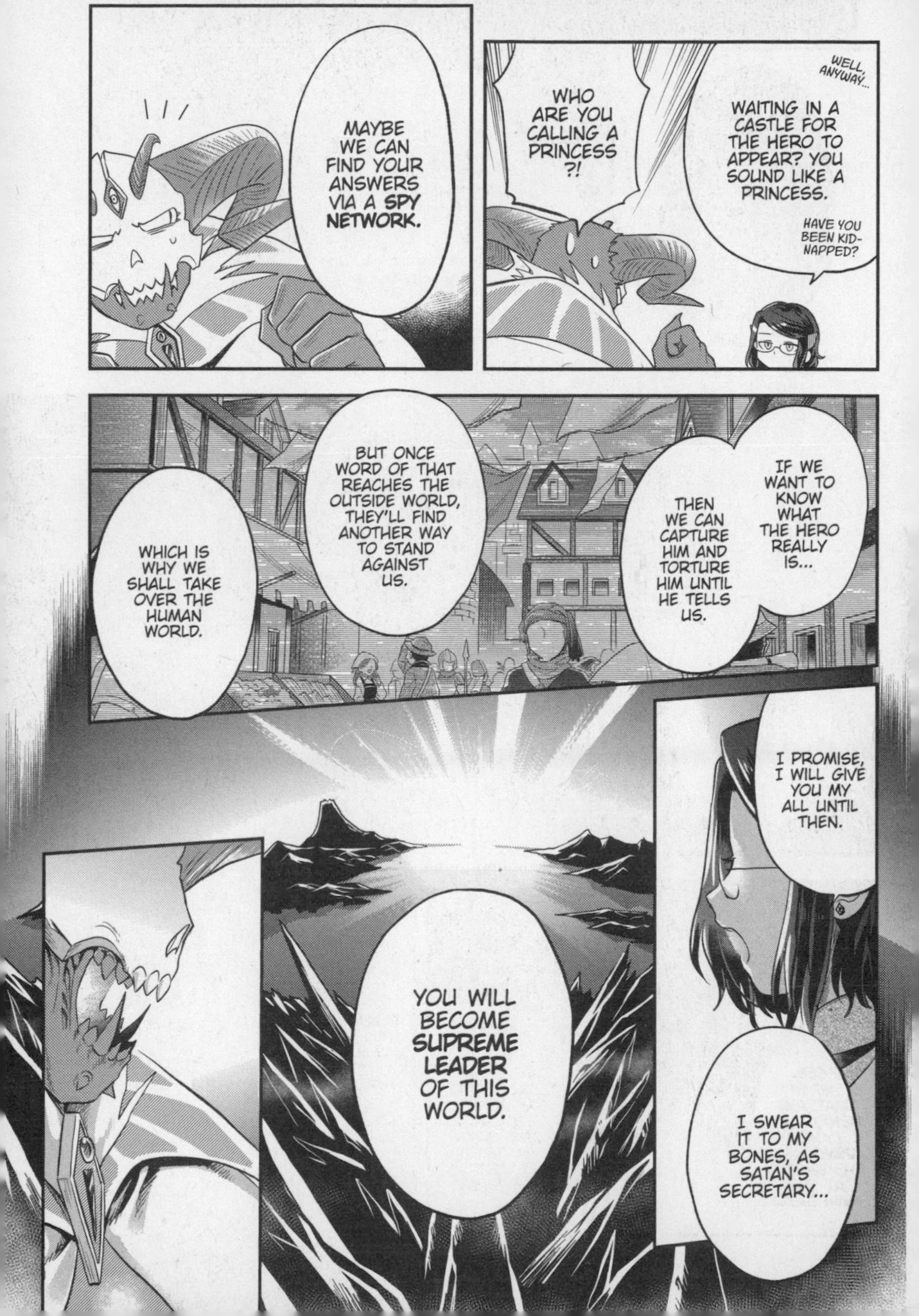

WELL, ANYWAY...
WAITING IN A CASTLE FOR THE HERO TO APPEAR? YOU SOUND LIKE A PRINCESS.
HAVE YOU BEEN KID-NAPPED?
WHO ARE YOU CALLING A PRINCESS?!
MAYBE WE CAN FIND YOUR ANSWERS VIA A SPY NETWORK.
IF WE WANT TO KNOW WHAT THE HERO REALLY IS...
THEN WE CAN CAPTURE HIM AND TORTURE HIM UNTIL HE TELLS US.
BUT ONCE WORD OF THAT REACHES THE OUTSIDE WORLD, THEY'LL FIND ANOTHER WAY TO STAND AGAINST US.
WHICH IS WHY WE SHALL TAKE OVER THE HUMAN WORLD.
I PROMISE, I WILL GIVE YOU MY ALL UNTIL THEN.
YOU WILL BECOME SUPREME LEADER OF THIS WORLD.
I SWEAR IT TO MY BONES, AS SATAN'S SECRETARY...

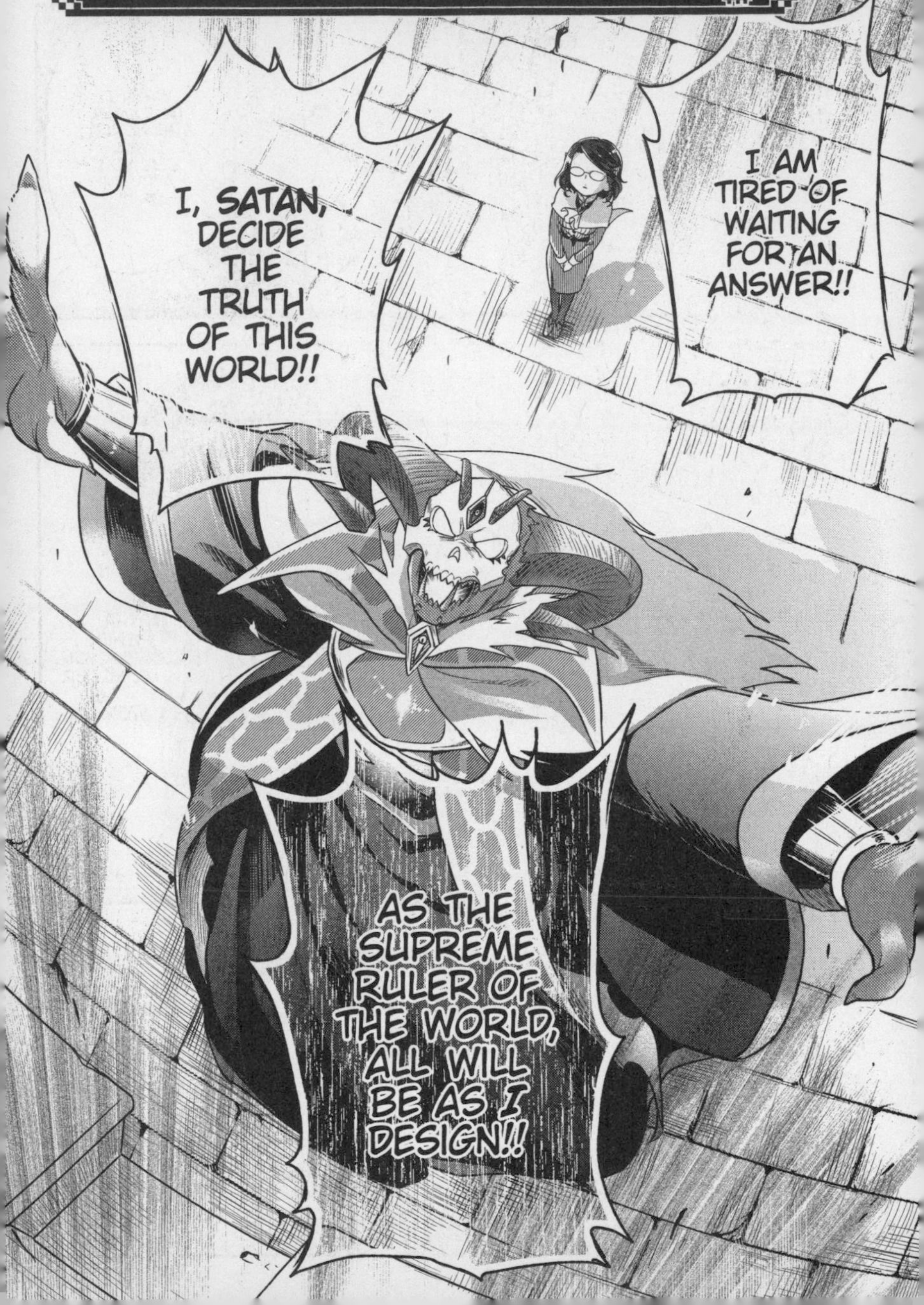
I AM TIRED OF WAITING FOR AN ANSWER!!
I, SATAN, DECIDE THE TRUTH OF THIS WORLD!!
AS THE SUPREME RULER OF THE WORLD, ALL WILL BE AS I DESIGN!!

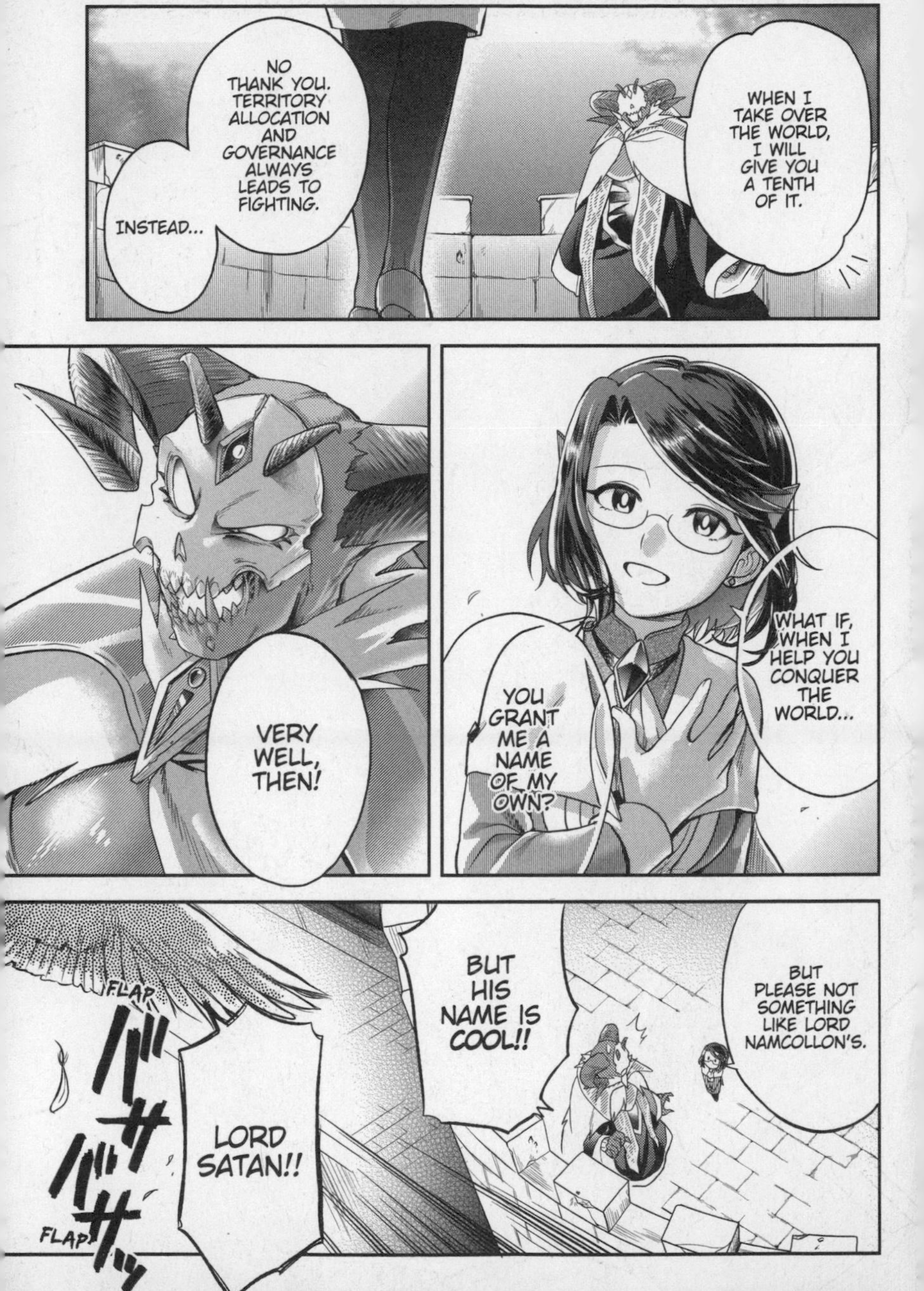
WHEN I TAKE OVER THE WORLD, I WILL GIVE YOU A TENTH OF IT.
NO THANK YOU. TERRITORY ALLOCATION AND GOVERNANCE ALWAYS LEADS TO FIGHTING.
INSTEAD...
WHAT IF, WHEN I HELP YOU CONQUER THE WORLD...
YOU GRANT ME A NAME OF MY OWN?
VERY WELL, THEN!
BUT PLEASE NOT SOMETHING LIKE LORD NAMCOLLON'S.
BUT HIS NAME IS COOL!!
LORD SATAN!!
FLAP
FLAP

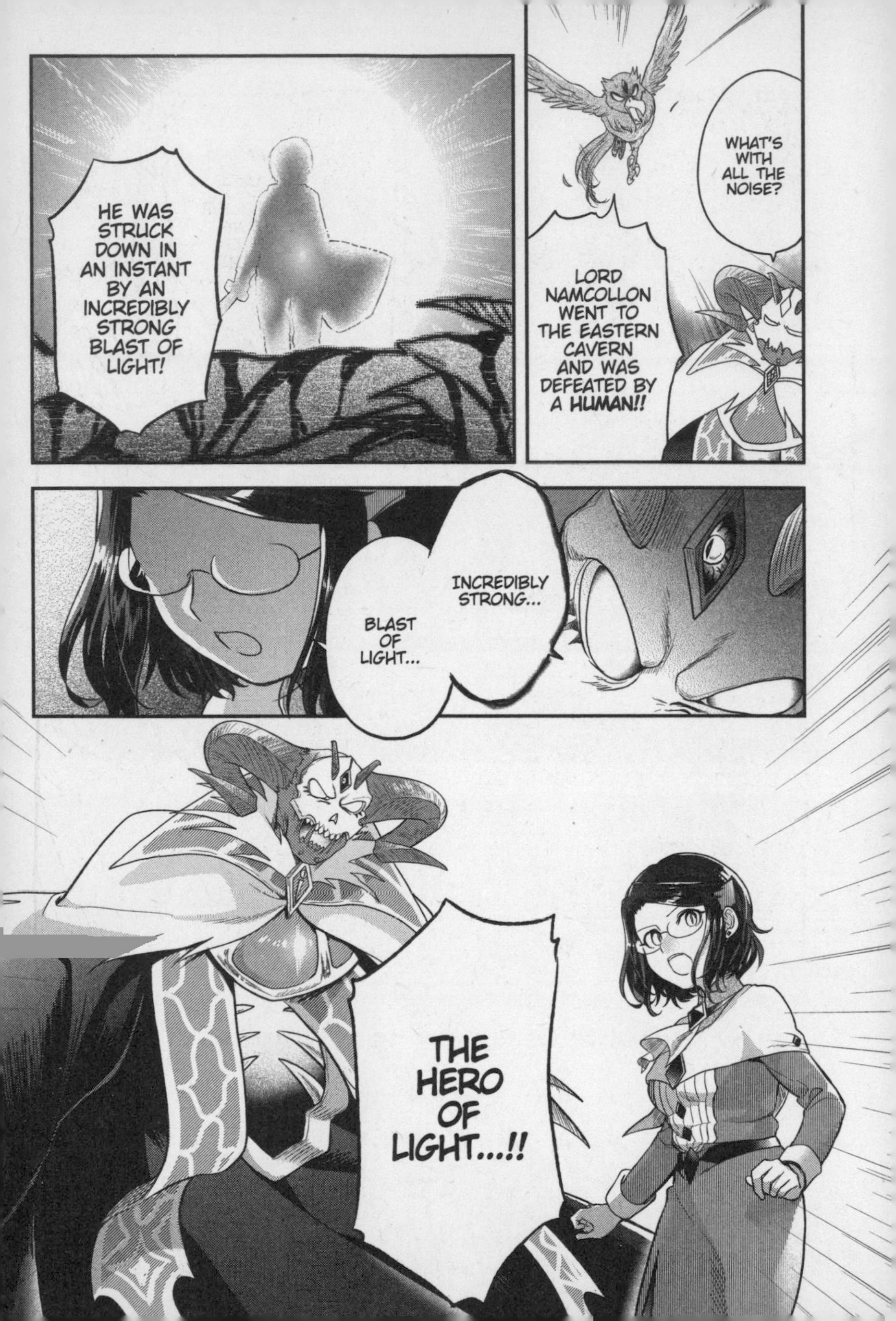

WHAT'S WITH ALL THE NOISE?
LORD NAMCOLLON WENT TO THE EASTERN CAVERN AND WAS DEFEATED BY A **HUMAN**!!
HE WAS STRUCK DOWN IN AN INSTANT BY AN INCREDIBLY STRONG BLAST OF LIGHT!
INCREDIBLY STRONG...
BLAST OF LIGHT...
THE HERO OF LIGHT...!!

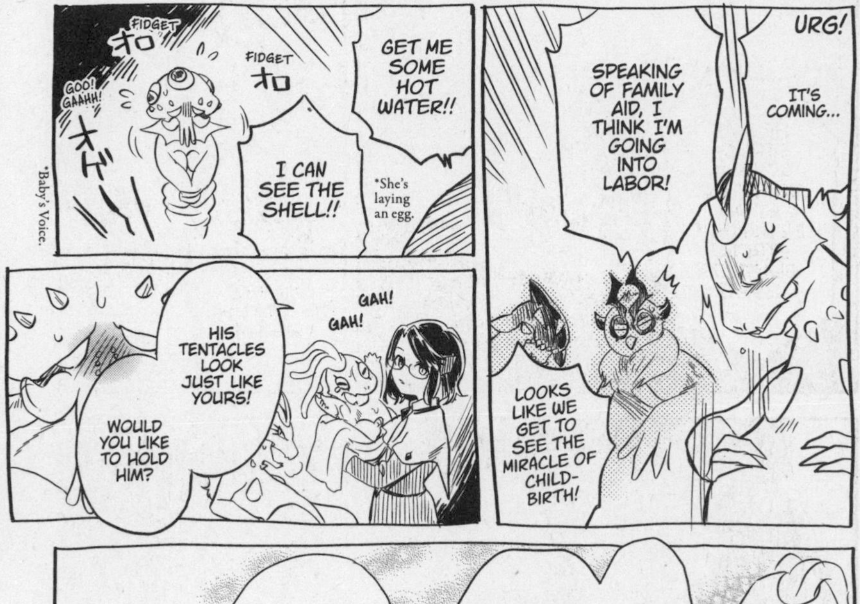
URG!
IT'S COMING...
SPEAKING OF FAMILY AID, I THINK I'M GOING INTO LABOR!
LOOKS LIKE WE GET TO SEE THE MIRACLE OF CHILD-BIRTH!
GET ME SOME HOT WATER!!
I CAN SEE THE SHELL!!
*She's laying an egg.
FIDGET オロ
FIDGET オロ
GOO! GAAHH!
オギャー
*Baby's Voice.
GAH!
GAH!
HIS TENTACLES LOOK JUST LIKE YOURS!
WOULD YOU LIKE TO HOLD HIM?
I'M GOING TO TRY...
LIKE, **SUPER HARD** TO BE AN AWESOME FATHER TO YOU THREE.
PLEASE BE THE BEST ROLE MODEL YOU CAN FOR THEM.
TENTACLES IS GOING TO TRY. = LOTS OF PREGNANT WOMEN. = NO ESCAPE!
SOMETHING LIKE THAT...?

CHILDREN ARE THE FUTURE OF THE DARK LORD'S ARMY.

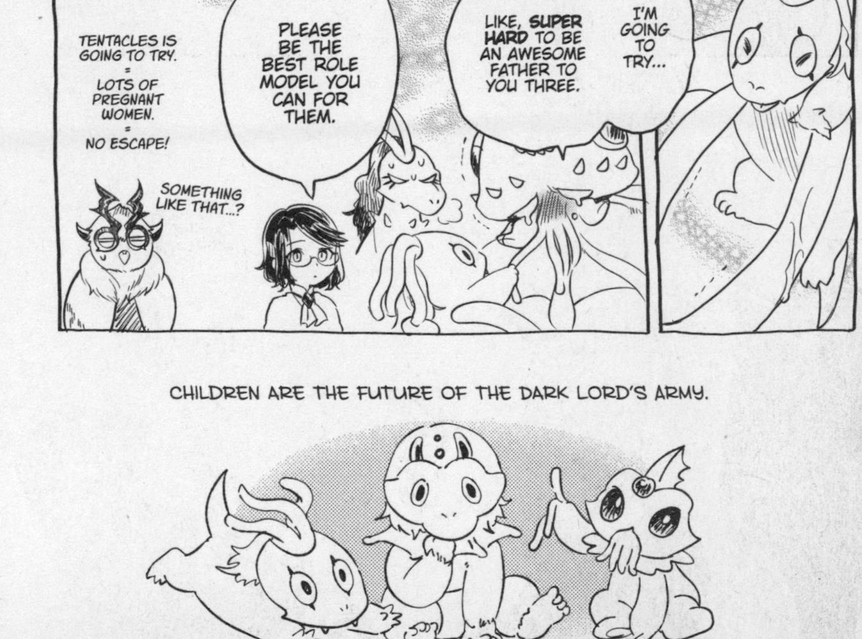

**SATAN'S SECRETARY**

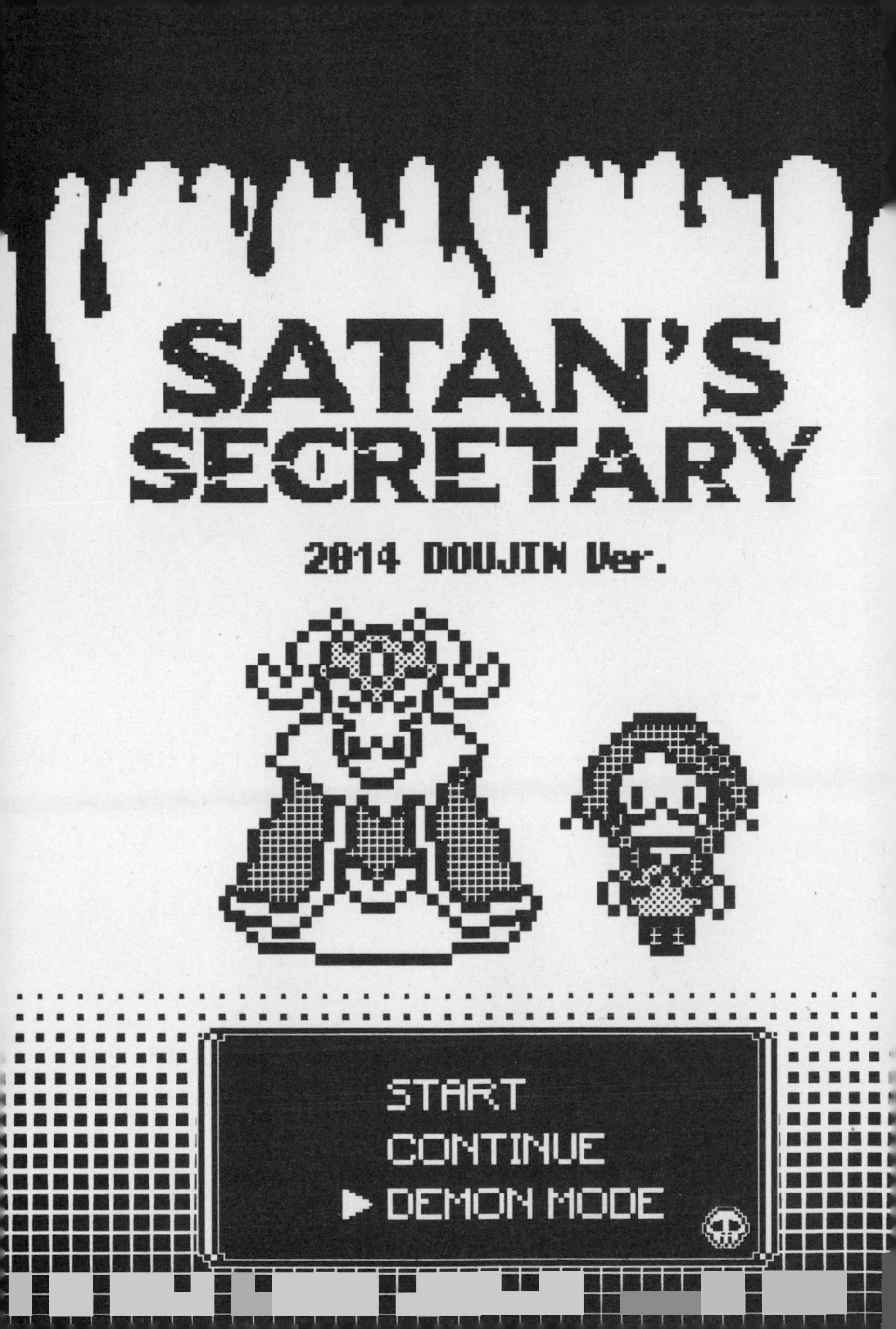
SATAN'S SECRETARY
2014 DOUJIN Ver.
START
CONTINUE
▶ DEMON MODE

# STRUGGLE FOR ME

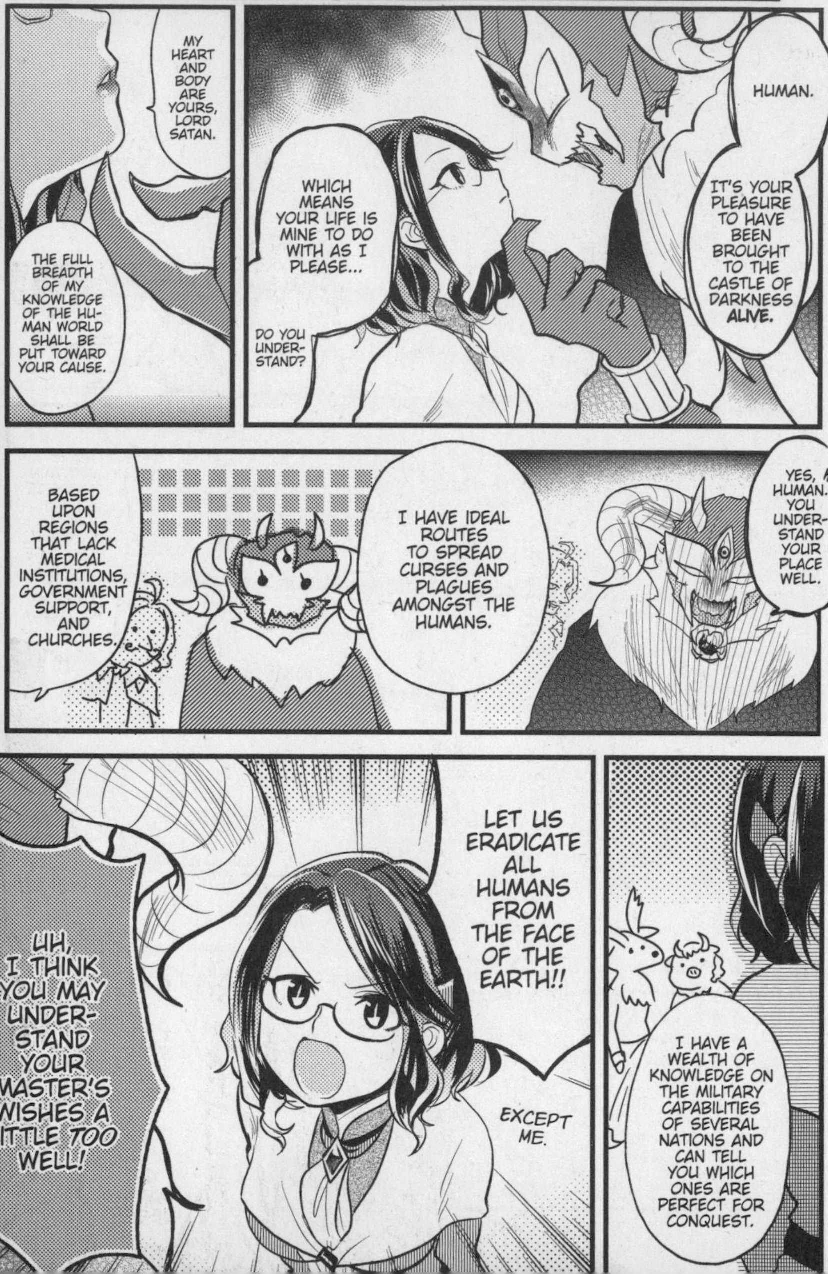

HUMAN.
IT'S YOUR PLEASURE TO HAVE BEEN BROUGHT TO THE CASTLE OF DARKNESS **ALIVE.**
WHICH MEANS YOUR LIFE IS MINE TO DO WITH AS I PLEASE...
DO YOU UNDER-STAND?
MY HEART AND BODY ARE YOURS, LORD SATAN.
THE FULL BREADTH OF MY KNOWLEDGE OF THE HU-MAN WORLD SHALL BE PUT TOWARD YOUR CAUSE.
HEH HEH...
YES, HUMAN. YOU UNDER-STAND YOUR PLACE WELL.
I HAVE IDEAL ROUTES TO SPREAD CURSES AND PLAGUES AMONGST THE HUMANS.
BASED UPON REGIONS THAT LACK MEDICAL INSTITUTIONS, GOVERNMENT SUPPORT, AND CHURCHES.
I HAVE A WEALTH OF KNOWLEDGE ON THE MILITARY CAPABILITIES OF SEVERAL NATIONS AND CAN TELL YOU WHICH ONES ARE PERFECT FOR CONQUEST.
LET US ERADICATE ALL HUMANS FROM THE FACE OF THE EARTH!!
EXCEPT ME.
UH, I THINK YOU MAY UNDER-STAND YOUR MASTER'S WISHES A LITTLE *TOO* WELL!

# THESE HORNS ARE NOT JUST FOR SHOW

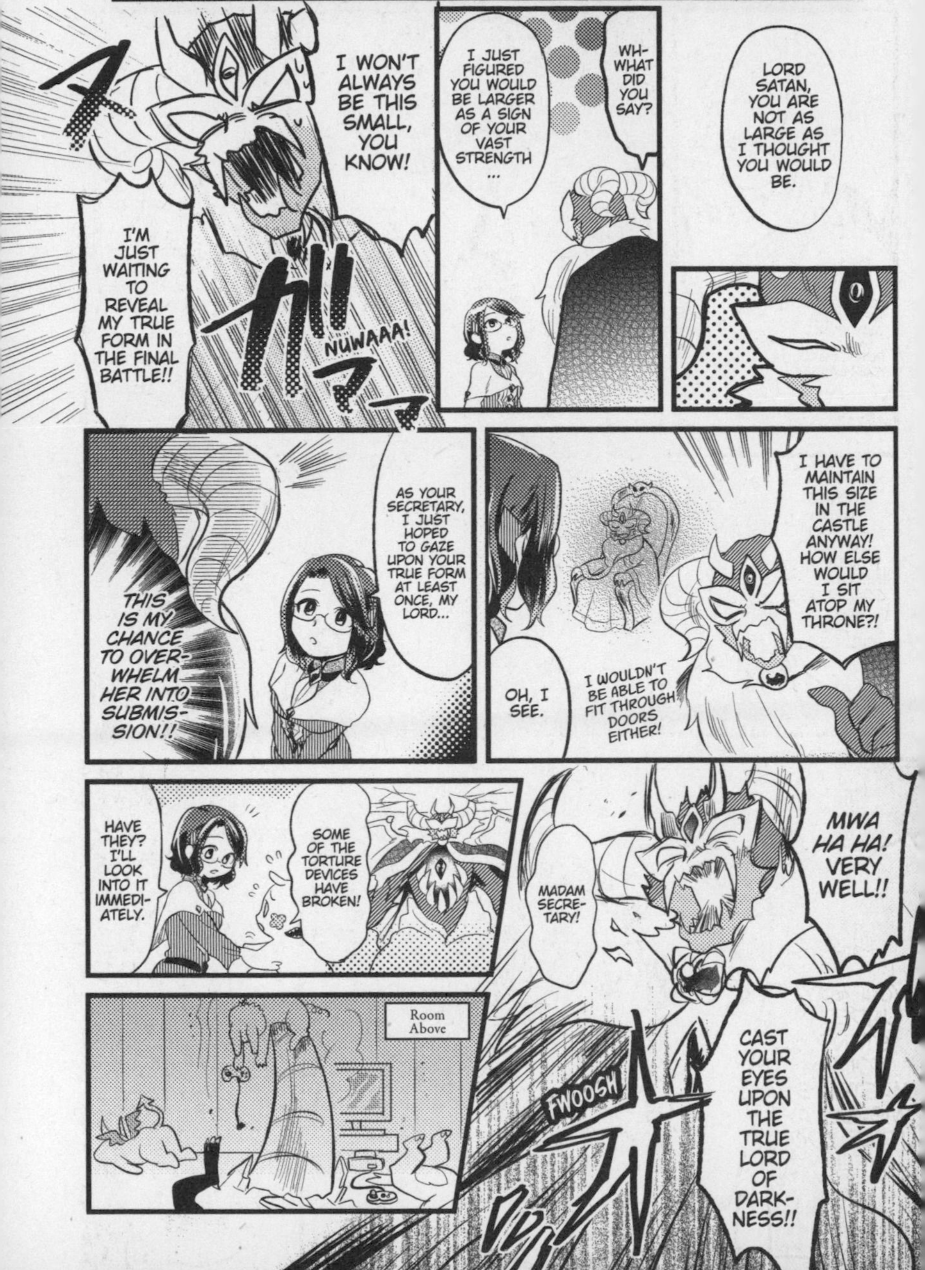
LORD SATAN, YOU ARE NOT AS LARGE AS I THOUGHT YOU WOULD BE.
WH-WHAT DID YOU SAY?
I JUST FIGURED YOU WOULD BE LARGER AS A SIGN OF YOUR VAST STRENGTH ...
I WON'T ALWAYS BE THIS SMALL, YOU KNOW!
I'M JUST WAITING TO REVEAL MY TRUE FORM IN THE FINAL BATTLE!!
NUWAAA!
I HAVE TO MAINTAIN THIS SIZE IN THE CASTLE ANYWAY! HOW ELSE WOULD I SIT ATOP MY THRONE?!
I WOULDN'T BE ABLE TO FIT THROUGH DOORS EITHER!
OH, I SEE.
AS YOUR SECRETARY, I JUST HOPED TO GAZE UPON YOUR TRUE FORM AT LEAST ONCE, MY LORD...
THIS IS MY CHANCE TO OVER-WHELM HER INTO SUBMIS-SION!!
MWA HA HA! VERY WELL!!
CAST YOUR EYES UPON THE TRUE LORD OF DARK-NESS!!
FWOOSH
MADAM SECRE-TARY!
SOME OF THE TORTURE DEVICES HAVE BROKEN!
HAVE THEY? I'LL LOOK INTO IT IMMEDI-ATELY.
Room Above

# THERE'S ONLY ONE RULE, DON'T TELL ANYONE!

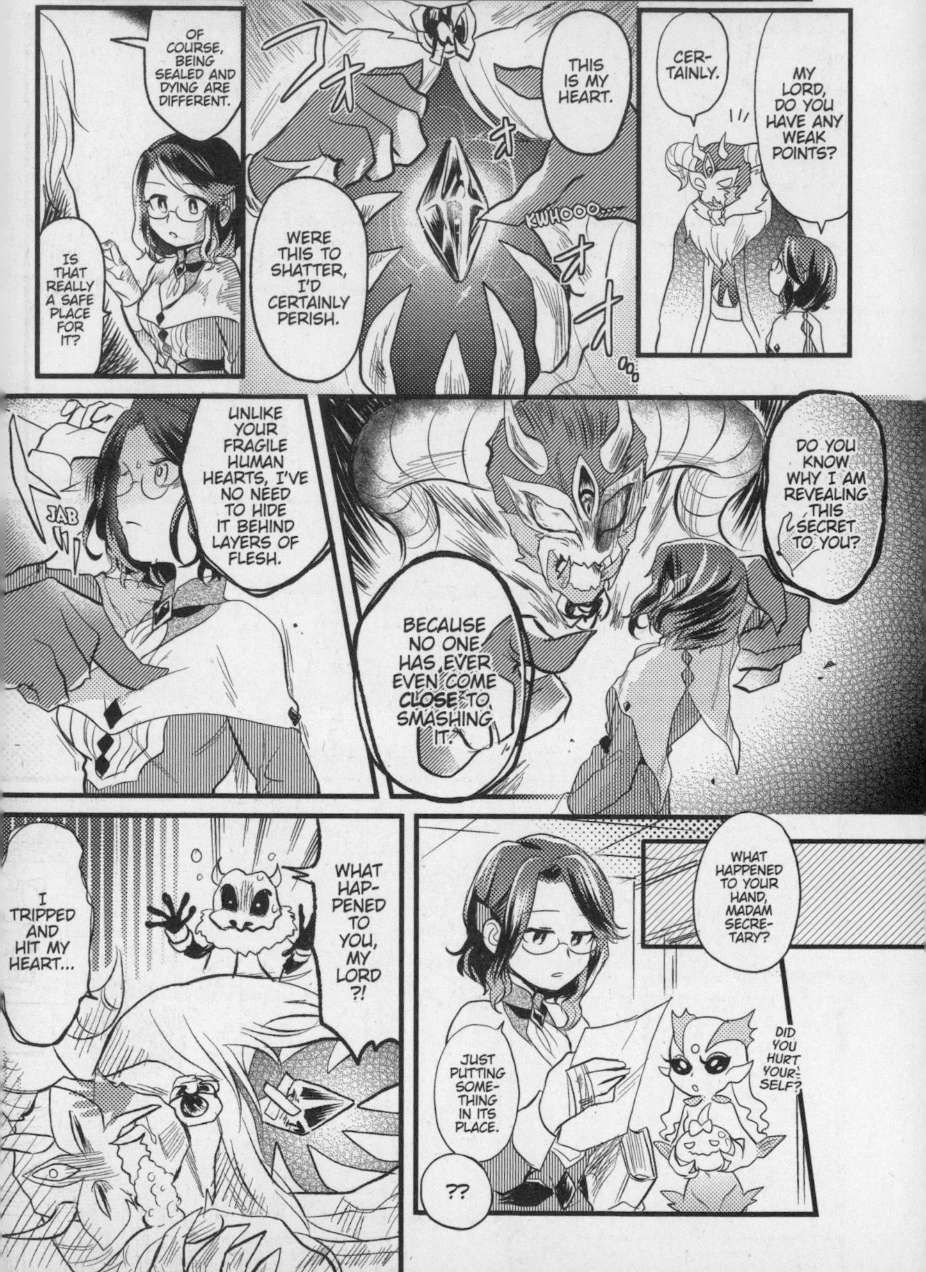

MY LORD, DO YOU HAVE ANY WEAK POINTS?
CERTAINLY.
THIS IS MY HEART.
KWHOOO...
WERE THIS TO SHATTER, I'D CERTAINLY PERISH.
OF COURSE, BEING SEALED AND DYING ARE DIFFERENT.
IS THAT REALLY A SAFE PLACE FOR IT?
DO YOU KNOW WHY I AM REVEALING THIS SECRET TO YOU?
BECAUSE NO ONE HAS EVER EVEN COME CLOSE TO SMASHING IT.
UNLIKE YOUR FRAGILE HUMAN HEARTS, I'VE NO NEED TO HIDE IT BEHIND LAYERS OF FLESH.
JAB
WHAT HAPPENED TO YOUR HAND, MADAM SECRETARY?
DID YOU HURT YOURSELF?
JUST PUTTING SOMETHING IN ITS PLACE.
??
WHAT HAPPENED TO YOU, MY LORD?!
I TRIPPED AND HIT MY HEART...

# MISTAKING PURE INTENTIONS

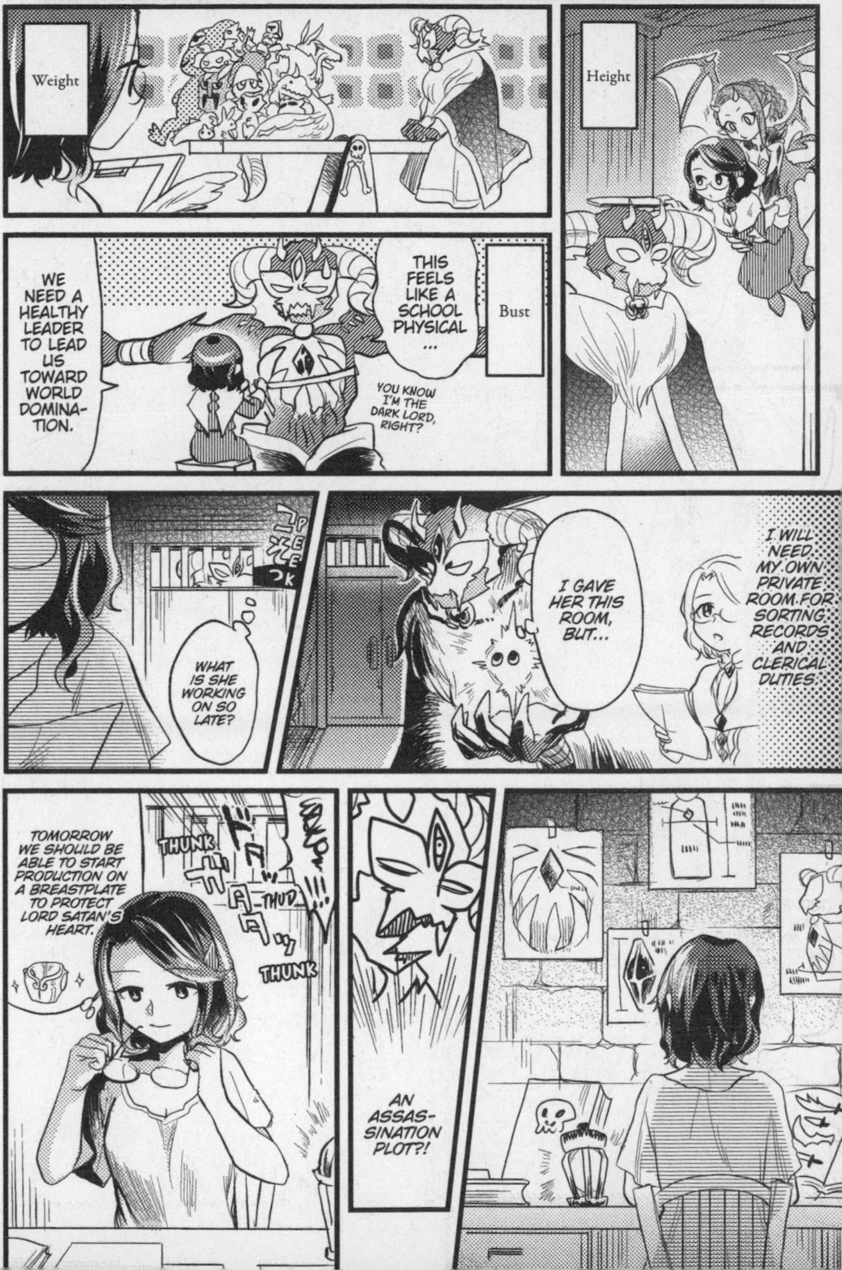
Height
Weight
Bust
THIS FEELS LIKE A SCHOOL PHYSICAL...
WE NEED A HEALTHY LEADER TO LEAD US TOWARD WORLD DOMINATION.
YOU KNOW I'M THE DARK LORD, RIGHT?
I WILL NEED MY OWN PRIVATE ROOM FOR SORTING RECORDS AND CLERICAL DUTIES.
I GAVE HER THIS ROOM, BUT...
PEEK
WHAT IS SHE WORKING ON SO LATE?
AN ASSASSINATION PLOT?!
THUNK
THUD
THUNK
TOMORROW WE SHOULD BE ABLE TO START PRODUCTION ON A BREASTPLATE TO PROTECT LORD SATAN'S HEART.

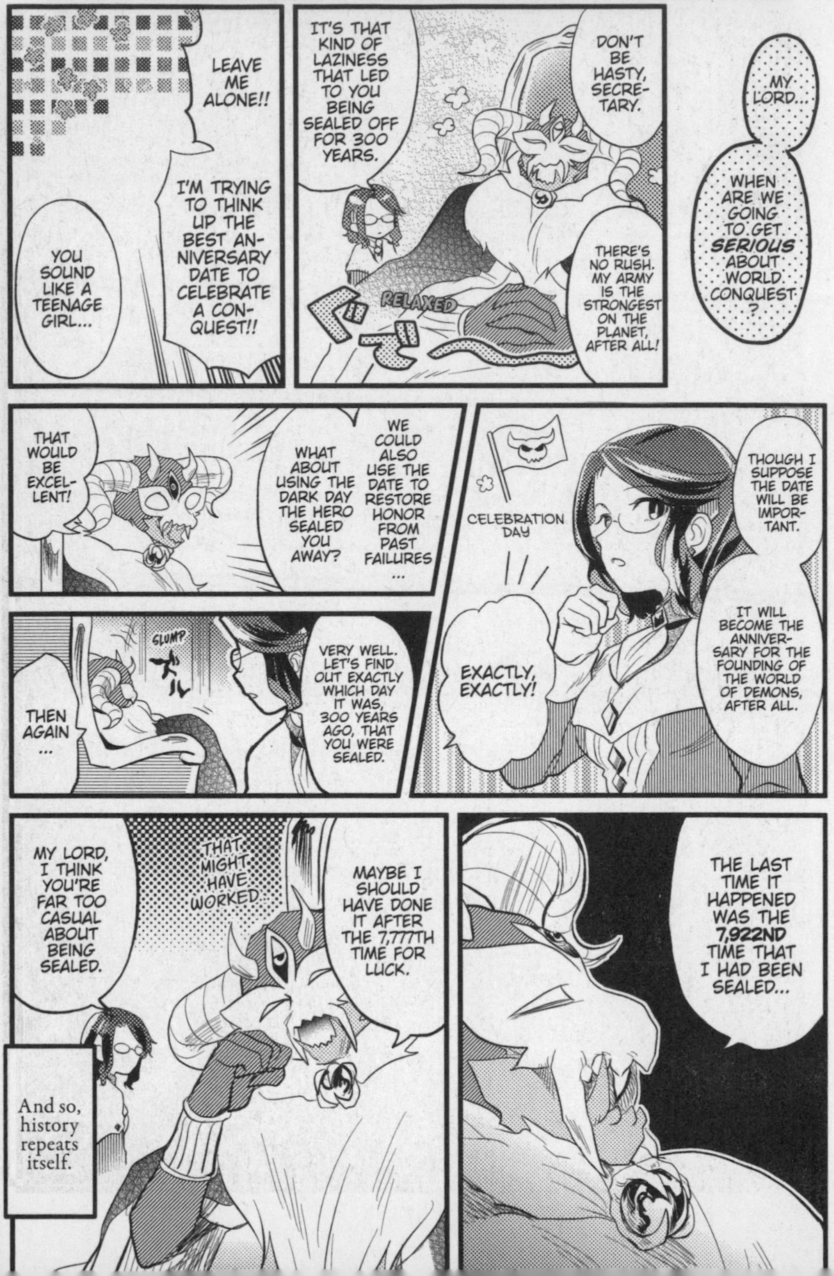
MY LORD...
WHEN ARE WE GOING TO GET **SERIOUS** ABOUT WORLD CONQUEST?
DON'T BE HASTY, SECRETARY.
THERE'S NO RUSH. MY ARMY IS THE STRONGEST ON THE PLANET, AFTER ALL!
IT'S THAT KIND OF LAZINESS THAT LED TO YOU BEING SEALED OFF FOR 300 YEARS.
RELAXED
LEAVE ME ALONE!!
I'M TRYING TO THINK UP THE BEST ANNIVERSARY DATE TO CELEBRATE A CONQUEST!!
YOU SOUND LIKE A TEENAGE GIRL...
THOUGH I SUPPOSE THE DATE WILL BE IMPORTANT.
CELEBRATION DAY
IT WILL BECOME THE ANNIVERSARY FOR THE FOUNDING OF THE WORLD OF DEMONS, AFTER ALL.
EXACTLY, EXACTLY!
WE COULD ALSO USE THE DATE TO RESTORE HONOR FROM PAST FAILURES...
WHAT ABOUT USING THE DARK DAY THE HERO SEALED YOU AWAY?
THAT WOULD BE EXCELLENT!
VERY WELL. LET'S FIND OUT EXACTLY WHICH DAY IT WAS, 300 YEARS AGO, THAT YOU WERE SEALED.
SLUMP
THEN AGAIN...
THE LAST TIME IT HAPPENED WAS THE 7,922ND TIME THAT I HAD BEEN SEALED...
MAYBE I SHOULD HAVE DONE IT AFTER THE 7,777TH TIME FOR LUCK.
THAT MIGHT HAVE WORKED.
MY LORD, I THINK YOU'RE FAR TOO CASUAL ABOUT BEING SEALED.
And so, history repeats itself.

# AFTERWORD

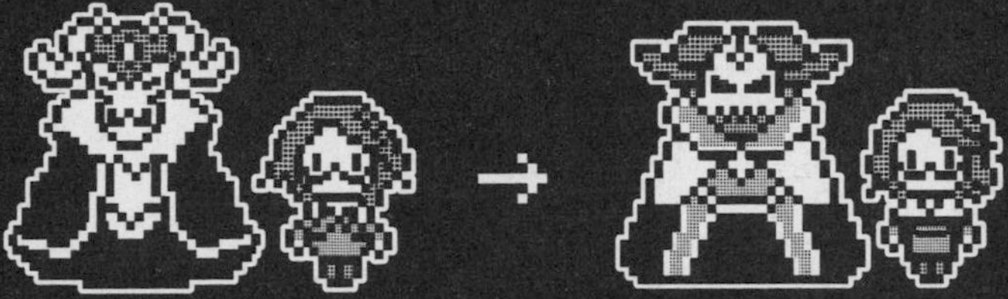

I FIRST WROTE *SATAN'S SECRETARY* IN 2014 JUST FOR FUN. IT WAS ORIGINALLY DISTRIBUTED AT A LOCAL DOUJINSHI FAIR, BUT I AM SO THRILLED I WAS ABLE TO GET HELP FROM SO MANY PEOPLE, INCLUDING MY EDITOR, AND NOW IT'S BEEN COLLECTED INTO THIS BOOK. I'M SO GLAD I GOT TO CONQUER THIS!

PLANNING HOW TO TAKE OVER THE WORLD IS REALLY HARD, AND MY RELEASE SCHEDULE IS REALLY TIGHT, BUT I WILL STEEL MY MIND AND WORK EVEN HARDER. THESE PATHETIC HUMANS WILL NOT DEFEAT ME!

THANK YOU SO MUCH! BIG THANK-YOU TO MY DESIGNER, MY SUPPORTIVE FRIENDS, EVERYONE AT THE PUBLISHERS, THE BOOKSHOPS, AND THE READERS.

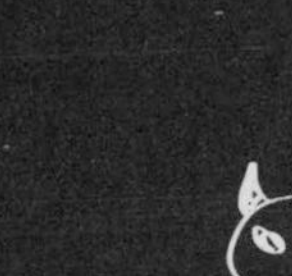

鴨鍋
かもつ

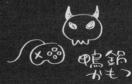

KAMOTSU KAMONABE

魔王の秘書 1巻

SATAN'S SECRETARY VOLUME 1

CONGRATULATIONS!

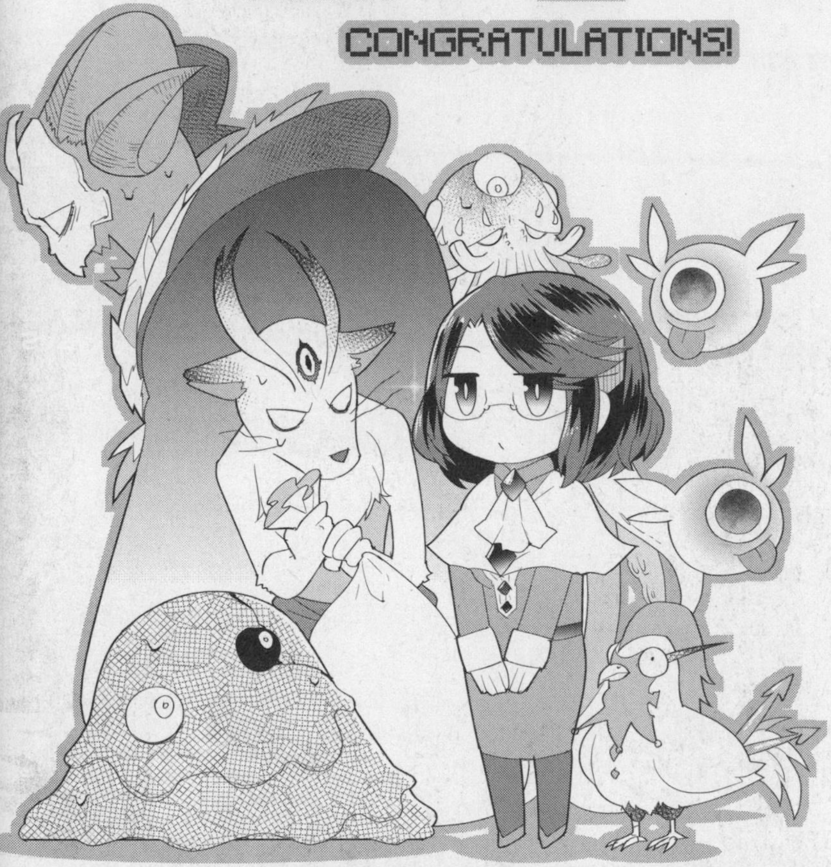

I HOPE YOU LOOK FORWARD TO MORE FROM THE USELESS SATAN, THE LOST SECRETARY, AND ALL THE DEMONS WHO JOIN THEM.

瀬野反人

KAMOTSU KAMONABE

## here Is No Crying in World Conquest!

swear this. Things are heating up but evil is certainly on its way.
his is not some myth nor fairytale, but the story that demons like
ourself face, the tale of darkness, of a Hero, and of conquest.
ou have forgotten how many months (years? centuries?) ago was it
at you became the Dark Lord.
nd now you, the Dark Lord, have a different reason to cry.
onquering the world is easy compared to this.
rom the swarm of humanity comes the genius Secretary of the
ark Lord's Army.
his is the RPG adventure of *Satan's Secretary*.

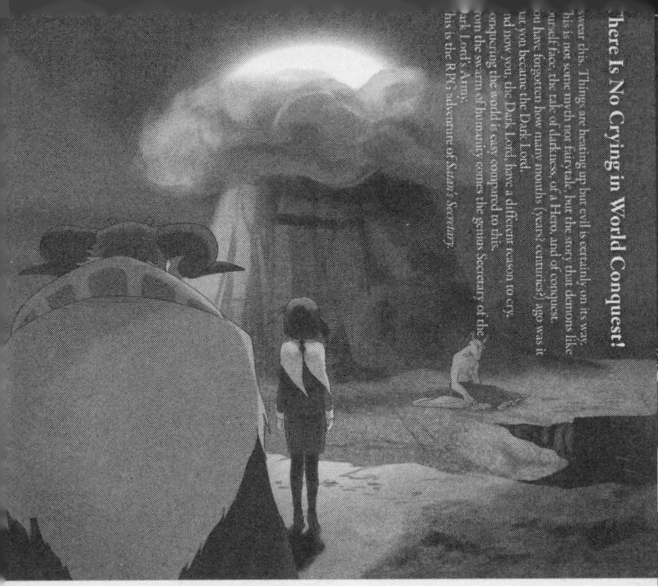

# SATAN'S SECRETARY

1

SATAN's SECRETARY

PRESENTED BY
KAMOTSU KAMONABE
VOLUME ONE

SEVEN SEAS ENT.

SATAN'S SECRETARY 1 VOLUME ONE KAMOTSU KAMONABE

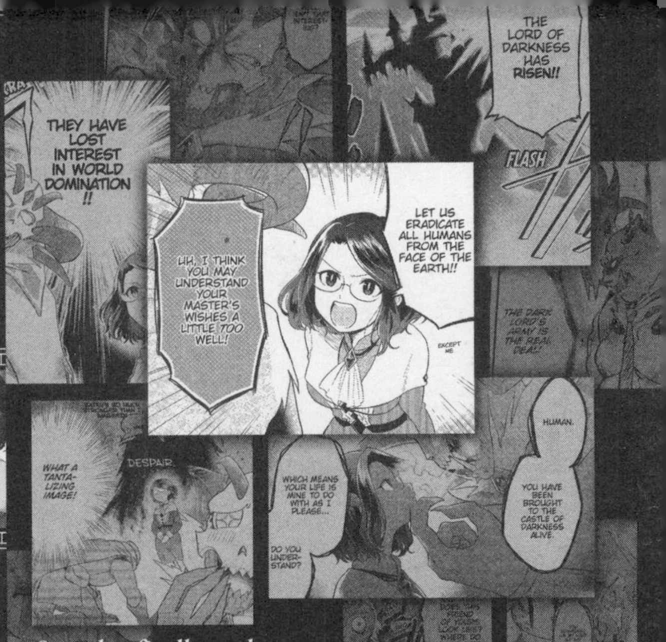
THE LORD OF DARKNESS HAS RISEN!!
FLASH
THEY HAVE LOST INTEREST IN WORLD DOMINATION !!
LET US ERADICATE ALL HUMANS FROM THE FACE OF THE EARTH!!
EXCEPT ME.
UH, I THINK YOU MAY UNDERSTAND YOUR MASTER'S WISHES A LITTLE TOO WELL!
THE DARK LORD'S ARMY IS THE REAL DEAL!
HUMAN.
YOU HAVE BEEN BROUGHT TO THE CASTLE OF DARKNESS ALIVE.
WHICH MEANS YOUR LIFE IS MINE TO DO WITH AS I PLEASE...
DO YOU UNDER-STAND?
DESPAIR.
WHAT A TANTA-LIZING IMAGE!

## Satan has finally awoken.

With the goal of world domination, the Prince of Darkness begins kidnapping humans to use as research subjects.
And as he does, he encounters someone completely unexpected--a Secretary!
She has unimaginable talent and is able to do her job with swift efficiency.
With this capable woman in hand...
The human world is in big trouble!

The JRPG style fantasy gag manga about Satan and a Secretary, that's all the rage on Twitter, is finally here!!

注意

This is a fantasy RPG based on Japanese products for a younger audience. Warning: A lot of love has been put into the parodies to existing games and companies. These have not been ethically reviewed, however all choices were made with careful consideration by the author. If there are any issues about original works please contact us with the address provided.

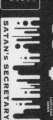

SATAN's SECRETARY

SEVEN SEAS ENTERTAINMENT PRESENTS

# SATAN'S SECRETARY vol. 1

### story and art by KAMOTSU KAMONABE

TRANSLATION
**Jennifer O'Donnell**

ADAPTATION
**Jamal Joseph Jr.**

LETTERING
**Erika Terriquez**

COVER DESIGN
**KC Fabellon**

PROOFREADER
**Brett Hallahan**
**Janet Houck**

ASSISTANT EDITOR
**Shannon Fay**

PRODUCTION ASSISTANT
**CK Russell**

PRODUCTION MANAGER
**Lissa Pattillo**

EDITOR-IN-CHIEF
**Adam Arnold**

PUBLISHER
**Jason DeAngelis**

MAOU NO HISHO VOL. 1
© Kamotsu Kamonabe 2016
Originally published in Japan in 2016 by EARTH STAR Entertainment, Tokyo.
English translation rights arranged with EARTH STAR Entertainment, Tokyo,
through TOHAN CORPORATION, Tokyo.

Seven Seas books may be purchased in bulk for promotional, educational, or
business use. Please contact your local bookseller or the Macmillan Corporate
and Premium Sales Department at 1-800-221-7945, extension 5442, or by
e-mail at MacmillanSpecialMarkets@macmillan.com.

Seven Seas and the Seven Seas logo are trademarks of
Seven Seas Entertainment, LLC. All rights reserved.

ISBN: 978-1-626928-68-8

Printed in Canada

First Printing: June 2018

10 9 8 7 6 5 4 3 2 1

FOLLOW US ONLINE: *www.sevenseasentertainment.com*

# READING DIRECTIONS

This book reads from *right to left*, Japanese style.
If this is your first time reading manga, you start
reading from the top right panel on each page and
take it from there. If you get lost, just follow the
numbered diagram here. It may seem backwards at
first, but you'll get the hang of it! Have fun!!

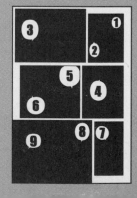

Satan ... ing th ... human woman with an unimaginable talent for organizing his demon army and keeping the conquest on track. But why would a mild-mannered woman like the Secretary betray the human race? And will Satan survive her strict schedule? Either way, the human world is in big trouble!

# IT'S A HELL OF A JOB!

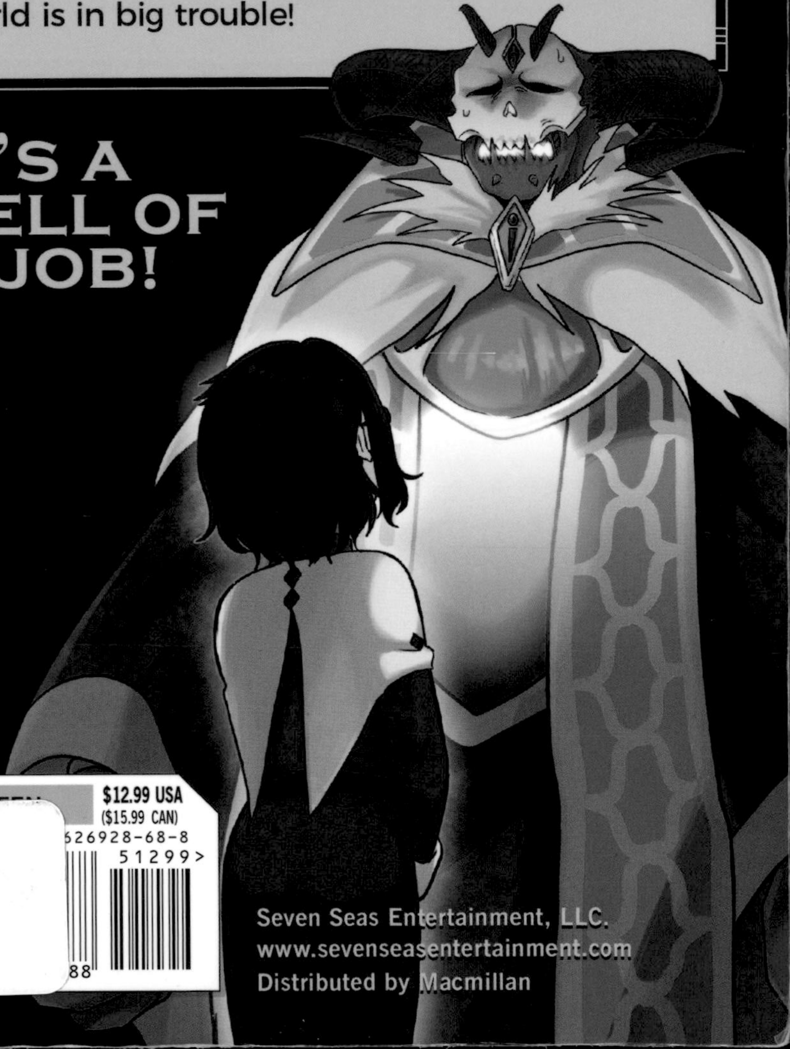

$12.99 USA
($15.99 CAN)
626928-68-8
51299>
88



Seven Seas Entertainment, LLC.
www.sevenseasentertainment.com
Distributed by Macmillan